LONDON

8th Edition

By Jason Cochran

FrommerMedia LLC

Frommer's London, 8th Edition

Published by:
Frommer Media LLC

ISBN 978-1-62887-517-1 (paper), 978-1-62887-518-8 (e-book)

Editorial Director: Pauline Frommer
Editor: Linda Cabasin
Production Editor: Cheryl Lenser
Cartographer: Roberta Stockwell
Photo Editor: Meghan Lamb
Indexer: Cheryl Lenser
Cover Design: Dave Riedy

Front cover: Big Ben clocktower in London.
Title page: Shad Thames.

For information on our other products or services, see www.frommers.com.

Frommer Media LLC also publishes its books in a variety of electronic formats. Some content that appears in print may not be available in electronic formats.

Manufactured in Malaysia

5 4 3 2 1

HOW TO CONTACT US

In researching this book, we discovered many wonderful places—hotels, restaurants, shops, and more. We're sure you'll find others. Please tell us about them, so we can share the information with your fellow travelers in upcoming editions. If you were disappointed with a recommendation, we'd love to know that, too. Please write to: Support@FrommerMedia.com

FROMMER'S STAR RATINGS SYSTEM

Every hotel, restaurant and attraction listed in this guide has been ranked for quality and value. Here's what the stars mean:

★ Recommended
★★ Highly Recommended
★★★ A must! Don't miss!

AN IMPORTANT NOTE

The world is a dynamic place. Hotels change ownership, restaurants hike their prices, museums alter their opening hours, and buses and trains change their routings. And all of this can occur in the several months after our authors have visited, inspected, and written about these hotels, restaurants, museums, and transportation services. Though we have made valiant efforts to keep all our information fresh and up-to-date, some few changes can inevitably occur in the periods before a revised edition of this guidebook is published. So please bear with us if a tiny number of the details in this book have changed. Please also note that we have no responsibility or liability for any inaccuracy or errors or omissions, or for inconvenience, loss, damage, or expenses suffered by anyone as a result of assertions in this guide.

CONTENTS

LIST OF MAPS

ABOUT THE AUTHOR

Jason Cochran also writes the award-winning Frommer's guide to Orlando, Walt Disney World, and Universal, and he is the author of the book *Here Lies America*. He was twice awarded Guide Book of the Year by the Lowell Thomas Awards (Society of American Travel Writers) and once by the North American Travel Journalists Association. His voice has reached millions of travelers since the mid-'90s, when as a long-term backpacker he wrote one of the world's first travel blogs, and for half a decade he co-hosted *The Travel Show* on WABC with Pauline Frommer. He is editor-in-chief of Frommers.com. For this edition, Jason would like to thank the following people for their invaluable contributions and companionship: Hilary and Steve Bowsher, Brian Fairbairn, Karl Eccleston, Alex Robertson Textor, and Sophie Collard. *www.jasoncochran.com*, @JasCochran

ABOUT THE FROMMER TRAVEL GUIDES

For most of the past 50 years, Frommer's has been the leading series of travel guides in North America, accounting for as many as 24% of all guidebooks sold. I think I know why.

Though we hope our books are entertaining, we nevertheless deal with travel in a serious fashion. Our guidebooks have never looked on such journeys as a mere recreation, but as a far more important human function, a time of learning and introspection, an essential part of a civilized life. We stress the culture, lifestyle, history, and beliefs of the destinations we cover, and urge our readers to seek out people and new ideas as the chief rewards of travel.

We have never shied from controversy. We have, from the beginning, encouraged our authors to be intensely judgmental, critical—both pro and con—in their comments, and wholly independent. Our only clients are our readers, and we have triggered the ire of countless prominent sorts, from a tourist newspaper we called "practically worthless" (it unsuccessfully sued us) to the many rip-offs we've condemned.

And because we believe that travel should be available to everyone regardless of their incomes, we have always been cost-conscious at every level of expenditure. Though we have broadened our recommendations beyond the budget category, we insist that every lodging we include be sensibly priced. We use every form of media to assist our readers, and are particularly proud of our feisty daily website, the award-winning Frommers.com.

I have high hopes for the future of Frommer's. May these guidebooks, in all the years ahead, continue to reflect the joy of travel and the freedom that travel represents. May they always pursue a cost-conscious path, so that people of all incomes can enjoy the rewards of travel. And may they create, for both the traveler and the persons among whom we travel, a community of friends, where all human beings live in harmony and peace.

Arthur Frommer

THE BEST OF LONDON

Whether you realize it or not, London shaped your destiny. There's hardly a quarter of the globe that London, as the seat of England's government, hasn't changed. The United States was founded in reaction to London's edicts. Australia's first permanent European settlers were London's criminals. Modern Canada, South Africa, and New Zealand were cultivated from London. India's course was irrevocably changed by the aspirations of London businessmen, as were the lives of millions of Africans who were enslaved and shipped around the world while Londoners lined their pockets with profits. That you bought this book, written in English somewhere other than in England, is evidence of London's reach across time and distance. And its dominion continues to this day: London is the world's most popular destination for foreign tourists.

London is inexhaustible—you could tour it for months and barely get to know it. Few cities support such a variety of people living in remarkable harmony. In 2016, this historically Christian country even elected a Muslim mayor, Sadiq Khan. That diversity makes London like a cut diamond: Approach it from a different angle each day, and it presents an entirely fresh shape and color. From famous stories to high style, London is many things in every moment.

But at this moment, London is embattled by monumental shifts—the passing of its beloved Queen Elizabeth II in September 2022 and the ascension of King Charles III, the Covid-19 pandemic and subsequent economic uncertainty, and Britain's exit from its membership in the European Union (a messy move that people call Brexit). These shifts are molding this place into something new, but as yet undefined. Few can be confident about how these waves of change will alter the color of the city and the mood of the nation. London is already an extremely difficult place to live. Locals still pay the highest rate in the world for their public transit, and it's still a brutally expensive city for housing—the average monthly rent for a one-bedroom flat outside the center of the city is £2,220, but the average salary is just £60,921. Will the city squeeze out the young and the poor? Are the high times coming to an end? For now, London waits.

St Margaret's Church has been the official church of the House of Commons since 1614, but behind it, Westminster Abbey has been a place of worship for a millennium.

LONDON'S best ATTRACTIONS

- **British Library** (p. 122): The finest and rarest books on the planet, plus the Magna Carta, are laid open for your eyes.
- **British Museum** (p. 126): Some of the most astounding treasures of the classical world are housed in one overwhelmingly glorious neoclassical building.
- **Churchill War Rooms** (p. 148): A time capsule of the tense days of World War II and the most advanced biographical museum in existence.

The encyclopedic British Museum collects masterworks and artifacts from almost every era of human history.

- **National Gallery** (p. 138): Some 2,000 masterpieces, the cream of Western European art, reside at what may be the best fine art collection in the world.
- **Natural History Museum** (p. 165): For kids, it's all about the dinosaurs, but this "cathedral of nature" has major chops as a research facility, too.
- **St Paul's Cathedral** (p. 183): Sir Christopher Wren's masterpiece is the icon of London and a shrine to historic events and people.
- **Tate Modern** (p. 179): Bankside's hymn to the "shock of the new," a former power station, makes an impression before you see a single artwork.
- **Tower of London** (p. 186): Britain's gruesome underbelly and its glittering Crown Jewels coexist in one sprawling city castle of stone.
- **Victoria & Albert Museum** (p. 169): Always evolving and growing, this is probably the world's finest collection of decorative arts.
- **Westminster Abbey** (p. 153): Be awed by Britain's ancient spiritual heart, where nearly 1,000 years of monarchs have been crowned and many are buried. The exciting **Queen's Diamond Jubilee Galleries** balcony museum recently opened for the first time.

LONDON'S essential EXPERIENCES

- **Promenading on South Bank:** In 1957, the Thames was declared "biologically dead." Today, it flows with life. Alongside it, as restaurants, bars, and creative developments continue to pop up, a walk along the South Bank from Westminster Bridge to Tower Bridge is newly one of the world's great promenades. The ever-changing perspective from Parliament to the Tower is ceaselessly inspiring.
- **Following in Royal Footsteps:** London is where some of the most famous characters in history played their scenes. Nearly every British monarch

Tate Modern is world famous for displaying contemporary art, but its Thames views can be just as inspiring.

3

since 1066 was crowned in **Westminster Abbey** (p. 153). Henry VIII strutted around **Hampton Court Palace** (p. 205), and the story of Queen Elizabeth II centers on **Buckingham Palace** (p. 147) and **Windsor Castle** (p. 323). And the story continues: The future King George VII and his siblings were diapered in **Kensington Palace** (p. 164).

o **Flying High on the London Eye:** Ride to the top of our generation's contribution to London's beloved attractions for a far-reaching shot of the cityscape. See p. 174.

o **Climbing the Dome of St Paul's Cathedral:** Wren's baroque masterpiece stirs emotion in everyone who lays eyes on its lead-coated wooden dome. But it's the climb to the Golden Gallery for a 360° panorama that will stay with you forever. As for Wren, he was forced to add the balustrade for Queen Anne. "Ladies think nothing well without an edging," he complained. See p. 182.

o **Immersing Yourself in World War II:** More than 80 years later, the Blitz still isn't far from many Londoners' minds. Dig into the power of their resistance at the superlative time capsule of the **Churchill War Rooms** (p. 148), the immersive **Museum of London Docklands** (p. 195), the floating military museum **HMS** *Belfast* (p. 181), and the top-secret code-breaking headquarters of **Bletchley Park** (p. 336).

o **Taking Afternoon Tea:** Look smart at **Brown's Hotel,** the **Goring, Fortnum & Mason,** or the **Langham** (p. 98), where the traditional tea ritual carries on as it did in Britain's colonial heyday.

o **Spending an Evening at a West End Theatre:** London is the theatrical capital of the world. The live stages of **Theatreland** around Covent Garden and Soho offer a combination of variety, accessibility, and economy—but the shows of the Fringe are where the future can be found. See p. 257.

Specialty foods and ready-to-eat meals from across the U.K. and Europe are sold at Borough Market.

LONDON'S best FOOD

o **Tucking into Honest British Ingredients:** After many lost years of too much boiled cabbage and bread, the English have fallen back in love with farm-fresh ingredients. The gastropub movement, epitomized by its still-potent pioneer, the **Eagle** (p. 84), is just the beginning. Delectable English traditional cooking can be found from the oldest establishments (**Rules,** p. 94) to neighborhood holes-in-the-wall (**Andrew Edmunds,** p. 87; **10 Greek Street,** p. 87).

The British Tea Guild Council bestows awards for best afternoon teas, and the Goring (p. 57) has earned the top prize in years past. Seen here is the hotel's special Platinum Jubilee–themed service from 2022.

A world of cheese awaits at Neal's Yard Dairy.

o **Sinking a Pint in a Traditional Pub:** From Tudor coaching inns to riverside taverns, London's pub culture spans the centuries. Raise a pint where Shakespeare did at **The George** (p. 113), raise one with Sir Ian McKellen at his pub **The Grapes** (p. 114), immerse yourself in an ale at Dr. Samuel Johnson's local **Ye Olde Cheshire Cheese** (p. 120), and drink in a Victorian jewel box of etched glass at the **Princess Louise** (p. 118). Then repeat. See "21 Pubs You'll Love" on p. 112.

o **Mining the Stalls at Borough Market:** The top port of call for foodies is the market under the railway by London Bridge station—not least for the free samples dished out by vendors keen to market their wares. It's gourmet heaven. See p. 105.

o **Enjoying the New English Comfort Food:** London's first Indian restaurant opened in 1810, and Asian food of every origin is now the capital's most popular genre of cuisine. The dozens of curry houses on **Brick Lane** (p. 110) pitch for your business at the curb; or take in a traditional meal at Covent Garden's **Punjab Restaurant** (p. 96), opened by an Indian wrestler back in 1947.

o **Chowing Down on Farmhouse Cheese:** England produces hundreds of artisan cheeses. Check out the West Country cheddars, red Leicester, and goat cheeses at such cheesemongers as **Neal's Yard Dairy** (p. 106) or eat a gloppy, gooey plate of raclette at **Kappacasein** (p. 105). But get your fill while you're here: You can't get it back through Customs.

o **Tasting Britain's Fading Traditions:** As young English diners insist on international fare and healthy options, the older ways of cooking become rarer. Whether it's the deep-fried goodness at the linoleum-lined "chippy" **Fryer's Delight** (p. 85), or the traditional "caff" of the **Regency Café** (p. 102), mid-century Britain is still steaming along—affordably.

LONDON'S best HOTELS

It's no exaggeration to say London has some of the world's best hotels.

o **Meet the Locals at a Family-Run B&B:** Mom-and-pop inns once ruled London. The new dominance of corporate hotels has all but extinguished the once-bright flame of local English hospitality. But you can still find some stellar homegrown homes where owners put you first, including the Valotis and Cabrals of the **Alhambra Hotel** in St Pancras (p. 46), the Beynons of Bloomsbury's **Jesmond Hotel** (p. 47), and the Goodsalls of **Lime Tree Hotel** in Victoria (p. 58).

o **Lose Yourself in a Grande Dame:** The first all-service grand hotel in Europe, the **Langham** (p. 63) was built in 1865, and it's still extending top-flight hospitality to guests with taste—and cash. **Claridge's** (p. 60) and **The Savoy** (p. 51) have attracted royalty and creative misadventures since the late 1800s. Best of all, you can tour their ground floors without being a guest.

o **Make the River Your Base:** Throughout London's history, the riverfront was mostly an unsavory industrial zone worth avoiding, but we're luckier in our times. Excellent hotels like **Bankside** (p. 65), **Sea Containers** (p. 66), and a new **Hoxton** (p. 68) have set up shop on the south end of Blackfriars Bridge, putting guests within quick reach of the Thames Path, Tate Modern, and St Paul's and the City.

o **Pay Less Than $90:** You may not think it's possible, but with advance planning, you can get a new, impeccably maintained private room in the center of town. Book way ahead with the British chains **Premier Inn, Travelodge,** or **easyHotel,** or with the imported budget brands **Ibis** and **citizenM,** and London is yours, cheap. See p. 38.

o **Sleep Where History Happened:** Rather than tear it down, Londoners would rather revitalize it. Be party to the spy stories at **St. Ermin's Hotel** (p. 57), rest under the swoony spires of Gilbert Scott's neo-Gothic **St. Pancras Renaissance Hotel** (p. 43), dine in a former church and wake up in its wood-paneled offices at the boutique charmer **L'Oscar** (p. 49), or relax in the onetime headquarters of the Ministry of Defence at the **Corinthia London** (p. 62).

o **Enjoy Style for Less:** A new mid-level style of European hotel gives

Queen Victoria and Prince Albert visited Claridge's hotel in 1860, 4 years after its original building opened. It still feels regal today.

you all you need in a stylish package without the dull corporate formula. At the **Resident** hotels (p. 53) and **Z Hotels** (p. 42), you'll surrender some space, but not the chic. Buzzy Dutch boutique **citizenM** (p. 38) has huge beds and a loopy personality, but a fair price.

LONDON'S best FOR FAMILIES

o **Cruising London's Waterways:** In addition to the grand River Thames, London has a working canal system that once kept goods flowing to and from the city's docks. The best value trips are on the **Thames Clipper** traversing the city's entire waterfront (p. 227) and on the **Regent's Canal** (p. 218).

o **Riding the Tiny Tube:** Climb aboard a segment of the miniature London Post Office Railway, which for 76 years shuttled mail under the capital's streets. It's part of the kid-oriented **Postal Museum** (p. 134).

o **Visiting Harry Potter:** Warner Bros.' deep dive into how it designed and made its blockbuster films, **The Making of Harry Potter** (p. 207), is one of the country's most popular family attractions, surpassing expectations, and a Gringotts section was added in 2019. Potterheads could happily spend a whole day here.

o **Losing Your Way in the World's Most Famous Hedge Maze:** The green labyrinth at **Hampton Court** twists and turns for almost half a mile. When you manage to extricate yourself, stroll through centuries of architectural styles at this stunning palace, home of many an English monarch. Don't forget to pick up a kids' activity trail. See p. 205.

o **Going Botanic in Royal Kew:** The **Royal Botanic Gardens, Kew,** house more than 50,000 plants from across the planet, including Arctic and tropical varieties. Youngsters will love the 200m-high (656-ft.) Treetop Walkway, up in the Gardens' deciduous canopy. See p. 206.

The movie set of Dumbledore's office at Warner Bros. is an enchanting part of the Harry Potter Studio Tour.

Kew Gardens bills itself as the most biodiverse place on earth—with good reason. Along with ornate flower beds (pictured), the Gardens' greenhouses nurture rare specimens thought to be extinct in the wild. One South African plant germinated from seeds gathered in 1806.

- **Asking How, Where & Why:** Inside South Kensington's **Science Museum** (p. 167), interactive exhibits keep inquisitive minds occupied. Or pilot a simulated ship at the kid-centric **National Maritime Museum** (p. 197), or learn how to drive a Tube train at the **London Transport Museum** (p. 136).

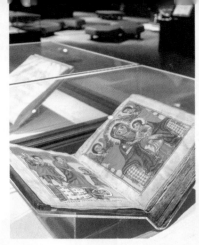
Eye-popping precious books are on display for free at the British Library.

- **Learning the Panto Lingo:** From November to early January, join one of Britain's most delightful holiday experiences: pantomimes, which are slapstick musical romps through famous stories, usually starring D-list celebrities. Hiss at villains, shout instructions for heroes, and giggle at good-natured drag performers, a traditional role called *the dame*. Try the **Theatre Royal Stratford** (www.stratfordeast.com), the **New Wimbledon** (www.new wimbledontheatre.net), the **Hackney Empire** (p. 264), or the **Richmond Theatre** (www.richmondtheatre.net).

- **Seeing Peter Pan in Kensington Gardens:** You'll feel like a character from a Victorian novel as you stand beneath Sir George Frampton's beloved 1912 statue of the boy who played the panpipe. There's no better way to admire and enjoy the "green lung"—the largest and most popular open space in the middle of a city that already holds the record for the most green space for a city of its size. See p. 218.

LONDON'S best FREE & DIRT CHEAP EXPERIENCES

- **Visiting the Great Museums:** London's best museums and galleries show off their permanent collections for free. Those include the **British Museum, National Gallery, National Portrait Gallery, Tate Britain, Tate Modern, Natural History Museum, Science Museum, V&A,** and the **British Library.** See chapter 5.

- **Taking in Fresh Air & a City View:** North of the River Thames, **Hampstead Heath** (p. 216) offers miles of woodland trails, historic pubs, and sumptuous mansions. In the southeast, the flower beds of **Greenwich Park** (p. 216) enjoy a panoramic sweep over the Thames.

- **Dining on the Cheap:** Away from the Michelin-starred hotspots, London is surprisingly well equipped with affordable, tasty places to enjoy a full meal for under £15. Among the best is the West End's most venerable budget pit stop, **Café in the Crypt** at St Martin-in-the-Fields church (p. 91).

Hampstead Heath is a popular fair-weather hangout.

- **The King of Libraries:** The **British Library** (p. 122) started as the monarch's private stash but now its doors yawn wide to the public with free exhibitions and priceless manuscripts that must be seen to be believed.
- **Catching a Free Event in the Center of the City:** From the **Lord Mayor's Show** to the **Notting Hill Carnival,** a large number of major public events cost nothing to attend. See "London Calendar of Events" (p. 365).

THE best HISTORIC EXPERIENCES

- **Meeting the Heroes & Villains of History:** Get face-to-face with a rogue's gallery from the past at the **National Portrait Gallery,** where faces seem to watch you across time with a sparkle in their eye. The gang's all here, from a supercilious Henry VIII to a pugnacious Hogarth to a sad-eyed Princess Diana, already fading into a memory. See p. 142. *(Closed until the spring of 2023.)*
- **Taking a Tour of Royal London:** From palaces and parks to the royal art collections, history, geography, and culture have been shaped—or owned—by centuries of aristocratic rule. You can see the best of it in a day, including the late Queen Elizabeth's favorite grocer, **Fortnum & Mason** (p. 232), plus any one of 800 other Royal Warrant holders (p. 240). Roam the very rooms used in daily life by kings and queens at **Buckingham Palace** (p. 147), **Hampton Court Palace** (p. 205), **Kensington Palace** (p. 164), and **Windsor Castle** (p. 323).
- **Peering into a Time Capsule:** Some museums preserve scenes that were frozen in time. No reconstructions or fakery here: You'll gaze upon authentic World War II military operations at the **Churchill War Rooms** (p. 148);

In 1856, the National Portrait Gallery began its collection by acquiring the only rendering of William Shakespeare thought to be painted from a sitting and not other sources. Since then, the Gallery has exhibited huge works (including one with 400 identified sitters), tiny ones (a thumbnail-sized picture of Henrietta Anne, Duchess of Orleans), and nearly 1,000 portraits of the late Queen Elizabeth II, many of them rare photographs.

admire the graves of great artists and the location of epic rituals at **West-minster Abbey** (p. 153); explore the secret cloisters of the **Charterhouse** campus (p. 191), founded in 1371 and only opened to tourists in 2017; see the home that made **Charles Darwin** want to stop traveling (p. 207); roam an intact battleship at the **HMS** *Belfast* (p. 181); and marvel at the treasure-crammed townhouse of a 19th-century collector (**Sir John Soane's Museum,** p. 144).

o **Shopping in the Grandest Department Stores of Them All:** And, no, it's not Harrods. **Liberty** (p. 234), founded in 1875 and moved to its current half-timbered, mock-Tudor home in 1924, and **Selfridges** (p. 236), both designed and built by Americans, redefined sales methods, liberated women from homebound drudgery, and played crucial roles in world history.

o **Imagining Domestic Life Through the Ages:** At the **V&A** (p. 169), gape at one of the finest collections of fine historic furniture in the world. But that's a museum—nothing immerses you in the past quite like the brain-bending role-playing of a night visit to **Dennis Severs' House** (p. 193).

SUGGESTED ITINERARIES & NEIGHBORHOODS

Few great modern cities are as multilayered, intricate, and unknowable as London, Western Europe's most populous city (8.8 million in 2021, the highest level since before World War II). Perhaps that's because history is knitted into its layout. London is mostly the haphazard product of blind evolution, which piled up over successive generations to produce a complicated metropolis.

As recently as the early 1800s, London—and by London, I mean what we now call the City of London, or the City, between St Paul's and the Tower—was a frenzied cluster where many lives, birth to death, were carried out within the same few blocks. The main streets ran south to the river (not east or west, as they do now), the smoke of industry was banished downwind to the east, and kings lived near the Thames for easy transportation. All around the City were dozens of villages, many of which retain their names as modern neighborhoods—and, if you're lucky, a whiff of their original personalities, but not of their original pestilence.

Quickly, London swelled to swallow its current territory. Yet because of ancient echoes, neighborhoods remain surprisingly small—many are just minutes across by foot, and even crucial streets can change names several times. It's still possible to stroll along and sense sudden shifts in energy and character. In many ways, London is still a complex system of hamlets. It's one of the many delights that makes it so surprising. It also means it can take a lifetime to scratch its surface.

Addresses sometimes reflect this improvisation; a building numbered 75 may sit across the street from one numbered 32. Despite this, it's immensely difficult to get lost. The City maintains some 1,200 Legible London map **"Finger Posts"** on sidewalks throughout town.

If you want a handheld map, forgo the oversimplified one your hotel might offer and don't tax your data plan. The most cherished paper map is the *London A–Z* (www.az.co.uk), first compiled by the indefatigable Phyllis Pearsall, who walked every mile of the City for the 1936 debut edition and commanded the resulting cartography empire until her death 60 years later. Its *London Mini A–Z*

Street Atlas (£6) fits into a pocket. Just be sure to call it the "A to Zed" or you'll get a funny look; in England, the last letter in the alphabet is, quite sensibly, pronounced so it will not rhyme with eight other letters.

LONDON IN 1 DAY

First of all, what were you thinking? If you're in town on a layover, didn't you know that many airlines will allow you to stick around for a few days at no charge? Never mind. What's done is done. Eat a huge breakfast and make your way to Tower Hill.

1 The Tower of London ★★★

Start here (p. 186) because it usually opens an hour earlier (9am) than most attractions. Spend about 2 hours making stops at the **Crown Jewels** and the **White Tower,** and snap that requisite photo of the **Tower Bridge** (p. 185) from the quay. Grab a triangle sandwich (the quintessential London lunch).

Tube it west on the Circle or District lines to Westminster.

2 Westminster Abbey ★★★

Allot a rushed 2 hours to see the effigies of kings and queens (p. 153). Of the **Chapel of Henry**

Even in daylight, the Tower of London can feel spooky. Mind the ravens!

VII, Washington Irving wrote: "Stone seems, by the cunning labor of the chisel, to have been robbed of its weight and density, suspended aloft as if by magic, and the fretted roof achieved with the wonderful minuteness and airy security of a cobweb." Outside, take in the **Houses of Parliament** (p. 148) and **Big Ben's Elizabeth Tower** from across the street. The latter just completed its first full restoration since 1859, and its faces have been returned to their original Prussian blue and gold colors.

Walk up Whitehall, passing No. 10 Downing St. (the walking tour on p. 283 will guide you).

3 The National Gallery ★★★

At **Trafalgar Square,** the symbolic heart of the city, you can finally see some of the world's most famous paintings in person (p. 138). Park guards ask tourists not to climb those famous bronze couchant lions, each of them 20 feet long, that surround Nelson's Column. Don't mount them—they're cracking.

London's Neighborhoods

Between 1872 and 1876, designer Edward Middleton Barry created this dramatic extension for the National Gallery. The opulent Barry Rooms are centered around a huge octagon and arranged in the shape of a Greek cross. Early staff worried that the architecture and vivid colors would draw visitors' focus away from the masterpieces.

From the Strand, head to the back of Charing Cross station and cross the Thames.

4 London Eye ★★

There's time for a revolution on London's favorite contemporary icon and the new focal point of national celebrations (p. 174).

Finish just north of the National Gallery, around Leicester Square.

5 West End Show ★★★

Curtains go up around 7:30pm (p. 257). Enjoy an ice cream during interval (intermission)—it's a custom. Afterward, hurry to a

Crown a day of sightseeing by viewing the heart of the city from the London Eye.

pub and raise a pint to a city where you've barely scratched the surface (see p. 112 for ideas).

LONDON ON A 2ND DAY

You're going to have to move fast, but you'll be able to see some highlights. Take the Tube to Mansion House, Blackfriar, or St Paul's.

1 St Paul's Cathedral ★★★

As you appreciate the underside of the dome, also appreciate the grave fact that before the 1940s, its exterior flanks were crowded with buildings. Bombings wiped away the structures that once hemmed it in.

A dome's-eye view of the splendor that is St Paul's Cathedral during services.

Cross the Thames on the Millennium Bridge (the walking tour on p. 302 will help).

2 Tate Modern ★★★

Here's a museum (p. 179) in a colossal structure with river views that can be more memorable and accessible than what's on display inside it. If it's summer, catch a matinee at **Shakespeare's Globe** (p. 222), just a few yards east; an afternoon pint across the bridge at the Art Nouveau **Blackfriar** (p. 113) will recharge you.

Take the Jubilee line from Southwark to Green Park.

3 Green Park ★★

Walk south through Green Park (p. 215) to behold the front of **Buckingham Palace** (p. 147); if you're here in March, you may be lucky enough to see fields of daffodils in bloom. Return to Piccadilly to browse the classy shops lining it, particularly **Fortnum & Mason** (p. 232), **Hatchards** (p. 238), **Cordings** (p. 241), and the haberdasheries of **Jermyn Street** just south.

Take the Tube's Piccadilly line (notice the century-old tilework) to Russell Square.

4 The British Museum ★★★

You'll spend the afternoon roaming its vast halls (p. 126), but you'll scarcely be able to wrap your brain around the age, rarity, and craftsmanship of what you see. Such aesthetic exertions may induce cravings for cream tea at its Great Court Restaurant or another pint at a Victorian valentine of a pub, the **Princess Louise** (p. 118).

Catch bus 55 toward Oxford Circus. Sit on the top level for the views!

5 Oxford Circus ★★

Wind up the afternoon with a dive into the bustling fitting rooms of the shops on **Oxford Street, Regent Street,** and **Carnaby Street** (p. 230),

Even if you don't catch the showy Changing the Guard ceremony, Buckingham Palace from the Mall is a sight to behold.

where you'll find a huge selection of cool clothes at what Londoners call "High Street" prices—meaning they're sane. Maybe get a cocktail at the 1940s-themed **Cahoots** (book ahead; p. 279) or walk southeast for a few minutes in Soho and have dinner at **Andrew Edmunds** (p. 87), a neighborhood gem with a changing menu that charges prices far below its rank, and afterward, stroll past the lights of **Piccadilly Circus.**

If you still have juice left, walk down Haymarket, turn left on Cockspur, and follow it down the Strand to Aldwych.

6 South Bank ★★★

Cross right using the Waterloo bridge and wander east along the popular promenade of **South Bank.** During the evening, couples stroll, theaters light, cafes buzz, and the water of the Thames glitters in the light reflected from the **Illuminated River** light installation (p. 275) and the ancient grey dome of St Paul's. It makes for an unforgettable evening.

LONDON ON A 3RD DAY

Follow the itinerary for 2 days in London, but add in one of the South Kensington museums, preferably the **Victoria & Albert (V&A)** (p. 169), and follow that with a walk through **Hyde Park** (p. 218) and a tour of the public areas of Prince William's London home, **Kensington Palace** (p. 164), in adjoining **Kensington Gardens.** Take the Tube or a bus to Westminster and dive into the time capsule of the **Churchill War Rooms** (p. 148). Follow that with a stroll along the South Bank from Westminster to London Bridge, taking your pick among the pubs and restaurants you find along the path.

AN ITINERARY FOR FAMILIES

London is low-rise and manageable, so anywhere except the financial centers (the City, Canary Wharf) are good places to stay with kids. But make sure they're ready to climb lots of stairs if you're taking the Tube. Also ask for kids' "trails" at the big museums: London's museums work hard to create materials that cater to children—maybe too much, as it's often at the expense of adult minds. Every major museum, no exceptions, also has an on-site cafe for lunch or refreshment.

Day 1: Double-Deckers & Thames Clippers

Forget expensive open-top tours: Start your day seeing Piccadilly Circus, Trafalgar Square, St Paul's Cathedral, the Tower of London, and much more for the price of bus fare on an antique, double-decker **Routemaster bus** with an old-style staircase on the end. Take route 15, every 15 minutes. Board at an endpoint, Trafalgar Square or Tower Hill, or a stop along the route. After visiting the **Tower of London** (p. 186), head to the ferry dock and see the city from the river on a **Thames Clipper** (p. 361).

Along with formal gardens (pictured), Kensington Palace is flanked on one side by a meadow of native wildflowers, including daisies, poppies, and campion, planted to give sustenance and shelter to the city's pollinators.

Disembark at **Tate Modern** (p. 179), which comes fully loaded for young exploration with family trails, a learning zone on Level 5, and some very cool video tablets for interpreting the art. Take the Tube to the West End for a **musical** (p. 258).

Day 2: Covent Garden & Coram's Fields

Make your way to Covent Garden's **London Transport Museum** (p. 136), where kids can pretend to drive a bus and explore other eye-level exhibits. Then bring your brood on a 15-minute walk north to the **British Museum** (p. 126) and hook them up with crayons and pads, exploration backpacks, and the special object collections tour geared to young minds. If they're the daring types, the mummies never fail to impress. Just east you'll find a city park just for children: The 7-acre **Coram's Fields** (www.coramsfields.org), which was set aside in 1739 for an orphanage at a time when 75% of London kids died before the age of 5. Its southern gate is where mothers once abandoned their babies in desperation. Today, no adult may enter without a child, and this once sad spot is now the scene of daily family joy; there's a petting zoo, two playgrounds for all ages, sand pits, and a paddling pool.

Day 3: The Brompton Road Museums

Today is devoted to exploration of the Brompton Road museums, a trio of world's-bests for kids: Take the Piccadilly line to South Kensington, where the **V&A** (p. 169) has hundreds of hands-on exhibits for kids (look for the hand symbol on the maps), such as trying on Victorian costumes or donning armor gauntlets. Next door, the plain-speaking signs and robotic dinosaurs of the **Natural History Museum** (p. 165) impress kids as much as the airplanes and space capsules over their heads at the

Coram's Fields, near the Foundling Museum, is dedicated to children in memory of the city's orphans.

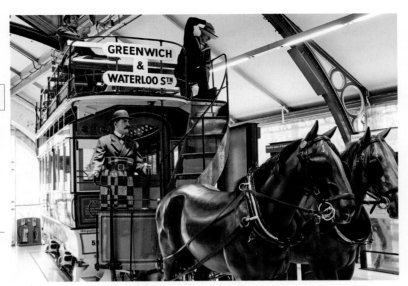

Kids will experience double-decker omnibuses at the hands-on London Transport Museum.

Science Museum (p. 167)—both institutions furnish even more kids' trails and activities for free. Go east on the Circle or District Tube lines to Temple, and you're at the dancing water jets (transformed in winter to a skating rink) of the **Somerset House** courtyard (home of the Courtauld Gallery; p. 136). If the weather doesn't suit that, the **London Eye**'s capsules are safe, climate-controlled, and move imperceptibly—the view will stimulate and inspire kids.

A DISCOVERY WEEKEND

The Frommer's guides are designed to give you a firm introduction to the sights, hotels, and restaurants that speak most to a visitor about what's going on in each destination. But authentic London doesn't begin and end with these pages, and if you dip into neighborhoods where more locals live, your visit will be immeasurably richer.

Day 1: Brixton & Bollywood

When Victoria was queen, families flocked to live near the incandescent lights of Brixton's Electric Avenue, which in 1888 became one of London's first shopping streets lit by electricity. Today, it's a boisterous immigrant community, timeworn and down-market but safe. By day, explore the glazed awnings of its markets, where to inhale the aroma of meat and spices is to walk through a portal to Jamaica, India, or China—and to be reminded that London, like few others, is a truly worldly city. In the evening, experience London's huge South Asian community—Indians are nearly 20% of the population, and one of Britain's richest men, Lakshmi Mittal, is Indian-born—by attending a Bollywood film at the Boleyn Cinema (www.boleyncinemas.uk; Tube: Upton Park), a historic 1938 Art Deco building and the second-largest Bollywood screen in a country that loves the genre.

Day 2: Go Football Mad or Cricket Crazy

London hosts 13 professional football (soccer) teams, more than any other city on Earth. From mid-August to mid-May, catch matches at some of the best Premier League teams: **Chelsea** (www.chelseafc.com), **Arsenal** (London's first club; www.arsenal.com), **Tottenham Hotspur** (www.tottenhamhotspur.com), **Fulham** (www.fulhamfc.com), or **West Ham United** (www.whufc.com), which took up residence in London Stadium, the former Olympic Stadium at Stratford. Filling the gap from April to September, and less likely to pelt you in the skull with a beer bottle, is cricket. Attend "test matches" at Marylebone's **MCC Lord's Cricket Ground** (www.lords.org) or Oval's **Surrey County Cricket Club** (www.kiaoval.com). The relatively young **T20 Blast** league (www.ecb.co.uk/T20-Blast), currently sponsored as the **Vitality Blast**, plays faster-paced "T20" versions of the game to appeal to fans who don't want a match to take all day. If you figure out how the game works, fill me in, won't you? It's a little like baseball—and a lot like watching grass grow.

Day 3: Ale, Yorkshire Pudding & Tough Questions

On Sunday afternoons, find a pub with an inviting garden for a traditional **Sunday Roast,** a spread of roasted meats with all the trimmings such as

Make like Ted Lasso and attend a football match to see Londoners at their most rambunctious.

Use the Code

London is chopped into geographic parcels, and you'll see those postcodes on street signs. The heart of the City, in postcode terms, is near the Chancery Lane Tube stop. From there, areas are given a compass direction (N for north, SW for southwest, and so on) and a number (but ignore that, since a number greater than 1 doesn't mean the area is in the boonies). In the very heart of town, addresses get an extra C for "centre," as in WC1, which is where Covent Garden is located. Every address in this book includes its postcode, which corresponds to the neighborhood in which you'll find it. Don't worry—you won't need to memorize these because each listing in this book also includes the nearest Tube stop to help you quickly place locations on a map. Here are some of the most common postcodes:

WC1 Bloomsbury

WC2 Covent Garden, Holborn, Strand

W1 Fitzrovia, Marylebone, Mayfair, Soho

W2 Bayswater

W6 Hammersmith

W8 Kensington

W11 Notting Hill

SW1 Belgravia, St James's, Westminster

SW3 Chelsea

SW5 Earl's Court

SW7 Knightsbridge, South Kensington

SE1 Southwark

SE10 Greenwich

EC1 Clerkenwell

EC2 Bank, Barbican, Liverpool Street

EC3 Tower Hill

EC4 Fleet Street, St Paul's

E1 Spitalfields, Whitechapel

E2 Bethnal Green

E14 Canary Wharf/Isle of Dogs

N1 Islington

NW1 Camden Town

NW3 Hampstead

Yorkshire pudding (a popover-like pastry) and gravy, washed down with copious amounts of beer. It's the more leisurely equivalent of brunch: After a long week of working to keep their exorbitantly priced shared flats, Londoners hang out at roasts all day, so it's always smart to reserve a place ahead of time. Some pubs also hold **quizzes,** another staple of British life. Form teams and answer trivia for lame prizes, but be warned: Foreigners always fold on the sports and politics questions.

Neighborhoods in Brief

London's neighborhoods were laid out during a period of wagon and foot traffic, when districts were defined in narrower terms than we define them today; indeed, for centuries people often lived complete lives without seeing the other side of town. Ironically, in our times, the Tube has done much to divide these districts from each other. Visitors are likely to hop a train between them and don't often realize how remarkably close together they really are.

Are these the only areas of interest? Not even close. Literally hundreds of fascinating village clusters abound, many with names as cherishable as Ponders End, Tooting, and The Wrythe. And considering that about 40% of Londoners now belong to an ethnic minority and more than 200 languages are spoken, the flavor of your experience shifts as you go. But visitors are likely to spend time here, and all are considered safe to walk around day or night.

BLOOMSBURY & FITZROVIA

Best for: *Museums, affordable inns, residential streets, universities*

What you won't find: *Evening entertainment, nightclubs*

Bloomsbury's dark-brick, white-sashed residential buildings and leafy squares date mostly from the Georgian period, when the district became the first in a chaotic city to be planned—it was an early version of the

In this aerial shot, some of London's historic maritime infrastructure—the Pool of London, Tower Bridge, and St Katharine Docks—are juxtaposed with some of the city's more progressive contemporary structures, such as the egg-shaped former City Hall by architect Sir Norman Foster.

From Arthur Frommer's *Europe on $5 a Day* (1957)

"All you've heard to the contrary, Londoners are among the warmest people of Europe, and London is a friendly and inviting city. It has charm and a polite- ness of attitude that belie its big-city status. You'll want to extend your stay. . . . Can you live in London on $5 a day? There's nothing to it."

modern suburban development. The refined air attracted the intelligentsia nearly from the start, and its two universities are both 19th-century institutions. The British Museum settled here, too. Bloomsbury became a place of remembrance on July 7, 2005; of the 52 who died in terrorist bombings that day, 26 perished underground on a Piccadilly line train between King's Cross and Russell Square stations, and 13 were killed on a double-decker bus passing through Tavistock Square. Bloomsbury's cozier sister Fitzrovia, similar in character but devoid of major attractions, lies on the western side of Tottenham Court Road. Famous residents included George Bernard Shaw and Virginia Woolf, who both lived (at different times) at 29 Fitzroy Square.

KING'S CROSS

Best for: *Budget hotels, trains heading north (and south to Paris), alternative/down-and-dirty nightlife, student housing, boutique shopping and dining*
What you won't find: *Green space*

In 2010, the area around King's Cross station was an unsavory tenderloin of porn stores and warehouses. Change came, as it often has in English history, from France: The Eurostar train now hurtles from and to France (and beyond) from this neighborhood, and its arrival revolutionized the local vibe. Behind the station, millions of pounds have just transformed once-derelict industrial infrastructure into Granary Square and the Coal Drops Yard, a canalside center for arts hotspots, restaurants, colleges, and tech HQs. Fans of Harry Potter know that the young wizard boards the Hogwarts Express at the (fictitious) Platform 9¾; the movie

versions shot at Platforms 4 and 5 but used prettier St Pancras station, next door, as a stand-in facade. Legend (surely apocryphal) says the Celtic queen Boudicca rests somewhere near Platform 8 of King's Cross.

MARYLEBONE & MAYFAIR

Best for: *Luxe shopping, hotels, restaurants, small museums, strolling, embassies*
What you won't find: *Historic sites, savings*

The middle-class hubbub of Oxford Street west of Regent Street divides high-hat Marylebone from its snobbish southern neighbor, Mayfair. Both play host to upscale shopping and several fascinating, if overlooked, museums, but there the similarities end. World-famous Mayfair, typified by hyperluxe bauble shops and blue-blood heritage (Queen Elizabeth II was born at 17 Bruton St. in a building that is no longer there), has a high opinion of itself as a starchy enclave of wealth, much of it from other countries. Yet Mayfair has less to offer the casual tourist, although it is the city's hot zone for cushy hotels. (The title of the musical *My Fair Lady* is witty wordplay on how its Cockney heroine, Eliza, would have pronounced "Mayfair lady.") Marylebone (*Marle-bun*), on the other hand, benefits from convenient Tube and bus connections and lively sidewalks crowded with evening celebrants, particularly around James Street. Also, thanks to a territorial local authority, its main shopping drag (Marylebone High Street) remains one of the last important streets in London that isn't awash with the ubiquitous corporate chain stores. Oxford Street was once the city's flagship shopping corridor but is in a slow decline; the western half between Oxford Circus and Marble Arch is the classier end, with marquee department stores such as Selfridges and Marks & Spencer.

SOHO, COVENT GARDEN & CENTRAL WEST END

Best for: *Shopping, restaurants, theater, cinema, nightlife, opera, free art (National Gallery and National Portrait Gallery), star sightings*

What you won't find: *Elbow room, silence*

London's undisputed center of nightlife, restaurants, and theater, the West End seethes with tourists and merrymakers. After work, Old Compton Street and Covent Garden overflow with people catching up with friends; by 7:30pm, the theaters and opera houses are pulsing; by midnight, the action has moved into the nightclubs of Leicester Square and lounges of Soho; and in the wee hours, you might find groups of partiers trawling Gerrard Street, in a teeny Cantonese Chinatown, drunkenly singing football-related shanties and hunting for snacks. Prim Trafalgar Square, dominated by the peerless National Gallery, has often been called London's focal point. On a sunny day, you'll find few places that exude such well-being.

WESTMINSTER, INCLUDING ST JAMES'S

Best for: *Historic and government sites, river strolls, St James's Park*

What you won't find: *Affordable hotels, a wide choice of restaurants*

Though it's near the West End, this area's energy is more staid. It's a district tourists mostly see by day. South of Trafalgar Square, you'll find regiments of robust government buildings but little in the way of hotels or food. Whitehall's severity doesn't spread far: Just a block east, its impenetrable character gives way to the proud riverside promenade of Victoria Embankment overlooking the London Eye, and just a block west, to the greenery of St James's Park, which is, in effect, the king's front yard, since Buckingham Palace is at the western boundary of this area. North of the park, the tidy streets of St James's are even more exclusive than Mayfair's, if that's possible.

THE CITY

Best for: *Old streets with new skyscrapers, the Tower of London, St Paul's, financial concerns*

What you won't find: *Nightlife or weekend life, ancient atmosphere*

Trafalgar Square is the unofficial meeting place of the city.

Technically, this is the only part of London that's London. Other bits, including the West End, are under the jurisdiction of different local governments, such as Westminster or Camden. The City, as it's called, is where most of London's history happened. It's where Romans cheered gladiators. It's where London Bridge—at least 12 versions—touched shore. It's where the Great Fire raged. And, more recently, it's where the Deutsche Luftwaffe focused many of its nocturnal bombing raids, which is why you'll find so little evidence of the aforementioned events. Outside of working hours, the main thing you'll see in the City is your own reflection in the facade of corporate fortresses; even most of the pubs close on weekends. Although it encompasses such priceless relics as the Tower of London, St Paul's Cathedral, the Tower Bridge, the Bank of England, and the Monument, many of the area's remnants are underfoot. The spiderweb of lanes and streets dates to the Roman period, with names that hint at their former lives (Walbrook is where the river Walbrook, now hidden underground along with Roman-era ruins on its shore, flowed down to the Thames; Honey Lane, Bread Street, Milk Street, and Poultry all once hosted food markets). Buildings have come and gone, but the veins of the City have pumped in situ for thousands of years.

THE SOUTH BANK, SOUTHWARK & BOROUGH

Best for: *Museums, memorable pubs, strolls, gourmet foods and wines*
What you won't find: *Shopping, parks*

During the recent rehabilitation of Southwark (*Suth*-urk) from a crumbling industrial district, its blighted power station became one of the world's greatest museums (the Tate Modern), a master playwright's theater was re-created (the Globe), and a sublime riverfront path replaced the coal lightermen's rotting piers. Now it's where London goes to fall in love. It's a 1-mile riverside stroll between the London Eye and the Tate Modern, and every step is a pleasure. Once-dank railway viaducts are now filled with cafes and reasonable restaurants; one of Western Europe's tallest skyscrapers, The Shard, lords over from above; and the nation's dramatic showpiece (the National

Theatre) anchors them at South Bank. But it's gratifying to see that some things never change: Borough Market, which attracts gourmet foodies from around the world, is the descendant of a market that fed the denizens of that medieval skyscraper over the water, London Bridge.

VICTORIA & CHELSEA

Best for: *Boutiques, low-cost lodging, town homes, wealthy neighbors*
What you won't find: *Transit options, street life, museums*

Victoria doesn't technically apply to the neighborhood around the eponymous train station—Belgravia (to the west) and Pimlico (south and east) take those honors—but the shorthand is common. Most of the area, which is residential or uninterestingly workaday, was developed starting in the 1820s in consistent patterns of white stucco-terraced homes. The area, recently redeveloped with glass office buildings, contains two outlier West End theaters, but little else. Just north, you'll face the brick walls of Buckingham Palace Gardens. Chelsea, to its south, has a history of well-heeled bohemianism—Oscar Wilde, James McNeill Whistler, and the Beatles all lived here—although it's known more as one of the city's most exclusive (and some would say insular) communities. A stroll past boutiques and pocket-squared residents on the King's Road, turning evermore corporate and indistinct, is not the adventure it was in the '60s.

KENSINGTON, KNIGHTSBRIDGE

Best for: *Museums, shopping, ultra-luxe boutiques, also-ran hotels*
What you won't find: *Historic sites*

Here, one expensive neighborhood genuflects to another, and barely anyone you meet was born in England. South Kensington and Brompton draw the most visitors to their grand museums; and Knightsbridge is where moneyed foreigners spend and show off—London now has, per capita, among the most billionaires in the world, nearly twice as many as New York or Moscow. They can't legally change most of the facades, so to satisfy their hunger for more space, the big trend among the rich is to burrow downward to build underground rooms—the "pleasure

The Best Days to Go

Not all of London's best areas are active every day of the week. Some places might be deserted, others too crowded, so plan your time better by matching your adventures with the right day for each one.

Better on weekends: Notting Hill, Houses of Parliament tours (p. 148)
Worse on weekends: Camden, Covent Garden
Better on weekdays: Camden, the Kensington museums

Worse on weekdays: Notting Hill
Better on Monday: West End ticket availability
Better on Thursday: Borough Market
Better on Friday: British Museum, National Portrait Gallery, National Gallery, V&A, and Tate Modern (when there's a late closing scheduled), Windsor (p. 323)
Better on Sunday: Speakers' Corner (p. 161), Brick Lane and Shoreditch, Sunday roast at a pub

caves" of Kensington. Privilege has long had an address in Kensington—that's a reason those edifying institutions were located here to begin with, away from the grubby paws of the peasants—but it also is home to a core of French expats; you'll find the cafes catering to them on Bute Street. Kensington Palace, at Kensington Gardens' western end, is where Prince William and Princess Catherine live when they're in town. When you travel west to Earl's Court, you experience a considerable drop in voltage. It's a frumpy zone, with undistinguished eats and sleeps; the rise of King's Cross and Shoreditch for younger travelers has reduced it to near-negligible stature. Your parents may have stayed here once, but you shouldn't have to.

SHOREDITCH, SPITALFIELDS & HOXTON

Best for: *Nightclubs, music, food of all types, galleries, clothing*
What you won't find: *Museums, parks*

If Mayfair is London's champagne, the East End 'hoods used to be its hangover. For centuries it was an impoverished slum for poor immigrants and shifty souls. Now Spitalfields (*Spit*-all-fields), named for its excellent covered market for bougie wares like tees with ironic designs (p. 255) is being consumed by an unstoppable cancer of soulless, open-plan office buildings from the City. It blends into Shoreditch, which was hipster heaven in 2015 but now wears a self-assured mask of counterculture for people with plenty of disposable income. Shopping,

restaurants, bars—it's all here now. Dalston, youngish and bohemian, is north of these, the factories-cum-lofts of Stoke Newington just north of that. Every few years, the younger set moves another neighborhood north, where they can most afford the rising rents. East of Spitalfields, in ancient homes that have long housed waves of immigrants (French, then Jewish, now South Asian), you'll find the famed restaurants of Brick Lane (p. 110), the cafes and dance clubs of the converted Old Truman Brewery, and the art-savvy neighborhood of Whitechapel. Prostitutes are out, £4.50 coffee is in—which may not be an improvement.

GREENWICH

Best for: *Museums, antique and food markets, river views, strolls, boats*
What you won't find: *Hotels, bustle*

Greenwich, on the south bank across from the Canary Wharf developments, retains the tranquility of a village, which it once was, before London enveloped it. The town has an illustrious pedigree as a royal getaway (it has the oldest royal park in London), as a scientific capital, and as one of the world's most crucial command centers. If it all sounds like a living museum, it is: On top of being a UNESCO World Heritage Site (Maritime Greenwich), the village is literally the center of time and space, since it inhabits the exact location of Greenwich Mean Time, and of longitude 0° 0' 0". Set away from Greenwich town there's the colossal O_2 dome, the city's iconic concert venue.

Other Popular London Neighborhoods

Mostly because of iffy transit connections (for example, service by a single Tube line that, should it go on the blink, would derail your vacation), this book doesn't focus on these neighborhoods as prime places to stay, but they're still vital parts of town.

BAYSWATER & PADDINGTON

Best for: Sub-par inns, international food, well-preserved Victorian thoroughfares

What you won't find: Attractions, non-chain stores, adorable Peruvian bears

Its whitewashed, terraced houses were briefly the most fashionable in the city (Churchill and Dickens were briefly residents), yet today, the sizable transient population of this area deprives it of sustained energy. Its shops are on the dismal side, its food cheap and tawdry, and its hotels tend to be for itinerant tradespeople. Crowning the muddle is Queensway, a shopping street containing Whiteleys, a 1911 department store edifice now converted into apartments for grotesquely wealthy tenants who will probably never be home. Although the interior of Paddington station is one of London's most beautiful train hubs (it was built by the architect Isambard Kingdom Brunel in 1838), the facade is obscured by a hotel; *Paddington* (2014) used Marylebone Station's more atmospheric entrance instead. Paddington Station is inconvenient to walk to, though the Elizabeth Line (p. 349) now visits it, and Heathrow and Windsor trains go from it.

DOCKLANDS

Best for: Development, ancient warehouses, super-cheap chain hotels

What you won't find: Street life, nightlife

Most of far east London along the north side of the Thames is ignobly called by a single, sweeping name: Docklands. Captain Cook set off on his explorations from here, and its hand-dug basins teemed with ships bearing goods from around the planet. Docklands made colonial Britain successful—and thus America, Canada, Australia, and South Africa, too. After a fallow generation, East London's pools are under constant redevelopment by corporations in stacks of fluorescent-lit office cubes, and the Olympics settled here in 2012 near the Stratford Tube stop. Away from the river, in salt-of-the-earth neighborhoods like Bethnal Green, Stratford, and West Ham, the city's Pakistani and Indian populations flourish, with marvelous but unglamorous food and shops.

ISLINGTON

Best for: Antiques, gastropubs, theater, street markets, cafes, strolls

What you won't find: Museums, hotels

Few neighborhoods retain such a healthy balance between feisty bohemianism and groomed prosperity, and almost none retain streetscapes as defiantly mid–20th century as Chapel Market. Islington's leafy byways are dotted with antiques dealers, hoary pubs with backroom theater spaces, beer gardens, and most pleasingly on a sunny day, pedestrian towpaths overlooking Regent's Canal. Why more tourists don't flood Islington is a mystery—and a blessing—but that hasn't stopped its ascendancy as a choice neighborhood for those with money.

CAMDEN

Best for: Alternative music, massive clothing markets, junk souvenirs, pubs

What you won't find: Elbow room, hotels, upscale restaurants

London's analogue to San Francisco's Haight-Ashbury District, it was big in the countercultured 1960s and '70s and is still grotty enough for Amy Winehouse to have expired in. The area's shoulder-to-shoulder markets, which hawk touristy hokum, cheap sunglasses, and £7 falafel in the former warehouses and stables serving Regent's Canal, can be overcrowded with bickering teens, and the sort of places where you feel compelled to carry your wallet in your front pocket. Tourists come more out of duty than for any true mission for commerce, and they cram the inadequate Tube stop on weekends. But I would endure it all for a bowl of hot fettuccine alfredo at The Cheese Wheel (West Yard, Camden Lock Place), where steaming fresh pasta is coated with cheesy richness by being tossed around in a giant 40kg (88-pound) wheel of Parmesan.

The neighborhood of Camden Town is one of the city's foremost adult playgrounds. Visitors and locals alike flock here to stroll the towpaths, eat and shop in bustling markets and stores, and party in lively pubs and music venues.

NOTTING HILL

Best for: *Markets, village vibes, restaurants, pubs, tourists, antiques*

What you won't find: *Well-priced shopping, museums, Hugh Grant in a bookstore*

Thanks partly to Hollywood, this westerly village-like nook that was once known to locals for race riots and, in 2017, the horrible Grenfell Tower fire, appears high on many checklists. Its Saturday Portobello Road market, the principal draw, is fiendishly crowded but short on truly wonderful wares. In fact, it's dead touristy. Like Camden, people go because they think they should. But if you feel compelled, Hugh Grant's blue door from *Notting Hill* (1999) is at 280 Westbourne Park Rd.

WHERE TO STAY

S ome cities are so great, very little can slow them down. London's standards for hotels are among the best in the world—in fact, there are more than 11,000 five-star rooms in the city. And the turbulence of recent years did little to dim those standards.

Through Brexit, the United Kingdom renounced its partnership with the E.U. The full financial ramifications for business, and therefore for business travelers, are still being determined. Residents have suffered much disruption, but for tourists, so far the result hasn't been a catastrophe. For the past few years, even through the pandemic, London's status as Europe's power city seemed unshakable and hotel inventory still grew by thousands of rooms. Once mass vaccination made travel possible again, London found itself right back on top. Hotel rates didn't drop—if anything, they rose about 30% on many nights as pent-up demand swamped availability. So it behooves you, the visitor, to use the rates in this book as a starting point and **check prices for yourself.**

Some ground rules: First, don't get caught up in the star ratings that hotels promote. In Britain, a hotel can earn an extra star simply because it serves food. In fact, the more stars a place has, the more likely it is to charge for something you won't use, so focus instead on the location and the price. Second, to save cash, look for smaller hotels that have been carved out of historic buildings, even if that means irregular-size quarters with tiny bathrooms. Third, to secure the lowest rates possible (usually found only on each property's website), timing is critical. Most chain hotels will grant a discount for purchases made many months in advance and for nonrefundable bookings, and family-run places tend to cut deals if you stay longer. The cheapest places are still family-run.

London's non-corporate hotels are good about sticking to their posted rates; in fact, every property is required by law to post the *maximum* rate (almost never charged) in the lobby. Corporate-run hotels are also unabashed about charging insanely high prices given any uptick in demand. Beware dates around the London Marathon (Apr), bank holidays, Wimbledon (June or July), New Year's, and summer. In London, it's almost always high season, and even winter months can see peak rates. The best way to save, even at luxury hotels, is to book as far ahead as possible.

Package tours tend to stash tourists in undesirable and inconvenient neighborhoods with poor food options. Past-their-prime

London-Wide Hotels

PRIMROSE HILL

CAMDEN TOWN

ST. JOHN'S WOOD

MAIDA VALE

LISSON GROVE

PADDINGTON

MARYLEBONE

FITZROVIA

ST. PANCRAS

BLOOMSBURY

SOHO

COVENT GARDEN

WESTMINSTER

MAYFAIR

ST. JAMES'S

KNIGHTSBRIDGE

BELGRAVIA

VICTORIA

WESTMINSTER

SOUTH KENSINGTON

KENSINGTON & CHELSEA

CHELSEA

PIMLICO

VAUXHALL

SANDS END

BATTERSEA

Camden Rd.
Chalk Farm Rd.
Camden Town
Camden High St.
Camden St.
Regent's Park Rd.
Prince Albert Rd.
Avenue Rd.
Finchley Rd.
Abbey Road
Mornington Crescent
King's Cross Station
York Way
Regent's Canal
London Zoo
REGENT'S PARK
Boating Lake
St. John's Wood
Wellington Rd.
Maida Vale
Lord's Cricket Ground
St. John's Wood Rd.
Park Rd.
Albany St.
Hampstead Rd.
Eversholt St.
St. Pancras Station
British Library
King's Cross St. Pancras
Gray's Inn Rd.
Euston Station
Euston Rd.
Euston
Euston Sq.
Gower St.
Russell Sq.
Guilford St.
Maida Vale Rd.
Marylebone Station
Marylebone
Baker St.
Regent's Park
Great Portland St.
Tottenham Court Rd.
Goodge St.
Bloomsbury St.
British Museum
Holborn
Warwick Avenue
Edgware Rd.
Harrow Rd.
Edgware Rd.
Marylebone Rd.
Marylebone High St.
Wigmore St.
Oxford Circus
Tottenham Court Rd.
Charing Cross Rd.
Paddington Station
Paddington
Sussex Gardens
Gloucester Pl.
Baker St.
Seymour St.
Oxford St.
Bond St.
Regent St.
Leicester Sq.
Covent Garden
Westbourne Terr.
Marble Arch
Bayswater Rd.
Piccadilly Circus
National Gallery
Charing Cross Station
Bayswater
Lancaster Gate
Park Ln.
Green Park
Pall Mall
Trafalgar Square
Charing Cross
Bayswater Rd.
Queensway
KENSINGTON GARDENS
Round Pond
HYDE PARK
The Serpentine
Embankment
Kensington Palace
Hyde Park Corner
GREEN PARK
Constitution Hill
ST. JAMES'S PARK
The Mall
Westminster
Westminster Bridge
Kensington Gore
Royal Albert Hall
Kensington Rd.
Knightsbridge
Harrods
Buckingham Palace
St. James's Park
Westminster Abbey
Houses of Parliament
Natural History Museum
Victoria & Albert Museum
Belgrave Square
Grosvenor Pl.
Victoria St.
WESTMINSTER
Cromwell Rd.
Brompton Rd.
Eaton Sq.
Westminster Cathedral
South Kensington
Sloane St.
BELGRAVIA
Victoria Station
Gloucester Rd.
Fulham Rd.
King's Rd.
Sloane Square
Sloane Sq.
Victoria Coach Station
Warwick Way
Belgrave Rd.
Tate Britain
Lambeth Bridge
Sydney St.
Royal Hospital Rd.
Chelsea Bridge Rd.
Lupus St.
Vauxhall Bridge Rd.
Pimlico
Vauxhall Bridge
Millbank
Edith Grove
Fulham Rd.
King's Rd.
CHELSEA
Chelsea Embankment
Grosvenor Rd.
Vauxhall
Stamford Bridge Stadium (Chelsea Football Club)
Battersea Bridge
Albert Bridge
Oakley St.
Chelsea Bridge
BATTERSEA PARK
Boating Lake
Thames
Queenstown Rd.
Wandsworth Rd.
Lansdowne Way
Battersea Park
Queenstown Rd. (Battersea)

① ② ③ ④ ⑤ ⑥ ⑦ ⑧ ⑨ ⑩ ⑪ ⑫ ⑬ ⑭ ⑮ ⑯ ⑰

neighborhoods this guide no longer favors include **Lancaster Gate, Earl's Court, South Kensington,** and **Paddington.** They were cool once, but now that so many hotels have opened in the middle of town, most of these areas' old hotels now plod through nights like zombies in search of continental breakfast. The hotels in this chapter strive to keep you out of those dead tourist-hotel zones and keep you close to the action.

Also, **do not stay by the airport** unless you're catching a flight; those hotels are too far away, and transit is too expensive.

A few hotels we name are crazy expensive, but they're included because there's something worth visiting in them even if you're not staying overnight. Most major hotels in London welcome non-guests to enjoy their afternoon teas, cocktail lounges, and fine restaurants, so don't be shy.

Accommodations are subject to a value-added tax (VAT) of 20%, which you cannot claim back. Happily, almost all small B&Bs include taxes in their rates. More expensive hotels (those around £275 or more) tend to leave taxes off their tariffs, which can result in a nasty surprise at checkout, so it never hurts to ask if the rate "excludes VAT."

Absolutely no London hotel charges a "resort fee" or its equivalent; that's a uniquely North American scam.

THE BUDGET HOTEL CHAINS

The chains are all over town. Expect reliable standards, decently sized rooms with private bathroom, and unbeatable lead-in rates for people who pay months ahead of time. Unfortunately, so many people habitually turn to these brands that closer to the dates of stay, prices usually rise far past the point of value. In addition to these names, look into **Motel One London–Tower Hill** (24–26 Minories, EC3; www.motel-one.com; ✆ **020/7481-6420;** doubles from £99–£140, often a 2-night minimum; Tube: Aldgate), a stylish and ultra-cheap but cramped German name with a single location in the somewhat bland, business-y neighborhood between Tower Hill and Aldgate East.

citizenM ★★★ My favorite affordable London chain is actually Dutch. Their glassy open-plan lobbies lined with shelves of orange-and-white Penguin classic paperbacks (which every self-conscious interior designer in London displays to denote postmodern intellectualism) churn day and night with people sipping fine coffee and telecommuting. Check-in is self-guided by kiosk, and rooms are compact—almost podlike—but arranged with genius. Expect massive platform beds piled with body pillows, curvy unit bathrooms

King's Cross to Enbankment Hotels

39

Quarters can be tight at citizenM, but excellent locations and intuitive design make up for the squeeze.

slotted into the space with calculated aplomb, and a bedside tablet that lets you control everything from motorized blinds to the color of the room's mood lighting. There's even a hefty library of free movies (including porn—like I said, it's Dutch). My favorite locations are Bankside (behind the Tate Modern) and Tower of London, where the rooms and a fab rooftop bar overlook said eternal fortress, which no other budget hotel does. The Shoreditch location is close to nightlife, so it's more expensive on weekends.

www.citizenm.com. 4 locations around London. From £89 double, £125–£277 more typical. **Amenities:** Free movies; free Wi-Fi.

easyHotel ★ Prefabricated room units differ only in how little space you're given—the smallest are 6 sq. m (65 sq. ft.), space only for a bed and a shallow breath. No phone, no hair dryer, no frills at all. Bathrooms are just plastic cubicles combining a shower, toilet, and sink in one wet closet. The cheapest rooms don't even have windows, and you cannot change the thermostat. Want your room serviced? You'll pay £5 each time. Wi-Fi is £5 a day. I find the no-nonsense atmosphere like camping in a refrigerator box, but some visitors swear this is how you do London ultra-cheaply while avoiding hostels. Reservations typically cost £50 for double rooms if you book 6 months ahead, and around £110 if you procrastinate. The Shoreditch outpost is the most expensive of the four city locations.

www.easyhotel.com. No phone reservations. 4 locations in central London. Rooms £40–£130. **Amenities:** Wi-Fi (£5/day, £10/3 days).

Hub by Premier Inn ★★   Sleek, cannily designed rooms (just 11.4 sq. m/123 sq. ft.) are tight as air locks, packing in a platform bed for two with storage underneath, a bright and clean-lined shower/toilet module, well-located power outlets and USB charging ports, a fold-down desk, and a lime green chair. The staff won't do much for you, but using an app, you can dim or extinguish the lights, watch TV (all movies are free—the Wi-Fi is mercury-fast, too), or turn on the "do not disturb" light. *Downsides:* You may not get a mobile phone signal and you won't be able to look out a window, but the location is unmatched and there's a cafe for breakfast (around £10). Deservedly, the best rates sell out months in advance—book online only. My favorite location: Covent Garden, steps from Trafalgar Square; the Brick Lane one is unusual because so few hotels are on that market-and-nightlife street.

www.hubhotels.co.uk. 10 locations around London. £59–£199 double. **Amenities:** Breakfast (charged); free movies; free Wi-Fi.

Ibis Hotels ★★   This 600-strong French chain by the Accor hotel giant is distinguished by utilitarian but cheerful decor. You'll get a double bed, bathroom with shower, climate control, a 24-hour kitchen, TV, phone, free Wi-Fi, at least one outlet, and a built-in desk. The breakfast charge varies per property (around £10 is typical), but food is usually served from 4am, making this a smart choice if you need to catch an early flight or train. The fresh-baked breakfast baguettes are delicious—hey, it's proudly French. My favorite location: Ibis London Blackfriars, which is usually a little cheaper than the others but still in walking distance to a lot. There's also **Ibis Styles,** the "all-inclusive" brand that is slightly more upscale and includes breakfast and Wi-Fi; and **Ibis Budget,** a bare-bones, shower-only crash pad once known as Etap or Formule 1; rooms there are ultra-simple (though with flair), sleep up to three people, and have free Wi-Fi and TV, but practically nothing else. Check the map before booking, as some of its locations are distant from central London.

https://ibis.accor.com. No English-reservations hotline. 24+ locations around London. Rooms £81–£278, varying by season and location. **Amenities:** Free Wi-Fi.

Point A Hotels ★   This modern-budget brand provides everything you need in a compact room but nothing else: power shower, round-the-clock reception, air-conditioning, bedside USB ports, a drop-down desk, hooks (but not a closet). Not all rooms have windows. The a la carte model keeps costs down but is no path to luxury. Still, the facilities are clean and designed with minimalist zip. Don't write off a windowless room's power to mediate jet lag. Too often, however, rates are around £175, which is too much for this simplicity—around £110 would be more reasonable. The "Westminster" branch (its most central one) is actually across the river by Waterloo.

www.pointahotels.com. No phone. 7 locations in the city. Rooms £85–£199. **Amenities:** Air-conditioning; continental breakfast; free access to local gyms; free Wi-Fi.

Premier Inn ★   The largest hotel chain in the country, Premier offers rooms (maximum of two adults) with a king-size bed, bathtub and shower with all-purpose shower gel, tea- and coffee-making facilities, TV, phone, iron, air-conditioning (sometimes), at least three outlets, and a desk. Increasingly, it requires you to check in at a kiosk, eliminating human interaction, so when you need something (the Wi-Fi can be a particular problem), a pleasant stay can collapse into an instant fail. Prices rise and fall according to how much demand the company thinks there will be, so quotes fluctuate wildly. Final prices can be too high for such a standard room, so the key is early booking. *Warning:* The cheapest locations are deep in distant suburbs, so consult a map before taking the bait of a low price. Search results are mixed with its much simpler Hub locations (see above). Favorite location: Bankside.

www.premierinn.com. ℰ **0845/099-0095.** More than 12 locations around the central city. Rooms £179–£380, depending on season and location. **Amenities:** Bar/cafe; free slow Wi-Fi, £5/day for high-speed Wi-Fi.

Travelodge ★   Rates start around £88 for a non-flexible reservation if you book 11 months ahead. That more than makes up for the thin amenities of this economy brand, which has some two dozen properties in Greater London. It's nicer than the American Travelodge brand, which isn't related to it. Expect king-size beds, bathtub and shower, TV (but no phone, hair dryer, or toiletries except hair/body wash), paid in-room movies, a wardrobe, at least one power outlet, and a desk. Breakfast, if your property offers it, is about £10 more (kids 16 and under free). "Family rooms" have a pullout couch for two kids but cost the same as a double. "SuperRooms" have upgraded fittings and a coffee-maker, and PLUS locations have a simple cafe/bar. If you're willing to stay in a quiet suburban neighborhood with a bit of a rail commute, the deals can be extraordinarily cheap. Favorite location: Covent Garden.

www.travelodge.co.uk. ℰ **08719/848-484.** More than 20 locations around the city. Rooms £169–£300, depending on season and location (lower if booked far in advance). **Amenities:** Bar/cafe (often); Wi-Fi free for 30 min. daily, 24-hr. access £3/day.

Z Hotels ★★★   Please say it "Zed," which rhymes with "bed." Now that you've got that down, here's the formula: ideal locations; extremely compact rooms, but lots of room under the duvets; glassy, sleek style; and a lobby that's always abuzz with breakfast, coffee, or free daily wine. The formula works because there are design smarts where they count: Shower nozzles swivel the way you need them to, towels are plump and copious, you can control your thermostat. They poured cash into the bedding and the 40-inch TVs but did without closets and drawers. The cheapest rooms may not have windows. Note that if you share a room with a platonic friend, bathrooms are enclosed only by panels of fogged glass. My favorite locations, for convenience: Soho, Trafalgar, Covent Garden, and Piccadilly.

www.thezhotels.com. 11 locations around the city. Rooms £80–£369. **Amenities:** Cafe/bar; air-conditioning; free evening wine and cheese; free Wi-Fi.

KING'S CROSS & BLOOMSBURY

King's Cross hotels are close to six important Tube lines, the Eurostar to mainland Europe, and the Thameslink (which goes to Gatwick). The area was once known for small, down-market rooms—the chain hotels, listed above, are particularly present here. But ongoing development of Pancras Square and Granary Square in the old industrial yards behind the train stations has turned the area into London's tech capital, and hotel offerings have expanded. **Bloomsbury**'s chocolate-colored Georgian brick townhouses are more classically London and lie within a 20-minute walk of Soho and Covent Garden. The rise of that area pretty much wiped Paddington and Earl's Court off the tourist's map for cheap overnights.

Expensive

The Montague on the Gardens ★★ It's not easy these days finding typically British mid-priced hotels that aren't mired in gloomy tour-group dinginess, but the conjoined townhouses of the Montague deliver Englishness in demonstration as much as in word. Downstairs, a large staff pays close attention to guest needs, and rooms, always tasteful and richly comfortable, are a mishmash of styles as if in a moneyed home. They're also a mix of sizes (including singles) given the charming age of the buildings, but they're silent, plush, and otherwise appointed with more than you'll need. It's comfortable, dignified, and a homey bolt-hole for central London explorations, with the British Museum literally across the road. It's family friendly as well.

15 Montague St., WC1. www.montaguehotel.com. ℂ **020/7858-7731.** 100 units. Rooms £221–£356. Tube: Russell Square. **Amenities:** Restaurant; bar; air-conditioning; free bottled water; free Wi-Fi.

St. Pancras Renaissance Hotel ★★ This Gothic redbrick palace, a terminal hotel for St Pancras railway station, was built as the Midland Grand Hotel in 1873 for £300 million in today's money and, astonishingly, had only four bathrooms shared by 600 bedrooms—an issue that has been amply and luxuriously corrected. Behold one of London's architectural masterpieces: Its meticulous 2011 restoration not only rescued a Victorian icon from neglect but also created an enviable property. Premium rooms have an unforgettable view down the ribbed, cast-iron cavern of the train shed, and you can watch Eurostar trains depart for Paris in your bathrobe. There, the epic Chambers rooms have 5.5m (18-ft.) ceilings and details such as (now-decorative) fireplaces, arched windows, and substantial wooden doors. Rooms in the new Barlow wing feel more corporate, lack those long views (the ones in lower categories have small windows), and suit business travel tastes—the real show is in the original building. Echoing public spaces are a gilt-and-tile parade of self-important Victorian excess, from the winged Grand Staircase to the lushly carved brasserie and the old wooden Booking Hall, now a popular, classy nightspot. The building was "too good for its purpose," lamented its architect, Gilbert Scott, whose own son went mad and died in one of the rooms. It's worth a wander even if you're not staying here—management knows it's a jewel, and it welcomes visitors.

Euston Rd., London, NW1. www.stpancrasrenaissance.co.uk. ℂ **020/7841-3540.** 245 units. £350–£540 double. Tube: King's Cross St Pancras. **Amenities:** Restaurant; 2 bars; indoor pool; gym; spa; free Wi-Fi in Chambers rooms, otherwise £15/day.

The Standard London ★★   The Standard burst onto London's scene in 2019, but inside, it's pure 1974. It has been designed to eye-pleasing extremes—in this case, to evoke that bygone era in all its shag-carpeted, spherical-lamped, olive-and-beige glory. Everything takes its cues from its brutalist building, which used to house the local city government but now time-warps young people to a groovier existence with a busy street-facing cocktail bar. It's an ideal addition for the ironic but moneyed dot-com overachievers who are moving into the new corporate offices around nearby Granary Square. The most affordable standard rooms are dubbed "Cosy," and at just 13 square meters (139 sq. ft.) and sometimes without windows, they're terrible rooms, so don't get suckered into one. But if you have the dosh, this is one place where an upgrade is worth it: The King Terrace rooms (from £425) have outdoor spaces (with outdoor spa tubs) that overlook the ostentatious glory of St Pancras, which itself is an over-the-top representation of the design immoderation of the

The Standard offers a mesmerizing view of glorious St Pancras station.

'70s—the 1870s, that is. There are few buildings in the world more worth staring at from your window. Ask for a corner Queen of Queen room, with a wraparound couch under its curvy windows. All categories are well-equipped, with their own Bluetooth wireless speakers and free loaner raincoats (Stutterheims). (Smart! Umbrellas get lost.)

10 Argyle St., NW1. www.standardhotels.com/london. ✆ **020/3981-8888.** 266 units. From £229 single–£489 double. Tube: King's Cross St Pancras. **Amenities:** 2 restaurants; bar; 24-hr. fitness center; in-room A/C; free Wi-Fi.

Moderate

Great Northern Hotel ★★   Of all London's railway terminal hotels, from the outside the Great Northern seems the plainest—and the smallest. Its crescent-shaped building went up quite early, in 1854, and as a consequence it isn't as bombastic as its brethren. Rooms aren't huge, but they have a smart modern edge that includes—daringly for a hotel—cream-colored carpeting. The smallest rooms are called "Couchette" because the sled-style queen beds, attached at head and foot to the walls, are said to have been inspired by railway sleepers. (Don't worry—they have much more space for your luggage, although the result is less spacious than the higher-category Heritage and Victorian rooms.) Etched glass and cute little curved banquettes complete the

HOW TO LOVE a historic townhouse hotel

Unfortunately, the once-famous English B&B is an endangered species. Neighborhoods that were dependable for cut-price lodging (Gloucester Place in Marylebone, Ebury St. in Victoria, Gower St. in Bloomsbury) are being renovated to attract the ultra-rich, converting to luxury apartments, or selling out.

The ones that survive usually occupy "listed" buildings. What does that mean? It means that it has historical or architectural importance—for example, it's an example of a fine Georgian townhouse or an original stately Victorian terrace home. To keep developers from knocking down a gem, "listed" buildings are protected. Changing anything requires permission, down to the color of the paint. American tourists who are unused to London's listed buildings often post huffy online reviews about the quirks that define townhouse hotels, penalizing London inns for being London inns. That hotel is not a dump! It's historic.

Rooms are small by American standards. Don't blame the current owners. Room subdivision happened on a wide scale after World War II, to fill a housing gap after so many buildings were bombed, and now even removing those slapped-up walls requires council (government) approval, which rarely comes. Sometimes it feels like the walls and the bed are in a death match for dominance, recalling the compactor scene in *Star Wars*. You are unlikely to have a closet.

Tip: The largest rooms usually face the front.

Bathrooms are even smaller. In the old days, guests shared bathrooms. To suit changing tastes, landlords installed booths containing the staples (toilet, shower, sink) into rooms that weren't designed to have them. Would you rather go back to sharing?

Don't expect an elevator, or "lift." It's not that they're too cheap to install one. In these historic houses, they're not even allowed. Assume you'll have to use the stairs. They may be narrower than you're used to. Rooms on higher floors require climbing, but they also receive more light, less noise, and often cost less.

Ceilings get lower as you go higher. Until the 20th century, the floors of fashionable townhouses served distinct functions. The cellar was for kitchens and coal storage. The ground floor was usually used for living rooms. The first and second floors were reserved for bedrooms, and the top floor was for servants and for the children's nursery, which accounts for the slightly lower ceilings there.

Not all windows are double glazed. You think you hear traffic now? Imagine when horses and carriages clattered up the cobbles at all hours. If you're a light sleeper, simply ask for a room at the back. Rooms on back stairway landings often don't adjoin other rooms, either, which takes care of other ambient noises.

allusions to trains. High-standard perks pack the other spaces—a good British restaurant, Plum & Spilt Milk (named after a color scheme, not service standards), is one, and a cozy cocktail bar is another. *Caveat:* If you're quoted a rate over £300 for its Couchette category, you can do better elsewhere.

King's Cross St Pancras Station, Pancras Rd., N1. www.gnhlondon.com. © **020/3388-0800.** 91 units. From £250 double, max. occupancy 2. Tube: King's Cross St Pancras. **Amenities:** Restaurant; bar; snack bar; free Wi-Fi.

The Megaro ★ This old office building has been tarted up with brassy colors and a cluttered exterior mural, but inside, the theme is spacious and virtually Scandinavian, with open wood floors, unadorned paneling, poppy-colored lighting, smart slide-out makeup desks and workspaces, complimentary in-room snacks, and fresh tea leaves for your cuppa. Rooms on the main road have killer views of St Pancras and the plaza in front of King's Cross (no. 504, a corner, is the best for that), but if traffic noise irritates you, go for one facing the other way (no. 508, with a small balcony, picturesquely peeks over the pipe chimneys of nearby townhouses). If you're traveling with a platonic companion, ask for a room in which your bathroom isn't encased in glass walls; some are, some aren't.

Belgrove St., WC1. www.hotelmegaro.co.uk. ✆ **020/7843-2222.** 49 units. £194–£325, save 15% on website. Tube: King's Cross St Pancras. **Amenities:** Restaurant; bar; free Wi-Fi.

Inexpensive

Alhambra Hotel ★★★   The comforting Alhambra is an inn with heart, and a top value in Frommer's ever since *Europe on $5 a Day*—if you want an example of the long tradition of family-run establishments in London, it's exemplary. Its proprietors, whose lineage has owned the land for decades, take pride in the business and they keep prices low. They survived the pandemic by converting the former breakfast area into three more rooms and lowering prices slightly. Picture simple, small, but dignified rooms squeezed into old spaces, but always spotless and freshened up with bright bedspreads, inviting royal-blue carpeting, built-in desks with chairs, flat-screen TVs (but no phones), free fiber-optic Wi-Fi, and in-room safes, all rarities for this price point. If you share a bathroom, there are plenty to go around. In winter, it's easy to negotiate rates down by as much as 30%.

17–19 Argyle St., WC1. www.alhambrahotel.com. ✆ **020/7837-9575.** 55 units. £75–£125 single, £82–£168 double, slight discount for nonrefundable reservations, take-away breakfast box £5. Tube: King's Cross St Pancras. **Amenities:** Free Wi-Fi.

Celtic Hotel ★★   A defiant and idiosyncratic holdout from the way British hospitality used to be, the Celtic is the domain of the dedicated Marazzi family, who have been robust figures in London's affordable-travel scene for generations. Few other hoteliers put as much heart into making sure guests are acclimated to London by answering questions, obliging special dietary requests, and filling bellies with a cooked breakfast that's so enormous (try the banana yogurt) that lunch might become optional. They have devoted regulars—and many of them, going back more than half a century, because the Marazzis owned a beloved budget place nearby, St Margaret's Hotel, for 56 years, before being forced out by gentrification. Their move to the Celtic retained the quirky features their fans love: Rooms don't have TVs or phones, furniture is endearingly mismatched, and the lounge is a hub for socializing with fellow guests. Add up to £23 if you don't want to share a shower or toilet. You must book directly.

62 Guilford St., WC1. www.celtichotel.com. ✆ **020/7837-6737.** 35 units. From £72 single, from £99 double. Rates include full cooked breakfast. Tube: Russell Square. **Amenities:** 2 lounges; free Wi-Fi.

Hotel Meridiana ★   This is what a value hotel should be: not lavish, but you happily get what you pay for. Walls can be thin, rooms truly teeny, and many share bathrooms, but everything is spotless and it's well-maintained. Heating and hot water are reliable, too, which isn't always the case in buildings of this age, and some rooms have drawers, another relative curiosity. If you just need a dead-cheap place to sleep where you'll have no regrets about hygiene, this no-frills B&B is a decent choice. You're unlikely to get as much value for the price elsewhere.

43–44 Argyle Sq., WC1. www.hotelmeridiana.co.uk. ☏ **020/7713-0144.** 27 units. From £62 single, from £106 double. Continental breakfast £5. Tube: King's Cross St Pancras. **Amenities:** Free Wi-Fi.

Jesmond Hotel ★★★   It's easy to have a soft spot for this place near the British Library. This author even stayed here often when he was just out of college (in room no. 3, a cozy single on the rear landing—still there, still snug). Back then, the Beynon family had a young son, Glyn. Today, Glyn is a grown family man, and he's in charge—and he's doing a proud job of updating the family B&B in a 1780s townhouse (ask him about its history) far beyond the expectations of its tariff range. He installed new bathrooms with all-new piping, accounting for the larger-than-average showers; he sound-

Affordable, clean, friendly, and recommended by Frommer's for over 60 years: the Jesmond Hotel in Bloomsbury.

proofed the front windows to keep out the roar of Gower Street's traffic. He also converted the former parlor, with its antique (nonworking) fireplace, into room no. 2, a spacious double. The Jesmond is a classic (four units share bathrooms), and in fact, has been a Frommer's selection ever since *Europe on $5 a Day* (when a room cost $3.20). Don't confuse this place with the Jesmond Dene, a B&B on Argyle Square—it's very good, too, but not as central.

63 Gower St., WC1. www.jesmondhotel. org.uk. ☏ **020/7636-3199.** 15 units. £87– £230 single, £110–£300 double, £220–£300 triple, £174–£380 quad, £470 quint; discounts for advance reservations and Jan/ Feb; often a 3-night minimum. Rates include full breakfast. Tube: Goodge Street. **Amenities:** Free Wi-Fi.

SOHO, COVENT GARDEN & WEST END

This is the middle of London. The part of town that offers everything you need outside your door. The area that also offers streets crawling with inebriated

THE ENGLISH CHARM OF pub hotels

There was a time, not so long ago, when most people didn't travel much. Hotels were not the massive industry they are today. In most English villages, though, if strangers needed a bed, they only had to look as far as the local pub, many of which maintained a handful of clean and serviceable rooms upstairs as part of the business. Many still do, and the tradition continues in London, too, but now on the level of boutique hotels, minus the fawning service, that blend old-fashioned charm with modern conveniences (except lifts—most of these old buildings can't have one). Don't be worried about noise, because the pubs downstairs (where you'll have breakfast, and which have usually been upgraded, too) close by 11pm. These will feel like your own secret discoveries.

The Bull & The Hide There's nothing old and fusty about rooms here, and there's a free "pantry" for drinks and snacks. A winery owns the whole business, and it's in a high-rise business district convenient to East London. 4 Devonshire Row, EC2. thebullandthehide. com. ℂ **020/7655-4805**. £179–£287. Tube: Liverpool Street.

Fox & Anchor The keyword is *plush*: Power showers, brass bathtubs, Hypnos mattresses. The Market Suite has a cute little terrace, too. The pub's frontage is a protected Art Nouveau masterpiece in tile. 115 Charterhouse St., EC1. www.foxandanchor.com. ℂ **020/7250-1300**. £189–£239. Tube: Farringdon.

Mad Hatter Hotel Mad Hatter offers big rooms, a high-quality pub below, and a stunning location (a block from the Thames) for the price. Big enough (30 rooms) that it's run like a hotel. It's busier on weekends. 3–7 Stamford St., SE1. www.madhatterhotel. co.uk. ℂ **020/7401-9222**. £148–£216. Tube: Southwark or Blackfriars.

The One Tun Eight fully modern, light rooms with a whimsical dog-and-deer style motif are above a gastropub that does pan-Asian dishes. Dickens named it The Three Cripples when it played Bill Sikes' drinking den in *Oliver Twist*. It has air-conditioning. 125 Saffron Hill, EC1. www.onetun.co.uk. ℂ **020/7405-1521**. £124–£225. Tube: Farringdon.

Also see the pub rooms of The Sanctuary House Hotel (p. 59) and The Grazing Goat (p. 99).

20-year-olds singing shanties in full voice when the pubs close. You may not care, because staying centrally can save on Tube fare more than it costs in shoe leather. Sunday through Thursday are the cheapest nights here.

Expensive

The Haymarket Hotel ★★ Bubbly colored textures, mismatched but impeccably selected furniture—this Firmdale property is like staying at the country house of a fabulous friend who has made a fortune in coffee-table books. This elegant (but never stuffy) choice takes its cues from nearby St James's and is regally situated in a cluster of rehabbed buildings beside the Theatre Royal Haymarket. It backs up its bright Modern English visuals with five-star features such as a sharp staff, indulgent showers, and an indoor swimming pool. There are no high-end choices closer to the West End action yet serenely removed from its tumult—it's the one property in the Firmdale group not to be routinely mobbed with cocktail-swilling fashion chasers, which makes it a delicious place to land and recharge after a tiring day.

1 Suffolk Pl., SW1. www.firmdalehotels.com. ☎ **020/7470-4000.** 50 units. Standard rooms £460–£750. Tube: Piccadilly Circus. **Amenities:** Bar/restaurant; fitness center; basement pool; free Wi-Fi.

The Londoner Hotel ★★   One of the biggest construction projects the West End has ever seen yielded one of the most full-featured and well-located hotels, rising eight floors above Leicester Square and extending another eight below it. Standard rooms, in soothing putty-and-taupe tones, are less spacious than what Americans are used to for the price—what else is new, London?—but are unquestionably quiet, beautifully designed for coziness, and luxurious. Compensating for their size, they hit all the luxury marks: wood paneling, inviting beds, marble bathrooms with heated robot toilets, plenty of charging ports. And if you're lucky enough to get a southern view, you can see the roof of the National Gallery and the Eye from your bed. Stay here, and you get access to a library-like lounge with nibbles and a bar for guests (The Residence) and a spa-connected indoor pool (free to use) ideal for melting away the stress from hours of treading city pavements or shouldering through the street life of the surrounding neighborhood on crazy weekend nights. You should make heavy use of those latter amenities, which grant the sense of exclusivity and indulgence that the hotel's image promises, to justify the cost.

38 Leicester Square, WC2. www.thelondoner.com. ☎ **020/7451-0101.** 350 units. From £548 double. Tube: Leicester Square. **Amenities:** 6 restaurants; cocktail bar; indoor pool; gym; spa; free bottled water; A/C; free Wi-Fi.

L'Oscar ★★★   The owners of L'Oscar poured huge sums into refurbishing the once-abandoned seat of the Edwardian-era Baptist church, and the expenditure shows in sumptuousness: beds stuffed with Icelandic eiderdown,

The swellegant lobby of L'Oscar, a charming hotel set in a historic former church and its offices.

whimsical Arts and Crafts paintings, recessed carpeting that averts tripping, delicate and iridescent fabrics in rich purples and gold, and nearly 500 crystal bird sculptures scattered throughout. Hidden in back, the former chapel under an octagonal dome is now a magisterial setting for food and cocktails. Windows are triple-glazed against London traffic, creating silent private domains. All that said, the energy is cordial and not stuffy, in the best boutique style—with only 39 rooms to oversee, staff won't neglect you. As is often the case in government-protected buildings like this one, each room is differently shaped (the ones on lower floors, in former offices, are the most lavish, with elaborate architectural carvings and details), but almost all have king beds. Superior category ones, at the still-very-comfortable bottom rung of the price ladder, only have a shower and not a tub. A top candidate for honeymoons and marriage proposal vacations.

2–6 Southampton Row, WC1. www.loscarlondon.com. ℘ **020/7405-5555.** 39 units. Rooms £477–£627 double. Tube: Holborn. **Amenities:** Restaurant; cocktail bar; free gym passes; A/C; free Wi-Fi.

ME London ★ The nine-story field of polished black marble in its core atrium is unlike any lobby you've ever seen, and its 10th-floor bar, Radio Rooftop, is ridiculously pretty in both panorama and clientele. An "Aura Manager" hands incoming guests prosecco and seeks to serve as a concierge, while bedside panels control everything from the temperature to the hue of the mood lighting. For all that folderol, bathrooms are huge, and rooms aren't small, either, even if the windows feel like pointed ship prows poking over the street. This luxury entrant by Spanish group Meliá is not a hotel for little kids—but if you wear your dresses tight and take your pre-clubbing coffee black, the place called ME may suit your preening self-image.

336–337 Strand, WC2. www.melondonhotel.com. ℘ **020/7395-3400.** 157 units. From £285 double. Tube: Temple. **Amenities:** Restaurant; 3 bars; in-room spa treatments; fitness center; A/C; free Wi-Fi.

Rosewood London ★★★ One of the city's most exclusive fine hotels is entered through a stone courtyard arch of a gloriously elaborate edifice (constructed with boundless pomp in 1914 as the Pearl Assurance insurance citadel). The foyer is amazingly sheathed in brass, and rooms are so quiet you could hear your champagne bubbles pop. They're also exquisite: Giant 46-inch flat-screen TVs are standard, as is Italian bedding you sink into like a swimming pool. Push a button to bring down your window blinds and sip homemade sloe gin from the minibar. Downstairs in the Mirror Room, there's a celebrated modernized afternoon tea, plus a gimmicky bar themed to Scarfe, a cartoonist who is London's modern-day version of Broadway's Al Hirschfeld. If it weren't for the hard reality of the tariff, it would all be enough to sour you on the rest of your life in this trying world.

252 High Holborn, WC1. www.rosewoodhotels.com/london. ℘ **020/7781-8888.** 262 units. Rooms from £688. Tube: Holborn. **Amenities:** Restaurant; bar; lounge; fitness center; spa; A/C; free Wi-Fi.

The Savoy ★ Few cities can claim hotels as iconic as the Savoy, which merits a visit even if you, like most people, cannot afford to stay there. There may be no more thrilling hotel entrance than the polished gleam of its porte cochere centered around a Lalique fountain. The service puts no foot wrong. Strange, then, that the details pander so—when you pay this much, why can't you have a real painting rather than a print textured to look like canvas? Why are there portraits of Hollywood stars in the famous Thames Foyer? Still, the Savoy has vibrated with high history, half Edwardian and half Jazz Age, since 1889. The American Bar has been a hushed laboratory for upscale cocktails for a century; its Simpson's in the Strand (closed during Covid-19) has been serving roast British dinners since 1828. Corny details can't erase how much happened here: Churchill puffing, Chaplin mugging, Wilde and Bosie dallying, Gilbert and Sullivan pattering in its theater, Monet and Whistler painting the Thames from their windows. Even if it sometimes feels like an imitation of itself, it's a landmark.

The Strand, WC2. www.fairmont.com/savoy-london. © **888/265-0533** (U.S.), or 020/7836-4343 (London). 268 units. Rooms from £739. Tube: Embankment or Temple. **Amenities:** 3 restaurants; 2 bars; indoor pool; gym; spa; business center; A/C; Wi-Fi £10/day.

Moderate

The Clermont, Charing Cross ★ The railway terminal hotel above Charing Cross Station opened a month after Lincoln's assassination and underwent many lives (and Blitz damage). Now the Charing Cross is a quiet, high-value hotel that dips its toes into luxury trimmings (heated bathroom floors, walk-in showers, Nespresso coffee, free minibars that include beer, and so forth), but even if rooms could use some refreshing, it doesn't rip you off. The location is spectacular and could command much higher rates: At the nexus of Trafalgar Square, Strand, the Covent Garden area, and the Embankment, you're truly spoiled. Breakfast (overcrowded) is taken with a view toward St Martin-in-the-Fields. Echoes of a more genteel age treat you to the grandeur of old London at a good price.

The Strand, WC2. www.theclermont.co.uk/charing-cross. © **020/7523-5052.** 239 units. Rooms £186–£442. Tube: Charing Cross or Embankment. **Amenities:** Restaurant; bar; business center; A/C; free Wi-Fi.

The Dilly ★ Here's a perfectly located, classically architectural grand dame hotel from the Edwardian era (opened 1908 as The Piccadilly Hotel) that, despite the affectations of its palatial stone exterior, remains accessible both in price and attitude to families and average folk. Kids are particularly welcomed: They're given "Dilly Explorers" packs with games upon arrival, and the house afternoon tea, served in a gorgeous solarium overlooking Piccadilly, is an adorable Peter Rabbit–themed affair featuring edible characters. The bones of this hotel are spectacular, if quirky: The building is a honeycomb of century-old event spaces and painted-over opulence just waiting to be rediscovered; in some rooms your bathroom is a few stairs up from your sleeping area; and in the lower levels there's a fitness center (shared with paying members from the general public) that has a giant pool, which is a rarity. Service can be iffy and the decor is about 10 years out of date, but the location is unbeatable and you get plenty of space for the price. When this place is updated to catch up with its possibilities, prices will shoot out of range. This hotel's moment of potential is your moment to seize value.

21 Piccadilly, W1. www.thedillylondon.com. ℰ **020/7734-8000.** 105 units. £239–£295 double. Tube: Piccadilly Circus. **Amenities:** Restaurant with cocktail bar; indoor pool; gym; spa treatments; loaner bicycles; free Wi-Fi.

The Fielding Hotel ★   The prime location, just steps from Covent Garden's food and shopping, is why you overlook the cramped, lift-less quarters at this average family-owned hotel. In this early-19th-century warren of tight staircases and fire doors, the sometimes slightly airless rooms snuggle you with a certain throwaway charisma. It's not top of the line, but it feels like home. Rooms no. 10, 20, and 30 are doubles with sitting areas that catch lots of afternoon light, thanks to their corner position and copious windows. Everything's en suite (mostly shower only, but three have tubs), and there are no common areas to speak of. *Trivia:* Oscar Wilde was convicted of gross indecency in the Bow Street Magistrates' Court next door.

4 Broad Ct., Bow St., WC2. www.thefieldinghotel.co.uk. ℰ **020/7836-8305.** 27 units. £135–£150 single, £175–£199 double, £315 double queen or full flat. Tube: Covent Garden or Holborn. **Amenities:** Free Wi-Fi.

The Piccadilly London West End ★   This impossibly central hotel is, impossibly, off the radar. It's not the most perfect place you'll ever stay, but it's solid, well-run, thoughtfully equipped, and you won't be sorry you booked it. Slotted into a gorgeous old Victorian building in the heart of Shaftesbury Avenue (amid theaters and Soho alike), you'd walk right by it if you didn't know it was there, but inside is a friendly independent hotel, smoothly soundproofed (carpets, upholstered headboards), that packs high-level room amenities (A/C, Nespresso coffee, safe, hand-held tablets with tourist info) into moderately priced rooms. For being in the pounding heart of the city, the hotel feels calmly sealed away once you're inside. We'd classify this one as a find.

65–73 Shaftesbury Ave., WC2. www.thepiccadillywestend.co.uk. ℰ **020/7871-6000.** 67 units. £244–£479 double. Tube: Piccadilly Circus or Leicester Square. **Amenities:** Restaurant/bar; spa; gym; A/C; free Wi-Fi.

The Resident Covent Garden ★★★   An exterior that looks like just another Victorian office edifice in fact conceals an intelligently designed and carefully serviced oasis (charcoals, woods, gentle stripes) that opened in 2019 and aims to deliver low prices without sacrificing sophistication. The brand calls the concept "affordable luxury." That's not just hooey. You get flat-screen TVs; free Internet; a free music library; some oversized showers; safes; very quiet rooms; lots of outlets; plenty of storage space; and, most helpfully, mini-kitchens with fridges, microwaves, and a kettle, so you can prepare simple meals. The location (on busy Strand) is solid because there's so much right out

the door. The lift gets a little too busy, but you gain back time with the fantasy location. Find other good Resident hotels in Soho (great for nightlife) and near Buckingham Palace.

51 Bedford St. at Strand, WC2. www.residenthotels.com. ℭ **020/3146-1790.** 57 units. Rooms from £229. Tube: Charing Cross or Covent Garden. **Amenities:** In-room mini-kitchen; A/C; free Wi-Fi.

Strand Palace Hotel ★

Once a desultory pillow mill favored by shuffling package tours and folks on lost weekends, recent renovations improved its appeal. This dowager finally got wise to its stellar location—right across from the Savoy, beside Covent Garden—and it renovated itself out of the 1980s and back to the land of the living. Service may always be standard-issue, rooms and their windows could be larger, but beds are great and everything is a fair value considering the rest of the market. And, for the first time since its 1908 construction (a period when guests did not expect a view out their window, mind you), rooms now have air-conditioning. You'll often find it on the hotel discounter sites.

372 Strand, WC2. www.strandpalacehotel.co.uk. ℭ **020/7379-4737.** 785 units. Rooms £192–£450; 4th night free when booked on its website. Tube: Charing Cross or Temple. **Amenities:** 2 restaurants; 2 bars; business center; fitness center; free national calls; free minibar (deluxe rooms); A/C; free Wi-Fi.

Victory House Hotel ★

The location is beyond central: behind a gorgeous 1898 French Renaissance facade on the north side of Leicester Square—it gets noisy at night outside, but doubled panes keep the clatter to a soothing murmur that satisfies most sleepers. The lobby is perilously small,

Because Victory House is set in a historic building, some of the rooms have quirky architectural details, like round windows.

and rooms can also be petite but in an acceptably cozy way, although not if you're quoted a price above £300. The bathrooms are a higher grade than most with White Company Noir toiletries and heated towel bars, the beds large even if the ceilings are low, and the perks pleasing (like free bottled water). There aren't many common areas to hang out in, but you never have far to go to be in the middle of it all.

14 Leicester Place, WC2. www.victoryhouselondon.com. ⓒ 020/3909-4100. 86 units. Rooms £145–£300. Tube: Leicester Square. **Amenities:** Bistro; access to nearby gym; A/C; free Wi-Fi.

Inexpensive

Assembly London ★★ Almost always reliable for a value-priced bed in the middle of the action, the Assembly is a well-designed hotel secret you won't want to share. Rooms are wee and sparse, to be sure, but they're modern (blonde wood, charcoal carpet, and subway-like tile in their little bathrooms) and clean, and because the Assembly inhabits a tower practically on top of the National Portrait Gallery, many of them have sublime views of the city. You won't get a phone, a desk, or even a lobby to speak of, but do you really need those? To compensate for the lack of TVs, the Wi-Fi is perfect, whip-quick, and free. You get a hip rooftop bar/restaurant with a splendid east- and south-facing panorama that you won't find at luxury hotels five times the price. The evening pursuits of the West End are at your feet, no commute required.

SEVEN TRICKS FOR saving

To save money on guesthouses and inns, obey seven simple rules:

1. **Book early.** Even at the swankiest places, prices can more than halve if you commit at least six months ahead.

2. **Off-season is cheaper.** Many big hotels have two seasons: April through September vs. October through March (excluding holidays). Prices will be 10% to 25% cheaper in winter. Interestingly, very few family-owned B&Bs and inns bother with this system, pricing uniformly.

3. **Stay longer.** I haven't found a family-run hotel that wasn't willing to lower prices for anyone staying more than 5 or 6 nights.

4. **The days matter.** Any given hotel tends to be cheaper at one time of week over another: weekends in business zones like The City, weekdays in touristy Soho.

5. **Go mom-and-pop.** Their rates usually include taxes, but big hotels' rates don't.

6. **Book directly.** The chains now tend to give the best rates if you do that. (That said, in Frommer's tests, Booking.com and HotelsCombined.com compare well to competitors, and Booking.com tends to include tax in its quotes, which helps.)

7. **Last-minute deals are rare but do exist.** Routes for looking into deals within a week of travel are Hotwire. com, Priceline.com, and the app Hotel Tonight.

Lower-priced rooms sleep two, and the very cheapest ("Snug") may not have a window, so pay another £20 to bump up to "Nest" for a window and 30% more space. The largest room, "Den," is almost three times the size of the smallest ones but costs about £60 more. Book direct for 5% off. Really, this is a crash pad extraordinaire.

27–31 Charing Cross Rd., WC2. www.assemblyhotels.com. © **020/3953-4251.** 139 units. Doubles from £139, largest rooms ("Den") from £199. Tube: Leicester Square. **Amenities:** Bar/restaurant; A/C; free Wi-Fi.

Seven Dials Hotel ★ Here, everything is little and no-frills: the stairway, the rooms, the charm. And correspondingly, the rates. There's usually barely enough storage space, a TV mounted on an armature, a basic writing desk, teeny clean bathrooms, and firm beds, albeit ones covered with dowdy bedspreads. Basement rooms don't have windows. Forget the lack of a lift and all the ways it's average and slipping year by year. Its footing on Monmouth Street, steps from a rainbow of pubs, boutiques, and food clustering around Covent Garden (light sleepers be warned), is without comparison. Dump your bags and go play, because the price is fair.

7 Monmouth St., WC2. www.sevendialshotel.com. © **020/7240-0823.** 18 units. £90–£140 single, £100–£170 double, sometimes there's a 3-night min. No breakfast. Tube: Covent Garden. **Amenities:** Free Wi-Fi.

BELGRAVIA & ST JAMES'S

Restaurant choices and attractions thin out in the areas west of Westminster Abbey, where domestic townhouses from a grander age hold court. The center of London's hotel action shifted out of this area in the last generation—the hotels that remain have survived because they're exceptional and see much return business. Guests here usually require Tube or bus rides.

Expensive

Dukes Hotel ★★ In St James's, a neighborhood not wanting for luxury bolt-holes, Dukes sets itself apart for coziness and clubby service. It's virtually hidden near Green Park in a tight lane beside Spencer House (p. 151)—so no views—which makes this 1908 classic feel like it exists in a world of its own. Beds are big and soft, bathrooms have those fancy mechanized Asian toilets, hallways wind and creak the way you'd want them to. Make a table reservation for the deservedly popular bar—Ian Fleming, creator of James Bond, is often said to have been a regular, so tourists flock to it. Potables are freshly mixed on a wooden trolley at your table, but do not order your martini "shaken, not stirred"—Bond's recipe is widely considered to be a way to ruin the vodka. Drinks in there are over £20 (but skimp on nothing), but the rooms upstairs are much more affordable than they ought to be.

35 St James's Place, SW1. www.dukeshotel.com. © **020/7491-4840.** 90 units. Rooms from £293–£555. Tube: Green Park. **Amenities:** Restaurant; bar; fitness center; morning newspaper; free Wi-Fi.

The Goring ★★   Only one five-star hotel had the Royal Warrant from the late Queen Elizabeth II for Hospitality Services. Only one has been run by the same family since it opened (in 1910). Only one hosted Kate Middleton, the wife of a future king and mother of another, in her final night as a single girl before she walked down the aisle of Westminster Abbey. This is the Goring, classic but not self-importantly so, assiduously appropriate in style and rich in expensive fabrics, down to the Gainsborough silk on the walls, yet still goofy enough to put a stuffed sheep in every room. The fleet of doormen wears bowler hats, and the signature canary-yellow china at its hotly pursued afternoon tea (4-month wait; p. 98) is made just for the hotel. The effect is something like an English country house, especially as you look out oversized windows at its blooming garden. When you're here, there's no mistaking you're steeping in London culture.

Beeston Place, SW1. www.thegoring.com. ✆ **020/7396-9000.** 69 units. Rooms £566–£727. Tube: Victoria. **Amenities:** Restaurant; bar; gym access; A/C; free Wi-Fi.

Hotel 41 ★★   A secret romantic nest only steps from Buckingham Palace, Hotel 41 is a hushed hideaway on the top floor of its moderately priced cousin, The Rubens. You take a tiny private lift and tread a snug network of creaking corridors to reach its heart, a two-level, galleried conservatory bedecked like something to make Henry Higgins purr: mahogany shelves, inviting seating, sculptural busts and an oversized globe, and a yawning sky-light to let the light in. There, staff makes the rounds, quietly addressing guests by name and filling glasses with champagne and plates with an endless flow of scones and hors d'oeuvres. People forget to go outside and see London. The rooms are equally individualized and top-flight: done nearly entirely in black-and-white and lacking nothing. There's no on-site restaurant or spa, and some rooms have no view to speak of—the focus is on intimacy, service, and discretion. The duplex Conservatory Suite, with a skylight over the bed, is popular with newlyweds and other nuzzlers.

41 Buckingham Palace Rd, SW1. www.41hotel.com. ✆ **020/7300-0041.** 30 units. Rooms £348–£540. Tube: Victoria. **Amenities:** Bar; free snacks; access to nearby gym; free Wi-Fi.

St. Ermin's Hotel ★★   No so long ago, it was a package-tourist misery locals nicknamed "St. Vermin's." But with a new owner, much investment, and a hookup to Marriott's points system, glory has been restored to this hand-some 1889 Queen Anne structure, a hotel since 1899. The lobby's latticed riot of plasterwork and sweeping Art Nouveau stairs is enough to make a tourist drop one's baggage to rhapsodize about the London-ness of it all, but the history is just as rich: The premises were long used as a headquarters for British spy efforts—Ian Fleming, the creator of James Bond, worked here. Room sizes vary wildly, from puny to palatial, so you may need the guidance of a live person to get the right one, but they're all quiet and well-appointed—not five-star but solidly four. Children are emphatically welcomed (family rooms are available), and there's an agreeably pubby bar on premises; the Tube is on

FACING PAGE: The Goring Hotel's footmen attend to personalized services for guests. Here, one serves a Pimm's Cup, a classic British cocktail for summer.

57

the same block and Westminster Abbey a 5-minute stroll east. Precious Old World British vibrations such as these are to be protected and patronized.

2 Caxton St., SW1. www.sterminshotel.co.uk. ℂ **020/7222-7888.** 331 units. Rooms £307–£528. Tube: St James's Park. **Amenities:** 2 restaurants; bar; fitness center; free Wi-Fi.

The Stafford London ★   When it opened in 1912, the intimate Stafford appealed to Americans on a European spree; it even named its yacht-clubby bar The American Bar. Today, renovated to business-class standards (its Mews outbuilding is a particular romantic zone, but all areas are quiet and have super-soft beds), this rambling hideaway down a cul-de-sac in St James's, a short passageway from Green Park, is still popular with Americans who become repeat guests, so it doesn't succumb to the arrogance rife in London's top-tier hotels. Having a subterranean wine cellar that's some 400 years old, which consequently empowers it to be the only hotel in London to retain its own Master Sommelier (only a few hundred people have ever attained that designation), goes a long way toward attracting a discerning, but not stuck-up, clientele.

16–18 St James's Place, SW1. https://thestaffordlondon.com. ℂ **020/7493-0111.** 127 units. Rooms from £384. Tube: Green Park. **Amenities:** Restaurant; bar; fitness center; free Wi-Fi.

Moderate

Lime Tree Hotel ★★   Matt and Charlotte Goodsall brightened a once-frumpy guesthouse near Victoria Coach Station into a place that feels as current as it is friendly. The conjoined brick townhouses are historic, so no lift is permitted and stairs are plentiful, but everything is updated with slate-and-white paint, fresh curtains, and touches such as bedside reading lights (but no tubs; only showers). If you have a first-floor room on the front, you'll have a small balcony over busy Ebury Street; in the quieter back, you'll overlook The Buttery, the house cafe in the cute flower garden. A basement room is larger than the others but has no view.

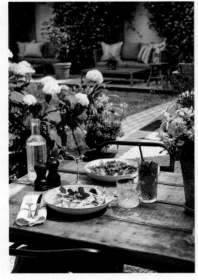

135–137 Ebury St., London SW1. www. limetreehotel.co.uk. ℂ **020/7730-8191.** 26 units. £125–£175 single, £170–£310 double, 3-night minimum stay often required. Breakfast not included. Children 4 and under not permitted. Tube: Victoria or Sloane Square. **Amenities:** Free Wi-Fi.

A meal in the garden of the family-owned Lime Tree Hotel.

SHOULD I pack IT?

Sanctuary House Hotel ★   Once, many pubs ran nondescript inns as sidelines. The pub here, where you take breakfast, is a truly typical Fuller's location (there are hundreds of them), but the hotel upstairs is a creaking, well-tended reward unto itself for value and charm, and the staff is unusually responsive for such a small property. The look plays up its Victorian origins with faux-antique telephones and plenty of handsome wood trim, but the modernized bathrooms and soft beds betray the fact that it's the beneficiary of some renovations by intelligent hoteliers. Even more miraculously, it's so near Big Ben that you can hear the bell peal.

33 Tothill St., SW1. www.sanctuaryhousehotel.co.uk. © **020/7799-4044.** 34 units. From £193 double including full breakfast, cheaper Sat–Sun. Tube: St James's Park or Westminster. **Amenities:** A/C; free Wi-Fi.

Inexpensive

Luna Simone Hotel ★   For many years, Luna Simone has been an affordable and reliable staple in this guide. A protected townhouse building with old metalwork on the banisters and oddly sized guest rooms, it has kept up by way of inexpensive furniture and basic amenities, but it's the thoughtful service that attracts many return guests. It's one of the last family-run inns in central London to still serve a complimentary (but simple) English breakfast. There's no lift or air-conditioning, but also no sharing of bathrooms. Cheap and cheerful, the way London used to do it—the owners have been at it since 1970.

47–49 Belgrave Rd., SW1. www.lunasimonehotel.com. © **020/7834-5897.** From £109 single, £149 double. Rates include breakfast. Tube: Victoria or Pimlico. **Amenities:** Free Wi-Fi.

MARYLEBONE & MAYFAIR

For visitors who want a balance of central location and private residential vibe, Marylebone's the place. A 10-minute walk takes you to the "smart" end of Oxford Street and Mayfair to the south, or the wide-open fields of Regent's Park to the north.

Expensive

The Beaumont ★★★   The proprietors call this relative newcomer "American-style," but you might peg it for Art Deco; after all, its 1926 facade was once the garage of Selfridges department store, the halls and lifts are full of glossy shots of bygone stars, and its bar and restaurant—serving duck egg hash at breakfast—strongly evoke a 1930s Los Angeles grill. Or maybe they mean that it's friendly, not stuffy—after all, the top-hatted doormen welcome you by name whenever you return, such as from Selfridges itself, steps away. Either way, it's a five-star hotel that benefits from the fact its guts were custom-built so rooms could be customized to be cutting-edge (free streaming movies, free minibar, heated bathroom floors). It's a top-quality luxury stay in a modestly sized hotel, but without the affected snottiness of some London properties. The Beaumont is most noted for Antony Gormley's geometric sculpture of a brooding man perched on one of its outcroppings—inside is an arty wooden suite that's favored by society spenders. You're more likely to love a "Classic" room facing the courtyard or a "Superior" facing the quiet street and a pocket park.

8 Balderton St., W1. www.thebeaumont.com. © **020/7499-1001.** 73 units. King-bed rooms from £590. Tube: Bond Street. **Amenities:** Restaurant; bar; fitness center with hammam and spa; free local calls; free movies; free Wi-Fi.

Claridge's ★★★   The redbrick Claridge's is the quintessential luxury Mayfair hotel, proudly proclaiming taste in discretion as administered through glittering Deco accents. The building dates to 1894 (when Gilbert & Sullivan's producer rebuilt it), but modern amenities are installed among the gilded plasterwork and (nonworking) fireplaces—neither floorboards nor exacting staff dare grumble. From the bathrooms (heated floors, high-tech toilet/bidets) to cavernous wardrobes and plump beds as wide as some studio apartments, there's not much to complain about. Its main lift is the last in central London to be operated by hand—there's a sofa inside should you tire during your five-level journey to the top floor—and its clubby cocktail bars and restaurant are favored by modern-day fashion icons (your Von Furstenbergs, your Jaggers, your Eltons) who detest the starched snobbery that can make the Ritz such a drag. Pedigreed unconventionality has always been a theme: In 1945, Winston Churchill declared suite 212 temporarily Yugoslavian territory so baby Prince Alexander II could claim to be born on home soil. Don't miss the lobby Christmas tree, designed each year by a new design luminary (in 2017, it was Karl Lagerfeld).

Brook St., W1. www.claridges.co.uk. © **020/7629-8860.** 203 units. Rooms from £750. Tube: Bond Street. **Amenities:** Restaurant; 2 bars; spa; fitness center; business center; free Wi-Fi.

Hyatt Regency London—The Churchill ★★ A strong choice for those with Hyatt points to redeem, it's a 2-minute walk from the back door of Selfridges department store, and many rooms recently received smart renovations with completely fresh bathrooms (robot toilets!) and truly well-selected art. Ten years ago, this circa-1970 building was a bit tired, but Hyatt has put the property on its front burner with millions of pounds in investment. Now it offers everything a five-star should, like all-night room service, and even if the location is a little off the main, it's still near the Tube, unquestionably comfortable, and run with snap for such a large place.

30 Portman Square, W1. http://londonchurchill.regency.hyatt.com. **℡ 020/7486-5800.** 440 units. Rooms £326–£500. Tube: Marble Arch. **Amenities:** 2 restaurants; bar; fitness center; tennis and jogging track in adjoining square; free Wi-Fi.

The Lanesborough ★★★ Once, I sneezed at the Lanesborough. Moments later, my butler—everyone has one here—flew to my side bearing a silver tray of hot tea, fresh-cut ginger on a porcelain plate, and acacia honey. And so it should be at one of the finest hotels in which I hope you will ever be so lucky to stay, where guest needs are meticulously anticipated and fresh-cut blooms are delivered to your bathroom counter the moment your back is turned. From 2013 to 2015, an £80-million renovation tore out every fixture and fully recrafted the interior with gilt, made-to-measure finery—like a mansion of Wedgwood china, Corinthian leather, and canopy king beds. It's an English pastiche for the super-wealthy, but a pitch-perfect one, and honeymoon nirvana. At the Lanesborough, intense formality dwells discreetly with new tech:

A dignified, comfortable guest room at the Hyatt Regency London–The Churchill.

TVs repose behind false paintings in gilt frames. Downstairs, near two portraits that, though unremarked, are actually originals by Sir Joshua Reynolds, moneyed regulars sip glasses of port dating as far back as 1778 and smoke £4,000 cigars in what many consider the world's best-stocked cigar lounge. Should the tariff at London's most expensive hotel understandably be out of your reach, at least stop by for the exquisite afternoon tea (p. 98) under the skylight of its magnificent Regency-style restaurant.

Hyde Park Corner, SW1. www.lanesborough.com. ℂ **020/7259-5599.** 93 units. Rooms from £955 including VAT. Tube: Hyde Park Corner. **Amenities:** Restaurant; bar; cigar lounge; fitness center; fresh fruit and water daily; free landline calls to U.S., Canada, and Europe; free Wi-Fi.

AND BEAR IN mind

London attracts the world's most spendy visitors, so it has one of the world's biggest supplies of luxury hotels. The choices below are comfortable indeed, and if they didn't have so much high-end competition, they'd be more prominently featured.

Brown's Hotel The rambling Brown's, in Mayfair, holds history in every creak: The first-ever phone call was placed from its ground floor. While staying here, Agatha Christie devised murders, Rudyard Kipling finished *The Jungle Book*, and Stephen King started *Misery*. It's an ideal choice for someone who wants a fine London hotel without enduring classist snobbery. 30 Albemarle St., W1. www.roccofortehotels.com. ℂ **020/7493-6020.** £485–£580 double. Tube: Green Park.

Corinthia Hotel London This 1885 building near the river was first the Hôtel Métropole and then the Ministry of Defence, but today it's a celebrity magnet, and perhaps managers have let this go to their heads—it charges 50% over its equals. You'll find a top jazz bar, one of the city's best spas, commodious quarters, and frequent stars. Whitehall Place, SW1. www.corinthia.com/london. ℂ **020/7930-8181.** Rooms from £600. Tube: Charing Cross.

Shangri-La Hotel at the Shard Staying here, on the 36th to 52nd floors of a glass-sheathed skyscraper, means that your room will be encased with floor-to-ceiling windows overlooking the city. You're a bird singing in a flawless, gleaming cage. When you take a bath (in your marble-coated washroom with heated floors), you may feel as if you're flying over the Tower of London, and when you swim in the horizon pool in the sky above St Paul's, the vista is so surreal that you may wonder if it's all a dream. 31 St Thomas St., SE1. www.shangri-la.com/london/shangrila. ℂ **020/7234-8000.** 202 units. King rooms from £670. Tube: London Bridge.

The Wellesley Knightsbridge The Hyde Park Corner ticket hall of the early Piccadilly Line once lay behind its iconic 1906 facade of arched oxblood-red tiles, although everything behind it has been exquisitely rebuilt in Super Art Deco for your comfort and, it must be said, for the egos of cigar fans—its attentions seem to revolve around its epic humidor lounge. Your 24-hour butler is just a button's push away and there's a Rolls Royce to take you within 1.5 miles—but no gym. 11 Knightsbridge, SW1. www.marriott.com. ℂ **020/7235-3535.** £565–£765 double. Tube: Oxford Circus.

The Langham ★★   The Langham has two claims to fame: It was the first grande dame hotel, in 1865, and it popularized afternoon tea. A lot has changed since then—for a while it was even occupied by the BBC. It was fully rebuilt in the early 1990s, so although you'll see a scant few Victorian touches, rooms are sized to modern standards while the huge three-building complex (the Regent Tower is the most secluded and has great views down Regent St.) maintains that unmistakable grande dame feel. Americans have always felt at home here, partly because it's not off-puttingly fussy while being comfortable. The Wigmore, its on-site pub, serves meals with piquant flavors, and its cocktail bar, Artesian, puts a playful twist on serious mixology. If you can, spring for a Club Level access, where you can get all three meals and free cocktails. It's a few short blocks from Oxford Street's best shopping.

1c Portland Place, Regent St., W1. www.langhamhotels.com/london. ✆ **020/7636-1000.** 380 units. Rooms £480–£720. Tube: Oxford Circus. **Amenities:** 3 restaurants; 2 bars; indoor pool; spa; fitness center; business center; free Wi-Fi.

The Zetter Townhouse, Marylebone ★★★   In nearly every way, it plays the part of the curious abode of an eccentric "wicked uncle" who collects oddities and likes to drink—each room has its own quirky character of antique mismatched furniture, hand-hung wallpaper, vintage glass photographic slides embedded in bathroom walls, and expensive punchbowl-set glassware. Yet the essence of this spot near Hyde Park and Oxford Street is fully modern, down to strong showers. Downstairs, the dusky, parlor-style lounge bar (Seymour's Parlour) keeps pouring coffees and well-made cocktails deep into the night. This is detailed luxury living with a frisky point of view, and it's a winkingly Londonish one at that; instead of a door hanger, you use a bowler hat painted with messages for the housekeeper ("NOT NOW"). There's another location in Clerkenwell, but this area has more going for it. *Tip:* The Studio Suite has a four-poster that could rival the Great Bed of Ware in the V&A, but the basement room has the least charm.

29–30 Seymour St., W1. www.thezetter.com. ✆ **020/7324-4567.** 24 units. Rooms from £245–£393. Tube: Marble Arch. **Amenities:** Bar/restaurant; free Wi-Fi.

THE SOUTH BANK & SOUTHWARK

From medieval times until about 2 decades ago, "respectable" Londoners wanted nothing to do with this once-industrial area. They all wish they'd bought property now. It's a terrific place to dwell in good weather, when it comes alive with walkers, booksellers, pub-goers, and playgoers. Furthermore, moderate hotels are proliferating: Brands such as Hilton, Holiday Inn, and Mercure are all along Southwark Bridge Road now. Don't forget the excellent citizenM (p. 38).

FINDING HOTELS online

If you contact the hotel directly, you'll usually not only get the lowest price, but you'll also have the power of negotiation.

Another danger of making a reservation through a third-party site: There are heaps of lousy budget options in London, particularly around Paddington and Earl's Court, that post misleading images, and it's easy to wind up in a seedy one. This is why you trust a book like Frommer's—we have been to every single place we recommend.

Most of the popular online travel agents have acquired each other to the point where the inventory doesn't change much between them. **Expedia** ate **Travelocity, Hotwire,** and **Orbitz. Hotels.com** ate **Venere. Priceline** ate

Agoda.com (but the latter delivers better results). Remember that a deal on an expensive hotel may not be a steal; as luxury hotels add star levels, they also add extra charges beyond the rate.

HotelsCombined.com, Kayak.com, and **Google Hotels** are "aggregator" sites that scan dozens of sites for deals and pull results together. If you hit them, don't feel pressured to hit Expedia and the like, because they include them in the search.

Because apps that don't have a browser-based interface are privy to deeper negotiated discounts, you might sometimes see lower price quotes on services like **Hopper, Hotel Tonight,** and the Instagram booking account **@Hotel**.

Expensive

Bankside ★★★   Bankside, part of the points-friendly Marriott Autograph Collection brand, is fresh and glassy and stylistically on-trend. Everything in this riverside tower has been thoughtfully but not pretentiously designed. There are corridor niches where water (still or sparkling) is always on tap, and instead of begging for ice, you just pick up the bucket that's always full and waiting there. Need housekeeping? Signal with your bedside tablet. Want champagne? The touchscreen vending machine will sell you a bottle (really). Contemporary art is a focus, both in the frisky stuff on the walls, in its gallery-like space that hosts changing artists and events, and in the pencil box of bespoke postcards on your desk that they'll mail for free. The restaurant, Artyard, is adventurous and delicious, too, with wicked clever cocktails (negronis that lilt with honey and truffles—wow) and a laid-back, airy personality. A lot of hotels are going up in this neighborhood, just a few steps from the Thames Path at the southern foot of Blackfriars Bridge, an ideal area if you want a central location without antique and cramped quarters. I'm a fan.
2 Blackfriars Rd., SE1. www.banksidehotel.com. ✆ **020/3319-5988.** 161 units. Rooms usually £367–£555. Tube: Blackfriars or Southwark. **Amenities:** Restaurant; bar; spa; fitness center; free Wi-Fi.

FACING PAGE: Despite the fact that Brown's Hotel has been favored by royalty, artists, world-famous scientists, and presidents since opening in 1837, the Mayfair institution doesn't feel like a stuffy museum—its Donovan Bar is one of the city's best. This lounge-like anteroom alongside its reception desk is as formal as Brown's gets.

65

Moderate

Park Plaza Westminster Bridge London ★   This glassy mega-hotel looks like a carburetor abandoned on a curb, but you won't believe the view from the "Big Ben View" rooms: straight down Westminster Bridge at the Houses of Parliament and Big Ben's tower, like a floor-to-ceiling fantasy. Otherwise it's a well-greased, impersonal formula (part of the Radisson network) that feels more like a convention center, and be warned that the cheapest "Atrium Facing" no-view rooms (scrutinize the room description) are starved of natural light. Still, it has a lot of rooms to fill, which means discounts in low season. Studio rooms have microwaves, fridges, and pullout beds, and there's a dark and soothing indoor pool.

200 Westminster Bridge Rd., SE1. www.parkplaza.com/westminster. **© 333/400-6112,** 800/333-3333 in U.S. 1,019 units. £130–£350 double, "Big Ben View" starting at £193. 3-night minimum in some periods. Tube: Waterloo or Westminster. **Amenities:** 2 restaurants; bar; indoor pool; fitness center; spa; free Wi-Fi.

Sea Containers London ★   The hotel anchor of the South Bank riverwalk, Sea Containers (once the Mondrian, but now simply named after its building, which was once a nerve center for oceangoing freight) is special because the vistas from its Thames-front units have no competition; book one and you'll feel like you're on a ship at water. That happens to be a theme here, coppery nautical motifs and all, some of which could use refreshing. There are plenty of appealing lifestyle embellishments (a basement first-run cinema, the rooftop 12th Knot bar, bottomless champagne brunch, the Lyaness bar serving

HOW TO GET YOUR HOTEL FOR free

What if I told you that you could spend 6 nights in London, airfare and hotel included, for $949 in winter and $1,249 in summer? It's called an **air-hotel package,** and it can cost about the same as airfare alone—except it *also* comes with hotel, breakfast, and often a tour or two thrown in. How do they do it? Contracted rates and bulk buying.

The lowest prices are from eastern American cities such as New York and Boston, but for a few dozen dollars more, you can leave from just about any other American city. You can also often extend the return by as much as a month without having to buy more hotel nights through them. The catch is this: Many of the least expensive hotel options are

pillow mills that have seen better days. For a little more peace of mind, upgrade to a slightly more expensive property.

The king of affordable air-hotel deals is **Go-Today.com** (www.go-today.com; **© 800/227-3235**), which usually offers 4- and 6-night packages to London, sometimes paired with other European destinations, including local flights between the cities (as low as $949 for 6 nights). Another: "Independent Vacations" from **Gate 1 Travel** (www.gate1 travel.com; **© 215/572-7676**). Scrutinize the airline-run vacation packages from the likes of **British Airways** and **American Airlines,** because those rates may not always be the cheapest.

experimental no-ice cocktails that have been hailed as the best in the world—seriously), but although the hotel esteems itself in its ironic stylings, it's in fact at its best when you use it to simply welcome the skyline into your bedroom—the restaurant opens to the river, and the famous riverfront path literally runs beside it. Rooms that face the water, not the back, are the only ones you should consider. It's decent for families, too, because so many room types interconnect.

20 Upper Ground, SE1. www.seacontainerslondon.com. (✆) **020/3747-1000.** 359 units. Rooms from £247. Tube: Blackfriars or Southwark. **Amenities:** Restaurant; 3 bars; spa; fitness center; free Wi-Fi (slow), fast Wi-Fi £7–£10/day.

Inexpensive

H10 London Waterloo ★★★   The sole London branch of a popular and well-run Spanish brand, the H10 is a recently built tower, so rooms are nicely sized and modern, with art that actually speaks of good taste, with a bonus of healthy floor-to-ceiling windows that let London in. Its flatiron shape means everyone enjoys lots of light, plus there's a fantastic eighth-floor terrace bar with London Eye views. The blocks nearby are slightly sleepy, but there's much choice within a 5-minute walk in most directions. It sells out frequently because it's worth the strong price.

284–302 Waterloo Rd., SE1. www.h10hotels.com. (✆) **020/7928-4062.** 177 units. From £145 double. Tube: Waterloo, Lambeth North, or Southwark. **Amenities:** Restaurant; 3 bars; spa; free Wi-Fi.

THE CITY & EAST LONDON

Not long ago, the City went to sleep at 7pm. Now, with Shoreditch and Spitalfields rapidly being developed, there are more reasons for creative types to linger by night. Some of London's prime party zones are, ideally, near hotels where rates bottom out on weekends. The Liverpool Street station area lacks character, but north of it, things get more lively. Just be wary of going *too* far east in East London: There are corporate choices in the Canary Wharf district and temptingly cheap rooms by the ExCeL convention center in the Docklands region, but they're intended for conference-goers, and from there it will take you a tedious 45 minutes to reach Piccadilly Circus by the Tube and DLR. If sightseeing is your aim, make Shoreditch your eastern cutoff.

Expensive

South Place Hotel ★★★   Plugged-in, stylish, and sexy: That's the City crowd this hotel goes for, and you'll feel that way, too. Rooms are much larger than the London usual, every inch was run through the design filter (those push-button blackout blinds!), and much of the art was commissioned by celebrated contemporary artists. Rooms, charcoal-grey with wool carpets, are large (especially the showers) and hushed, and you'll find plenty of outlets, AV connections, and a huge bed you can flop around in. The two acclaimed restaurants and several bars, and the hotel's terraces with retractable roofs, lure lively professionals who work in the area. On Sundays, there's no food to be found for blocks, but the scenes of Old Street and Shoreditch are 10-minute walks away.

3 South Place, EC2. www.southplacehotel.com. ✆ **020/3503-0000.** 80 units. From £265–£545 double. Tube: Moorgate or Liverpool Street. **Amenities:** 2 restaurants; 3 bars; guests' lounge; gym; spa; business center; free in-room movies; free Wi-Fi.

Moderate

Apex City of London ★★★   An excellent contemporary boutique brand from Scotland that appeals to high standards for space and style, Apex is a friendly and peaceful urban retreat that actually looks like its website's pictures. You'll find it literally steps from the Tower of London, and a few rooms glimpse the Tower Bridge—if you score a room with a balcony, it's worth the slight price upgrade. It's handsomely designed in hardwood and walnut, with bathrooms larger than many B&B guest rooms, including walk-in power showers. The only downside is this part of the City is deader than Old Marley in the off hours, which is why it can be a steal on weekends. The **Apex London Wall,** just as good but often even cheaper, is on the side streets north of handy Bank station, and the **Apex Temple Court,** off Fleet Street, is also tops (and closer to the West End).

No. 1 Seething Lane, EC3. www.apexhotels.co.uk. ✆ **020/7702-2020.** 179 units. £191–£515 double, best prices Sat–Sun. Tube: Tower Hill. **Amenities:** Restaurant; bar; fitness center; free local calls; free Wi-Fi.

Canopy by Hilton London City ★★   A very good 2021 addition to the hotel landscape on the edge of East London, Canopy is much less corporate than a standard Hilton. This airy property was custom-built, not slotted into an ancient edifice, so it's able to give us rooms that are as spacious as we demand, including plenty of accessible facilities. It goes not for Business Travel Anonymous but for something closer to Tech Worker Loft Chic, with exposed concrete rafters, London-inflected art, furniture that evokes midcentury modern, an indoor/outdoor rooftop cafe with killer views, and sustainable sensibilities such as water refill stations instead of wasteful plastic water bottles. Walk 10 minutes north, and you're in the nightlife of Spitalfields; 10 minutes south, and you're at the flank of the Tower of London. It's a strong big-brand hotel that's more about style than conformity—but you can still use Hilton points to pay for it.

11–15 Minories St., EC3. www.hilton.com. ✆ **020/3988-7480** or 888/225-9644 in the U.S. 340 units. £177–£325 double. Tube: Aldgate East, Aldgate, or Tower Hill. **Amenities:** 2 restaurants; cocktail bar; loaner bikes; fitness center; free Wi-Fi.

The Hoxton, Shoreditch ★★   The 2006 advent of "the Hox," which specializes in compact rooms that pack in style and cleverness, changed the way London thought of budget lodging, and now, international brands ranging from Marriott's Moxy to Hilton's Canopy steal its shtick. You sleep on a platform bed under exposed brick walls and you get pegs instead of a closet. You bathe under a rain shower that might be in a futuristic cylinder. Your continental breakfast is delivered each morning via a bag you hang on the door, which can make you feel like a monkey in a hipster zoo, and there's free water and milk for your little fridge and an hour of free telephone calls a day, even if you call internationally. The lobby is intended to be the chief social space: A grill, a bar, and coffee and free Wi-Fi flowing at all hours make it as much a gathering place for digital nomads as it is a way station for tourists. Just as good, but near the British Museum, is **The Hoxton, Holborn** (199–206 High Holborn, WC1; ℂ **020/7661-3000;** Tube: Holborn). New in 2019: **The Hoxton, Southwark,** in a purpose-built, loft-like tower a quick walk to the riverfront (40 Blackfriars Rd., SE1; ℂ **020/7903-3000;** Tube: Southwark). Book as far ahead as possible to keep the price down; £300 is probably too much for these cool but scaled-back services.

1 Austin St., E2. www.thehoxton/london.com. ℂ **020/7550-1000.** 208 units. Rooms £189–£369. Tube: Aldgate or Tower Hill. **Amenities:** Restaurant; 1 hr. free calls; free Wi-Fi.

Montcalm East ★ The slotted and angular arrangement of windows on the tower it inhabits is a little weird and overly experimental and there's not much touristic to see in the immediate vicinity, but there's still enough that's good about this 2021 newcomer: mood-lit contemporary rooms with automatic curtains, rain showers, an indoor pool, high-level views, and participation in the Bonvoy system of Marriott points. Even the smallest standard room is about 25 square meters (270 sq. ft.), which is bigger than you'd find in most brick-built hotels closer to the ground. The public spaces lean into the contemporary art that the area is known for—if you'd like to experience London as if you've got a condo in a newly built high-rise, it scratches that itch well. The neigh-

New architecture near Old Street at the Montcalm East.

borhood is popular during post-work drinks but is otherwise still figuring itself out amid redevelopment that includes this building, and the food and nightlife of Shoreditch are a 5-minute walk east.

151–157 City Road, EC1. www.montcalmeast.com. ℂ **020/3837-3000.** 288 units. From £234–£359 double. Tube: Old Street. **Amenities:** Restaurant; cocktail bar; indoor pool; fitness center; spa treatments; A/C; free Wi-Fi.

The Hoxton coddles its guests with fun quirks and decor you'd want in your own home. The public areas are simultaneously fashion-forward and cozy enough to camp out in for a few hours with your laptop and a good novel.

Inexpensive

The Corner London City ★   This tiny Dutch-made design hotel, origi-nally operated as Qbic, is a wacky antidote to other formula budget hotels. Everything you need—bed, outlets, bathroom with a rain shower, TV—is part of a prefabricated bed/bathroom structure that dominates the center of the room. The cheapest rooms, called "Snug," don't have a window—did you need one? Because those rooms can be less than £75 if you snag them first. It's not a capsule hotel, just one that came up with a funky multipurpose bed unit: Your lamp is made out of petrified garden hose, your clothing rack a strange ladder/planter of some sort—it's freaky fun, although it has been steadily aging since its 2013 debut. There are free coffee and tea machines on every floor and a preposterously arty lobby where organic continental breakfast is served. You'll be within walking distance to Spitalfields/Shoreditch (15 min.) and the Tower of London (15 min.).

42 Adler St., E1. www.thecornerlondoncity.co.uk. © **020/3021-1440.** 171 units. Rooms £73–£202, discounts on its website. Tube: Aldgate East. **Amenities:** Lounge; free cof-fee; free Wi-Fi.

Shoreditch Inn ★   Look, we're not saying it's the pinnacle of hospitality, but it is an affordable, clean crash pad in an economic environment that's increasingly hostile to those. Encumbered by none of the lifestyle obsessions that paralyze its navel-gazing neighbors, it's no-frills, tidy, and fit with little touches that distinguish it as a standout of its price class: double-glazed win-dows (to muffle Shoreditch revelry), quality toiletries, and roomy quarters. That it's in the middle of the action, especially on weekends, and that its front rooms overlook a church from 1740 have me wondering when the dream will end and the owners will put the price out of reach. They could ask for more money. Don't tell them. We need this place.

1 Austin St., E2. www.shoreditchinn.com. © **020/3327-3910.** 14 units. £141–£199 dou-ble. Rates include continental breakfast. Tube: Shoreditch High Street or Hoxton. **Amenities:** A/C; free Wi-Fi.

RENT A PLACE

Way before Airbnb, England had a tradition of hosted accommodation. Partly because of the post-Blitz housing crunch, Londoners considered it normal to make a few pounds by welcoming strangers into their homes. This fast-fading tradition may work for you if you've got a car, because staying in Zone 3 or 4 may enable you to park it cheaply. What's included? At the minimum, a bed and breakfast. Everything else depends, because homestays are as unique as the hosts themselves. Plenty of English people would rather offer their place with a broker they know than list it on Airbnb. The sharing economy and Covid-19 have, however, revolutionized what tourists demand. Most tourists now want to be undisturbed in their own private room, and they find them via sites like Airbnb or Vrbo, so most of the old B&B agencies have folded. There is still

The London Bed and Breakfast Agency (www.londonbb.com; ✆ **01474/708-701**), though. It specializes in finding trustworthy hosts for single female travelers: between £70 and £120 in Zones 1 to 3. There's also **Homestay.com,** on which anyone in any place can post a listing for their spare rooms, but it's user-generated and hosts aren't vetted closely beforehand. It posts hundreds of options in London.

Those who don't want to rent a room in a home can rent a whole flat. When you arrive, you'll often find a folder that schools you in the best local shops and restaurants, and you may encounter neighbors keeping an eye on the place and on your welfare (at one property I know of, the owner herself pops round and pretends to be a helpful neighbor), which is an advantage if you want to learn more city secrets. Many properties have minimum stays of 5 to 7 nights. In London, renters such as **Airbnb.com, Vrbo.com, FlipKey.com,** and **Housetrip.com** (the last two are owned by the same company) now rival nice hotels in price, so they're less of a value unless you're traveling with a group. For a layer of protection, British-based **City Relay** (www.cityrelay.com; ✆ **020/3865-0599**) populates its listings to Airbnb and HomeAway but has an actual Earl's Court storefront where you pick up keys, serving as a responsible intermediary. To find safe and friendly options for LGBT travelers and renters, the **Mister B&B app** (www.misterbandb.com; download via Google Play or Apple App Store) has arranged rentals since 2013.

Because London apartments are in such high demand, there is little incentive for owners to upgrade facilities, so on the low end of the market, expect clean but scruffy places with well-used, cheap vacation-home furniture. For higher-quality results, we recommend booking through a London rental specialist—one who has vetted the unit and has a relationship with its owner. Large, well-appointed units go from around £125 to £490 a night—for places that sleep up to eight people. Discounts often kick in after 6 to 8 nights.

The recommended **New York Habitat** (www.nyhabitat.com; ✆ **212/255-8018** in U.S.) represents hundreds of flats and has a licensed, U.S.–based office. Units for two range from £80 to £250, but they come larger, too.

London Perfect (www.londonperfect.com; ✆ **888/520-2087** in the U.S.) has class and its flats, many of which feel like living spreads from lifestyle magazines, are extremely well maintained; owners who allow fittings to become dated are cut from the roster. Prices start around £240 a night for studios and one-bedrooms sleeping up to four people, largely in tony neighborhoods like South Kensington and Chelsea. There's usually a 7-night minimum. The best of the 30-odd homes represented by **Coach House Rentals** (www.chslondon.com/london; ✆ **020/8355-3192**) are in West London.

A high-end renter, **One Fine Stay** (www.onefinestay.com; ✆ **800/808-5830** in the U.K., 855/553-4954 in the U.S.) shoots its flats as if it's photographing a fashion spread, which tells you something about its target market. Central

London digs start at £250 a night, with impeccable design and service to match.

Now on to a few "aparthotel" companies that own their own units. My favorite is **Lincoln Suites** (37–39 Kingsway, WC2; https://thelincolnsuites. com; ☏ **020/3995-0080**; from £180; Tube: Holborn), in a handsome five-story stone building close to Covent Garden. Its range, which goes from studio to one-bedroom apartments, is well-appointed in an updated style, and you get unusual extras like free streaming movies, underfloor heating, and little kitchens including dishwashers. Rooms on the lower ground floor don't have windows, but they're cheapest. The same owner also has **Stow-Away Waterloo** (137 Lower Marsh, SE1; www.stow-away.co.uk; ☏ **07591/829-835;** from £179; Tube: Waterloo), where an off-putting concept is in reality quite comfortable and private: It's a four-level stack of 20 shipping containers, plus a lift, that have been wholly transformed into current-design, climate-controlled, private living spaces with a kitchen, a two-person dining table, and a window at one end covered by electric-control blinds. This excellent execution is geared toward visitors who don't need services—the site is unmanned (it shares a lobby with a lively restaurant that's open late, but Lincoln Suites, which is across town, handles issues remotely)—although there are free laundry machines.

More: **Citadines** (www.citadines.com; ☏ **0800/376-3898,** 833/443-2785 in the U.S.) runs corporate-style, personality-free hotel rooms fitted like little long-stay business apartments, and it has five locations citywide. In order of centrality: Trafalgar Square, The Cavendish, Holborn–Covent Garden, Barbican (cheapest, from £120), Islington (newly built in 2019), and South Kensington.

Cheval Residences (www.chevalresidences.com; ☏ **020/3725-5333**) owns high-quality, fully serviced apartments with the poise and quality of a luxury hotel. It's in four neighborhoods in the city, but the most envy-inducing is the glassy Three Quays overlooking the Thames and the Tower of London. One-bedrooms there start at £300 a night, sliding up to three bedrooms sleeping six.

HOME EXCHANGES

You'd be surprised how many Londoners are dying to visit your own stomping grounds, and if you make contact with the right people, you can swap homes (sometimes simultaneously). It sounds strange, but nothing tends to get stolen because swappers often become good friends. Not just that, but neighbors will often pop by to check up on you, so you have a built-in source of insider advice.

So which club should you choose? Here are the biggies, in alphabetical order:

HomeExchange.com (sos@homeexchange.com): This slick service claims 450,000-plus homes in 159 nations. This is important because the more members, the more potential swaps. Results can be broken down by interest. It costs $175 a year for Americans to list.

HomeLink.org: Popular with British and Australian travelers (with reps in many countries) since 1953, this service costs Americans $105 per year.

Intervac (www.intervacus.com; info@intervacus.com): Intervac has been around for almost 7 decades and its claim to fame is that some 80% of its listings are international (30,000 families are represented), which means (as it puts it), "you compete with fewer Americans for overseas properties." Access to all listings is $115 a year, but you can take a limited 21-day trial for free.

Additional exchange sites include **SabbaticalHomes.com,** catering to academics; and **HomeAroundtheWorld.com,** for gays and lesbians (£45 for a year; operations suspended during the pandemic). Or you could roll the dice with a website like **CouchSurfing.com,** on which folks (generally younger) offer spare space to visitors. That's free, but there is no vetting system, so consider the risks before taking an offer.

CHEAP COLLEGE ROOMS

Staying in college housing over holiday periods is an ideal budget saver for visitors of any age. Reservations are accepted starting in spring. At all of them, expect a wood-frame bed with linen, a desk, a dresser, an in-room sink, the possibility of an equipped kitchen (although it might be shared), an en suite bathroom (usually), laundry facilities, breakfast (often at a reasonable charge), Wi-Fi, and phones in the room or in the hall.

London School of Economics (www.lsevacations.co.uk; ℂ **020/3437-0050**): Check these out first. Its six properties are in fine condition, with the dignity that you'd expect of a school that trains the world's power players in business. Rooms rent cheaply (£50–£88) for July, August, and the first chunk of September. A few rooms may be available at Christmas or Easter, too.

Some single "private accommodation" rooms at **City University London** (www.city.ac.uk/accommodation; ℂ **020/7040-5060**) are available from early July to early September. Prices from £160 a week.

University College London (www.ucl.ac.uk/residences; ℂ **020/7529-8975,** or 020/7387-4537): Its dorms, clustering in Bloomsbury, are less prestigious than LSE's, but they aren't depressing. From late June to September, 11 residences are available starting at £41 to £80, but not all rooms have private bathrooms.

King's College (info: www.kingsvenues.com; booking: https://webbandb. kcl.ac.uk; ℂ **020/7848-1700**): Four halls are available for short rental from late June through mid-September. Kitchens but no utensils, no air-conditioning. They rent for around £50 to £70.

International Students House (229 Great Portland St., W1; www.ish.org. uk; ☎ **020/7631-8300;** Tube: Great Portland Street): Part dorm, part subdued hostel, rates start at £80 per night. Bathrooms are shared, female-only rooms are available, and some rooms are co-ed but partitioned. Other academic choices are more private.

WHERE TO DINE

I n 1957, Arthur Frommer visited London for his seminal *Europe on $5 a Day*. His report was gloomy: "With great despair, this book recommends that you . . . save your money for the better meals available in France and Italy. Cooking is a lost art in Great Britain; your meat pie with cabbage will turn out just as tasteless for 40¢ in a chain restaurant as it will for $2 in a posh hotel." The report today is happily quite different: Bon appétit!

4

As it turns out, good cooking wasn't a lost art at all. True, there are still plenty of places you'll find a crappy meal, but it's cabbage dishes that have become the lost art. Now that London swarms with people from across the world, you'll find nearly every style of cuisine—ask any Londoner for their favorite restaurant and it's bound to be a foreign food. In recent generations, British consumption of sugar, potatoes, and flour has halved. Countless restaurants now serve ingredients fresh from the farm. Even most of the major museums (listed starting on p. 122) run cafes that, surprisingly, more than pull their weight.

There is bad news. Prices keep shooting skyward—meals can cost about 15% to 20% more than they cost in 2019—and the most popular restaurants, unable to keep up given a labor market made weaker by Brexit (which made it harder for continental Europeans to work here), are so busy that it's increasingly important that you make reservations in advance for everything except casual grab-and-go meals.

London's greenie culture still thrives, and virtually every menu will have plenty of dishes for **vegetarians** to eat. The situation for **vegans** isn't quite as obvious, but cooks here are well-educated, so most kitchens understand **vegan** dietary requirements. The news is just as good for people with **food allergies:** A majority of potentially irritating ingredients are marked when you buy pre-made food at the major shops, and nearly every server will quiz you about your allergies when you order.

A late-night dining culture is not universal here, so don't be surprised if a kitchen closes by 9:30 or 10pm (check ahead if you intend to eat late).

Do not rely on Google, Yelp, or Apple Maps to find places. Online inventory is often incomplete, opening hours are often totally wrong, and the results leave out some non-chains. You can

sometimes find some meal deals
on **OpenTable.co.uk** and **Square
Meal.co.uk.**

There are plenty of flashy places
where tourists can't get a table or
where the party dies after the star
chef moves on. But each place in
this book has demonstrated endur-
ance, will welcome out-of-towners,
and was chosen to say something
about London of the moment—
you'll taste what it's like to eat like
a Londoner today.

BLOOMSBURY, FITZROVIA & KING'S CROSS

These areas north of the central tourist district are more residential and consequently less of a scene than other parts of town can be, but now that the hip
developments around Granary Square, north of King's Cross, are coming
online, the scenesters are beginning to follow.

Moderate

Dishoom ★ INDIAN   The unlikely recipe of Irani and Indian food (plus
some Malay and Indo-Chinese) in a convivial semi-industrial atmosphere
might not automatically strike you as a necessary niche, but Dishoom has
been nothing less than a smash in Britain since its 2010 debut. Now it has five
locations in London, all particularly popular as go-tos for a moderately priced,
fun, casual meal. Far from being a standard curry slinger, its modern flavors
bend expectation, and certainly back up the success. An accommodating
range of dishes comes sweet and tangy, with ginger and garlic, grilled or
green, from kebabs to tikkas to Bombay street food; many people order two
or three. They're backed up by a smart cocktail list of original concoctions
such as the Kohinoor Fizz (made of gin, gooseberry syrup with lime, and a
kiss of Aperol). The Covent Garden location (12 Upper St., Martin's Lane,
WC2; © 020/7420-9320; Tube: Leicester Square) often has an off-putting line
out the door, so I prefer this one, which has a full cellar bar where you can
wait for your table and also gives you a good excuse to explore the newly
rehabbed and on-trend warehouses of Granary Square.

5 Stable St., N1. www.dishoom.com. © **020/7420-9321.** Main courses £10–£16. Mon–
Wed 8am–11pm; Thurs 8am–midnight; Sat 9am–midnight; Sun 9am–11pm. Reservations recommended. Tube: King's Cross St Pancras.

Honey & Co. Bloomsbury ★★ MIDDLE EASTERN   It's packed for
good reasons. First, the food on its changing menu brilliantly adapts Middle

London-Wide Restaurants

BARNSBURY

DE BEAUVOIR TOWN

Grand Union Canal

SOUTH HACKNEY

VICTORIA PARK

ISLINGTON

Angel

Pentonville Rd.

HOXTON

HAGGERSTON

Cambridge Heath

See "East London Restaurants and Pubs" map

CLERKENWELL

SHOREDITCH

Old St.   Old St.

BETHNAL GREEN

Bethnal Green

FARRINGDON

Farringdon   Barbican

Chancery Lane

High Holborn

HOLBORN

The Barbican Centre

Moorgate

Liverpool St. Station

Liverpool St.

Shoreditch

Whitechapel

Mile End Rd.

STEPNEY

WHITECHAPEL

Commercial Rd.

CITY (LONDON)

THE CITY

St. Paul's Cathedral

Mansion House

Bank of England   Bank

Aldgate East

Aldgate

Leman St.

Temple

Blackfriars

Fleet St.

Blackfriars Station

Fenchurch St. Station

Cannon St. Station

Cannon St.

Monument

Fenchurch St.

Tower Hill

Royal Mint

Cable St.   Shadwell

Shadwell

SHADWELL

WAPPING

Thames

BANKSIDE

Southwark

SOUTH BANK

Waterloo Bridge

Waterloo

Waterloo Station

SOUTHWARK

Borough

13 14

12

11

10

9   15 16

Tower Gateway

HMS Belfast

Tower of London

Tower Bridge

London Bridge

Tooley St.

18

Wapping

22 →

21 →

20

Rotherhithe

BOROUGH

Lambeth North

17

Long Lane

19

BERMONDSEY

Bermondsey

ROTHERHITHE

SOUTHWARK PARK

Borough Rd.

8

Elephant & Castle

NEWINGTON

New Kent Rd.

SOUTHWARK

Southwark Park Rd.

Raymouth Rd.

LAMBETH

ELEPHANT & CASTLE

LAMBETH

Grange Rd.

Kennington

WALWORTH

South Bermondsey

KENNINGTON

The Oval (Surrey County Cricket Ground)

Oval

Old Kent Rd.

CAMBERWELL

PECKHAM

The Anchor Bankside **12**	Maltby Street Market **19**
Boisdale **4**	Market Hall Victoria **5**
Boro Bistro **14**	The Market Porter **13**
Borough Market **13**	The Marquis of Granby **7**
Caravan **10**	The Mayflower **20**
Dishoom **1**	Mercato Metropolitano **8**
E. Pellicci **23**	The Old Brewery **21**
Flat Iron Square **9**	Padella **11**
The George Inn **15**	The Prospect of Whitby **22**
Gong **16**	Regency Café **6**
The Jones Family Kitchen **3**	Restaurant Story **18**
North Sea Fish **2**	Vinegar Yard **17**
The Grapes **22**	

West End Restaurants

The crowd-pleasing Dishoom does updated takes on street food and specialty cocktails.

Eastern dishes to London palates. Spectacular lamb shawarma is tender as brisket and spiked with pomegranate and mint, and is served in a little pot with hot and soft pita. Chicken dumplings come in a broth that smells like love. The "strawberry spliff" dessert proves that berries, phyllo, mint, and olive oil go well together. This place, which gained such a following it published several successful cookbooks, moved from the southern tip of Regent's Park (it now runs its old place at 52 Warren St. as a teeny grocery store for spices and the like) to here in 2022 partly to alleviate crowding. It's still busy, so make a reservation or miss out on this assured, sometimes revelatory, meal. Walk-ins are usually seated in the window or outside.

54 Lamb's Conduit St., WC1. www.honeyandco.co.uk. ✆ **020/7388-6175.** Main courses £16–£24 at lunch, £22–£25 at dinner. Tues–Sat 9am–10:30pm. Reservations strongly suggested. Tube: Russell Square.

Noble Rot ★★ BRITISH   East of the British Museum and 2 blocks from the Charles Dickens Museum, behind an old storefront amid the transporting upscale boutiques of Lamb's Conduit Street, spend a languid meal sampling spectacularly well-chosen wines, cheeses, and sublimely fine slices of Spanish hams. There are also a few changing British-drawn dishes like gnocchi with wild garlic, baked Scottish cod, and Middlewhite pork chops. It's perplexing how such simplicity can yield such a delightful few hours and make you wish you lived like this every day—the experience has proved so lovely that Noble Rot even supports its own food-and-lifestyle magazine. Once it got popular, it also opened a second location in Soho at 2 Greek St., W1 (✆ **020/7183-8190**).

East London Restaurants & Pubs

Beigel Bake **4**
Blacklock **1, 15**
City Social **11**
Darwin Brasserie
  at Sky Garden **14**
Duck & Waffle **10**
Eataly London **9**
Emilia's Crafted Pasta **13, 16**
Lyle's **3**
Poppies **5**
The Pride of Spitalfields **8**
Rochelle Canteen **2**
St John Bread and Wine **6**
Searcys Helix Restaurant
  at The Gherkin **12**
The Ten Bells **7**

SHOREDITCH

ISLINGTON

Old St.

THE CITY

WHITE CHAPEL

Tower 42

Bank of
England

Mansion
House

Monument

Cannon St.
Station

London Bridge

Tower
Gateway

Tower of
London

Tower Hill

Fenchurch Street
Station

Aldgate

Aldgate East

Whitechapel
Art Gallery

Liverpool St.
Station

Moorgate

Old Spitalfields
Market

Dennis Severs'
House

Shoreditch
High Street

Hoxton

83

Check the menu for that only-in-Britain freshness warning about some of the meat selections: "Game may contain shot."

51 Lamb's Conduit St., WC1. www.noblerot.co.uk. ☏ **020/7242-8963.** Set menus £18 for 2 courses and £22 for 3 courses; plates £12–£32. Mon–Sat noon–2:30pm and 6–9:30pm. Reservations strongly suggested for dinner. Tube: Russell Square.

North Sea Fish ★★ SEAFOOD   Don't expect a linoleum-lined chippy, but a classy fish market-cum-restaurant, hidden on a lost-in-time side street. Every hotel manager within a walkable radius has recommended it pretty much since it opened in 1977. Portions are huge, and there's always a selection of fresh fish (sole, salmon, halibut, and so on). If you need a healthier option, you can also get your fish grilled. Try the terrific homemade tartar sauce, or, for fans of little fishies, sample grilled sardines with salad. Here, take-away is about half the price of sitting down.

7–8 Leigh St., WC1. www.northseafishrestaurant.co.uk. ☏ **020/7387-5892.** Main courses £14–£29. Mon 5–9pm; Tues–Sat noon–2:30pm and 5–9:30pm. Tube: King's Cross St Pancras or Russell Square.

Savoir Faire ★★★ FRENCH   After braving the rummage sale of mediocre gastronomic clip joints around the British Museum, patrons are known to smugly proclaim this their "discovery"—omitting the reality that it's been presenting what it correctly terms "affordable gourmet" since 1995. How could anyone have ignored this bistro-style traveler's gift, where nothing is processed and everything is made-to-order? Meals are more than reliable; in this area, they're miracles on plates. The menu might include ample portions of nimbly executed dishes like pan-roasted duck magret, bouillabaisse, tequila-lime chicken, or beef bourguignon so tender you wonder if they've got Julia Child's ghost back there.

42 New Oxford St., WC1. www.savoir.co.uk. ☏ **020/7436-0707.** Main courses £5–£20; 2-course set menu £24–£27. Sun–Thurs noon–10pm; Fri–Sat noon–11pm. Tube: Holborn or Tottenham Court Road.

Inexpensive

Bill's ★ INTERNATIONAL   A 5-minute walk from the British Museum and handy for many uses—all-day brunch, lunches, dinner, feeding kids, or downing cheap cocktails. In few other London establishments will you find mac-and-cheese, burgers, flatbreads, shawarma, and Caesar salad on the same menu. Two-course set menus, if you choose one, are £14, and three courses cost £17. Bill's is a lifesaver when you're in need of drama-free, family-friendly grub served briskly, which is why you'll be glad to hear there are also locations near Piccadilly Circus (36–44 Brewer St., W1), in Southwark (Victor Wharf, Clink St., SE1) and not far south of Buckingham Palace (6 Cathedral Walk, SW1). Plus, there's free Wi-Fi.

St Martin's Courtyard, WC2. www.bills-website.co.uk. ☏ **020/2742-2981.** Main courses £10–£16. Mon–Sat 8am–11pm; Sun 9am–10pm. Tube: Covent Garden.

The Eagle ★★ TRADITIONAL BRITISH   By now, the trend is so widespread that the term *gastropub* is meaningless, but foodies note: That trend began here in 1991 (or so most agree), in Clerkenwell, a then-ungentrified area between Bloomsbury and Islington. So old are this place's roots that it actually makes a cameo in the nursery rhyme "Pop Goes the Weasel": "Up and down the City Road/In and out of the Eagle/That's the way the money goes/Pop goes the weasel." You'll be happy for your money to go here. Behind the bar of a bare-to-the-wood corner saloon, rebuilt in 1901, the sometimes-surly staff prepares a changing selection of about a dozen flavorful dishes a day, from the likes of pork loin salad to pan-roasted sole to the house specialty, the insidiously spicy Bife Ana steak sandwich dripping with marinated garlic and onion. Tables are shared (it's bad for groups), menu by blackboard only (sometimes it's posted on Instagram: @eaglefarringdon), furniture reassuringly shabby and mismatched. Order at the bar and relax with a beer, because here, the food's the thing, and it arrives on its own schedule, not much pomp about it.

159 Farringdon Rd., EC1. www.theeaglefarringdon.co.uk. *(C)* **020/7837-1353.** Main courses £10–£21. Mon–Fri noon–3pm and 6:30–11pm; Sat 12:30–3:30pm and 6:30–10:30pm; Sun 12:30–3:30pm. Reservations required for parties of 4–10. Tube: Farringdon.

The Fryer's Delight ★★ TRADITIONAL BRITISH/TAKE-AWAY   In our age, no one would dare name their joint something as hydrogenated as The Fryer's Delight. Fortunately, this joint is not of this age. It's a true old-world chippy, where the fry fat is from beef drippings, chips come in paper wrappings, the wooden booths and checkered floor date to the lean postwar years, and the men behind the counter are almost callously gruff. Prices are anachronistic, too: Nothing's more expensive than £6.20, and most are under £5. Order yours with mushy peas. It's a 10-minute walk east of the British Museum; look for the logo of a codfish tipping his bowler hat (seriously).

KEEPING THE BILL low

If you're watching your money, bear in mind these cultural differences:

Avoid eating in   By law, restaurants must charge you a higher tax rate if you eat on premises, so the take-away menu is always cheaper.

Avoid overtipping   Credit card slips may have a line for a tip, even if the tip was already built in (if it is, it'll be about 12.5% and the description may be as subtle as "discretion"). Only tip (10%–20%) if the menu says "service not included" or similar.

Avoid soda   It can cost more than £3.50, no refill, or even more now that the government taxes beverages with more than 50g of sugar per liter.

Avoid rice dishes   It's customary to pay £2 to £3 for a side dish of plain rice, even if you think it should come with what you ordered.

Avoid water   Well, avoid it bottled. If you just order "water," waiters may bring expensive bottled water, so if you want it for free, specify "tap water."

Avoid cocktails   Mixed drinks can cost a dizzying £10 to £17, and because pours are standardized, they're usually of the same middling strength. If you do drink, stick to beer (£5–£7 a pint) or wine (around £7 a glass).

One of the most well-reviewed fish-and-chips shops in the greater city, **The Golden Chippy,** is out east in Greenwich (p. 197), so plan to drop by if you're including those attractions in your visit (62 Greenwich High Rd., SE10; www.thegoldenchippy.co.uk; *℃* **020/8692-4333;** daily 11am–11pm; £11–£15).

19 Theobald's Rd., WC1. *℃* **020/7405-4114.** Main courses £4–£7. Mon–Sat 11:30am–10pm. Tube: Holborn or Chancery Lane.

SOHO & LEICESTER SQUARE

Visitors spend much time around here, in the dining and entertainment hub of London. Despite the miasma of culinary also-rans, from junky steam-table buffets to overpriced bistros, you'll still find a queue for nearly every afford-able restaurant in the hours before showtimes. If you have theater plans, you should try to book an advance reservation, but the cheapest places don't take them. London's touristy (and pan-Asian) Chinatown sits between Shaftesbury Avenue and Leicester Square, but don't hope for a luxury dining experience there.

Expensive

Bocca di Lupo ★ ITALIAN   Stripped-down Italian expertly conceived and delivered like tapas: This simple, classy conceit—and its chipper buzz, and that long, alluring bar in front of the open kitchen—have made it a main-stay in Soho since 2008. The menu might be printed twice a day to keep up with the availability of fresh ingredients (or with the adventurous ideas: squirrel ravioli has been known to make appearances, while sea bream carpaccio and cream of langoustine and red prawn risotto appear more reliably). If one of them fails to impress, you didn't pay much for it, so it's easy and fun to try another. The rich concepts hail from around Italy, and the region of origin is marked, like wine, to help guide your palate. The wine list, too, isn't ignored. It's among the best in town for this price.

12 Archer St., W1. www.boccadilupo.com. *℃* **020/7734-2223.** Small plates £9–£13; large plates £14–£32. Mon–Sat noon–3pm and 5–11pm; Sun noon–3:30pm and 5–9:30pm. Reservations strongly recommended. Tube: Piccadilly Circus.

The Ivy ★ TRADITIONAL BRITISH   A West End tent-pole since 1917, with guests ranging from Coward to Cumberbatch, this is where London thespians pretend to slum it, lifting hamburgers alongside cognac beneath its iconic wood paneling and harlequin mullioned windows. "The Ivy is like a safari park in which the rare and exotic creatures are nurtured," wrote the *Guardian.* At its sumptuous flatiron bar—you can drink at it, but you're required to eat something, too—spotting celebrities, should there be any (try after 9pm), is made all the more subtle. The menu of Ivy classics (shepherd's pie, fish-and-chips) has been embellished with Asian-ish notions (barbecued squid salad, Bang Bang chicken with peanut chili sauce), which only accentuates the bohemian posture. From the glass jug on the bar, order a "100 Year Legacy," which is a never-ending cocktail—a Martinez, an archaic variation

LONDON food chains I RECOMMEND

London, like so many other cities, is experiencing an economic shift that squeezes out mom-and-pop establishments in favor of better-heeled chains; you'll see these mid-priced, kid-friendly names on storefronts wherever you go. They're delicious and most are English-owned, so rely on them as well:

- **Busaba:** Peppy noodles and Asian dishes at communal tables.
- **Carluccio's:** New York–style Italian. Tile walls, pasta, fish, meats, coffees.
- **Farmer J:** Affordable mixed bowls and 3-course food trays sourced mostly from British meat and veg farms.
- **Franco Manca:** Well-priced pizza on soft sourdough crust. Its pies aren't

frozen first, and it's better than **PizzaExpress**, which is prevalent but inferior.

- **Giraffe:** Every kind of comfort food, extremely family-friendly, can get noisy.
- **Leon:** Free-trade, organic alternative to fast food includes "hot boxes" of Moroccan meatballs, halloumi wraps, and "superfood" salads.
- **M&S Simply Food:** Marks & Spencer's (p. 236) stand-alone shops for sandwiches, hit-or-miss ready-made dishes, and well-selected inexpensive wines.
- **Wagamama:** Hearty noodle bowls eaten at shared long tables.
- **Wahaca:** Substantial Mexican done well with British-grown ingredients.

of a Manhattan made with gin—dispensed from a communal spout and added to as time goes on. There are licensed versions of The Ivy spreading around town, but this is where the original has been planted since World War I.

1–5 West St., WC1. www.the-ivy.co.uk. © **020/7836-4751.** Main courses £17–£38. Set menu (Mon–Fri 2:30–6pm) 2 courses £26.50, 3 courses £31.50. Mon–Fri noon–11pm; Sat 11:30am–11pm; Sun 11:30am–10:30pm. Reservations recommended. Tube: Leicester Square or Covent Garden.

Moderate

10 Greek Street ★★★ CONTEMPORARY EUROPEAN   Sometimes, restaurants get it so right—from friendly and knowledgeable staff to unfussy surroundings to pure, clean, well-made food—that you wonder why they can't all be this way. The menu, all choices a top value for the money, changes but the impeccable standards don't: Frequent standouts include whole lemon sole with samphire (an edible coastal plant) and artichokes, lamb, Gloucester Old Spot pork, Hereford beef, elderflower sorbet, a continuous trickle of fresh-baked breads, and an affordable wine list chosen with as much care as the fish and meat cuts. If it seems full, just sit at the tiny bar.

10 Greek St., W1. www.10greekstreet.com. © **020/7734-4677.** Main courses £12–£25; pizzas £15. Tues–Sat noon–10:30pm. Tube: Tottenham Court Road.

Andrew Edmunds ★★★ BRITISH   The relaxed, townhouse–style storefront, a study in natural woods and candlelit purity, has been going since 1985, enduring most likely because it hasn't caved to Soho trendiness and its

Date night? Andrew Edmunds is romantic and atmospheric.

stupendous wine list is priced fairly. Chairs don't match, staff isn't in uniform, and the menu is hand-scribbled daily with a haste that belies the effort the chef puts into sourcing farmhouse meats and preparing seasonal ingredients. Expect choices along the lines of skate wing with cauliflower and capers, free-range Aylesbury duck breast, and artichoke spaghetti with wild garlic and almond pesto, plus the occasional nose-to-tail adventure. Superb dessert cheeses are selected from area farms. It's very London.

46 Lexington St., W1. www.andrewedmunds.com. *(C)* **020/7437-5708.** Main courses £16–£28. Mon–Fri noon–3:30pm and 5:30–10:30pm; Sat 12:30–3:30pm and 5:30–10:30pm; Sun 1–4pm and 6–10:30pm. Reservations essential; dinner accepted a month ahead, lunch accepted 3 weeks ahead. Tube: Piccadilly Circus or Oxford Circus.

Blacklock Soho ★★ MEATS   Blacklock presents an existential challenge to American barbecue fans who think they're the world's best meat masters: The extravagant "meat mountain" roast (as *Food Insider* puts it) served here is piled precariously atop browned potatoes and Yorkshire pudding and walloped with gravy, a spectacle that made Blacklock a destination for unabashed carnivores. All the meat is raised sustainably in Britain, and the entire animal is used one way or another. Appetites won't sustain themselves for long in the face of such fresh-seared profligacy. If your palate requires steeling, order a cocktail from the traveling trolleys. Although you do get a lot of protein for your pound, there's not a lot for vegetarians other than a token dish, such as barbecued halloumi, and some rich sides like cauliflower with four cheeses ("arriving to the table bubbling like Mount Vesuvius," the menu promises).

Make advance bookings for the Sunday roast. The formula works so well that further locations have been launched at 16a Bedford St., WC2 (© 020/3034-1394; Tube: Covent Garden) and 28-30 Rivington St, EC2 (© 020/7739-2148; Tube: Old Street) and in the City (13 Philpot Lane, EC2; © 020/7998-7676; Tube: Monument), but this is the location that's stashed in a former basement brothel, which in terms of indulgence seems fitting in a way I can't articulate.

24 Great Windmill St., W1. https://theblacklock.com. © **020/3441-6996.** Chops £5; steaks £12–£18; Sunday roast £14–£24. Mon–Fri noon–3pm and 5–11pm; Sat noon–11pm; Sun 11:45am–8pm. Tube: Piccadilly Circus.

Blanchette ★ FRENCH   Divinely assembled French-styled tasting plates focus on ingredients: things like grilled, flavor-rich beef *onglet* (hanger steak) with snails or mushrooms, grilled asparagus with aged Comté cheese, delightful cheese beignets, hot bread delivered in a brown paper bag with soft butter spread with a wooden paddle. The food may be crafted, but there's no fussiness in the welcome nor in the bespoke funky-pop soundtrack. The look is much like a casually urbanized French farmhouse of rough wood and exposed brick; a long bar under caged light bulbs is ideal for tasting charcuterie and cheese and sipping wine and cocktails. The set menu (Mon–Fri noon–3pm and 5–6pm and Sat 5–6pm) brings you three courses for under £20.

9 D'Arblay St., W1. www.blanchettesoho.co.uk. © **020/7439-8100.** Small plates £7–£12; larger plates £16–£31. Mon–Sat noon–11pm. Tube: Oxford Circus.

Brasserie Zédel ★★★ FRENCH   When you enter via its grand staircase, you'll feel like Toulouse-Lautrec in search of tonight's muse: The always-lively, gilt-and-marble cellar dining room, awash in *fin-de-siècle* statements like platter mirrors and vested waiters, is a perfect piece of Paris off Piccadilly. This is not a crusty survivor but a pitch-perfect modern scene that was crafted out of a huge space in what was once the Regent Palace, which in 1915 was the largest hotel in Europe. Menu choices are as authentic as Pernod, pastis, oysters, quiche Lorraine, and sublimely seasoned steak tartare (often, the first thing I order upon arriving in town). The adjoining **Bar Américain,** a 1930s Art Deco treasure by an architect survivor of the *Lusitania,* does indulgently uptight cocktails and champagne, while its 80-seat cabaret, **Le Crazy Coqs/Live at Zédel** (p. 271) is an elegant venue that does matinees and evening shows. This *rêve* of London's historic connections to European high life is not nearly as expensive as it feels, and its Gallic poise only adds to the deliciousness.

20 Sherwood St., W1. www.brasseriezedel.com. © **020/7734-4888.** Main courses £12–£25; 2 courses £13; 3 courses £17.25. Mon–Sat noon–11pm; Sun noon–4pm. Reservations recommended. Tube: Piccadilly Circus.

Ceviche ★★★ PERUVIAN   This hopping Peruvian hangout serves indescribably vibrant flavors that are punchy, citrusy, and unrepeatable anywhere else you've eaten. Favorite small plates include the *don ceviche* sea bass made with wickedly sour *limo chili* tiger's milk (a tart South American marinade;

Step into the glamour of Belle Époque Paris at welcoming prices at Brasserie Zédel.

no felines involved), and the succulent *anticucho* skewers of beef heart marinated in *panca chili* marinade. Once your tongue tastes its first vibrant zip, you'll feel compelled to come back. They now give diners a spoon to lap up leftover tiger's milk—probably because I kept begging.

17 Frith St., W1. www.cevichelondon.com. © **020/7550-9364.** Small plates £7–£15. Mon–Sat noon–11:30pm; Sun noon–10:30pm; kitchen closed Mon–Thurs 3:40–5pm. Reservations suggested. Tube: Piccadilly Circus or Tottenham Court Road.

Ducksoup ★★ INTERNATIONAL   The sort of invisible hidey-hole you have to be told about, tiny little Ducksoup feels like "your" spot. The metal grille on the windows, world-weary checkerboard flooring, and life-beaten walls make it look like a greasy cafe that would sling a fry-up at you, but instead, there's a funky wine list and solid, whole-food selections, which change daily, such as grilled artichoke with lemon and capers, ricotta *gnudi* (cheese dumplings), and chargrilled bream. The room feels like a London that went out with Thatcher, but dishes sit solidly within London's 21st-century gustatory passions.

41 Dean St., W1. www.ducksoupsoho.co.uk. © **020/7287-4599.** Plates £15–£25. Mon 5–10pm; Tues 5–10:30pm; Wed–Sat noon–3pm and 5–10:30pm; Sun noon–5pm; bar open later. Tube: Tottenham Court Road.

Inexpensive

Bar Italia ★★ COFFEE/ITALIAN   Italians settled Soho in the 1940s, and before they decamped for the suburbs, they installed a set of mod, gleaming coffee bars and cafes. This straggler from 1946 is a haunt of slumming celebrities and artists, yet modest enough for the rest of us. While this institution is busy all day—making simple sandwiches, delivering pastries—it swells with revelers after midnight. Even Rome doesn't have bars that steam, press, and shuffle coffee across the clock with such gusto. "Like everything in this city that Londoners really enjoy, it reminds us of being abroad," quipped the *Guardian*. Whatever; it practically leaks hipness.

22 Frith St., W1. ℭ **020/7437-4520.** Coffee £3–£4; pizza £10–£11; panini £7. Mon–Sat 6:30am–4:30am; Sun 6:30am–2am. Tube: Leicester Square.

Café in the Crypt ★ INTERNATIONAL   Super-central and unquestionably memorable, it's the tastiest graveyard in town! Under the sanctuary of the historic St Martin-in-the-Fields church at Trafalgar Square, atop the graves of 18th-century Londoners—fret not, the former occupants were moved elsewhere decades ago—one of the West End's sharpest bargains is served. The menu at this dependable 200-seat cafeteria changes monthly, but the large portions always include a few meat pies, a vegetarian choice, soups, salads topped with meats, and sweet apple crumble with custard; there's also fish-and-chips on Friday. The church keeps the draft beer and the wine (even by the bottle) flowing. This may be the only crypt you'll ever enter that's fun, delicious, and a lifesaver—at least for your budget.

Trafalgar Sq., WC2. www.smitf.org. ℭ **020/7766-1158.** Main courses £7–£15. No cash. Mon 10am–6pm; Tues 10am–7:30pm; Wed 10am–4pm; Thurs–Sat 10am–7:30pm; Sun 11am–5pm. Tube: Charing Cross.

Reliable cheap eats at the subterranean Café in the Crypt.

Gordon's Wine Bar ★★★ INTERNATIONAL   The atmosphere is matchless at this vaunted and vaulted casual wine bar, one of London's worst-kept secrets. It was established in 1890 (when Rudyard Kipling lived upstairs) and, thank goodness, hasn't been refurbished since—look in the front window and you'll see untouched champagne bottles intentionally left to grow furry with dust. These tight, candlelit cellars beneath Villiers Street are wallpapered with important newspaper front pages from the mid-20th century—the Crystal Palace blaze, the death of King George VI—and the wood barrels behind the bar are filled with port on tap (a *schooner* is small, a *beaker* is larger). Everything is suffused in a mustardy ochre from more than 42,000 past evenings of indoor tobacco smoke (no longer legal). Music is not played—not that you could hear it over the din of conversation. Pick a bottle of wine (it's affordable) from one of the binders and they'll give you the glasses, and for a light meal, select from a marble table of English and French cheeses or a steam table of hot food. In good weather, the event expands outside along Embankment Gardens with casual alfresco fare such as barbecue and sweet potato fries. (The stone arch was built around 1625 as a palace gate on the Thames, but its mansion is long gone and the river moved 46m/150 ft. south.) Come down in midafternoon, well before offices let out, or you won't secure seating.

47 Villiers St., WC2. www.gordonswinebar.com. © **020/7930-1408.** Cheese plates £9–£20; shared plates £14–£30. Mon–Sat 11am–11pm; Sun noon–10pm. Food: noon–9pm. No reservations. Tube: Charing Cross or Embankment.

Mildreds ★ VEGETARIAN   Packed since 1988, it's where vegetarians with palates go. The menu (all three meals) is ever-changing but always assembled with more care than the usual beans and tofu: Sri Lankan sweet potato and lime cashew curry, wood-roasted mushroom and ale pie, and green falafel with sour cherry and pistachio rice are three samples from its international menu. If you don't do onion or garlic, there's a thoughtful menu just for you. Big bowls and plates, appetizing presentation, and a vibe like home have secured Mildreds a following even among carnivores—it even had a pretty cookbook published. Save room for the cheesecakes or puddings—you won't believe they're gluten-free. You'll find another location near Trafalgar Square at 79 St Martin's Lane, WC2 (© **020/8066-8393;** Tube: Leicester Square), but this is the original, in a townhouse from the 1700s.

45 Lexington St., W1. www.mildreds.co.uk. © **020/7494-1634.** Main courses around £15. Mon–Sat 9am–11pm; Sun 9am–10pm. Tube: Tottenham Court Road or Piccadilly Circus.

Rasa Sayang ★★ SINGAPORE/MALAYSIAN   When you need something quick, flavorful, and filling in Chinatown or the Theatre District, this super-casual spot is superior to most of the other fast-casual Asian restaurants in Chinatown, and the service is less haughty. Rich and flavorful street food–inspired dishes abound like Malay *nasi lemak* with fragrant coconut rice,

Gordon's Wine Bar is rarely this empty. But even when you're fighting the crowds, it's one of the most atmospheric, charming hiding places in the West End to tuck into a cheese plate and a good cabernet.

spicy/noodly *laksa* soup bowls, fluffy roti *canai* stringy flatbread, stir-fry noodles, and Singapore spicy crab.

5 Macclesfield St., W1. www.rasasayangfood.com. © **020/7734-1382.** Main courses around £13. Mon–Thurs noon–2:30pm and 5–10pm; Fri–Sat noon–10pm; Sun noon–9pm. Tube: Piccadilly Circus.

COVENT GARDEN

The area was once more interesting, but CAPCO, which governs the leases, has adopted a policy of squeezing out oddballs in favor of imported brands such as Shake Shack, Le Pain Quotidien, Apple, and Balthazar. The food within the market is tourist-priced, but if you simply must eat there, head to the lower level where you'll find £6 *tartines* (open-faced sandwiches) at **Chez Antoinette** and good cheese at the **Crusting Pipe** wine bar.

Expensive

J. Sheekey ★★ SEAFOOD   Smartly turned-out waiters prep you with so many specialized fish-eating utensils that your place setting starts to look like a workstation at Santa's workshop. Such presentational flourishes are appropriate to theaterland, where Sheekey has been a classic for years, and although prices aren't generous, portions and quality are. The least expensive main dish, fish pie, is fortunately its trademark, but there are plenty of other choices, from shrimp-and-scallop burgers to a delectable lemon sole, plus a changing slate of game and meats for the fish-averse. Despite all the fuss, children are welcomed.

28–35 St. Martin's Ct., WC2. www.j-sheekey.co.uk. © **020/7240-2565.** Main courses £23–£46. Lunch and late-night set menu: 2 courses £25, 3 courses £30. Mon–Sat noon–11:15pm; Sun noon–10:15pm. Reservations recommended. Tube: Leicester Square.

Rules ★★ TRADITIONAL BRITISH   For a high-end kitchen that takes British cuisine seriously, go with an icon. Rules is London's oldest restaurant (est. 1798), and its patrons have included Graham Greene, Charles Dickens, Evelyn Waugh, and Edward VII, who regularly dined here with his paramour Lillie Langtry. (The management is less than discreet about it; the nook they used is named for him.) Being a major stop on the tourist trail has gone slightly to its head and it's steeped in its own hype; beer comes in a "silver tankard," for example, and the landmarked rooms are an over-dressed Georgian yard sale of yellowing etchings, antlers, and rich red fabrics. But what's on the table is indisputably high-class: English-reared meat like haunch of venison, whole roast squab or grouse (it serves 18,000 game birds annually), and cocktails like that famous

Delivery Apps

After a long day of trooping through museums and up and down stairs in the Tube, you're forgiven if you just want to put your feet up. These apps are favored by Londoners for finding nearby take-away or food delivery services: **Deliveroo, Just Eat, UberEATS,** and **Getir,** which delivers groceries like Instacart does in the U.S.

one made of tonic, juniper, and quinine. Its nearest rival, **Simpsons-in-the-Strand** at the Savoy hotel (p. 51), has been going since 1828.

35 Maiden Lane, WC1. www.rules.co.uk. ℭ **020/7836-5314.** Main courses £22–£43. Tues–Sat noon–11:30pm; Sun noon–10pm. Reservations recommended. Dress code: smart casual; no shorts. No children 9 and under admitted after 7pm. Tube: Covent Garden.

Moderate

Browns ★ TRADITIONAL BRIT-ISH In London, there's a Browns for fashion and a Brown's Hotel, but Browns the spacious brasserie is the Browns you can afford. Installed in the former Westminster County Courts, this high-quality, Brighton-based English chain serves updated English food and imported beer. The globe lanterns, enormous mirrors, and staff buttoned into crisp white oxford shirts impart the sense of a Gilded Age chophouse. Expect lots of indul-gently hearty dishes such as lobster risotto, steak and Guinness pie, fish-and-chips, or a nice fat burger with Irish cheddar. A sense of tradition—starchy, but the kind that's welcoming to tourists—is the main product here.

Surf and turf at Browns brasserie.

82–84 St Martins Lane, WC2. www.browns-restaurants.co.uk. ℭ **020/7497-5050.** Main courses £14–£29; 2-course pre-theater meal (Mon–Fri noon–5pm) £16; bottomless brunch until 2pm Fri–Sun from £40. Mon–Wed 10am–11pm; Thurs–Fri 10am–midnight; Sat 9am–midnight; Sun 9am–10:30pm. Tube: Leicester Square.

Flat Iron ★★★ STEAK For a mere £12, you get an absolutely perfect 200g (7-oz.) steak or steakburger, a cup of salad, a serving of beef-dripping popcorn, and on the way out the door, a cone of caramel ice cream topped with shavings from a block of dark chocolate. No wonder there's a queue at peak hours. The menu is focused—no chicken, no pork, and sorry, vegetari-ans—plus good cocktails and well-suited side dishes. Specializing makes the cooking expert and the juicy meat is over-the-top delicious. The beef comes from conscientiously raised British cows, and each week, 7 tons of it are served at Flat Iron's several locations (others include one near the British Museum at 9 Denmark St., off Tottenham Court Rd.; 17 Beak St., off Carnaby St.; and 88–90 Commercial St. in Spitalfields). This version by Covent Gar-den is the best for killing time before your table is ready—and it's also one of the few locations that serve the ice cream.

17/18 Henrietta St., WC2. https://flatironsteak.co.uk. No phone. Main courses £12. Wed–Thurs noon–11pm; Fri–Sat noon–11:30pm; Sun–Tues noon–10:30pm. No reserva-tions. Tube: Covent Garden or Leicester Square.

The Jones Family Affair ★★ BRITISH   This multilevel, pop art–filled Affair brings a groovy, convivial steakhouse vibe to the neighborhood near the National Gallery. If you love beef, the way JFA's Josper grill can almost mystically seal in the flavors of its Yorkshire longhorn could blow your mind, but then again, the oxtail burger might do it instead. It's not just about beef, though; fish, duck, and pork (that's cut like beef) are also knowingly prepared in generous portions. Most proteins come from The Ginger Pig, a network of principled farmers. Sides such as truffled mac-and-cheese and lemon-and-mint courgettes fill out the traditional cuisine goals, and the lengthy list of creative cocktails, many of them gin-based or riffs on traditional English quaffs, seal the deal. When you're in Belgravia, its sister restaurant, **Jones Family Kitchen** (7–8 Eccleston Yards, SW1; ✆ **020/3929-6000;** https://jones familykitchen.co.uk), in an off-street courtyard south of Victoria Station, delivers many of the same pleasures, but with more space to stretch out for conversation.

40–42 William IV St., WC2. https://jonesfamilyaffair.co.uk. ✆ **020/3750-2121.** 2-course set menu £20, 3-course £24 before 6pm; lunch main courses £10–£24, dinner mains £15–£35. Mon 5pm–midnight; Tues–Sat noon–midnight. Tube: Charing Cross.

Inexpensive

Punjab Restaurant ★★★ INDIAN   Do not be deceived by looks. This is not a hack kitchen sponging off the Covent Garden tourist trade—this place predates the recent curry trend, which is why it survived the crest of the popularity wave. Punjab has been cooking since 1947, when it was opened by Gurbachan Singh Maan, a wrestler, and moved to this location in 1951 to serve the bureaucrats of the India High Commission during a tumultuous political period. Now, his fourth generation runs it with striking professionalism. It proclaims itself the oldest North Indian restaurant in the U.K., and staff have worked here for decades. Cooking is light on the oil and *ghee*. Meats and tandoori (the oven was installed in 1962) are well marinated, and so they arrive tender. The menu is cheeky, too: "If you have any erotic activities planned for after you leave us, perhaps you should resist this sensational garlic *naan*." Reserve ahead on weekends.

80 Neal St., WC2. www.punjab.co.uk. ✆ **020/7836-9787.** Main courses £10–£18, sometimes a £18 per person minimum. Mon–Sat noon–11pm; Sun noon–10pm; last orders 15 min. before closing. Tube: Covent Garden.

MAYFAIR & MARYLEBONE

It's hard to find a dining establishment in these high-toned hoods that isn't overpriced, swooning with self-importance, and wooing a clientele that's better-connected than you are. The "in" spots seem to change with the trends, but you may rely on—and be welcomed by—these stalwarts.

Expensive

Hide ★★★ CONTEMPORARY   One of the city's most celebrated chefs, Ollie Dabbous, oversees this ambitious, three-level destination, arranged in a

Flowery avocado toast at Hide.

sparse Scandinavian style, where he has plenty of space to throw money at ideas and allow diners to absorb the ministrations of his army of staff, including a dozen-plus sommeliers. The wine list from Hedonism, one of the city's most comprehensive wine stores, is one of the largest in the world (more than 6,000 bottles—you will splash out in more ways than one). Choose the street-level, a la carte Hide Ground, serving all three meals, afternoon tea, and baked creations; or Hide Above, overlooking Green Park, for fine-dining tasting menus; Hide Below is the bar and wine cellar (try the martini made with birch sap instead of ice). Any choice will wow, with dishes weaving acid and richness to deliver amazements that always belie the deceptively plain menu descriptions. This is what happens when a talent is given full license to play—you get a menu full of headliners. Charred asparagus in meadowsweet and hay buttermilk with praline; 7-year aged Simmenthal beef tartare with nasturtium, tobacco, and molasses; miso-glazed goose or turbot in verbena and a sauce made of its own bones; a saffron-indulged bouillabaisse that has caused many a grizzled food critic to exalt like the Pythia channeling Apollo. Don't expect any dish to loiter on the menu for long, because Dabbous has built the perfect personal theme park for inventing new thrills. He's thought of everything, down to the phone chargers in the tables and the lighting, which (for real) intentionally eliminates shadows so you can properly Instagram your dinner, because once the mastery of the cooking is complete, each plating yields a second work of art. Make reservations as far ahead as you can.

85 Piccadilly, W1. www.hide.co.uk. © **020/ 3146-8666.** Main courses £28–£48; 7-course tasting menu £140; wine pairings from £65. Mon–Fri 7:30am–1am; Sat 9am–1am; Sun 9am–11:30pm. Last food orders at 11pm. Reservations required. Tube: Green Park.

KOL Restaurant ★★★ CONTEMPORARY MEXICAN You may not think you came all the way to London for Mexican food, but you've almost certainly never had it prepared so experimentally and innovatively by a chef so laden with awards. Young

Clever British/Mexican fusion dishes at KOL restaurant.

STEEPED IN TRADITION: afternoon tea

Afternoon tea is an overpriced tourist's pursuit, to be sure, but that doesn't mean it's not delightful to pass the time by pretending to be fancy. Arrive hungry and you'll be served a never-ending banquet of scones, clotted cream, pastry, light sandwiches, and a bottomless brewed torrent. Dress up, if you please, and be discreet about photos. Hundreds of places throw teas, but these are among the most transporting, legendary, or best located. Most places will add champagne for £15 to £20 more.

Brown's Hotel This Mayfair institution, open since 1837, offers exacting execution and a handsome paneled room that Victoria loved having tea in, but it's not overly snooty. It veers trendy, mounting additional themed teas according to a posted schedule. www.roccofortehotels.com. ✆ **020/7518-4006.** Noon–4:30pm; £65. Tube: Green Park. Also see p. 62.

Fortnum & Mason The venerable department store on Piccadilly has sold tea for 3 centuries, so naturally in its Diamond Jubilee Tea Salon, nibbling off duck-egg-blue china and serenaded by grand piano, you choose from 150 tea types, many of which are supplied to the other hotels on this list. The crowd can be touristy. www.fortnumandmason.com. ✆ **020/7734-8040.** Tea served all day; £70. Tube: Green Park. Also see p. 232.

The Goring Near Buckingham Palace, it serves on its own bespoke canary-yellow china in your choice of the blood-red lounge, the airy conservatory, or the garden. Book at least 3 months ahead, but sit as long as you want once you're there. www.thegoring.com. ✆ **020/7396-9000.** Mon–Fri 3:30–5pm; Sat 1–4pm; Sun 1–5pm; from £60. Tube: Victoria. Also see p. 57.

Great Court Restaurant, The British Museum Enjoy more sensibly priced scones under the courtyard's central glass canopy. It's a gorgeous but casual setting you're sure to visit anyway. www.britishmuseum.org. ✆ **020/7323-8990.** Daily 11:30am–5pm (last sitting 4pm); £22. Tube: Russell Square. Also see p. 126.

Santiago Lastra, *GQ*'s Chef of the Year for 2021, has received worldwide acclaim for rendering traditional Mexican dishes, but solely using British ingredients. The ideas are masterful, bursting with flavor, and repeated at no other restaurant on Earth: You might have a squid-and-rhubarb ceviche, a mole with blackcurrant, or langoustine tacos with sauerkraut, all tinged with a spicy kick grown right in the United Kingdom. KOL is a tiny place where cooking is performed amid the diners, and the experience is highly prized; reservations open early each month for timings two months hence (i.e., June 1 for August seatings). *Warning*: If you don't show up for your booking, you're docked £90 as if you'd gone.

9 Seymour St., W1. https://kolrestaurant.com. ✆ **020/3829-6888.** Set menus of 6 or 9 courses £90–£125 with optional supplements. Seatings Tues 6–9:15pm; Wed–Sat noon–1:45pm and 6–9:15pm; Sun noon–2:30pm. Tube: Marble Arch.

Le Gavroche ★★★ FRENCH There are always newcomers in Mayfair hoping to capture the vanity crowd, and trendy styles with fresh young chefs rise and burn out, but Le Gavroche remains the top choice for classical French

Houses of Parliament Take tea overlooking the Thames in the modern Terrace Pavilion rooms behind the House of Commons. www.parliament.uk/visiting. © 020/7219-4114. Generally 2 and 3:45pm on a scattered schedule; £30 adults, £15 kids 12 and under, plus price of tour. Tube: Westminster. Also see p. 146.

The Lanesborough Dazzling in every way, from the delicacy of the pastry to the airy Regency frills of the conservatory glass overhead, for cozy class this Knightsbridge hotel institution defeats the Ritz by a strong scone's throw, I'd say. www.lanesborough.com. © 020/7259-5599. Mon–Thurs 2:30–4pm; Fri–Sat noon–4pm; Sun 3:30–4:30pm; £65. Tube: Hyde Park Corner. Also see p. 61.

The Langham The first London hotel to initiate the custom (in 1865) is still top quality, but it's also one of the most commercial, having branded itself with a Wedgwood partnership. There's a children's version with a literary theme. www.palm-court.co.uk. © 020/7636-1000. 5 seatings Wed–Sat 12:30–5pm; £62. Tube: Oxford Circus. Also see p. 63.

The Milestone The antiqued, library-like Park Lounge overlooking Kensington Gardens is your stop if you're near Kensington Palace. It doles out doggy boxes for guests who can't finish— a courtesy that's uncommon at teas. www.milestonehotel.com. © 020/7917-1000. 3 seatings 1–5pm; from £65. Tube: High Street Kensington.

The Ritz The only way most of us can afford the formal gilding, mirrors, and boisterous floral arrangements of the Ritz, at 150 Piccadilly, is to submit to the machinelike attentions of the servile waiters in its gilded Palm Court (1906). They process 400 people daily over a range of hours the gentry would actually find unseemly for tea. It's fancy but the mood is chilly. No jeans or sneakers, with jacket and tie required for men. Book 6 to 8 weeks ahead. www.theritzlondon.com. © 020/7300-2345. 5 seatings 11:30am–7:30pm; £67. Tube: Green Park.

cuisine. Its leader, Michel Roux, Jr., is the son of the chef who founded the restaurant in 1967. The famous cheese soufflé is still there after all these years. Also on the menu: Scottish salmon with kohlrabi and miso puree, roast veal loin, and butter-poached lobster tail, plus desserts including hot passion fruit soufflé with white chocolate ice cream. The cheese board is exemplary. It's all beautifully presented and served with style. The wine list is a master class in top French vintages, and is kind to the purse on lesser-known varieties. It all takes place in a comfortable, conventional basement dining room that may be too old-fashioned for some, but is endearingly classic to those who have cherished this place for over a half century.

43 Upper Brook St., W1. www.le-gavroche.co.uk. © 020/7408-0881. Main courses £40–£63; tasting menu £180 (without wine). Tues–Sat 5–10pm. Reservations required. Dress code: smart (no T-shirts or sportswear). Tube: Marble Arch.

Moderate

The Grazing Goat ★ BRITISH A block north of Oxford Street, this farmhouse-style gastropub (light wood, bare tables, a bar, strong but casual

food halls OF FAME

Inspired by the markets and food trucks of the United States, London has welcomed a multicourse banquet of gourmet gatherings that function like foodie markets for fresh, ready-to-eat creations. Some of the best:

Borough Market The king of foodie meccas; the one all the others wish they were. See p. 105. Tube: London Bridge.

Camden Markets The down-market choice—mostly cheap and simple—but bountiful. Star attraction: The Cheese Wheel, where hand-rolled tagliatelle is tossed in a bowl made of a huge truckle of melting Parmesan. See p. 252. Tube: Camden Town.

Eataly It's the Italian eater's paradise that itself is devouring the world. 135 Bishopsgate, EC2. www.eataly.co.uk. Mon–Sat 9am–11pm; Sun 9am–10pm; last entry 1 hr. before closing. Tube: Liverpool Street.

Flat Iron Square A stone's throw from Borough Market, this small but reliable spot (under brick arches and with a yard) is good for grubby pubby fare like pizza, burgers, taproom beers. 45 Southwark St., SE1. www.flatironsquare. co.uk. Tues–Sat noon–11pm; Sun noon–8pm. Closed Mon. Tube: London Bridge.

Maltby Street Market Purveying gorgeous flavors such as "bad brownies" oozing salted caramel, egg-shaped waffles, and "African volcano" hot sauce. Partly outdoors amid the railway vaults south of the Tower Bridge. Maltby St., SE1. www.maltby.st. ℂ **020/7394-8061.** Sat 10am–5pm; Sun 11am–4pm. Tube: London Bridge or Bermondsey.

Market Hall Victoria Some 14 restaurants, bars, and seating for 300 in an Edwardian baroque shopping arcade vacated by a nightclub. Don't miss the rooftop bar. Terminus Place, 191 Victoria St., SW1. www.markethalls.co.uk.

WHERE TO DINE

service) attracts a varied crowd for wine or a locally brewed pint, quality house-cured meats, and classic British proteins such as rotisserie beef, venison, chicken, fish-and-chips, and the title character served with a raisin-mustard *jus*. The all-day Sunday roast (beef, pork, or lamb) with all the trimmings is swishier than what a pub serves, but a tonic for feet run weary by shopping at nearby Selfridges. *Hidden B&B gem alert:* Upstairs are eight country-house-inspired rooms, each with a king bed and free Wi-Fi (from £220, but don't expect such attentive service upstairs).

6 New Quebec St., W1. www.cubitthouse.co.uk. ℂ **020/7724-7243.** Main courses £19–£32. Mon–Sat 7:30am–11pm; Sun 7:30am–10pm; kitchen closes 1 hr. prior to close, bar closes 1 hr. later. Tube: Marble Arch.

Inexpensive

The Hard Rock Cafe ★ AMERICAN   You'll find one in every city from Key West to Kuwait. Its burgers (though excellent) nudge £18, it's cramped, and much of the so-called memorabilia consists of instruments played once and tossed aside. But this Hard Rock was the world's first, opened in 1971, so there is a grudging authenticity. And you don't have to eat here to take a free tour of its museum, The Vault (daily 1–9pm), packed with historic guitars.

Mon–Tues 9am–10pm; Wed–Fri 9am–11pm; Sat 10:30am–11pm; Sun 10:30am–10pm. Tube: Victoria.

Market Hall West End   A one-time BHS department store off Oxford Street is now the U.K.'s biggest food court, with food stalls, four bars, a tap-room, a terrace with a retractable roof, a demonstration kitchen, and—just to raise the game—proper forks, knives, and glassware. 9 Holles St., W1. www.market halls.co.uk. Mon–Tues 11am–10pm; Wed–Sat 11am–11:30pm; Sun 11am–8pm. Tube: Oxford Circus.

Mercato Metropolitano   Dedicated to small producers and emerging chefs, this former factory space has been a smash since its 2016 opening. Fresh-baked wood-fired pizzas, cocktails, and beers, all sorts of world food, and a filling overuse of the term *artisan*. 42 Newington Causeway, SE1. www.mercato metropolitano.co.uk. © **020/7403-0930.**

Mon–Thurs 8am–11pm; Fri 8am–midnight; Sat 11am–midnight; Sun 11am–10pm. Tube: Elephant & Castle.

Seven Dials Market   A 5-minute walk north of Covent Garden, it invites thriving street-food vendors to wow palates in a Victorian banana-and-cucumber warehouse. 35 Earlham St., WC2. www. sevendialsmarket.com. Mon–Tues 11am–10pm; Wed–Sat 11am–11pm; Sun 11am–9pm. Tube: Covent Garden or Leicester Square.

Vinegar Yard   Under the gleaming monolith of the Shard, Vinegar Yard is a friendly mix of top-level street food, local beers, art installations, and pop-up shops. There's a covered area for poor weather, and on weekends it adds a flea market. Last orders at 9pm. 72–82 St Thomas St., SE1. www.vinegaryard.london. Mon–Tues 5–10pm; Wed–Sat noon–10pm; Sun noon–8pm. Tube: London Bridge.

This is the original, dare I say *legendary* location, so it's the one you should favor; the one at 225–229 Piccadilly opened in 2020 and there, you have to eat in a not-very-historic basement.

150 Old Park Lane, W1. www.hardrock.com. © **020/7514-1700.** Main courses £12–£19. Sun–Fri noon–10pm; Sat noon–11pm. Reservations recommended. Tube: Hyde Park Corner.

BELGRAVIA, KENSINGTON & WESTMINSTER

South Kensington near the museums is a particular disappointment; the museums offer insultingly overpriced food services while most nearby establishments are not a culinary credit to such fine institutions. If you must eat in South Ken, scout around the cafes at Exhibition Road around the Tube stop; look into frenetic local tapas chain **Casa Brindisa** (7–9 Exhibition Rd., SW7; www.brindisakitchens.com; © 020/7590-0008); or try **Franco Manca** (91 Old Brompton Rd.; www.francomanca.co.uk; © 020/7584-9713), a local brand that does pizza on sourdough crust. Otherwise, the pickings are ripe with the usual chains.

Moderate

Boisdale ★★ SCOTTISH   Richly done up in red and green like an all-year manifestation of the coziest Christmas, Boisdale makes a year-round gift of the best of Scottish cuisine, from whisky to neeps. It's big on brilliantly prepared fish (the delicately fried calamari with pickle and Tellicherry chili mayo is a starter standout), aged steaks, and oysters, but the accompaniments are compelling as well, even when they're as minor as the rich yellow table butter or the thrice-cooked chips with Bloody Mary ketchup. It's all served atop crisp tablecloths by heedful servers in rooms festooned with etchings and antlers—a masculine scene, to be sure, and the setting for many a power lunch by homesick Scots working in London, many of whom seem to know the staff by name. There may be no finer place in the city to try properly prepared haggis—you can even get a vegetarian version of it as a burger. And surprise—it also supports an excellent jazz-and-standards cabaret (ticketed separately) that attracts excellent vocalists and musicians nearly nightly.

15 Eccleston St., SW1. www.boisdale.co.uk. ℰ **020/7730-6922.** Lunch main courses £11–£32; dinner main courses £18–£32. Mon 5–11pm; Tues–Fri noon–1am; Sat 5pm–midnight; Sun noon–2:30pm. Reservations recommended. Tube: Victoria.

Inexpensive

Regency Café ★★★ TRADITIONAL BRITISH   The mid-20th-century "caff" diner, once a staple of London life, is rapidly being swept into Formica

The colorful-as-a-kilt dining room at upscale Scottish restaurant Boisdale.

heaven by trendy bistros. Among the few holdouts still doling out classic English breakfasts all day is the 1940s Regency, a discount-Deco requiem to a lost age in yellowed white tiles and bolted-down plastic chairs. This isn't a gustatory treasure (the fryer is in heavy use, white bread heaped high, sausage a food group); it's an anthropological one. Big-value food including £2.90 burgers or homemade meat pie is prepared with lightning speed, and your order is jarringly bellowed so that you can come fetch it. For another marvelous "caff," see E. Pellicci (p. 110).

17–19 Regency St., SW1. https://regencycafe.has.restaurant. *℃* **020/7821-6596.** Main courses £2.70–£6.75. Mon–Fri 7am–2:30pm and 4–7:15pm; Sat 7am–noon. Tube: Pimlico or Westminster.

THE SOUTH BANK & CITY

For a casual street-food meal, head behind the Southbank Centre for the Southbank Centre Food Market, a collection of changing food stalls cooking up curries, duck confit burgers, sausages, and other cheap and ready-to-eats. It runs Friday through Sunday, starting around noon and wrapping up by about 8pm (6pm Sunday).

Expensive

Restaurant Story ★★★ MODERN BRITISH   This is how a meal here might begin: Instead of handing you a menu, your server lights a white taper on your table and begins serving dishes by that candlelight. A few courses in, as it burns down, comes the reveal: That was no ordinary candle (I won't give away the secret), and all of a sudden, you realize you are actually amid a sensational parade of tricks of the tongue and deliberate gastronomic *trompe l'oeil*. The dramatic and whimsical flourishes are by hot talent Tom Sellers, who, astonishingly but deservedly, earned a Michelin star within 5 months of Restaurant Story's 2013 opening for his narrative-as-meal concept and earned a second one 9 years later. Everyone receives a tasting menu that's tailored to their palate, formulated out of English ingredients and inspired by memories and moments from Sellers' English upbringing. It sounds pretentious, but it is, in fact, one of the most sensational nights you may ever spend in a restaurant. It's a high-wire act few other chefs would be capable of and yes, it's pricey, but few other places I think would be so worth it.

199 Tooley St., SE1. www.restaurantstory.co.uk. *℃* **020/7183-2117.** 10 courses £185. Mon 6:30–11pm; Tues–Sat noon–5pm and 6:30–11pm; in Dec, also Sun 6–11pm. Reservations essential. Tube: London Bridge or Bermondsey.

Moderate

Caravan ★★ INTERNATIONAL   Housed in a former metal box factory a short walk from Tate Modern, the industrial-feeling and cheerfully casual Caravan is always busy but glows with the *joie de vivre* of quality ingredients and flavorful combos. It roasts its own coffee (and does a brisk business on that alone) and bakes its own goods—the jalapeño cornbread is moist and kicky—and pushes its tapas-size dishes into fun flavor realms like coconut-lime chicken salad, sourdough pizzas, hearty veggies-and-chutney bowls, and bulgur-and-halloumi fritters. The original location, cavernous but with a particularly pleasant patio, is found in the Granary Square shopping-and-dining development near the Regent's Canal, a short walk north of King's Cross station (1 Granary Square, N1; ☎ **020/7101-7661;** Tube: King's Cross St Pancras).

Great coffee and casual fare at Caravan.

30 Great Guildford St., SE1. www.caravan restaurants.co.uk. ☎ **020/7101-1190.** Small plates £7–£10; pizzas £12–£15; large plates £16–£21. Mon–Thurs 8am–11pm; Fri 8am–midnight; Sat 9am–midnight; Sun 9am–4pm. Tube: Southwark or London Bridge.

Padella ★★★ ITALIAN   Eaters go wild for its succulent and savory pasta dishes—there's always a line curling out the front door into this one-room fishbowl alongside Borough Market. Once you're in, you mount a stool at a counter (facing the cooks is best, but it'll be too busy for you to be choosy) and get busy delighting yourself from a brief list of small-plate superstars like creamy gnocchi with nutmeg butter, *pici cacio e pepe* (cheese-and-pepper pici noodles), and pappardelle with a ragù of 8-hour Dexter beef shin from Ireland, plus a few tap wines and beers. You'll be happier with two plates than with just one. For the best shot at quick seating, try daily around 9pm or Sundays before opening. If you're within walking distance, you can often use the free WalkUp app to add yourself to the waiting list; otherwise, check in using the QR code at the doorway. There's a second, just-as-busy location at 1 Phipp St., EC2, in Shoreditch (closed Sun–Mon; Tube: Old Street).

6 Southwark St., SE1. www.padella.co. No public phone. Main courses £5–£13.50. Tues–Sat noon–3:45pm and 5–10pm; Sun noon–3:45pm and 5–9pm. Tube: London Bridge.

Inexpensive

Boro Bistro ★★ FRENCH/ALGERIAN   The aimlessly gawping crowds at Borough Market might exhaust you, but a relaxing chill-out spot can be found very near the grounds. Downstairs in the brick vaults between the Market and Borough High Street just east of Southwark Cathedral, this European-with-a-pubby-twist bistro is many visitors' fast favorite for Roman-esque atmosphere. Lit by candles that have accumulated wax over countless nights, you dine at funky, weather-beaten wood tables on cocktails, wines, and craft beers; shared platters (Corsican coppa, baked Camembert); burgers (the house version is draped with Comté cheese); and odds-and-ends alternatives (croque monsieur, spicy Parmesan chicken wings, orange salad with mint and red onion). In nice weather, the terrace is ideal for a drink, and in cold weather, there are heaters and fleece blankets.

6–10 Borough High St., Bankchambers, Montague Close, SE1. www.borobistro.co.uk. ℗ **020/7378-0788.** Dishes £4–£12. Tues–Sat noon–11pm; Sun noon–10pm; kitchen breaks 3–6pm Mon–Thurs. Reservations suggested. Tube: London Bridge.

Borough Market ★★★ INTERNATIONAL   Countless visitors cite it as a highlight of their London vacations. This popular complex combines Victorian commercial hubbub with glorious, farm-fresh flavors, rendered as finger food for visitors. If there's any country that has farming down, it's England, and this market is its showplace. About a dozen greenmarket vendors sell their country meats, cheeses, and vegetables beneath its metal-and-glass canopy all week long, but the market really blooms Thursday through Saturday, when more than 100 additional vendors unpack and the awe-inspiring scene hits its swing. The least crowded time is Thursday between 11am and noon; Saturdays are plain nuts. It's best to pay with cash—most dishes are around £7 to £10—and you'll eat standing up. Buy a flute of prosecco from one of the vendors selling it and feel your palate lighten. Some don't-miss stops (you'll find more of your own):

o   Under the Victorian glass canopy of Three Crown Square, **Le Marché du Quartier** (www.marketquarter.com) does duck confit sandwiches.

o   Sample never-exported cheeses like melt-in-your-mouth **Bath soft cheese** (www.parkfarm.co.uk).

o   **Shellseekers,** the fishmonger by the door to Roast, is known for hand-dived Dorset scallop, served in its own shell and topped with a bacon and sprout stir-fry; a bathtub-big pot of paella bubbles at its neighbor **Bomba.**

o   Artisan cacao in drink and food at **Rabot London** on Bedale Street.

o   **Roast** (www.roast-restaurant.com; mains £20–£40), which runs an expensive restaurant upstairs, has a stall for rich meats such as roast pork belly with crackling, or Bramley applesauce and beef with horseradish cream.

o   At **Maria's Market Café,** the second-generation proprietor slaves over a stove making fresh *bubble* (a mushy version of home fries) for vendors and visitors alike.

o   The **Brindisa Grill** booth (www.brindisa.com), facing Stoney Street, feeds a steady line of punters its grilled chorizo sandwich with oil-drizzled pequillo peppers from Spain.

o   Especially on weekends, dozens of **kiosks** for fresh-cooked foods fill the northern yards, with picnic tables and seating.

o   Outside on Stoney and Park streets, by the well-stocked **Market Porter** pub (p. 105) and casual sit-down restaurant **Elliot's,** are more finds: **Kappacasein** dairy from Bermondsey (www.kappacasein.com), which melts

4

WHERE TO DINE

The South Bank & City

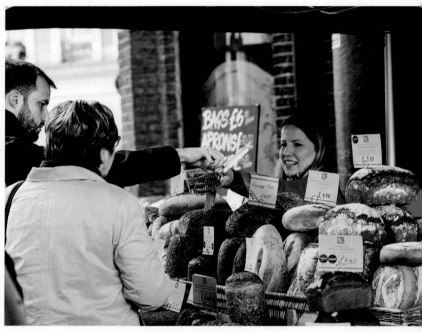

Fresh bread for take-away at the marvelous Borough Hall.

great wheels of Ogleshield cheese into decadent *raclette*; **Monmouth Coffee Company** (www.monmouthcoffee.com), for 40 years one of London's most revered roasters, which sends tasters around the world to monitor the single-source growers of its beans (it no longer uses disposable paper, so bring your own cup or they'll rent you one); and **Neal's Yard Dairy** (www.nealsyarddairy.co.uk), the gold standard for English cheese, tended by clerks in caps and aprons.

It's easy to explore on your own, but tours are also popular. Food writer Celia Brooks leads one that's officially recommended by the Market (www.celiabrooks.com; 3 hrs.; £116), but other good ones are led by Eating London (p. 223), London Food Tour (www.londonfoodtour.com; £75), and Chubby Fellow, who does a general tour and another that's all about cheese (www.chubbyfellow.com; £80). There has been a market on this very spot since the 1100s. Welcome to its story.

8 Southwark St., SE1. www.boroughmarket.org.uk. © **020/7407-1002.** Mon–Wed 10am–3pm; Thurs 11am–5pm; Fri noon–6pm; Sat 8am–5pm. Tube: London Bridge.

Emilia's Crafted Pasta ★★ ITALIAN   There's not much good to eat around the Tower of London, so this marvel is most welcome. Just east over the approach to Tower Bridge is an atmospheric maritime enclave known as

St Katharine Docks, dug by hand for cargo ships in the 1820s. Under cast-iron columns in a former goods vault, this speedy-service open kitchen makes succulent and indulgent pasta fresh daily with no preservatives. It's easy to love the truffled cacio e pepe, pancetta carbonara, green beans bathed in creamy green pesto, and ethereal tiramisu. Emilia's is ultra-casual but tiny (just a few tables that spill onto the waterfront in good weather, plus six bar seats), so make a booking in advance for your Tower trip. Its neighbors on the Docks include some other worthwhile cafes and premium coffee shops. Another useful location is a 10-minute walk north (77 Alie St., E1; *©* **020/7702-9944;** Tube: Aldgate East or Aldgate).

Unit C3, Ivory House, St Katharine Docks, E1. www.emiliaspasta.com. *©* **020/7481-2004.** Main courses £9.50–£14. Sun–Thurs noon–9:30pm; Fri–Sat noon–10pm. Reservations recommended. Tube: Tower Hill or Tower Gateway DLR.

EAST END & DOCKLANDS

Much of the city's most exciting cooking for a fun night out has migrated to Shoreditch and Spitalfields, leaving Mayfair to cater to the expense-account gourmets and Soho to feed the beery hordes.

Expensive

Lyle's ★★ BRITISH The kind of place where chefs like to eat, where the dishes appear simple and fluid and yet require authority to accomplish, Lyle's

THE world COMES TO LONDON

Those fortunate enough to have traveled broadly know how sadly rare it is to find places where people of wildly different colors, religions, and nationalities can live together in relative harmony. London, though, like New York City, Toronto, or Sydney, is certifiably multi-ethnic, with some 300 languages and 45 distinct ethnic communities. (By 2030, it's predicted, half the city's population will be foreign-born.) It's a fine opportunity for some culinary world travels of your own. Here are the Tube or rail stops for some of the major concentrations:

Bangladesh Bethnal Green, Whitechapel

Caribbean Brixton, Willesden Junction

Egypt Shepherd's Bush

Ghana, Nigeria, Congo, West Africa Seven Sisters, Hackney Central, or Hackney Downs (National Rail)

India, especially northern Southall (National Rail)

Ireland Kilburn

Kenya Barking

Kurdistan Manor House

Lebanon Shepherd's Bush

Nigeria Peckham Rye (National Rail)

Persia Edgware Road

Poland Hammersmith, Ealing Broadway

Somalia Streatham (National Rail)

Sri Lanka and South India Tooting (National Rail)

Syria Shepherd's Bush

Turkey Dalston Kingsland and Stoke Newington (National Rail)

Vietnam Hackney Central or Hackney Downs (National Rail), Old Street

TALL orders

London's skyscrapers are sprouting like bamboo, and with them, dining aeries. Top-floor restaurants are too sophisticated to bother with bottom-feeder grub—these places compete with terrific cuisine that's a pleasure to eat. The prices are higher because the views are. Reservations are suggested for all of them.

City Social   *The scene:* The quintessential Special Occasion restaurant: ambience, style, exquisite plating by award-winning chef Jason Atherton, dizzying prices. *The view:* on the 24th floor among the City skyscrapers, with a clear view of the Shard and the Gherkin. It's also worth a trip for its bar. Tower 42, 25 Old Broad St., EC2. www.citysociallondon. com. © **020/7877-7703.** Mains £32–£48. Tues–Fri noon–2:30pm and 6pm–9:30pm; Sat 5–9:30pm. Tube: Liverpool Street.

Darwin Brasserie   *The scene:* The atrium atop the "Walkie-Talkie" is like an upscale mini-mall of evening pursuits, including thump-thump-thump beats at

Sky Pod bar and a seafood place, Fenchurch. Our choice, Darwin, has an honest menu (lamb, chicken, pork, fish) on an elevated floor where some of the horizon may be obscured by the tower's drooping-eyelid roofline, but it's still pretty. (Soak in the panorama from elsewhere in the atrium after dinner.) *The view:* the Tower of London, the Thames, the Shard, and beyond. Sky Garden, 36th Floor, 20 Fenchurch St., EC3. www.skygarden. london. © **0333/772-0020.** Dinner main courses £17–£26. Mon–Tues noon–10pm; Wed–Thurs 9am–10pm; Fri–Sat 8:30am–10:30pm; Sun 8:30am–9:30pm. No cash. Reservations required. Tube: Monument or Bank.

Duck & Waffle   *The scene:* All day and night—yes, it's 24 hours, and doubles as a skilled *cocktailerie*—it cycles through shared-plate menus that lean toward richness. *The view:* It's a little inland from the Thames, so the nearest views are of the Gherkin and the City. 40th Floor, 110

has a short, changing New British-meets-Nordic menu, but it runs deep with inventiveness and delicacy: lemon sole with buttermilk and sea aster (a salt marsh plant), raw beef with mussels that's actually chopped beef with shellfish emulsion, soured cream with chocolate as a dessert. Dishes are neatly creative, but flavors remain clean, even if the blank loft space in which they're served is a bit factory-like. If things are busy, you can always sit at the bar. Tea Building, 56 Shoreditch High St., E1. www.lyleslondon.com. © **020/3011-5911.** Lunch: mains £14–£32; dinner: 6-course set dinner £89. Tues–Sat noon–2:15pm and 6–9pm. Reservations recommended. Tube: Shoreditch High Street or Liverpool Street.

Moderate

St John Bread and Wine ★★ TRADITIONAL BRITISH   Hand in hand with the gastropub trend is "nose-to-tail" eating. That's a polite way to say you'll be eating various animal body parts, resulting in tastes that were commonplace to agrarian English ancestors (heart, cockscomb, marrow, whole pigeon) but are new to most North American tongues. I personally hate it, but it's always on the foodie dream lists. Most places charge, um, an arm and a leg for it, but you can sample it at this lower-priced offshoot of the influential St John restaurant (still running in Smithfield), which in the 1990s brought

Bishopsgate, EC2. www.duckandwaffle. com. ✆ **020/3640-7310.** Sharing plates £9–£13. Tube: Liverpool Street.

Gong *The scene:* Take cocktails, small bites, and sashimi on the 52nd floor of the Shard in this tight little bar, and London's highest, atop the Shangri-La Hotel (p. 62). *The view:* sweeping eastern panorama from Southwark, including London Bridge Station, the Tower of London, and Tower Bridge. 35th floor, The Shard, 32 London Bridge St., SE1. www.gong-shangri-la.com. ✆ **020/7234-8208.** Dinner main courses £24–£40. Mon–Wed 4pm–12:30am; Thurs–Sun noon–1am. Tube: London Bridge.

The Oxo Tower *The scene:* Behold, a gratitude-inducing panorama over the Thames from an Art Deco landmark which, like Tate Modern, was once a power station. The associated bar, casual brasserie, and restaurant (pick one) are favorites for celebrating special occasions. *The view:* St Paul's and the City

from South Bank, not too high up. 22 Barge House St., SE1. www.oxotower restaurant.com. ✆ **020/7803-3888.** Bar bites £10–£20; Brasserie mains £20–£30; Restaurant mains £22–£43. Mon–Wed 11am–10:30pm; Thurs 11am–11pm; Fri–Sat 11am–midnight; Sun noon–10:30pm. Reservations essential. Tube: Blackfriars or Waterloo.

Searcys Helix Restaurant at The Gherkin *The scene:* Very James Bond. You provide ID, clear security, and ride a few lifts in The Gherkin to arrive at a former member's club duplex with floor-to-ceiling glass—a view forbidden to the public until 2018. The food is the freshest English fare, the wines immaculately chosen. *The view:* slowly being swallowed by a building boom. 39th floor, The Gherkin, 30 St Mary Axe, EC3. https://searcysatthe gherkin.co.uk. ✆ **0330/107-0816.** 2 courses £45; 3 courses £59. Mon–Sat noon–2pm and 6–9pm; Sun 10am–4pm. Tube: Liverpool Street.

back British cooking in a big way. Walls are simple white, chairs are plain wood, the menu is posted afresh daily, and the kitchen staff is serious about food and wine, no matter its form. Experience dishes like cold lamb with chicory and anchovy, smoked sprat (sardines) with horseradish, and laver bread (made with seaweed) with oats and bacon. A meal here can be an adventure (ever eaten dandelion?).

94–96 Commercial St., E1. https://stjohnrestaurant.com. ✆ **020/7251-0848.** Main courses £15–£28. Daily noon–3pm and 6–9:30pm. Reservations recommended. Tube: Aldgate East or Shoreditch High Street.

Inexpensive

Beigel Bake ★★ BAKERY The city's most famous take-away bakery, Jewish or otherwise, never closes but there's often a line. Watching the clerks slice juicy chunks of pink salt beef in the window, then slather it onto a beigel with pickle slices and some nostril-clearing mustard (£5.70), is an attraction unto itself, and once you eat one, you may dream of it forevermore. The queue moves quickly even if time doesn't—the phone number on the sign out front still posts an area code that hasn't been active since 2000. The patronage is a microcosm of London, ranging from bikers to hipsters to arrogant yuppies to

Brick Lane: 24-Hour Playground

Brick Lane, named for its medieval status as a source for bricks, was once a Jewish area but has become so strongly identified with immigrants from the Indian subcontinent that its name has transcended geography to become a shorthand term for England's South Asian population. In the span of just a few blocks, most of which have signage in both English and Bengali, lines of Indian restaurants jockey for business. No discerning Londoner would claim that any serve the city's best Indian cuisine, and most of them are in fact run by Bangladeshi or Pakistani entrepreneurs catering to a milder English notion of northern curries. (If you want something more modernized, try **Gunpowder** [https://gunpowderrestaurants. com], a block west on Commercial Road at White's Row.) But it's nonetheless a fun place to leverage competition and sit down for a bargain meal in a happening hood. Bring your own wine, though, because most are run by Muslims who don't sell alcohol. By day, the connecting Dray Walk is a short block of sophisticated boutiques and laid-back cafes. On weekends, it hosts blocks upon blocks of markets for vintage clothes, books, food, and art—Sundays are good for hours of browsing and noshing (www.sundayupmarket.co.uk).

people just scraping by. Its beigels (*bi*-gulls) are not as puffy or as salty as the New York "bagel" variety, and they even come filled for £2 to £3—or just 40p for a plain one. Its pastries are gorgeous, too: The chocolate fudge brownie, less than £1.50, could be nursed for hours.

159 Brick Lane, E1. ✆ **020/7729-0616.** Daily 24 hr. Tube: Shoreditch High Street.

E. Pellicci ★★★ TRADITIONAL BRITISH London's tradition of mid-20th-century diners, or "caffs," is quickly being gentrified into nostalgia, but this fry-up on deeply authentic and unflashy Bethnal Green Road has been run by the affable Nevio family since 1900. Some of them were born upstairs, and the matriarch of the family has commanded the kitchen since 1966. The Deco interior, a greasy spoon fantasia of sunburst icons, chrome, and primrose, was carved by a regular in 1946 and is now protected by law. You'll be boisterously welcomed with open arms— Mama, cooking Italian specialties such as cannelloni, may wave to you from the kitchen—and you'll spend a happy meal sharing a table with locals

Do a classic English breakfast at E. Pellicci, a long-running "caff."

("Where are you from?" "Looks like rain tomorrow"), sipping the best cuppa tea you ever had. As proof of your acceptance by the regulars, after you're done you may be sent out with a parting gift of homemade cake. There's no more iconic "caff" in town, and certainly none happier.

332 Bethnal Green Rd., E2. https://epellicci.co.uk. *℮* **020/7739-4873.** Main courses £4.60–£14. Mon–Sat 7am–4pm. Tube: Shoreditch High Street or Bethnal Green.

Poppies ★★ SEAFOOD   Big crispy portions flopping on big oval plates eaten with a big knife and fork to big 1950s sock-hop music: The franchise-ready Poppies does for British fish-and-chips what peppy jukebox diners have done for mid-20th-century American food. Amusingly, it wraps its chips in custom-printed newspaper since it's now illegal to use the chemical-laden real thing. For all its plastic theatricality, it hews to authenticity: The chief dish, cooked to order, is sustainably caught and sourced from third-generation fishmonger T. Bush at Billingsgate Market. For those whose palates swerve differently, there's also chicken, the chance to try jellied eels, and Minghella ice cream hailing from the Isle of Wight. Try the Soho location (55 Old Compton St., W1; *℮* **020/7734-4845;** same hours) for strolling the West End with chips.

6–8 Hanbury St., E1. www.poppiesfishandchips.co.uk. *℮* **020/7247-0892.** Main courses £9–£22. Sun–Wed 11am–10pm; Thurs–Sat 11am–11pm. Tube: Shoreditch High St. or Liverpool Street.

Rochelle Canteen ★★ BRITISH   A sublime secret is hidden away, discovered only if you ring a doorbell beside a green door in a brick wall. You'll pass through the grassy yard of an 1880s school, and in the old bike shed, join a daytime garden party. The changing menu is rigorously British and fresh, yet without flourish: green pea soup, roast sirloin, leek and Wigmore cheese tart, fish-and-chips, chicken and wild garlic pie. Your companions will be high-functioning artists, designers, and professionals, many of whom now

---

SAVE BREAD WITH sandwiches

You'll go all day without crossing paths with a bobby or a Cockney, but you can't walk a block in London without passing a sandwich shop. The cheapest ones are what I call the **triangle sandwiches,** which are ready-made, sliced diagonally, and sealed into triangular containers. They are made fresh every day by the million, cost less than £6, and can rescue both time and money during your busy touring schedule.

A few ubiquitous chains in the triangle sandwich trade:

- **Gregg's** (www.greggs.co.uk): Its sandwiches are average in every way, but it also does pies and hot meat rolls.
- **Marks & Spencer** (www.marksandspencer.com): Lots of cheap stuff, well done, and around dinnertime, markdowns up to 50%.
- **Pret A Manger** (www.pret.com): Clever flavors, with gourmet fixings in snazzy combination, and ubiquitous.

lease space in the former school, plus the occasional kid, if they behave as well as a Victorian child. In fine weather, it's easier to find a seat because dining spills outdoors, the better to enjoy jugs of rhubarb and ginger fizz.

Rochelle School, Arnold Circus, E2. www.rochelleschool.org. © **020/7729-5677.** Main courses £13–£15. Daily 9–11am and noon–3pm; Wed–Sat also 6–7:30pm; closing changes seasonally. Reservations suggested. Tube: Shoreditch High Street.

21 PUBS YOU'LL LOVE

Pubs are the beating heart of British life, as they have been for centuries. Your neighborhood hangout is called your "local," but many of the oldest premises have been so well-loved (or so well-bombed) that their original features are gone. Most are now company-owned, depressingly standardized—far too many British pubs have stripped out ceilings and carpeting to expose ductwork and wood in a feeble attempt to look "modern."

The following pubs, however, should do you right. All of them serve food of some kind (burgers, meat pies, and the like—but most take last food orders by 8:30pm) for at least part of the day; you usually order at the bar, where you receive a numbered tag for your table so that servers can find you.

Pubs commonly charge around £6 for a pint of the favored serving size—about 20 American ounces—and the ABV percentage tends to be strong. Guinness is Irish (and takes about 2 minutes to pour properly, in two stages). A good cask ale is a specialty you must try while you're in England. Cask ale is not refrigerated because it's stored in the cellar, where the temperature is right for the fermentation process to continue until the drink hits your glass. Cask ale is drawn using stiff hand-pumped taps, and it only stays fresh for a short time, like bread or pastry—so don't be surprised if the one you select has already run out. To find pubs that persevere in the dying art of pouring old-fashioned cask ales, visit the **Campaign for Real Ale** (www.camra.org. uk). Basic mixed drinks like gin and tonic ("G&T") are also served, but mixers are charged extra, and don't expect a generous pour because measures are standardized—for true cocktail bars run by seriously skilled experts, see the list on p. 278. Pubs have bottled beer and cider, too. When the bell is rung, it's last call—as early as 11pm—and the landlord *will* turf you out.

The Anchor Bankside ★★ This Thames-side patio in sight of St Paul's dome is perhaps the most popular spot in London at which to sit on the water with a fresh-pulled pint. There's been a tavern here at least since the 1500s, when Londoners ferried to Southwark for bear baiting, gardens, brothels, and Shakespeare (the playwright surely would have known the place). Diarist and royal confidant Samuel Pepys is said to have watched London burn to the ground from the safety of this shore in 1666. The industrial Anchor brewery that subsumed it for 200 years was cleared away in the 1980s, and a spacious (but always crowded) riverside terrace was added. Beer snobs kvetch that it's become a tourist draw, particularly in fine weather, but that's all right with me;

pubs have always been hangouts for the hoi polloi, and few of them so perfectly meld abundant history with an enviable location.

34 Park St., SE1. www.greeneking-pubs.co.uk. © **020/7407-1577.** Mon–Wed 11am–11pm; Thurs–Sun 11am–11:30pm; Sun noon–10:30pm; food served until 10pm (Mon–Sat), 9:30pm (Sun). Tube: London Bridge.

The Argyll Arms ★★   Having a beer in here can feel like drinking in a bejeweled red velvet box, thanks to the acid-etched glass screens that subdivide the busy bar into dignified drinking areas. Originally installed in 1895 to prevent brawls between the working and middle classes (at a time when even Underground rides were segregated), the screens somehow survived the 20th century. Drinks are £1 more than they should be, but it's one of the prettiest pubs in London, and its location southeast of Oxford Circus makes it an easy stop.

18 Argyll St., W1. www.nicholsonspubs.co.uk. © **020/7734-6117.** Mon–Thurs 10am–11:30pm; Fri–Sat 10am–midnight; Sun 10am–11pm. Tube: Oxford Circus.

The Blackfriar ★★★   Deservedly protected by landmark status, this 1904 Art Nouveau masterpiece (also spelled the Black Friar) is as jolly as the fat friars that bedeck it in bronze, wood, and glass. A short walk from St Paul's, it was once snuggled down a few dark alleys, but neighboring demolitions liberated it; now it's blessed with a noisy outdoor patio and walls of windows bathed in afternoon sunshine from over the Thames. The back saloon was designed for the upper classes, hence its exceptionally overbaked interior in marble and bronze; the undulating front bar, where pop music plays and pub crawls frequently pass through, is extraordinarily well-stocked with a range of cask ales and cider. Pricey food is shuttled from the upstairs kitchen via a hand-cranked dumbwaiter.

174 Queen Victoria St., EC4. www.nicholsonspubs.co.uk. © **020/7236-5474.** Mon–Fri 10am–11pm; Sat 9am–11pm; Sun noon–10:30pm. Tube: Blackfriars.

The Coal Hole ★   A onetime haunt of actor Edmund Kean, who drank himself to an early curtain, was rebuilt in 1904 in the Arts and Crafts style and is still a hangout for performers at the adjoining Savoy Theatre. Use the entrance in back, by the stage door, to access the clubbier lower level. The antique streetlamp on the Strand is a vestige of an experimental gaslight piping system that burned off sewage gases before the farty stink could overcome citizens. Bottoms up!

91–92 Strand, WC2. www.nicholsonspubs.co.uk/thecoalholestrandlondon. © **020/7379-9883.** Sun–Wed 10am–11pm; Thurs 10am–11:30pm; Fri–Sat 10am–midnight. Tube: Charing Cross or Embankment.

The George Inn ★★★   Unquestionably one of the most important ancient pubs still standing, the George traces its lineage to at least 1542, when a map of Southwark first depicted it; the Tabard Inn, where Chaucer's pilgrims gathered in *Canterbury Tales,* was then a few doors south (it's gone now). Shakespeare knew it (check out Pete Brown's 2012 book *Shakespeare's Local*), and Dickens memorialized it in *Little Dorrit.* The oldest section, a galleried wood-and-brick longhouse, dates to 1677, built after a horrific fire swept the district.

The George Inn pub was once an inn for long-distance carriage travelers.

It later functioned as an 18th-century transit hub, its courtyard encircled with a tavern, a hotel, stables, wagon repair bays, and warehouses; the rise of a railway nearly destroyed it, and only one side of the complex survives. (The National Trust now protects it.) Sip ale in the low-ceilinged timber-and-plaster chambers, or sit in the cobbled courtyard, in the Shard's shadow, and soak up the fading echoes of history.

75–77 Borough High St., SE1. www.greeneking-pubs.co.uk. © **020/7407-2056.** Mon–Thurs 11am–11:30pm; Fri–Sat 11am–midnight; Sun noon–10:30pm; food until 10pm Mon–Sat, 9pm Sun. Tube: London Bridge.

The Grapes ★★ It's in every way a classic that is cherishable in that inimitable English way—Victorian wooden bar with stools, red carpeting, worn plank floors, a blissful lack of clanging "fruit machines." But then again, that tiny back porch with a smashing riverfront panorama of a bend in the Thames all but waves a magic wand over it. If you find it all preposterously winsome, you wouldn't be alone—it's ridiculously narrow and jams at peak hours, but come at noon and it's a dream. Charles Dickens, who partied here, wrote about it in *Our Mutual Friend*, and the wizardly Ian McKellen loved it so much (he lives nearby, so it's been his local for decades) that when it came up for sale, he and his ex-boyfriend teamed up to buy it and preserve it. Sir Ian is known to pull pints and host Monday's quiz night when he's not performing somewhere. The prize is £50 in drinking money, which you'll find delightful to spend here.

76 Narrow St., E14. www.thegrapes.co.uk. © **020/7987-4396.** Daily noon–11:30pm; food served until 9:30pm. Tube: Limehouse DLR or Westferry DLR.

The Grenadier ★★★   They say this was the Duke of Wellington's local bar and the unofficial clubhouse for his regiment, hence the battlefield artifacts on display; they also say someone was beaten to death here for cheating at cards, hence the routine ghost sightings. This tiny plank-floored, currency-festooned pub/restaurant, pretty as a picture in a cobbled mews, comes off like a boozer in some upcountry village, with only 15 places at its pewter-topped island bar. Once a haunt for servants of the surrounding townhouses, clientele these days skews toward an international mix of students and businessmen. The pub is also said to be known for its Bloody Marys (I think they're over-rated). To find it, head down Grosvenor Crescent from Hyde Park Corner station, hang a hard right just before Belgrave Square onto Wilton Crescent, and take your first right onto Wilton Row.

18 Wilton Row, SW1. www.greeneking-pubs.co.uk. © **020/7235-3074.** Mon–Sat 11am–11:30pm; Sun noon–11:30pm; food served until 9:30pm. Tube: Hyde Park Corner.

The Lamb ★   Quiet, not too touristy, this east Bloomsbury choice (where Ted Hughes took Sylvia Plath on their early dates) is representative of a neighborhood local that still has some prime Victoriana from the old days. Check out the rare sunburst etched-glass snob screens obscuring the bar, built so you don't have to look the help in the eye. Or put 50p in the polyphon in the corner—that's a musical metal disc that works like a music box and was the gramophone of a century ago. The carpet is a tired tartan, the walls lined with sepia photographs of long-forgotten stage actresses, and the cask beers are out-of-the-ordinary enough to intrigue.

94 Lambs Conduit St., WC1. www.thelamblondon.com. © **020/7405-0713.** Mon–Wed 11am–11pm; Thurs–Sun 11am–midnight; Sun noon–10:30pm; food served noon–9:30pm. Tube: Russell Square.

The Lamb and Flag ★★   Too tiny and thronged after work to supply much respite, it is nonetheless the epitome of a city pub, tucked down an atmospheric brick alley and blessed with an original fireplace. It has been known throughout the centuries as both the Coopers Arms and the Bucket of Blood (the latter because it hosted illegal prizefights in the early 1800s), and its building is said to be Tudor in origin. No one can prove it, because it was heavily rebuilt in the 1890s. You'll find the pub on a lane just east of the intersection of Floral and Garrick streets, near Covent Garden. But you probably won't find a place to sit unless you start drinking after lunch, which the regular patrons on its memorial wall surely did.

33 Rose St., WC2. www.lambandflagcoventgarden.co.uk. © **020/7497-9504.** Mon–Sat 11am–11pm; Sun noon–10:30pm; food served until 9pm. Tube: Covent Garden or Leicester Square.

The Market Porter ★   Amid the gastronomic mayhem of Borough Market, this lovely old timber-beamed boozer is a fine place to drink in any time of the week. In fact, more times than most pubs, because its location earned a special license to open at 6am when vendors are working. Sundays and off-hours are pleasant for sitting by a double-sided fire drinking one of its nine

A pub has stood on this site since 1583, and the Grapes occupies a building from the 1720s that somehow survived the Blitz. It mostly served as a pub for Limehouse dock workers, but it has toasted luminaries including Charles Dickens (who described it as "a tavern of dropsical appearance") and its current co-owner, the actor Sir Ian McKellen.

traditional ales (choices change) or eating upstairs—ingredients all come from the market. It can also act: It appeared as the Third Hand Book Emporium in the third Harry Potter film.

9 Stoney St., SE1. www.themarketporter.co.uk. ℭ **020/7407-2495.** Mon–Fri 6–8:30am and 11am–11pm; Sat noon–11pm; Sun noon–10:30pm; food served until 1 hr. before closing (until 5pm Sun). Tube: London Bridge.

The Marquis of Granby ★   Amusingly, since the 1800s some pubs near the Houses of Parliament have been equipped with a "division bell," which rings—rather like a fire alarm—to warn socializing MPs they have only 8 minutes to scurry back to vote. The custom is gradually being replaced by an app, which is disappointing. Other pubs that retain their division bells—St Stephens Tavern on Bridge Street across from Big Ben, the Red Lion on Whitehall—are cloyingly touristy, but not the Marquis. A single-room pub with bare floorboards and high wood walls, it's a hangout for government types (and their lobbyists) and prides itself on real hand-pumped ale.

41 Romney St., SW1. www.nicholsonspubs.co.uk. ℭ **020/7227-0941.** Mon–Fri noon–11pm; Sat noon–5:30pm. Tube: Westminster or Pimlico.

The Mayflower ★   The story goes that in 1620, local resident and sea captain Christopher Jones was recruited by some dissenters, who boarded his ship the *Mayflower* alongside this pub (then it was the Shippe; the current building is from the 1700s) to set sail to Southampton and thence to the New World. It's hard to imagine, and otherwise it's a fairly traditional pub (oak beams, wood paneling) with real ales and a fire. Its extension dock over the Thames is a worthy place to raise a pint and survey your personal slice of the river on a summer day or for its popular Sunday roast (reserve ahead for that). Would the Pilgrims have called it a sin? Surely, but they were no fun.

117 Rotherhithe St., SW16. www.themayflowerrotherhithe.com. ℭ **020/7237-4088.** Mon–Sat 11am–11pm; Sun noon–10:30pm; food served until 10pm (Sun until 9pm). Tube: Rotherhithe.

The Old Brewery ★★   In 2010, a new microbrewery named Meantime took up residence in Sir Christopher Wren's palatial Old Royal Naval College (a stately UNESCO World Heritage site where the Paris scenes in 2012's *Les Misérables* were shot), which sits on the Thames in outlying Greenwich. It occupied the very brewery building that once furnished Napoleonic War veterans with their three daily pints. Now, the Old Brewery, run by respected British beermaker Young's, serves drinks on a large outdoor patio, and seasonal English fare inside. The beer selection isn't as rewarding as it once was, but on a sunny day, there are few places more dreamy for a pint in Maritime Greenwich (p. 197).

The Pepys Building, Old Royal Naval College, SE10. www.oldbrewerygreenwich.com. ℭ **020/3437-2222.** Mon–Sat 10am–11pm; Sun 10am–10:30pm; food served until 10pm. Tube: Cutty Sark DLR.

The Pride of Spitalfields ★★   Lovingly shabby, with a tired floral carpet and weary red upholstered banquettes, the backstreet boozer east of Brick

Lane is the embodiment of a homey pub pulling pleasing pints. The upright piano is rarely played (recorded classic punk is preferred), the sewage system is finicky, the beer bottles are dusty, but the goings-on are lively and neighborly. Unlike in some neighborhood joints, they understand tourists, so if you're friendly, you'll have fun. Jack the Ripper suspect James Hardiman, a "cats meats vendor," drank here when it was called the Romford Arms. Your choice of victuals will be more mainstream; in the afternoon, you can get cheap salt beef for a few pounds.

3 Heneage St., E1. ℃ **020/7247-8933.** Mon–Tues and Thurs–Sat 11am–midnight; Wed 11am–11pm; Sun noon–10:30pm. Tube: Aldgate East.

The Princess Louise ★★★   This Victorian fantasia just south of the British Museum is worth a visit even if you don't drink. Its lost-in-time feeling begins with the proud signage, a traditional marquee of gold lettering on black. The 1891 interior has been miraculously maintained in mint condition: Morris & Son etched glass, mirrors, mahogany privacy screens, cast-iron bar, Corinthian columns, Simpson & Son mosaic tile floor. Even the men's room marble urinals are legally protected from alteration. There's no music or TV, mobile phones are sternly discouraged, and all of the libations are by the resolutely old-fashioned Samuel Smith, which has been brewing since 1758 in Yorkshire and still draws its water from its original well.

208 High Holborn, WC1. ℃ **020/7405-8816.** Mon–Fri 11am–11pm; Sat noon–11pm; Sun noon–6:45pm; food served Mon–Thurs noon–2:30pm and 6–8:30pm, Fri noon–2:30pm. Tube: Holborn.

The Prospect of Whitby ★★   The oldest riverside pub in London has much to entice you: a pedigree that stretches back to 1520, during the reign of Henry VIII. A 400-year-old stone floor. A backstory that includes a seamy stretch as a den for river smugglers, thieves, bare-knuckle boxers, and cock fighters. The replica scaffold commemorating the hanging of infamous pirate Captain Kidd beside the pub in 1701. A client list ranging from Charles Dickens (of course) to Richard Burton (of course), Princess Margaret (again, of course), and artists J. M. W. Turner and Whistler, who both captured the view from its confines. Not enough? If all of that doesn't convince you of its appeal, take note that it's fully reputable now, partly due to the popularity of its two creaky but spacious floors and its big side yard, where you can kick back with wide Thames views and great old-growth trees—look out for a replica scaffold that commemorates the many bankside executions that happened around here. Over weekends, it can get overly crowded, so to share the atmosphere with fewer souls, come on a weekday.

57 Wapping Wall, E1. www.greeneking-pubs.co.uk. ℃ **020/7481-1095.** Mon–Sat 11am–11pm; Sun noon–9pm; food served until 9pm. Tube: Shadwell DLR.

The Salisbury ★   The Covent Garden/Leicester Square location is unbeatable, and the ornate exterior and interior are unmistakably Victorian—ostentatious, just-how-drunk-was-the-designer Victorian, to be precise. Thrill to the Grecian urns in the brilliant-cut glass, the pressed-copper tables, and the nymphs entwined in the bronze lamps. No wonder it was long a favored place for furtive meetings between gay men back when homosexuality was illegal, and then an actual gay pub when that archaic law was abolished. Now it's a haunt for all types of customers, including families but especially the city's theatrical community, and a suitable pit stop for any West End exploration. It does burgers and fish-and-chips, too, albeit by the corporate recipes of the Taylor Walker pub company. Theater fans should check out the cellar, which is papered with posters, many of them rare, from 1980s and '90s shows.

90 St Martin's Lane, WC2. www.greeneking-pubs.co.uk. ✆ **020/7836-5863.** Mon–Thurs 11am–11pm; Fri–Sat 11am–midnight; Sun 11am–10:30pm; food served until 10pm. Tube: Leicester Square.

The Ship & Shovell ★★   One of the most endearing configurations for any pub you'll ever see, it's cleft in two by an alley trod by commuters on their way to Charing Cross. On the north, there's a traditional Victorian-style space, and on the south, a cozier room with a languidly sloping floor and private snugs. A cellar links the halves. The bewigged, tubby chap on the swinging sign is Admiral Cloudesley Shovell who, in 1707, wrecked his ship and drowned 800 sailors, which certainly gives the interior's nautical theme an ignoble context. It's special for another reason, too, being one of the few pubs in town to pour Dorset ales from Hall & Woodhouse, a family brewer dating to 1777.

1–2 Craven Passage, WC2. www.shipandshovell.co.uk. ✆ **020/8391-1311.** Mon–Sat 11am–11pm; food served Mon–Fri noon–3:30pm, Sat noon–4pm. Tube: Charing Cross or Embankment.

The Ten Bells ★   It's said that Annie Chapman, one of Jack the Ripper's victims, downed her last beer at this Spitalfields boozer, while another, Mary Kelly, picked up her clients outside; for an icky period in the 1970s, the pub

Affable publicans at The Ten Bells, where Jack the Ripper's final victim drank her last pint.

capitalized on infamy by being renamed for their slayer. These days, the toilets are a bigger threat to health and safety than Jack the Ripper ever was. The pub's Victorian tilework has been restored, and now it's a busy waterhole where the clientele is young, the furniture casually mismatched, and the partying ever more intense as the evening advances. Nicholas Hawksmoor's Christ Church, which towers next door, silently observes the latest mortals at play.

84 Commercial St., E1. www.tenbells.com. ☏ **020/7247-7532.** Sun–Wed noon–midnight; Thurs–Sat noon–1am. Tube: Liverpool Street.

Ye Olde Cheshire Cheese ★★★   Just the sort of rambling, low-ceilinged tavern you imagine London is full of (and was, once), it was built behind Fleet Street in the wake of the Great Fire in 1666; steady log fires and regularly strewn sawdust make it smell like it's still burning. In later generations, it played regular host to Dr. Samuel Johnson (who lived behind on Gough Square), Charles Dickens (who refers to it in *A Tale of Two Cities*), Yeats, Wilde, and Thackeray. You can get pretty well thackered yourself today: There are six drinking rooms, but the cozy front bar—of pallid light, candles in the fireplace, and antique paintings of dead fish—is the most magical. Observe the stuffed carcass of Polly the Parrot, enshrined above the bar since 1926: Her "adept use of profanity would have put any golfer to shame," according

Ye Olde Mitre, hidden off the street in a hard-to-find courtyard, is one of London's coziest pubs.

to her obituary in the *New York American*. ***Note:*** Don't confuse this place with the Victorian-era Cheshire Cheese pub at Temple.

Wine Office Ct., off 145 Fleet St. ℂ **020/7353-6170.** Mon–Sat 11am–11pm. Tube: Blackfriars, Temple, or Chancery Lane.

Ye Olde Mitre ★★★ Suspended in a hidden courtyard and seemingly between centuries, this enchanter—no TVs, no music—was once part of a great palace mentioned by Shakespeare in *Richards II* and *III*. The medieval St Etheldreda's Chapel, its surviving place of worship, stands outside. This extremely tiny pub (established in 1546 but built in its present form in 1772) has two entrances that feed either side of the bar. The one on the left grants you access to "the Closet," a fine example of a semiprivate sitting area called a "snug"; the one on the right brings you face-to-face with a glass case containing a blackened stump said to be part of a cherry-tree maypole that Elizabeth I danced around. (Yeah, right, drink another one.) Suck down a house specialty: pickled or Scotch eggs. To find the pub, look for a little alley among the jewelry stores on Hatton Garden, between 8 and 9 Hatton Garden.

1 Ely Ct., off Ely Place, EC1. www.yeoldemitreholborn.co.uk. ℂ **020/7405-4751.** Mon–Fri 11am–11pm. Tube: Farringdon or Chancery Lane.

EXPLORING LONDON

Engaland was a top dog for 500 years, and London is where it kept its bark. Many of the world's finest treasures came here during the Empire and never left. Riches built this city. The major attractions could by themselves occupy months of contemplation. But the sheer abundance of accumulated wealth—layer upon layer of it—means that London boasts dozens of exciting smaller sights, too. You could spend a lifetime seeing it all, so you'd better get started.

The heavily promoted **London Pass** (https://londonpass.com) gets you into a bevy of attractions and a Golden Tours sightseeing bus for a fixed price (such as £79 a day or £103 for 2 days), but is unlikely to pay off in the small amount of time you're given to use it. The pass might say "one-day," but remember most attractions are only open for 8 hours of it. Only the version that lasts 6 days (£157 adult, £102 child, some discounts online) would potentially pay off, but still only *marginally* and only if you barely pause to eat.

Historic Royal Palaces operates Hampton Court (p. 205), Kensington Palace (p. 218), Kew Palace (p. 208), and the Tower of London (p. 186). An annual membership pass will possibly save you money if you plan to see several of them; do the math (www.hrp.org.uk; ℭ **020/3166-6000;** £62 one adult, £94 two adults, £82 for one adult plus up to six children, £122 two adults plus up to six children).

BLOOMSBURY, FITZROVIA & KING'S CROSS

In the same neighborhood, bear in mind **Queer Britain** (2 Granary Square, N1; https://queerbritain.org.uk; free admission; Wed–Sun noon–6pm; Tube: King's Cross St Pancras), which opened in 2022. This space, which is dedicated to the history of LGBTQ+ people, is still getting its legs, and there's no permanent collection on display, so whether you want to go will depend on whatever the temporary exhibition is.

The British Library ★★★ MUSEUM   One of the planet's most precious collections of books, maps, and manuscripts, the British Library holds approximately 150 million items and adds 3 million each year, so when it puts the cream (about 200 items) on display,

Pandemic-related staffing woes have caused some attractions to **shorten operating hours,** so it pays to check ahead and see if the hours posted in this guide have been expanded.

Children's prices generally apply to those 15 and under. To qualify for a **senior discount** (often expressed as a **"concession"**), you usually must be 60 or older. **Students** require ID for discounts. Some places offer **Family**

Tickets with discounts for up to three kids with adults. Museums may post prices that include a voluntary **"gift aid"** donation; British citizens get tax back for it but you don't, so no one will mind if you ask to have it removed.

In addition to closing on public holidays and on December 25 and 26 (Boxing Day), some heritage properties open only in the summer.

you will be astounded. The **Treasures of the British Library,** at the Sir John Ritblat Gallery, displays these in a cool, climate-controlled suite of black cases and rich purple carpeting. It ought to be mobbed, but isn't. The trove changes whenever something needs to be taken out of the light, but these have been there, and might be when you are:

TOP DON'T-MISS EXHIBITS AT THE BRITISH LIBRARY

Delicate paper artifacts are frequently taken off display for preservation, but look for some of these holdings:

- Two of the four known copies of the **Magna Carta,** 800 years old in 2015
- The **Gutenberg Bible** from 1455
- The Beatles' first lyric doodles: "A Hard Day's Night" on Julian Lennon's first birthday card (with a choo-choo on it) and "Yesterday," which had the working title of "Scrambled Eggs"
- The **Diamond Sutra,** the oldest known printed book, which was found in a Chinese cave in 1907 and was probably made by woodblock nearly 600 years before Europeans developed similar technology
- The desk **Jane Austen** used to write her novels
- The *Codex Sinaiticus,* one of the two oldest Christian Bibles (the Pope has the other) and illuminated manuscripts from Buddhism, Jainism, and Islam
- Milton's contract for *Paradise Lost* (he ended up getting paid just £10)
- A letter from Elizabeth I to James VI of Scotland warning him not to open diplomatic relations with Spain
- Captain Robert F. Scott's diary of his failed South Pole exploration, found on his body
- **Michelangelo**'s letter to his nephew telling him he had finished *The Martyrdom of St. Peter,* and pages from **Leonardo da Vinci's notebook,** in mirror writing
- Works in the hand of **Mozart, Handel** (his *Messiah*), **Oscar Wilde, P. G. Wodehouse, Mary Shelley, Sylvia Plath, Chopin, Bela Bartók,** and others
- An 11th-century copy of ***Beowulf*** on vellum, in Old English; it's the only surviving manuscript, written when Ethelred the Unready was king.

5

EXPLORING LONDON | Bloomsbury, Fitzrovia & King's Cross

London-Wide Attractions

See also "West End & Westminster Attractions" map

The King's Library, some 85,000 tomes assembled by King George III, floats in a glassed-in central tower and forms the core of the collection, like Thomas Jefferson's library does for Washington, D.C.'s Library of Congress—which means that the king who lost America and a principal engineer of that loss provided the seeds for their respective nations' libraries. The hall contains the **Philatelic Exhibition,** 500 drawers containing thousands of rare stamps.

You can't handle books unless you're a scholar, but the Library encourages anyone to hang out in its public spaces. In addition to the Treasures, the Library presents about 150 annual talks featuring celebrities and historians and some strong temporary exhibitions (about £16; check www.bl.uk/whats-on), including ones on Gothic horror, punk, gold, and comic books. Twice a day (barring Covid-19 restrictions), you can book a tour (about £10) of the facilities, although for all the hype over its supposedly brilliant architecture, the men's and women's washrooms are on opposite sides of the building and the whole place is riddled with little staircases.

96 Euston Rd., NW1. www.bl.uk. © **01937/546-546.** Free admission. Mon–Thurs 9:30am–8pm; Fri 9:30am–6pm; Sat 9:30am–5pm; Sun 11am–5pm. 1-hr. tours, when available, are bookable at www.bl.uk/events. Tube: King's Cross St Pancras.

The British Museum ★★★ MUSEUM   Founded in 1753 and first opened in 1759 in a converted mansion, the British Museum is as much a monument to great craftsmanship as it is to the piracy carried out by 18th- and 19th-century Englishmen who, on their trips abroad, plundered whatever goodies they could find and then told the bereft that the thievery was for their own good. Yet the exquisite taste of these English patriarchs is unquestionable, and now the British Museum may be the museum to beat all the rest. In fact, most years it's the top attraction in the country—5.9 million people visited in 2019. Put on your walking shoes because it's not the king of museums for nothing.

Strategies for British Attractions

Many of London's biggest museums are free to enter, but there's a catch: To make up the cash they miss out on, they find lots of other revenue streams. Some institutions charge a few pounds for printed **maps** (to get around that, take a digital photograph of the posted floor plan in the lobby and use that as a guide). They also charge £15 or more for the most interesting **temporary exhibitions;** the most popular ones sell out ahead, so do some advance planning online using the What's On section of museum websites. Since the pandemic began, museums are relying upon **QR codes** for everything from ticketing to information, so make sure your smartphone supports scanning those. If you can, download the free **Smartify** app, because more museums are using it to power their tours instead of maintaining their own apps (bring your own earbuds). Fortunately, the British funding model also gives museums an incentive to operate superlative **shops,** publish wonderful keepsake guidebooks, and run gorgeous **cafes** that even attract people off the street—you'll never go hungry at the major attractions.

The British Museum

1. Great Court
2. The Reading Room
3. Rosetta Stone
4. The Parthenon Sculptures ("Elgin Marbles")
5. Statues of the Nereid Monument
6. Mausoleum of Halikarnassos
7. Lindow Man
8. Treasures of Sutton Hoo
9. Clocks and Watches
10. Egyptian Rooms
11. Asia Galleries
12. Enlightenment Gallery

Americas
Ancient Egypt
Ancient Greece and Rome
Asia
Britain and Europe
Middle East
Themes

UPPER FLOOR

Great Court Restaurant

91 11 90
66
10
61 62 63 64 65
59 58 57 56 55 54 53
73 52
72 51
71 7 50
70 49
69a 69 40 8 41
68 37 38 39 47 46
9
48

GROUND FLOOR

Sainsbury Exhibitions Gallery

30
34
24 26 27

20 6
21
18 19 9 4 1
4 18b 5 22 1
2
Reading Room
18 17 23 8 4 12
18a 1
16 3
10 7 4
15 2
14
Great Court
18 1
13 6 2a
12 11 3

Main Entrance
Great Russell Street

Because museum staff will do nothing beyond ensuring you aren't touching things or misbehaving (even the info desk just reads off the website), it's imperative that you do advance research and learn the background of the things you see. Also take advantage of the schedule of daily talks and exhibitions either online or posted in the Great Court. These include a bevy of freebies: 15 daily **Eye-Openers** (40 min.), focused on particular rooms; 20-minute **Spotlight tours** about major holdings (such as the Rosetta Stone or the Parthenon marbles) on Friday evenings; and **Hands On,** which actually allows you to touch some ancient things (11am–4pm).

This museum is so full that it risks being relentless or dull if you don't have context, and unfortunately, curators don't give you much to go by. They want you to buy things instead. **Maps** range from £2 to £6 depending on the level of guiding information you want, and even those are oversimplified. For a free and better one, scan the QR code at the info desk to bring up one on your phone (Wi-Fi is also free); another QR code brings you to an audio guide of highlights. Books from its gift shop may also help. A simpler path is to pay £5 to download the material on the British Museum Audio app, which details 300 of the most popular items for free and charges an add-on of £2–£3 for themed walking tours. The app is less than ideal and books from the shop offer more detail, but it's cheaper than the £7 tablets this place used to rent before the pandemic.

Dominating the glass-roofed **Great Court** like a drum in a box, the cream-and-gold round **Reading Room,** completed in 1857, was once part of the British Library containing King George III's exemplary book collection. Patrons had to apply for tickets, and they included Lenin and Karl Marx, who developed their political theories here; other habitués included Bram Stoker, Sir Arthur Conan Doyle, and Virginia Woolf, who wrote upon entering "one stood under the vast dome, as if one were a thought in the huge bald forehead which is so splendidly encircled by a band of famous names." You can't get inside unless you have a ticket to an event being held in it. The **Great Court Restaurant** above the Reading Room serves full afternoon tea from 11:30am to 4pm for £24 (otherwise meals are £23 for two courses, £29 for three courses, and kids meals are £14 for two courses; reserve online or at ℘ **020/7323-8990**). To the right as you enter the Court, don't miss the paneled King's Library rooms (1827), now known as the **Enlightenment Gallery** and brimming with cabinets of curiosities retrieved from the ends of the earth by the likes of Captain James Cook himself.

Other holdings are grouped in numbered rooms by geography, with an emphasis on the Greek and Roman Empires, Europe, and Britain. Given the rarity and beauty of this massive collection, it feels perverse to call anything a highlight, but these are some that the museum itself names as standouts.

TOP DON'T-MISS EXHIBITS AT THE BRITISH MUSEUM

o The museum's most famous, and most controversial, possessions are the so-called **Elgin Marbles,** gingerly referred to as the **Sculptures of the Parthenon** (rooms 18 and 19) to disguise imperialist provenance. These

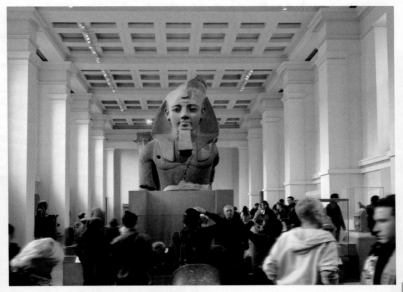
The British Museum has the largest collection of ancient Egyptian objects outside Egypt, and its mummies have thrilled children since Victorian times.

slab sculptures (called friezes and metopes), plus some life-size weathered statuary, once lined the pediment of the famous Parthenon atop Athens' Acropolis. After being defaced (literally—the faces were hacked off) in the 500s by invading vandals (okay, not the East Germanic Vandal tribes—these guys were Persian), the sculptures suffered further indignities in a 1687 gunpowder explosion before being sawed off and carted away by Lord Elgin. They're laid out in the gallery in the approximate position in which they appeared on the Parthenon, only facing inward so you can admire them. Greece ceaselessly demands their return, but the British have argued that they're better cared for in London. The smog-burnt portions left behind in Athens, despite their glossy new galleries, make a muddy issue of conservation and politics even murkier.

o Fragments of **sculptures from the Mausoleum at Halikarnassos,** one of the lost Seven Wonders of the Ancient World, loom in room 21. They're colossal in the original sense—one horse's head measures 2.1m (7 ft.) long.

o The pivotal **Rosetta Stone** (196 B.C.), in room 4, is what helped linguists crack hieroglyphics, and its importance to anthropology can't be exaggerated. Napoleon's soldiers found it in Egypt in 1799, but the British nabbed it in 1801. Consider it his first Waterloo.

o At the back of the ground floor, in room 24, find the giant **Hoa Hakananai'a.** It was plucked from Easter Island in 1868 and stood outside, under the portico, for nearly 80 years before being brought indoors. So much for the "we take care of things better" argument.

The Great Court of the British Museum is a striking melding of classic and contemporary architecture. Look up: Some 3,312 triangular glass panels, each a slightly different size and shape, protect the historic Reading Room and visitors alike from the famously moody English weather.

- The grisly array of **Egyptian Mummies** in rooms 62, 63, and 64 petrifies living children, and on your visit these galleries will be thronged as usual. In addition to the wizened corpses, there are painted coffins; the hair and lung of the scribe Sutimose, dating to 1100 B.C.; and scarabs galore. In room 64, check out the body from 3400 B.C., found in a fetal position without a coffin, which was preserved by dry sand. Beside it is another one, 400 years younger, that rotted to soil because it was laid to rest in a basket.
- Kids stare moon-eyed at crumpled, leather-faced **Lindow Man** in room 50; he was discovered, throat slit, in a Cheshire bog nearly 2,000 years after his brutal demise. Preserved down to his hair and fingernails, he looks like he could spring to life and pound the glass of his case.
- Nearby (room 49) is the **Mildenhall Treasure,** a hoard of new-looking silver Roman tableware unearthed by Gordon Butcher, a Suffolk farmer, as he plowed fields in 1942; the saga of how he was cheated of his fortune was chronicled by writer Roald Dahl. (Yes, pillage is something of an underlying theme in this place.)
- The Anglo-Saxon treasures unearthed in 1939 at the **Sutton Hoo** hoard, a discovery dramatized in the 2021 Ralph Fiennes film *The Dig,* are in room 41.
- The **Lewis Chessmen** (room 40), cartoonish and made from walrus ivory, are whimsical favorites dating from the 12th century.

JEREMY BENTHAM'S "auto icon"

England's own Ben Franklin, **Jeremy Bentham** (1748–1832) was a philosopher, a progressive, a subversive, a prison reformer, a supporter of suffrage and the decriminalization of homosexuality, an educator, and a pen pal of U.S. President James Madison. Bentham worked to enable equal access to courts and schools, and he coined the words *international* and *maximize*—he codified *codification* itself.

He was so ahead of his time that he refuses to stay in the past: His will stipulated eternal access to his corpse—a gift that would keep on giving, really. Starting years before his death, he purportedly carried around a pair of glass eyes that were intended for his future "Auto Icon" (auto = self, icon = image), which would represent him forever. After he expired, his body was dissected for students. In 1850, a colleague dressed his remains and Bentham's severed head was placed between his own feet on proud and ghoulish display. There his remains remain, in a lobby at University College London. His skeleton is hidden under his original clothing and gloves. Unfortunately, his noggin was clumsily preserved and kids kept swiping it (in 1975, some hooligans held it for a £10 ransom), so today it's stashed in the vaults, and instead, you'll see a disturbingly lifelike waxwork head staring blankly with those long-pocketed blue eyeballs. His new doughy face, which looks quite a bit like his enlightened philosophical predecessor Benjamin Franklin, sagely observes the current scholarly crop at UCL from beneath a straw hat. You'll find this weird display attracting no attention whatsoever from the socializing scholars in the UCL Student Centre at 27–28 Gordon Square (Tube: Euston Square).

- The **oldest known map** in the world, by the Babylonians, was carved on a clay tablet in the 6th century B.C. and now resides in room 55.
- Room 70, on Level 3, contains many remarkable holdings: the bronze **head of Roman Emperor Augustus,** found in the Sudan and unsettlingly lifelike (it still has its eyeballs of glass and stone); the **Portland Vase,** a black, cameo-glass jug that would be very difficult to make even today; beside that, the historically important **Warren Cup,** a 1st-century silver chalice graphically depicting homosexual sex (and voyeurism of same) in relief; and a 3rd-century Roman **crocodile-skin suit of armor.**

Great Russell St., WC1. www.thebritishmuseum.org. ⓒ **020/7323-8299.** Free admission. Sat–Thurs 10am–5:30pm; Fri 10am–8:30pm. No wheeled luggage, no checked items larger than 40cm x 50cm. Tube: Tottenham Court Road, Holborn, or Russell Square.

Other Bloomsbury Area Attractions

The Charles Dickens Museum ★ MUSEUM   Although Dickens moved around a lot, his last remaining London home, which he rented for £80 a year for less than 2 years when he was 30, is now his testament. A museum since 1925, and restored to a period look with a few family pieces, these five floors double as an education on what a stylish early Victorian home was like. This is where Dickens lived when his celebrity got a kick-start (*Oliver Twist* and *Nicholas Nickleby,* arguably his biggest hits, were written while he was in residence) and he experienced formative loss (his sister-in-law Mary Hogarth, age 17, died suddenly and mysteriously in his arms in the guest bedroom; 8 months later, he named his first daughter after her and later, he patterned Little Nell in *The Old Curiosity Shop* after her). As you inspect his desk from later in his life, his commode chair, and (incongruently in the middle of the nursery) window bars from a prison that housed his spendthrift dad, an unpleasant realization sets in: Charles Dickens was a brilliant storyteller, maybe the most gifted in the history of the English language, but he was also kind of a jerk. Tough on his kids and publicly cruel to his wife—he seems to have preferred both her sisters to her and everyone knew it—his equal talent seems to have been for ego. Still, as you behold the specially designed podium he brought with him on performance tours that sold out wherever he went, a fuller picture of the brash, boundless talent will form for you. Definitely pay the surcharge for the audio tour, because the free leaflet doesn't cut it.

48 Doughty St., WC1. www.dickensmuseum.com. ⓒ **020/7405-2127.** Admission £12.50 adults, £10.50 seniors and students, £7.50 children 6–16. Wed–Sun 10am–5pm; last admission 1 hr. before closing. Tube: Chancery Lane or Russell Square.

The Foundling Museum ★★ MUSEUM   Small but devastating, it tracks the history of the Foundling Hospital, which took in thousands of orphans between 1739 and 1953. This was a period in which kids were treated like rubbish: For example, in 1802 a law was passed limiting the time children could work in mills—to 12 hours a day. By that measure, the benefactors were actually helping kids by locking them in this borderline prison—the kids were

Where the great storyteller spun his yarns—the Charles Dickens Museum.

treated poorly to discourage mothers from giving them up. Don't miss the heartbreaking cases of tokens that mothers left at the doorstep with their babies. These tiny objects, into which a lifetime of hopes was imbued, never made it to their children lest they compromise anonymity. Also take the time to listen to the oral histories by some of the last kids to be raised by the Hospital; at the time of recording, they were elderly but still obviously quite shaken. Upstairs is the exquisitely rococo Court Room (1745) and a modest but respectable collection of 18th- and 19th-century English works (Hogarth, Reynolds, Millais), which, because this was an institution that attracted well-positioned benefactors, was one of the first permanent art exhibitions in the world. Today, the museum also brings in temporary exhibitions exploring the relationship between adult artists and children. The composer Handel loved the Hospital: He frequently performed his *Messiah* as a benefit for the facility (a 1754 score is on display). The former exercise grounds, now called Coram's Fields, are still the domain of the child; adults are not permitted to enter without a kid in tow. Perhaps not at all coincidentally, J. M. Barrie's original *Peter Pan* play had 8 Grenville Street (demolished 1938), across Brunswick Square, as the Darling home, where the orphan Peter Pan flew into the nursery in search of his shadow.

40 Brunswick Sq., WC1. www.foundlingmuseum.org.uk. (✆) **020/7841-3600.** Admission £9.50 adults, £7.50 seniors and students, free for children 15 and under; higher posted prices include a voluntary donation. Tues–Sat 10am–5pm; Sun 11am–5pm. Tube: Russell Square.

Hunterian Museum ★ MUSEUM   This ghoulish exhibition at the Royal College of Surgeons, now 2 centuries old, chronicles the life's work of John Hunter (1728–93), who elevated surgery from something your barber dabbled in to something a saw-wielding, germ-spreading "scientist" would, ahem, undertake. These are the gruesome bodily explorations that led to some of the most important discoveries in Western medicine. It's a macabre scene, crowded with thousands of specimens, including extinct animals, all tastefully presented in a modern, gleaming hall that was just lavished with a multiyear renovation (the new facility opens in 2023). Most of your time will be spent squeamishly perusing black-lidded jars of human and animal pathology and anatomy (many originally obtained by grave robbers, a common practice then), plus a bone-grinding collection of crude surgical instruments that could rattle even the steeliest physician. Look for the cross-section of a chicken's head that Hunter grafted with a human tooth. Such Frankenstein projects were his stock in trade. In 1783, when a 7-foot, 7-inch man named Charles Byrne heard Hunter would seek his corpse after he died, he tried to escape that fate by being buried at sea in a lead-lined coffin; Hunter bribed fishermen to fetch it, and here the poor man's skeleton now hangs. As part of the history of surgery, you'll also find an ill-conceived amputation buzz saw. In its first use, it became slick with blood, slipped, and lopped off a nurse's hand; both patient and nurse were killed by subsequent infection. Name another museum that can match an exhibit like that!

35-43 Lincoln's Inn Fields, WC2. www.rcseng.ac.uk/museums. ✆ **020/7405-3474.** Free admission. Check ahead for hours, but they're likely to be Tues–Sat 10am–5pm. Tube: Holborn.

The Petrie Museum of Egyptian Archeology ★★ MUSEUM   Britain made a lot of mistakes when it comes to Egypt, and not just with Suez. Almost as soon as "explorers" could break into ancient tombs, they would lose track of thousands of things they discovered or leave poor information about how they found them. Since the 1800s, University College London has worked to properly collect, identify, and date more than 80,000 artifacts; roaming its treasure-crammed cases, some of which are stocked with items that still stump scholars, can be awe-inspiring. From the cotton Tarkhan dress last worn 5,000 years ago to Roman funerary portraits painted in beeswax, the things one finds in these stacks could blow a mind.

Malet Place, University College London, WC1. www.ucl.ac.uk/culture/petrie-museum. ✆ **020/3108-9000.** Free admission. Tues–Fri 1–5pm; Sat 11am–5pm. Tube: Goodge Street.

Postal Museum & Mail Rail ★★ MUSEUM   In an industrial patch of central London no tourist usually wanders into, you can now find two well-done attractions in one, and both are perfect for kids. The first holds exhibits about the social history of mail delivery in the country, from origins (Henry VIII was once the only guy allowed to get mail) to antique vehicles to old "pillar" post boxes to Arnold Machin's sculptures of the young Queen Elizabeth II photographed to make stamps. There are lots of things for kids to press and bang, including a pneumatic tube that sends messages whizzing in an overhead tube across the hall, and there's a mail-themed play space, which costs a little extra. But the most memorable aspect of a visit will be a 20-minute loop on the Mail Rail, a little-seen 22-mile underground line that from 1927 to 2003 was used to deliver millions of letters a year. A short portion (with recorded narration and a plastic dome over the carriages, which are as tiny as the train in the kiddie section of a carnival, so please refrain from being tall) now carries curious tourists on a 1-mile looping journey 70 feet below the streets. (Claustrophobes can see what riders do by getting an Exhibitions Only ticket and watching what they missed on screens near the boarding platform.)

15–20 Phoenix Place, WC1. www.postalmuseum.org. © **0300/0300-700.** Full admission £17 adults, £12 ages 16–24, £10 ages 3–15; £1 discount if purchased online. Audio guide £3 on your own smartphone. Wed–Sun 10am–5pm. Tube: Farringdon or Chancery Lane.

Wellcome Collection ★★ MUSEUM Once upon a time, there was a very strange Midwestern pharmacist named Henry Wellcome. Henry got very wealthy and developed a taste for hoarding medical oddities, such as Napoleon's toothbrush, hair from George III, oil paintings of childbirth, and Japanese sex toys. When he died, he bequeathed a flashy museum for them, which now makes for a highly amusing hour's visit. Besides the permanent collection, there's always an offbeat temporary exhibit or two, pertaining to the human body and its uses—recent ones were on sex research, the psychology of magic tricks, and corpse forensics. It's usually surprisingly compelling.

183 Euston Rd., NW1. www.wellcomecollection.org. © **020/7611-2222.** Free admission. Tues–Wed and Fri–Sun 10am–6pm; Thurs 10am–8pm. Tube: Euston Square, Warren Street, or Euston.

The Hardy Tree

In 1866, as laborers dug their way through his churchyard to create the new St Pancras Station, the Vicar of St Pancras noticed with horror that they were tossing aside thighbones and skulls. His cemetery contained the remains of Mary Wollstonecraft, Johann Christian Bach, Sir John Soane, and Ben Franklin's son, the last colonial governor of New Jersey, so the Vicar assigned a young architecture student named Thomas the unenviable task of overseeing the relocation of some 8,000 bodies. As he worked, Thomas carefully arranged their discarded headstones around a tree. The tree survives, and today its trunk grows around the markers. Now it is called the Hardy Tree—you see, young Thomas, who created this eerie living monument, was about to become the famous novelist Thomas Hardy. (St Pancras Old Church, Pancras Rd., NW1; www.posp.co.uk; © **020/7424-0724;** Tube: King's Cross St Pancras.)

SOHO, COVENT GARDEN & WEST END

The Courtauld Institute of Art Gallery ★★★ MUSEUM   Art historians consider the Courtauld one of the most prestigious collections on Earth, yet the tourist masses don't know it, which makes for a very pleasant visit. The small two-level selection is supreme, with several masterpieces you will instantly recognize. Among the winners are a version of Manet's scandalous *Le Déjeuner sur l'herbe,* depicting a naked woman picnicking with two clothed men, and the artist's *A Bar at the Folies-Bergère,* showing a melancholy barmaid standing in front of her disproportionate reflection. There are multiple works by Cézanne and Toulouse-Lautrec, and Tahitian paintings by Gauguin. Degas' *Two Dancers on a Stage* is iconic, as is Van Gogh's *Self-Portrait with Bandaged Ear.* Especially rare is a completed Seurat, *Young Woman Powdering Herself,* which depicts his mistress in the act of dressing and initially included his own face in the frame on the wall—he painted over it with a vase of flowers to avoid ridicule.

The Courtauld Gallery has an exceptional collection of Impressionist (and other European) art.

Somerset House, Strand, WC2. www. courtauld.ac.uk. No public phone; email: galleryinfo@courtauld.ac.uk. Admission £9 adults, seniors and children 18 and under free. Advance booking recommended but not required. Daily 10am–6pm; last admission 45 min. before closing. Tube: Temple.

London Transport Museum ★★ MUSEUM   Try to imagine London without its wheeled icons: the red double-decker bus, the black taxi, and the Tube, which are the best of their kind in the world and a draw for visitors. In Covent Garden's soaring cast-iron-and-glass 1871 flower-selling hall (Eliza Doolittle would have bought her flowers here), the vehicles' development and evolution are traced with excellent technology (lots of ambient sounds and video displays, although some are getting grubby or outdated) and detail (there are even fake horse apples beneath the antique carriages). You can board a fleet of intact landmark vehicles, such as Number 23, a steam locomotive that powered the Underground in its most unpleasant days ("a form of mild torture," wrote the *Times* then); also on display are plenty of the system's famous Edwardian and Art Deco posters, many of which are art unto themselves. Designers will appreciate the background on Johnston, the distinctive typeface created in 1916 for the Underground by Frank Pick, which could

West End & Westminster Attractions

Apsley House **4**
The Benjamin Franklin
House **16**
Buckingham Palace **7**
Churchill War Rooms **18**
Cleopatra's Needle **15**
The Courtauld Institute
of Art and Somerset
House **14**

Handel & Hendrix Museum **3**
The Household
Cavalry Museum **17**
Houses of Parliament **20**
Jewel Tower **21**
London Transport Museum **13**
National Gallery **10**
The National Portrait Gallery **11**
The Queen's Gallery **7**
Royal Academy of Arts **8**
The Royal Mews **6**
Sir John Soane's Museum **12**
Speakers' Corner **2**
Spencer House **9**
Tate Britain **22**
The Wallace Collection **1**
Wellington Arch **5**
Westminster Abbey **19**

Somerset House

Once a naval complex and later where Londoners came to settle taxes, **Somerset House** (Strand, WC2; www.somerset house.org.uk; ✆ **0333/320-2836;** Tube: Temple) is now a favored cultural hangout and home of the Courtauld Institute of Art Gallery. The courtyard, beneath which lie the foundations of a Tudor palace, has a grove of 55 ground-level fountains that delight small children, and it's the scene of popular summer concerts, screenings, talks, and a winter ice rink. Guided 30-minute tours (£5; book ahead online) go most Tuesday and Saturday afternoons from the information desk in the Seamen's Hall. Also look for changing exhibitions (either free or around £10 adults, £8 seniors and students, depending on what's on). The Victoria Embankment terrace overlooking the Thames (from across the street) can be enjoyed for free.

now be considered London's unofficial font. Along the way, you'll learn a great deal about shifts in London life; you may even feel a twinge of embarrassment about the state of your own town's public transportation. It's a must for fans of London history and a good place to entertain children—but if you're childless, you'll need patience. The gift shop, which doesn't require a ticket, is exemplary, and full of fun stuff like posters, Tube-themed clothing, and items made from the Underground's seating upholstery (called *moquette*).

Covent Garden, WC2. www.ltmuseum.co.uk. ✆ **020/7565-7299.** Admission £21 adults, £20 seniors and students, free for young people 17 and under. Daily 10am–6pm; last admission 45 min. before closing. Tube: Covent Garden.

National Gallery ★★★ MUSEUM   When the bells of St Martin-in-the-Fields peal each morning at 10am, the doors promptly open on one of the world's greatest artistic fireworks shows—each famous picture follows an equally famous picture. Few museums can compete with the strongest, widest collection of Western European paintings in the world—one of every important style is on display, and it's almost always the best in that genre. There are 2,300 works, which is plenty to divert you for as long as you can manage, although most visitors just wander around without getting properly close to the brushwork. Be different.

FINDING WORKS: This stupendous institution is marred by lazy presentation; it's very difficult to find the works you want to see. The map (£2) is a poor value that omits works. Directional signs lack room numbers, and the museum is so popular (nearly 6 million people most years) that staff is mostly concerned with controlling visitors, not edifying them. It's almost like they want you to wander confused and unenriched, which is why I strongly suggest preparing for your visit by searching for the Highlights from the Collection section on its website and the short spotlight videos on its YouTube channel (nationalgallerylondon), where you can learn to appreciate a little of what you'll be seeing. To find any specific painting, use your smartphone to look it up under Search the Collection on the museum's website; if it's on display, the gallery number will appear under Key Facts. The museum offers free Wi-Fi,

The National Gallery is chockablock with Western Europe's elite masterpieces, like this work by George Seurat.

but it may not work, and it doesn't offer a place for you to recharge your phone after you've done all that work.

LEARNING ABOUT WORKS: Posted signs are awfully straitlaced. You can glean a little more information if you download the Smartify app (free; bring earbuds) and point your phone at works you want to learn more about. The website has some touring trail suggestions, but your visit would be best illuminated by some expert input. Check the info desk for events, such as the **10-Minute Talks** about a single work (Mon–Fri 4pm); 45-minute **Lunchtime Talks** (1pm) about a specific work or artist; storytelling for kids; or the few hour-long tours (check the schedule online). Permanent displays are supplemented by temporary exhibitions, one free and one paid (£8–£18). The Gallery schedules most family activities for Sundays. The two restaurants are top-quality but overpriced, and besides, the view from the restaurant at the National Portrait Gallery next door (see below) is better. But don't miss the superlative gift shops, which will print you a color-matched custom copy of any of the 1,200 works or even mail a framed version home.

Galleries imperceptibly surge through time in a clockwise arrangement. The best course is to start in the Sainsbury Wing (the first wing upon your entrance from Pall Mall East), which will order viewings more or less chronologically.

TOP DON'T-MISS EXHIBITS AT THE NATIONAL GALLERY

○ Piero della Francesca, one of the most sought-after Renaissance painters, is represented by *The Baptism of Christ* (1450s, room 61 in the Sainsbury

National Gallery Highlights

13th to 15th-century paintings
16th-century paintings
17th-century paintings
18th-Early 20th-century paintings

Creative Space

Learning Gallery

West Wing

Sunley Room

East Wing

Central Hall

Room 1

Sainsbury Wing

The Ambassadors, Hans Holbein the Younger **4**

The Arnolfini Portrait, Jan Van Eyck **63**

The Baptism of Christ, Piero della Francesca **61**

Bathers at Asnières, Georges Seurat **43**

Christina of Denmark, Duchess of Milan Hans Holbein the Younger **4**

The Entombment, Michelangelo **8**

The Execution of Maximilian, Edouard Manet **44**

The Fighting Temeraire, J.M.W. Turner **34**

Marriage à la Mode, William Hogart **35**

The Martyrdom of Saint Sebastian, Piero del Pollaiolo **59**

An Old Woman, Quinten Massys **5**

Samson and Delilah, Peter Paul Rubens **18**

Self Portraits, Rembrandt **22 and 23**

Sunflowers, Vincent van Gogh **43**

Venus and Mars, Sandro Botticelli **58**

Whistlejacket, George Stubbs **34**

Wing). With its then-advanced use of light and foreshortening, its faces verge on bemusement, and the dove, representing the Holy Spirit, seems to fly straight at viewers.

o After Sandro Botticelli fell under the spell of the hardline reformer Savonarola, he burned many of his finest paintings in the Bonfire of the Vanities and changed to an inferior style, so his best works are rare. *Venus and Mars* (1485, room 58 in the Sainsbury Wing), depicting the lovers reclining, is one of them.

o Michelangelo's *The Entombment* (ca. 1500, room 61) is unfinished but powerful. The feminine figure in the red gown is now thought to be St John, but it's hard to know for sure, since the artist favored strong masculine traits.

o King Henry VIII sent his trusted portrait painter, Hans Holbein the Younger, to Brussels to capture an honest likeness of 16-year-old *Christina of Denmark, Duchess of Milan* (1538, room 12), so he could decide if she was pretty enough to marry. She declined *his* proposal, and as a happy consequence, survived to 1590.

o Nearby, Holbein's *The Ambassadors* (1533, room 4) is full of symbolic riddles that refer to the French guy on the left, and famous for a stretched image of a skull that can only be viewed in proper perspective from the side. Get close; the fine brushwork extends even to the feathers on the shoes.

o Kids love Quinten Massys' grotesque, porcine *An Old Woman* (*The Ugly Duchess;* 1513, room 46), thought to be a satire on ladies who try to look younger than they are, but possibly a woman suffering from a disease.

o Among other works, Rembrandt van Rijn shows two self-portraits. One at age 34 (1637, room 22) is pridefully detailed to declare ego—he even gives himself a single name like the Renaissance masters. By age 63 (across the same room), he's in simple clothes and broadly dolloping paint with a palette knife. The pair makes for a universal story of preening youth giving way to confident old age.

o Edouard Manet's *The Execution of Maximilian* (1867–68, room 44) was sliced into five sections after the artist's death, but Edgar Degas reassembled what he could find; the missing patches lend the firing-squad scene further tension.

o J. M. W. Turner's *The Fighting Temeraire* (1839, room 34), depicting a proud sailed battleship being towed for scrapping by a filthy steam-engine boat. As echoed by Q in *Skyfall* as he met James Bond in front of it, it's a national symbol for the decline of the Empire's glory days and the rise of industrialism. A few paintings over, George Stubbs' cryptic, life-size portrait of rearing stallion *Whistlejacket* stops everyone in their tracks; it was painted in 1762 for its proud owner.

o William Hogarth's lurid *Marriage à la Mode* (1743, room 35), is a lurid soap opera of marriage, infidelity, greed, disease, and poisoning told in six satirical paintings.

Your visit to London's major museums will be a lot better if you do these things *before* leaving home.

o **Check what temporary exhibitions are on.** You'll need a ticket, and they sell out.

o **Print maps from the website.** It costs £2 to £3 to pick one up, and they're not worth it because they lack detail.

o **Pick a few items you want to see.** Not just so you can find them (they often move around). Also, signage may be weak and curators unavailable. The more you know, the more you'll love what you see.

o **Check the times for talks and kids' events.** London's museums are generally abuzz with activities. Make sure you don't miss the good ones.

o The Gallery is rich in Peter Paul Rubens, with some 25 works attributed to him. His *Samson and Delilah* (1609–10, room 18) is known for Samson's muscular back and Delilah's crimson robe.

There's much more: George Seurat's almost-pointillist *Bathers at Asnières* (1884, room 43); Monet's *The Water-Lily Pond* (1899, room 41); Van Gogh's *Sunflowers* (1888, room 43); the Pollaiuolo brothers' *The Martyrdom of Saint Sebastian* (1475, room 59); Jan van Eyck's instantly recognizable *The Arnolfini Portrait* (Sainsbury Wing, room 63), a mysterious but fabulously skillful depiction of light that dates to 1434 and looks years ahead of its time. **Brueghels** (room 26; bring your reading glasses to see the crazy details). **Cézannes. Uccellos.** There's so much good stuff here that you may want to go twice during your visit, and the Gallery is centrally located, so you can.

Trafalgar Square, WC2. www.nationalgallery.org.uk. ✆ **020/7747-2885.** Free admission. Mon–Thurs and Sat–Sun 10am–6pm; Fri 10am–9pm. Tube: Charing Cross or Leicester Square.

The National Portrait Gallery ★★★ MUSEUM   On paper, the concept of a portrait gallery sounds like Field Trip Hell. But actually, you'll be surprised how the best works capture the sparkle of life behind these charismatic shapers of history. Here, the names from your high school textbook flower into flesh-and-blood people, and the accompanying biographies are so sublimely evocative that subjects come alive. In 2019, the NPG began an intense refit geared toward expanding exhibition space into a Victorian-era building previously used as offices. The museum isn't slated to re-emerge until spring 2023.

One of the gallery's most instantly recognizable paintings is the **Darnley portrait of Elizabeth I** (1575), in which the Virgin Queen's face is, as we all expected, a ghostly white—except conservators have recently discovered that in her time her skin was originally painted much rosier, almost normal, but the colors faded. Right away, it becomes clear that our perceptions of these once-breathing people are about to be reshaped. The troublesome **Henry VIII** is shown in several likenesses. One is a delicate 1537 paper cartoon by Hans Holbein the Younger (for a mural at Whitehall—a rare survivor from that palace), in which the king suspiciously peers with flinty grey eyes—hinting at a shiftiness that His Majesty probably couldn't recognize in his own likeness, but that all who knew him feared. One painting of **King Edward VI,** painted when he was 9, is executed in a distorted perspective (called anamorphosis) that requires it to be viewed from a hole on the right side of its frame, which is original. You'll also find **George Washington** (he was born an Englishman, after all) and one of the only authoritative images of **Captain James Cook,** who was so pivotal in colonial expansion. Look for the **Chevalier D'Eon,** a male diplomat and fencing champion who lived as a woman in the late 1700s; for the adorable little nose of pugnacious **William Hogarth** in his terra-cotta bust; and for the sketch of **Jane Austen** by her sister Cassandra—friends said it stank. The **Brontë Sisters** appear together in an 1834 portrait found folded atop a cupboard in 1914; their alcoholic brother Patrick Branwell Brontë painted himself out, but his ghostly image is eerily reappearing. The genius of artist John Singer Sargent is immediately apparent in the 1894 likeness of poet **Coventry Patmore;** with just a few spare brush strokes, you feel like you know the old fella.

Fortunately, the portraits don't stop when cameras were invented. The ever-divisive **Margaret Thatcher** is here; **Princes William** and **Harry** make appearances in a 2009 sitting, wearing the uniform of the Household Cavalry; and **Beatrix Potter** (1938), pictured in front of some sheep, looks as soft and kind as the gran you wish you had. Modern portraits (an impressionistic **Ed Sheeran; Kate Bush** in a 1978 chromogenic print) change often because there's not enough room to show everything. Just about everything can be photographed (never with flash) or purchased as a poster in the gift shop.

Late Shift evenings (Fri 6–9pm), with DJs, talks, live music, and dozens of people lounging on gallery floors in sketching sessions, are great fun and a

It's Free!

All of the following attractions charge no admission fees for their permanent collections. Not a shabby lineup!

smart way to free up daytime hours to see more attractions. Also consider the rooftop Portrait Restaurant (☎ **020/7312-2490**), which has a breathtaking view of Nelson's Column and Big Ben's tower—it's better than the National Gallery's.

St Martin's Place, WC2. www.npg.org.uk. ☎ **020/7306-0055.** Free admission. Sat–Thurs 10am–6pm; Fri 10am–9pm; last admission 45 min. before closing. Tube: Leicester Square.

Sir John Soane's Museum ★★ MUSEUM   A doorman will politely request that you deposit your bags. With good reason: These two townhouses on the north side of Lincoln's Inn Fields are so overloaded with furniture, paintings, architectural decoration, and sculpture that navigation is a challenge. The Georgian architect, noted for his egotistic neoclassicism (the Bank of England) as much as for his aesthetic materialism, bequeathed his home and its contents as a museum for "amateurs and students," and so it has been, looking much like this since 1837. It's as if the well-connected eccentric had just popped out to purloin another Greek pilaster, leaving you to roam his groaning wood floors, sussing out the *objets d'art* from the certifiable treasures. His oddball abode, which his will decreed must be left precisely as it was on the day he died, is a melee of art history in which precious paintings and sculpture jostle for space like baubles in a junk shop. Ask to join a tour of the **Picture Room,** built in an 1823 expansion, so you can watch its false walls be opened, revealing layer upon buried layer of works (such as William Hogarth's eight-painting *The Rake's Progress,* a documentary of dissolution) filed inside false walls. Look sharp for Canalettos (which often fetch £9 million at auction) and a J. M. W. Turner (ditto). Curation appears convoluted and haphazard: The guides swear that although sunshine appears to pour onto the masterpieces through skylights, there are UV filters—yet architectural fragments from Whitehall Palace are plainly betrayed to the elements in the courtyard ("It was never covered because that's the way he wanted it,"

Scholar . . . or imperialist hoarder? The overstuffed abode of Sir John Soane.

a guide says). You have to wonder how Soane could legally acquire antiquities such as the sarcophagus of Pharaoh Seti I, carved from translucent limestone but stockpiled for £2,000, and stash him in his cellar near the kitchen. And you won't know because nearly nothing is marked. (Just how the Hogarth hoarder wanted it, too.) Full description books are £10, but the £3 version is oversimplified. Surf the simulated museum at http://explore.soane.org to get preacquainted, or, most helpfully, take a guided 1-hour tour (£16; noon; book ahead). All in all, a visit reminds you of the unseemly way in which privileged Englishmen used to stuff their homes with pilfered art as a way of stocking up on a sense of superiority—but that doesn't mean it's not wondrous.

13 Lincoln's Inn Fields, WC2. www.soane.org. ✆ **020/7405-2107.** Free admission. Wed–Sun 10am–5pm, last entry 4:30pm; tours at noon (book ahead online). Tube: Holborn.

Other West End Attractions

The Benjamin Franklin House ★ HISTORIC HOME   The only surviving residence of the portly politico is a sort of architectural preserve. Shocker: Franklin lived in this boardinghouse by the Thames for nearly 16 years, without his wife—he was here for the Boston Tea Party, the enactment of the Stamp Act, and his invention of the armonica—and it was only the Revolution (and a major international scandal) that forced him from his adopted home back to the Colonies. For much of his life Franklin was a fervent Loyalist who, even as late as 1775, felt the differences between Britain and the Colonies could be settled in "half an hour." Tours are conducted by a young actress playing the landlady's daughter, Polly Hewson, who became such a dear friend that she moved to Philadelphia and was with him when he died. In empty rooms, Polly tells wistful tales as recordings chime in with voices from her memory. Rewards are mixed. Exhibits are sparse (one exception is the ghoulish deposit of human bones in the backyard, likely left over from dissections by Franklin's doctor neighbor). It's humbling to see how this giant man made do with such small quarters. The worn wooden staircase, on which he got his exercise when French trollops weren't available, is so well preserved it feels ghostly.

36 Craven St., WC2. www.benjaminfranklinhouse.org. ✆ **020/7839-2006.** Fri–Sun 10:30am–5pm. Admission and tour (required) £9.50 adults, £8 seniors and students, free for children 11 and under. Tours Fri (architectural tour without performance; £2 cheaper) and Sat–Sun (historical tour), reservations required. Tube: Embankment or Charing Cross.

The Temple Church ★★ CHURCH/HISTORIC SITE   For 900 years, this remarkable little sanctum has been a cradle for legal and religious liberties around the world. The oldest part, the Round, was built in 1185 by the Knights Templar from the Crusades. Back then, they were considered the good guys, so when befuddled King John ran afoul of his barons, he sought

CLEOPATRA & "eros"

Two monuments in the West End have been enchanting visitors for years. When he finished his legendary fountain in the middle of Piccadilly Circus in 1893, sculptor Alfred Gilbert thought the playful, maritime-themed sculptures on its base would be celebrated. Audiences, however, have minds of their own: They responded instead to the archer god on top. But they got even that bit of admiration wrong—they thought he represented **Eros**, god of erotic love, when Gilbert had actually intended Anteros, god of requited love. Today, Piccadilly Circus isn't a roundabout anymore—it's an interchange—but the ceaseless tourist crowd photographing Gilbert's misunderstood masterpiece at least puts the circus back into Piccadilly. Gilbert's fabulous fountain is now dry and full of McDonald's wrappers, but his misidentified god blesses the city as an icon. (Tube: Piccadilly Circus.)

The original Cleopatra's Needles obelisks—which Cleopatra had nothing to do with—were erected in Heliopolis, Egypt, around 1450 B.C., and inscriptions were added 200 years later. The Romans moved the granite spires to Alexandria, where they toppled and were buried in the sand, which preserved them until the early 1800s. After a perilous delivery, London's 224-ton **Cleopatra's Needle** was erected here on the river in 1878 (New York City got one in 1881, and a third went to Paris). Two sphinxes were installed to guard it (some say backward, because they face the sculpture, not away from it). Just 140 years here wrecked what 20 Saharan centuries didn't: Pollution has rendered the hieroglyphs illegible. In 1917, German bombs scarred the western sphinx. The cast-iron benches in the area were installed in preparation for its arrival in the 1870s. Look closely; you'll find sphinxes and camels hidden in the armrests. (Tube: Embankment or Temple.)

sanctuary here and, under protection of the Knights, hammered out the details of the Magna Carta, which gave common law rights to the people that they had never had before. America owes the basis of its Constitution to this building. You can see the stone effigies of nine of the Knights scattered in the Round. Horribly, on May 11, 1941, a Nazi incendiary bomb wrecked this precious place; many of the beautifully carved effigies are now as lumpen and faceless as corpses from Pompeii. The reconstruction of the Temple, which is still a working church serving the legal community in the surrounding Inner and Middle Temple Inns of Court (to which all English barristers must belong), was exacting. Notice how the Purbeck Marble columns, sourced from the same Dorset mine as the originals 700 years before, lean slightly according to the architect's plans from the 1200s. It also has world-famous acoustics, a sublime organ, and a top-notch choir, so if you come, time your visit to coincide with the music schedule.

Inner Temple, EC4 (in the quad south of the intersection of Fleet St. and Chancery Lane). www.templechurch.com. ✆ **020/7353-3470.** Admission £5 adults, £3 seniors and students, free for children 16 and under. Generally open Mon–Fri 10am–4pm, but check ahead because hours shift weekly. Tube: Temple or Blackfriars.

WESTMINSTER & ST JAMES'S

For information on the **Changing the Guard** ceremony, please see p. 214.

Buckingham Palace ★★ PALACE If you were to fall asleep tonight and wake up inside one of the **State Rooms,** you'd never guess where you were. Is it opulent? No question. But if gilding, teardrop chandeliers, 18th-century portraits, and ceremonial halls could ever be considered standard-issue, Buckingham Palace is your basic palace. The mild tastes of the late Queen Elizabeth II—call it "respectable decadence" of yellows and creams and pleasant floral arrangements, thank you very much—is partly the reason. Remember, too, that much of this palace was built or remodeled in the 1800s—not so long ago in the scheme of things—and that the current Royal Family considers Windsor to be their real home. That's right: Buckingham Palace is a mere *pied-à-terre.*

All tickets are timed and include an audio tour that rushes you around too quickly. (If you want to see highlights of the formal gardens, tours go half-hourly on Mon and Thurs–Sun, and that's another £11.50.) The route threads through the public and ceremonial rooms at the back of the Palace—nowhere the Royal Family spends personal time (and besides, tours are held only when they're in Scotland, 2 months a year). Highlights include the 50m-long (164-ft.) **Picture Gallery** filled mostly with works amassed by George IV, an obsessive collector; the 14m-high (46-ft.) **Ballroom,** where Queen Elizabeth II conferred knighthoods; the parquet-floored **Music Room,** unaltered since John Nash decorated it in 1831, where the late queen's three eldest children were baptized in water brought from the River Jordan; and a stroll through the thick **Garden** in the back yard. It's definitely worth seeing—how often can you toddle around the spare rooms in a king's house, inspecting artwork given as gifts by some of history's most prominent names? And monarchists will simply adore the gift shop, full of premium products to which the Windsors have deigned to attach their approval, from tea seats to fuzzy animals. But it's no Versailles. If you're in London any time other than August or September and spot the royal standard of red, gold, and blue flying above, you'll at least know the king is home. If it's the Union Jack, he's gone.

Buckingham Palace Rd., SW1. www.royal collection.org.uk. ✆ **020/7766-7300.** Admission £30 adults, £19.50 students, £16.50 children 5–17. Discounts online if you visit The Queen's Gallery and Royal Mews on the same day. Generally open for 10 weeks starting in late July. July–Aug daily 9:30am–7:30pm; Sept daily 9:30am–6:30pm; last admission 1 hr. 15 min. before closing. Occasional brief openings outside of summer; check website. Tube: Victoria or Green Park.

Lion and unicorn on the gate of Buckingham Palace.

Churchill War Rooms ★★★ MUSEUM/HISTORIC SITE   One of London's most fascinating museums is the secret command center used by Winston Churchill and his staff during the most harrowing moments of World War II, when it looked like England might become German. We regard the period with nostalgia, but a staggering 30,000 civilians were killed by some 18,000 tons of bombs in London alone, and more than 65,000 innocent people were killed in Britain as a whole. Here, in the cellar of the Treasury building, practically next door to 10 Downing St., the core of the British government hunkered down where one errant bomb could have incinerated the lot of them.

When the war ended, the bunker was abandoned, but everything was left just as it was in August 1945. When it came time to make it a museum, everything was intact—from pushpins tracing convoy movements on yellowed world maps to rationed sugar cubes hidden in the back of a clerk's desk drawer. Although the hideout functioned like a small town for 526 people, with sleeping quarters, kitchens, radio rooms, and other facilities that would enable leaders to live undetected for months on end, it feels a lot more like your old elementary school, with its painted brick, linoleum, and round clocks. Now and then, you'll hear atmosphere sounds such as footsteps or whistling (even though Churchill strictly forbade whistling down here).

Midway through, you disappear into the **Churchill Museum,** surely the most cutting-edge biographical museum open at this moment. Exhaustively displaying every conceivable facet of Churchill's life (his bow tie, his bowler hat, and even the original front door to 10 Downing St.), it covers the exalted statesman's life from entitled birth through his antics as a journalist in South Africa (where he escaped a kidnapping and became a national hero) to his stints as prime minister. It's a warts-and-all encyclopedia. You even learn his favorite cigar (Romeo y Julieta) and brandy (Hine). The entire museum is atwitter with multimedia displays, movies, and archival sounds, but the centerpiece will blow you away: a 15m-long (50-ft.) Lifeline Interactive table, like a long file cabinet illuminated by projections, that covers every month of Churchill's life. Point the touch slider at a date, and the file "opens" with 4,600 pages of rare documents, photos, or, for critical dates in history, animated Easter eggs that temporarily consume the entire table (select the original Armistice Day or V-E Day to see what I mean). You could play for hours, dipping into his life day by day.

Clive Steps, King Charles St., SW1. www.iwm.org.uk. © **020/7930-6961.** Admission £26.35 adults, £23.60 seniors 65 and over, £13.15 children 5–15, posted prices are higher and include a voluntary donation. Sept–June daily 9:30am–6pm; July–Aug daily 9:30am–7pm; last admission 1 hr. before closing. Tube: Westminster or St James's Park.

Houses of Parliament ★★ LANDMARK   In olden days, England's rich overlords got together at the king's house, Westminster Palace, to figure out how to manage their peasants. Over time, the king was forced out of the proceedings and most of the Palace burned down. What remains is constructed to express the might of Empire power and the lofty aesthetics of Gothic Revival architecture. Luckily, the nation allows you to tour a dozen

Westminster & St James's

EXPLORING LONDON

It's nearly impossible to take a bad photo of the Houses of Parliament.

stately halls and even to wander through its vaunted House of Lords and House of Commons when they're not in session. There are now two ways to see it: Choose a 100-minute guided group tour, which presents the usual issues of audibility and pace, or take it easy with the 2-hour audio guide (and eavesdrop on groups whenever you want).

The historical highlight is massive **Westminster Hall,** one of the world's most precious spaces and a UNESCO World Heritage Site, built in 1097 by William Rufus, son of William the Conqueror. Richard II commissioned its cherished oak hammer-beam ceiling before he was deposed in the 1390s. Charles I, William Wallace, Sir Thomas More, and Guy Fawkes were all condemned in it, monarchs lie in state in it—and your role in it is to pick up your audio tour. The rest of the Palace is roughly divided into three areas: those for the **House of Lords** (whose members inherit seats upholstered in rose, with an unbelievable gilt sitting area where Queen Victoria would preside on designated occasions); the **House of Commons** (by far the more powerful, elected by the people, but plainer, with seats of blue-green under a hanging forest of microphones); and some flabbergasting lobbies, sitting rooms, and the **Robing Room** (golds, browns, burgundies), which the Sovereign flits through when he shows up once a year to kick off sessions. You walk right onto the floor of both Houses. Many delicious details are elucidated, from the knock-marks on the Commons door made by the Crown's emissary, the Black Rod, to the line in the carpet members may not cross when in the throes of vigorous debates. Booking ahead is advisable; otherwise, try your luck for openings at the ticket office next to the Jewel Tower, across the street.

Overseas visitors are permitted to observe some debates, but the wait can be as long as 2 hours (line up outside the Cromwell Green visitor entrance). Check ahead, since security concerns may cause the government to review public access. The website also posts times of lower-level "Westminster Hall debates" in a committee room, where anyone can come on a first-come, first-served basis. Question Time is only allowed for U.K. residents by previous arrangement with their MP or a Member of the House of Lords.

Sorry, but Elizabeth Tower (1859) beside the Houses—it contains the 13½-ton bell known as Big Ben plus four smaller bells—is usually only open to U.K. residents. If the green Ayrton Light atop it burns, Parliament is sitting after dark. But see it soon: This entire aged complex is in dire shape and will close for several years after 2025 for a much-needed restoration; it frequently catches fire, and chunks of masonry keep shearing off. Make your own metaphors.

Bridge St. and Parliament Sq., SW1. www.parliament.uk/visit. ✆ **020/7219-4114.** Guided tours £29 adults, £24.50 seniors and students 16–18, £13 children 5–15, free for children 4 and under, add £2 if booked the same day. Audio tours £22.50 adults, £19.50 seniors and students, children 5–15 free with paying adult and additional children £9.50 each. Tours: Sat and most weekdays during Parliamentary recesses; times vary; always check ahead. Reservations recommended. Tube: Westminster.

Spencer House ★★ HISTORIC HOME   Currently controlled by the Rothschild banking company, which hosts diplomatic and corporate events here, this lush home is the only surviving London mansion with an intact 18th-century interior; tours let you see the ground floor and a portion of the first floor. The house was begun in 1756 as a love nest by Diana Spencer's ancestors (and, by extension, the future king's); its lavish gilt and carved decor repeatedly invoke the symbols of fidelity and virility. Great War damage spooked the Spencer clan, who moved out in the 1920s, and since then, they've gradually transferred the most precious elements to their estate at Althorp, 193km (120 miles) north of the city, and replaced them with equally fantastic facsimiles—the library fireplace, for instance, took 4,000 hours to carve. The original Painted Room suite was once at the V&A. Tours are limited to 20, so book ahead.

27 St James's Place, SW1. www.spencerhouse.co.uk. ℂ **020/7514-1958.** Tours £15 adults; £12 students, seniors, and children 15 and under; reservations essential. Sun 10am–4:30pm; closed Aug. Tube: Green Park.

Tate Britain ★ MUSEUM   Tourists often wonder about the difference between the Tate Modern and this, its sister upstream on the Thames. Well, the Modern is for contemporary art of any origin, and the Britain, besides its calmer and more civilized affect, is mostly for British-made art made after 1500. Its art is far more approachable than the esoteric stuff at Bankside, and

Tate Britain's elegant spiral staircase, which was sunk into the floor of its original 1897 rotunda during a 2013 refurbishment, adds a curvy, theatrical sweep to the galleries' retrospective of mostly British art.

The Tate-to-Tate Boat

The most fun way to get between the Tates is not the Tube (a circuitous route) but the **Tate Boat** (www.tate.org.uk/visit/tate-boat; ℭ **020/7887-8888;** £8.70 adults, £14.80 return; half-off kids 15 and under, Oyster rate 10% off, Oyster with Travelcard one-third off), a 220-seat catamaran that zips along the Thames every 40 minutes between the Tate Britain and the Tate Modern during gallery opening times. Along the way, it supplies camera-ready views of the London Eye and the Houses of Parliament. Tate's entertainment! The route is RB2, sold at the piers.

you'll see plenty of grade-A work, though not many recognizable masterpieces. Britain has a historic knack for collecting masterpieces, not so much for creating them, so a lot of the work here is rich with relevance but highly imitative of classical styles.

Descriptions are usually pedantic ("this picture bridges the historical and the sublime"), and paintings are usually hung salon-style, many at such an altitude that lighting glare makes them inscrutable. But that could change with a much-needed 2023 rehang (a few galleries may be closed for that), which also aims to address marginalization, diversity, and historical context in ways the museum has never tackled before.

Beloved paintings are constantly being removed, a frustrating habit with Tate, but some masterpieces can be relied upon. Look for these: Turner's trenchant *The Field of Waterloo* was painted in 1818, 3 years after the battle; its shadowy piles of corpses, and of bereaved family members searching them, is still considered a daring exposure of the true price of war. The oil-on-canvas *Carnation, Lily, Lily, Rose* by John Singer Sargent depicts children holding paper lanterns so luminous that when it was first exhibited in 1887, its worth was instantly recognized and it was purchased for the nation. John Everett Millais' depiction of a drowning *Ophelia* is also considered a treasure for its phenomenally tricky depiction of water; the artist painted the plants in the summer so he'd get them right and waited until winter to paint his model, Elizabeth Siddal (or Siddall), a hat-shop girl, in a tub of water. Naturally, she caught a severe cold (he paid for her doctor's bill after her father threatened to sue). Kids love the double vision of *The Cholmondeley Ladies*, two new mothers "born the same day, Married the same day, And brought to Bed the same day"; look closely and you'll realize they're not identical. Check out the sculptures, too, including forms by **Henry Moore,** who gets a couple of rooms, and **Barbara Hepworth.** But the crowning attraction here is the **Turner Galleries,** with their expansive collection of works by J. M. W. Turner. Turner (1775–1851), the son of a Covent Garden barber, was a master of landscapes lit by gauzy, perpetual sunrise, and the dozens of paintings testify to both his undying popularity and his doggedly British tendency to convey information mostly by implication. Turner's work is lovely, if sleepy (the precise landscape painter John Constable called them "airy visions

Westminster Abbey

0 — 100 ft
0 — 30 m

RAF Chapel

Tomb of Henry VII

Tomb of Mary Queen of Scots

Tomb of Elizabeth I

Lift to Triforium (Queen's Diamond Jubilee Galleries)

Shrine of St Edward the Confessor

Chapter House

High Altar

Sanctuary

North Doorway (Entrance)

North Transcept

Poet's Corner

Quire

To College Garden

Organ Gallery

Cloister Garth

North Aisle

South Aisle

Nave

Coronation Chair

Deanery

Dean's Yard

Bookshop

West Doorway

---

painted with tinted steam"), but it's best appreciated if you understand its influence on subsequent artists. An underground cafe can supply quick sustenance (the neighborhood doesn't offer much to eat).

Millbank, SW1. www.tate.org.uk/britain. ⓒ **020/7887-8888.** Free admission. Daily 10am–6pm. Tube: Pimlico.

Westminster Abbey ★★★ HISTORIC SITE/CHURCH   If you have to pick just one church to see in London—nay, one church in the entire *world*—this is the one. The echoes of history are mind-blowing: The current building dates from the 1200s, but it was part of a monastery dating to at least 960. Every English monarch since 1066 has been crowned here (with three minor

exceptions: Edward V, Edward VIII, and possibly Mary I). There are 17 monarchs interred here (deaths dating from 1066 to 1760—the crypts are overstuffed, so now they go to Windsor), as are dozens of great writers and artists. Even if England's tumultuous history and the thought of bodies lying underfoot don't stir your imagination, the interior—in places, as intricate as lace—will earn your appreciation. A visit should take about 3 hours and should begin early, since entry lines (1.3 million tour a year) can be excruciating.

Unlike St Paul's Cathedral (p. 182), which has an airy, stately beauty, the much smaller Westminster is more like time's attic, packed with artifacts, memorials, tombs, and virtuosic shrines—a confluence of God, art, and dense history. It's easy to feel overloaded after just a few minutes. Take your time and don't get swept along in the current of visitors. Let them pass. There are stories to be told in every square meter of this place—name another building where there is such a staggering continuity of a nation's heritage.

A visit is likely to start with a welcome from a volunteer; the Abbey follows the Benedictine tradition, which dictates a warm reception for everyone. It's also still a functioning Anglican spiritual center, so there may be calls for prayer or moments of silence as you tour. You'll be in the Nave, passing Darwin's resting place (just after the first blue gate), and it only accelerates from there. Bombastic tombs abound; take your time absorbing their colonialist self-importance. Google one and you'll unravel a tale, such as the one Thomas Banks sculpted (1789) for Sir Eyre Coote, commander of the British Forces in India—"death interrupted his career of glory." Although Coote's battles of conquest slaughtered thousands of Indians, he is attended by a weeping, naked savage. All that ponderous stone, yet he (like many others memorialized in the Abbey) is not even buried here—he's in Hampshire.

The royal tombs are clustered in the region of the High Altar, where coronations and funerals are conducted. The most famous rulers of all time are truly *here*—not in story, but in body, a few inches behind marble slabs. Some are stashed in cozy side chapels (which once held medieval shrines before Cromwellians bashed them to pieces during the Reformation; some vandalism is still visible), but the oldest are on the sanctuary side of the ambulatory (aisle). The executed **Mary, Queen of Scots** was belatedly given a crypt of equal stature to her rival, **Elizabeth I,** by Mary's son **James I,** who gave himself only a marker for his own tomb beneath **Henry VII**'s elaborate resting place. Some **Stuart and Hanoverian monarchs** are also here (Charles II, Queen Anne, William and Mary) but don't have elaborate tombs. James I's infant daughter Sophia, who died aged 3 days, was given a creepy bassinet sarcophagus in the Lady Chapel (peer into it using a mirror).

The audio tour only picks up highlights, and that pushes you along too quickly if you're truly interested. The *Treasures of Westminster Abbey* book in the gift shop is useful for identifying oddities and learning about people

FACING PAGE: Dragons, lions, and other fearsome creatures act as waterspouts on the facade of Westminster Abbey. In February 2022, the Abbey's Twitter account requested suggestions for names for the most distinctive ones—Gargoyle McGargoyle-Face and Boris were two of the most popular entries.

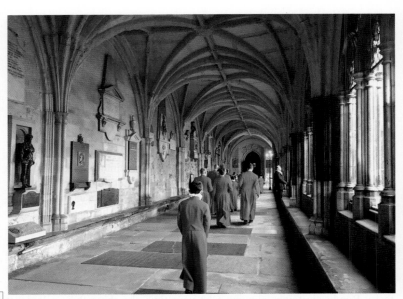
Westminster Abbey is not only an iconic historic site, but it's also a busy house of worship.

buried under them, but it's £17. If you have questions, approach anyone in a red robe; they're "vergers," or officers who attend to the church. They lead 90-minute **guided tours** (up to four times daily between 10:30am and 2pm, for a £10 add-on; book when you arrive at the Abbey), and if you stump them, you may win an invitation to the atmospheric Library, a creaking loft that smells of medieval vellum and dust, where an archivist can answer you.

The South Transept is **Poet's Corner,** where Britain's great writers are honored. You'll see many plaques, but 60% (Shakespeare, Austen, Carroll, Wilde, the Brontës) are merely memorials. The biggest names who truly lie underfoot are Robert Browning, Geoffrey Chaucer (he was placed here first, starting the trend), Charles Dickens, Thomas Hardy (without his heart, which was buried in Dorset), John Gay, Rudyard Kipling, George Frideric Handel (who popularized the use of the Abbey as a concert venue), Dr. Samuel Johnson, Laurence Olivier, Edmund Spenser, and Alfred, Lord Tennyson. Ben Jonson is commemorated here, but is actually buried in the Nave near Isaac Newton, Charles Darwin, and the new genius on the block, Stephen Hawking. Also in the Nave, in the northwest corner, look out for a batch of prime ministers underfoot.

TOP DON'T-MISS EXHIBITS AT WESTMINSTER ABBEY

o That oak seat in the last niche before your exit is the **Coronation Chair.** Unbelievably, nearly every English monarch since 1308 has been crowned on this excruciating-looking throne. The slot under the seat is for the 152kg (336-lb.) Stone of Scone, said to have been used as a pillow by the Bible's

Jacob, and a central part of Irish, Scottish, and English coronations since at least 700 B.C. After spending 7 centuries in the Abbey (except for when Scottish nationalists stole it for 4 months in late 1950), the Stone was returned to Scotland in 1996, where it's on view at Edinburgh Castle. It will return for every future coronation.

o **Oliver Cromwell,** who overthrew the monarchy and ran England as a republic, was buried with honors behind the High Altar in 1658. Three years later, after the monarchy was restored, his corpse was dug up, dragged to Tyburn (by the Marble Arch), hanged, and decapitated. The body was then tossed into a common grave, and its head put on display outside the Abbey. (Didn't they realize he was already dead?) Today his much-abused cranium is at Sidney Sussex College in Cambridge. Cromwell's daughter, who died young, was mercifully allowed to remain buried in the Abbey. In the window above the grave, look for a hole that was left after a 1940 Blitz bombing.

o The **High Altar,** with a mosaic floor laid in the year 1268, is where coronations take place. The actual event sounds glamorous, but it's actually excruciating for everyone involved: Some 8,500 spectators are packed into this small space, and the monarch's crown weighs a brutal 5.5 pounds.

o The **Quire** is where the choir sings; it comprises about 12 men and 30 or so boys who are educated at the adjoining Westminster Choir School, the last of its type in the U.K. The wooden stalls, in the Gothic style, are Victorian, and are so delicate they're dusted using vacuum cleaners.

A 2018 addition opened a very old space to the public for the first time. It's the 13th-century **Triforium,** a horseshoe-shaped attic 70 feet up with an astounding view down the length of the sanctuary—a lift tower was grafted to the venerable building just for it. This once-dusty aerie is now the mind-blowing (and lightly trafficked) **Queen's Diamond Jubilee Galleries.** You'll find such fascinating stuff as Prince William and Kate's marriage license and a crowd of the startlingly lifelike wax effigies used in centuries of notable funerals to show the masses what their heroes looked like—many, like Mary II, wearing their *original* garments. Back on the ground, look also for the panel concealing the **Chapter House,** which was made between 924 and 1030 and is Britain's oldest door. Time seems suspended in the **Cloister,** or court-yard. Writer Aphra Behn was buried in the East Cloister near the steps of the church when she "dyed" in 1689 (her wry inscription: "Here lies a Proof that Wit can never be Defence enough against Mortality."). Even better gardens are hidden away: Look for the fragrant and fountained **Little Cloister Garden,** blackened by 19th-century coal dust, and beyond that to the right, the wide **College Garden** (open Tues–Thurs), a tempting courtyard with daffodil beds, green lawns, and five plane trees dating to 1850 and discovered only by those in the know (now that's you). The garden is thought to be Britain's longest-established one, having been cultivated for nearly a millennium. **Westminster School,** started by the abbey's monks in the 1300s, stands nearby; past students include Christopher Wren, Edward Gibbon, John Gielgud, and pop musicians Thomas Dolby and Gavin Rossdale. (Incidentally, there haven't been monks in this complex for 550 years, yet Londoners persist in calling it an "Abbey.")

Get a real sense of the majesty of the space at a service. Evening prayer services with choirs from around the world are at 5pm weekdays; sung Eucharist is on Sundays at 11am, plus a Sunday organ recital at 5:45pm and evening service with simple hymns at 6:30pm (but check ahead; services are sometimes shuffled to smaller, but equally historic, chapels). Holy Communion is daily at 8am, Matins are at 10am, and Evensong is Saturdays at 3pm. There's also a daily Eucharist at 12:30pm in the Nave. In the **Cellarium** cafe, afternoon cream tea is just £7.50 and starts in late morning, and full lunch is served. Next door, pop into **St Margaret's Chapel** (free), which the monks built in 1523 so they'd be left alone in peace. The Germans didn't comply: Some southern windows were destroyed by a bomb and were replaced by plain glass, and in addition to damage to the north wall, Pew 3 remains charred.

Broad Sanctuary, SW1. www.westminster-abbey.org. ✆ **020/7222-5152.** Admission £25 adults, £22 seniors and students, £11 children 6–17, free for children 5 and under; price includes audio guide; access and prices may be reduced if portions of the Abbey are being used for official business. Queen's Diamond Jubilee Galleries £4.50 adults, free for young people 17 and under. Generally open Mon–Tues and Thurs–Fri 9:30am–3:30pm; Wed 9:30am–6pm; Sat 9:30am–1:30pm, but check the online calendar; last admission 1 hr. before closing. Closed Sun for worship. Check ahead for closures. Tube: Westminster.

Other Westminster & St James's Attractions

Jewel Tower ★ HISTORIC SITE   Built around 1365, it's one of only two remnants left from the 1834 fire that ravaged the Royal Palace of Westminster. Minor and easily overlooked, this three-level stone tower, once a moat-side storehouse for Edward III's treasures, has walls so thick it was later considered an ideal setting for taking accurate measurements. So, you'll see some explanation of weights-and-measures standards and some relics dug up from the moat (including a 1,200-year-old sword, and a bulbous bottle from the Sun, a 17th-c. tavern where Samuel Pepys drank).

Abingdon St., SW1. www.english-heritage.org.uk. ✆ **020/7222-2219.** Admission £6 adults, £5.30 seniors and students, £3.60 children 5–15; posted prices are higher and include voluntary donation. Apr–Sept Wed–Sun 10am–5pm; Oct–Nov 2 Sat–Sun 10am–5pm; Nov 3–Mar Sat–Sun 10am–4pm. Tube: Westminster.

The Queen's Gallery ★ MUSEUM   Every monarch inherits the mother of all art collections—one million items including 7,000 paintings, 30,000 watercolors, and half a million prints, to say nothing of sculpture, furniture, and jewelry—but the late Queen Elizabeth decided to show many of them to the public. Only a tiny fraction is here; the booty is also in palaces such as Kensington and Hampton Court, and on loan. The few works (budget 1 hr.) are undoubtedly exceptional (one of the world's few Vermeers, a Rubens self-portrait given to Charles I, glittering ephemera by Fabergé), but depending on what temporary exhibition supplements them, they may not be the cream of what the crown owns, and it may bore kids.

Buckingham Palace Rd., SW1. www.royalcollection.org.uk. ℃ **020/7766-7301.** Admission £17 adults, £11 students 18–24, £9 children 5–16; discounts online if you visit The Queen's Gallery and Royal Mews on the same day. Thurs–Mon 10am–5:30pm; last admission 4:15pm. Tube: Victoria.

The Royal Mews ★ MUSEUM   Most visitors pop in to what amounts to the king's garage in about 15 minutes. You'll see stables fit for a you-know-who (they barely smell at all) and His Majesty's Rolls-Royces (many of which, at King Charles III's behest, run on green fuels). You'll also overdose on learning about regulations for when this set of harnesses may be used and when that leather must be polished.

Buckingham Palace Rd., SW1. www.royalcollection.org.uk. ℃ **020/7766-7302.** Admission £14 adults, £9 students 18–24, £8 children 5–17; discounts online if you visit The Queen's Gallery and Royal Mews on the same day. Thurs–Mon 10am–5pm; last admission 4pm. Tube: Victoria.

MARYLEBONE & MAYFAIR

Alexander Fleming Laboratory Museum ★ HISTORIC SITE   It was here in this room, in 1928, that a dashing young Scottish microbiologist, Alexander Fleming, came back from vacation to discover a wayward bacteria had contaminated a petri dish. This annoyance was fortunately recognized as a eureka moment, because it's when he realized what penicillin was and what it could do. Since World War II, it has saved millions of lives. Fleming's museum is super old school: crisp elderly volunteer docents, a clunky and barely audible film from decades ago, recalcitrant hours. But it's real, since it has never been renovated and the stuff in Fleming's lab was actually his. He moved out in 1933, but his equipment was kept and put back in 1993. In addition to his teeny lab, which preserves his microscope, you also visit a small exhibit explaining how the rescue of mankind went down—one fellow medical professional ate a little of the new mold to prove it was safe. "Tastes like Stilton!" he declared, and they're still not sure if the intruding bacterium flew in from Praed Street or fluttered up from the mold lab that was once where you just bought your entry ticket. Although management would hate knowing I said so (and you can't take any pictures, so don't try), the museum is a part of the active maternity ward where Prince George, Princess Charlotte, and Prince Louis were born (for a while, Fleming's lab was for diaper storage and as a nap room for obstetricians). When you depart, you actually walk through it, past rushing nurses, beaming parents, and babies who will live long, healthy lives because of the accident that happened in the room you have just been in.

St Mary's Hospital, 135a Praed Street, W2. www.imperial.nhs.uk/about-us/who-we-are/fleming-museum. ℃ **020/7886-6528.** Admission £4 adults, £2 seniors and students. Mon–Thurs 10am–1pm; call ahead to ensure the hospital is open for tourists. Tube: Paddington.

Apsley House ★★ HISTORIC HOME   This is how you'd be rewarded if you became a colonial war hero: You'd get Hyde Park as a backyard. In 1815, Arthur Wellesley defeated Napoleon and became the Duke of Wellington, and later prime minister. The mansion, still in the family (they maintain private rooms), was filled with splendid thank-you gifts showered upon him by grateful nations, including a thousand-piece silver set from the Portuguese court. Still, he never seemed to get his nemesis off his mind: Under the grand staircase stands a colossal nude statue of Napoleon that the little emperor despised; the Duke cherished it as a token of victory. Apsley's supreme art stash, which was largely looted by the French from the Spanish royal family and never went home, includes a few works by Jan Brueghel the Elder, Diego Velasquez's virtuosic *The Waterseller of Seville* (you can understand why it was the artist's favorite work—just looking at it makes you thirsty); and Correggio's *The Agony in the Garden,* in a case fitted with a keyhole so the Duke could open it and polish it with a silk hankie. The Duke and his best friend lived here together after their wives died, and the whiff of faded masculine glory pervades the place like cigar smoke. In other circumstances, the Duke and Napoleon, who both liked fancy finery and fancier egos, would have been buddies. If you're also visiting Wellington Arch (p. 164), a joint ticket will save a couple of pounds.

149 Piccadilly. www.english-heritage.org.uk. ✆ **0870/333-1181.** Admission £11.60 adults, £10.40 seniors and students, £6.90 children 5–17 (including audio tour); posted prices are higher and include voluntary donation. Apr–Oct Wed–Sun 11am–5pm; Nov–Mar Sat–Sun 11am–5pm. Check ahead for closures. Tube: Hyde Park Corner.

Handel & Hendrix Museum ★ HISTORIC HOME   Here's a pleasant *Messiah* complex. This Mayfair building, the German-born composer's home from 1723 (he was its first tenant) to his death in 1759, has lived many lives—before the museum's 2001 opening, conservators chipped 28 layers of paint off the interior walls to uncover the original grey color. In its day, it was a factory for his celebrity: Handel would compose in one room, debut his work in another (there are still frequent performances; check the website), sleep in a third, and sell scores and tickets to the public from a ground-floor shop. None of the furniture was his, but Handel fans should investigate the composer's collection at the Foundling Museum (p. 132), where he was a crucial patron. In 2016, the museum expanded to encompass the top floors of a neighboring building, where legendary guitarist Jimi Hendrix lived in 1968 and 1969. Here, in a cozy flat, his girlfriend Kathy Etchingham tried to give him his first stable home; here he made music and love, entertained, filmed interviews (which gave curators images to reconstruct it down to the last detail)—and played Handel records to absorb the genius of his neighbor across the centuries. But Etchingham's nurturing efforts were to no avail; soon after they broke up, he died at age 27 in Notting Hill. *Note:* The complex is slated to be closed until 2023. Prices and hours are from 2019 and listed as guidance.

25 Brook St., W1. www.handelhendrix.org. ✆ **020/7495-1685.** Admission £10 adults, £5 children 5–16. Mon–Sat 11am–6pm; last admission 5pm. Tube: Bond Street.

Two musical geniuses are honored at the Handel & Hendrix Museum. Jimi's bedroom, re-created as it was in 1968–69, has exact models of his turntable and speakers.

Royal Academy of Arts ★ MUSEUM   Britain's first art school, founded in 1768, relocated here to Burlington House, a Palladian-style mansion away from Piccadilly's fumes (it has a few bars and an exclusive restaurant, The Keeper's House). In 2018, it completed a renovation that connected an adjacent building, linked it with modern elements such as polished concrete and picture windows, and forged a warren of grand spaces in which to put some previously stored works on display (the Royal Academy Collection Gallery contains those, plus the only marble sculpture by Michelangelo in Britain, an unfinished circular relief of Mary with the babies Jesus and John). Although it's one of London's oldest arts institutions, or perhaps because it is, the Royal Academy is not the most rewarding of the creative palaces. Your interest in the topic of its current paid exhibition will be key (£14–£20 tickets for those). The biggest event, and always worth it, is the annual **Summer Exhibition,** which without fail since 1769 (even in 2020—just late) has displayed the best works from anonymous submissions; careers are made by it. The cafe to the left when you first enter is a secret place to charge your phone. Don't miss the wooden red "Phone Box No. 1" tucked behind the stone front gate—it was the 1924 prototype for what we now recognize as an international icon.

Burlington House, Piccadilly or 6 Burlington Gardens, W1. www.royalacademy.org.uk. ✆ **020/7300-8000.** Free admission. Tues–Sun 10am–6pm; last admission 30 min. before closing. Tube: Piccadilly Circus or Green Park.

Speakers' Corner ★ LANDMARK   Near the northeast corner of Hyde Park, where Edgware Road meets Bayswater Road, Londoners of yore congregated for public executions. By the early 1800s, the gathered crowds were jeering at hangings instead of cheering them, and the locale's reputation for public outcry became entrenched. An Act of Parliament in 1872 finally legitimized it as a place of free speech, and its tradition of well-intentioned protest has evolved into a quirky weekend attraction. Laborers and suffragettes fomented social change here, but these days, you're more likely to encounter a rogues' gallery of idealists and religious nutters. Anyone can show up, always on Sunday mornings after 7am, with a soapbox (or, these days, a stepladder), plus an axe to grind, and orate about anything from Muslim relations to the superiority of 1970s disco—but if they don't have the wit to appease the crowd, they stand a good chance of being teased, or at the very least vigorously challenged. In true British style, most speakers refrain from profanity. Even the heckling is usually polite. ("Communists, violent racists, vegetarians," reported Arthur Frommer in 1957. "They undergo the finest heckling in the world, a vicious repartee. . . .")

Tube: Marble Arch, exits 4, 5, 8, or 9.

The Wallace Collection ★★★ MUSEUM   A little bit V&A (decorative arts and furniture), a little bit National Gallery (paintings and portraits), but with a boutique French flair, the Wallace celebrates fine living in an extravagant 19th-century city mansion, the former Hertford House. Rooms drip with chandeliers, clocks, suits of armor, and furniture, usually of royal provenance, and there's not a clunker among the paintings. While other museums were stocking up on Renaissance works, this collection's originators, visionaries of sorts, were buying 17th- and 18th-century artists for cheap, and now its collection shines. You might recognize Jean-Honoré Fragonard's *The Swing* (Oval Drawing Room), showing a maiden kicking her slipper to her suitor below. Peter Paul Rubens' *The Rainbow Landscape* is also here (East Drawing Room), as is the world's most complete room of furniture belonging to Marie-Antoinette (Study; look for her initials hidden around a keyhole on one cabinet). Thomas Gainsborough's *Mrs. Mary Robinson "Perdita"* (West Room) depicts the sloe-eyed actress in mid-affair with the Prince of Wales; she holds a token of his love, a miniature portrait, in her right hand. If she exudes suspicion, it's for good reason—the Prince dumped her before the paint was dry. Don't miss the

A French mantel clock from around 1774 at the Wallace Collection.

DEATH TAKES A holiday

If you're a major musical star, stay away from London! It seems a disproportionate number of singers have met untimely ends here (especially in the summer). These houses aren't open to the public, but their grim pasts make them music landmarks:

- **June 22, 1969, 4 Cadogan Lane, Belgravia** (Tube: Sloane Square): **Judy Garland** overdosed on barbiturates (Seconal) and expired in the bathroom of the two-room flat owned by her fifth husband of 3 months, Mickey Deans. The public outpouring of grief, and its suppression by police in New York City, is credited with starting, or at least fueling, the gay rights movement as we know it today.

- **September 18, 1970, 22 Lansdowne Crescent, Notting Hill** (Tube: Notting Hill Gate): In a basement flat of the Samarkand Hotel, **Jimi Hendrix** washed down nine Vesperax sleeping pills with alcohol. An ambulance was summoned, but arrived too late. The plot thickened 26 years later, when the last person to see him alive, girlfriend Monika Dannemann, was found asphyxiated in a car in Seaford, East Sussex, not long after being accused in court of keeping secrets about Hendrix's final moments.

- **July 29, 1974 and September 7, 1978, Flat 12, 9 Curzon Place, Mayfair** (Tube: Hyde Park Corner): **"Mama" Cass Elliot** of The Mamas and the Papas was found dead in between solo performances at the London Palladium in a flat owned by songwriter Harry Nilsson, who wasn't home. Contrary to lore, she didn't die by choking on a ham sandwich but from a heart attack in her sleep brought on by morbid obesity (she was 165cm/5'5" and weighed 108kg/238 lb.). Four years after Elliot's death, **Keith Moon**, drummer of The Who, died in the same flat. His undoing: chlormethiazole edisylate, a prescribed anti-alcohol drug. Horrified that two of his friends should die while borrowing his apartment, Nilsson quickly sold it to Moon's bandmate Pete Townshend.

- **July 23, 2011, 30 Camden Square, Camden** (Tube: Camden Town): After a period of abstinence, **Amy Winehouse** binged on vodka and succumbed to alcohol poisoning in her bedroom in this 2,500-square-foot townhouse, where she'd lived only a few months. Security guards were there but thought she was only sleeping. For years afterward, fans would leave bottles and cans of booze outside as a macabre tribute.

Great Gallery, a stupendous tour de force of world-class old master paintings. Red folders contain descriptions of pictures, and gold ones are for furniture—the information even tells who owned them before they got here. Be in the Ground Floor State Rooms at the top of the hour, when a chorus of golden musical clocks announce midday direct from the 1700s. Download the free Bloomberg Connects app (free Wi-Fi; bring earbuds) for an audio guide. The Wallace Restaurant, in the covered courtyard, has an exemplary atmosphere but stupidly high prices.

Hertford House, Manchester Sq., W1. www.wallacecollection.org. © **020/7563-9500.** Free admission. Daily 10am–5pm. Tube: Bond Street.

Wellington Arch ★ LANDMARK   When it was finished in 1830, it was intended as a triumphal entry to central London (Marble Arch, at Hyde Park's northern corner, was originally Queen Victoria's triumphal entry to Buckingham Palace). Now it's the equivalent of a shrug. Minor anecdotes of its relocation and the switch from Wellington's original statue on top to a smaller statue (*Peace Descending upon War,* the largest bronze sculpture in Europe) are all this handsome landmark can muster in its little museum, which also discusses the period when the Arch served as a police station. If you buy a joint ticket with the Apsley House (p. 160), across Piccadilly, you'll save a couple of pounds; you can take an elevator up with the admission price.

Hyde Park Corner, Apsley Way, W1. www.english-heritage.org.uk. © **020/7930-2726.** Admission £6 adults, £5.30 seniors, £3.60 children 5–17; posted prices are higher and include voluntary donation. Apr–Oct Wed–Sun 10am–5pm; Nov–Mar Wed–Sun 10am–4pm. Tube: Hyde Park Corner.

KENSINGTON & KNIGHTSBRIDGE

Kensington Palace ★ PALACE   Most people know it as the place where Princess Diana raised Princes William and Harry with Prince Charles from 1984 to 1996, but until fall 2022 it was where Prince William, Kate, George, Charlotte, and Louis lived when they were in town. It has been a royal domicile since 1689, when William and Mary took control of an existing home (then, this was in the country, far from town, to ease William's asthma) and made it theirs. Handsome and haughty, with little of the gilding and symmetry that defined later English tastes, the redbrick palace is not as ostentatious as you might expect. It has been constantly reused over time, so on your multimedia-led guide, you'll see three areas grouped by historical era: the **King's State Apartments,** pegged to King George III and Queen Caroline and the early 1700s; the **Queen's State Apartments,** centered on Mary II and the turn of the 18th century; and **Victoria: A Royal Childhood,** which explores the room where the long-lived queen was born, raised, and groomed to rule before her ascension in 1837. (Frankly, Victoria could use her own full museum, not just these spare rooms containing a few castoffs from her youth.)

But because this palace *has* been reused so often over time, there isn't much original furniture left, a shortcoming that curators try to distract you from: For example, roaming "Palace Hosts" will teach you how to bow properly in the Presence Chamber or play antique games of chance in the King's Drawing Room. There's very little signage to tell you what you're looking at or even what time period you're meant to be considering, but each room has a red-bound Room Guide (sometimes it's hard to find) that briefly describes objects and art they did manage to bring in.

Thankfully, the walk-through includes the magnificent King's Staircase, lined with delicate canvas panels whose perimeters are rigged with tissue paper slivers that will tear as a warning of shifting or swelling. The staircase is considered so precious that it wasn't opened to the public until 2004, 105 years after the rest of the palace first accepted sightseers. Outside in the

Sunken Garden, there's a new statue of Diana (unveiled in 2021); inside, you'll also see photos of royals and of gowns worn by Queen Elizabeth II, Diana, and Princess Margaret, who lived here as well. Overall, though, if you're short on time, this palace has seen better days.

Kensington Gardens, W8. www.hrp.org.uk. ℭ **084/4482-7777.** Admission £20 adults, £10 kids 5–15, including audio tour. Mar–Oct Wed–Sun 10am–6pm; Nov–Feb Wed–Sun 10am–4pm; last admission 1 hr. before closing. Tube: High Street Kensington or Queensway.

Natural History Museum ★★ MUSEUM   The commodious NHM, which attracts 5.2 million visitors in a normal year (mostly families, and by far the most of the three big South Ken museums), is good for several hours' wander, but you'll have plenty of company. In all ways, it's a zoo. You get a hall of dinosaur bones, a taxidermist's menagerie, racks of rocks, and case after case of stuffed stuff. Mostly, you'll encounter the wildest creatures of all: lurching, wailing, scampering children in all their varieties, because everything here, down to the simplified signage and touchable replicas, is pitched to kids on field trips. Most of the discussion here, and throughout the museum, is aimed at a child's mind, with signs answering such unasked questions as why we study nature. On weekends and school holidays, the outdoor queue can be an hour long, so go at opening.

Even if you don't give a hooey about remedial ecology, the main, cathedral-like Victorian building, started in 1873 and now called **Hintze Hall,** is unforgettable: Columns crawl with carved monkeys whimsically clinging to the terra cotta and plants creeping across 162 ceiling panels. The star gallery is probably the **Dinosaurs (Blue Zone),** where heavy crowds slog through one-way walkways past replicas including the 26m-long (85-ft.) **Dippy,** a 1905 plaster cast of a *Diplodocus carnegii* found in America. Some of the dinosaurs are robotic, which can scare small kids. More academic: At the top of the stairs, the **Treasures** gallery holds such historically meaningful stuff as a dodo skeleton and Britain's only moon rock. The pretend kitchen full of hiding places for insects and **Creepy Crawlies** (the **Green Zone**) are longtime visitor favorites, as is the **Red Zone** (the Earth Galleries), anchored by a toned-down, ride-along mock-up of a Japanese supermarket jolted by the 1995 Kobe earthquake. The **Darwin Centre**'s Cocoon looks like a seven-story egg laid in the back atrium; hidden inside are some 20 million bottled specimens (including those that came back on the *Beagle*) on 27km/17 miles of shelves, which you will not see unless you book a £25 "Spirit Collection" tour in advance (daily; 45 min.).

The museum's brainiacs even cultivate a wildlife garden and pond (the **Orange Zone;** open Apr–Oct) that attract a range of English creatures and flowers. All that plus two requisite ceiling blue whales, one of which is a replica in the Mammals section and the other a genuine skeleton, strung up in Hintze Hall, from an animal that was grievously injured by whalers and washed up on an Irish beach to die in 1891. They named it "Hope."

Cromwell Rd., SW7. www.nhm.ac.uk. ℭ **020/7942-5000.** Free admission but £5 suggested donation, timed reservations suggested but not required. Daily 10am–5:50pm. Tube: South Kensington.

Architect Alfred Waterhouse conceived of the Natural History Museum as a cathedral to nature. He purposefully created halls large enough to house the gargantuan skeletons that were being discovered and collected in the Victorian era, but he also lavished the walls with small, whimsical details that can only be seen up close.

Royal Albert Hall ★★ CONCERT HALL   In addition to being a great concert venue, the Royal Albert is also one of London's great landmarks, and you don't need a seat to enjoy it. Conceived by Queen Victoria's husband Albert, it opened in 1871, a decade after his death from typhoid (Vicky was so distraught that she didn't speak at the opening ceremonies). If you don't mind stairs, you can take a 1-hour tour. The hall contains such oddities as Britain's longest single-weave carpet (in the corridors), the Queen's Box (still leased to the monarchy), and a spectacular glass dome (41m/135 ft. high and supported only at its rim). Only groups can go backstage, however: Some 320 performances a year are presented, many with less than 24 hours' set-up time, and a flow of sightseers would be in the way, but for some of those very rare quiet days (about 20 a year), true backstage tours may be bookable online.

Kensington Gore, SW7. www.royalalberthall.com. © **020/7589-8212.** Free admission to lobby, tours £16.25 adults, £14.25 seniors and students, £8.25 children 5–16. Tours available most days; times vary, generally 10am–4pm. Tube: South Kensington.

Science Museum ★★ MUSEUM   It's really two museums, one old-fashioned and one progressive, that have been grafted together and embellished with a few tacky gimmicks and blatant corporate propaganda, but it's a firm family favorite. So many interesting exhibitions are on display here that you'll probably run out of time. The old-school section, which began collecting in 1857 and is split over six levels, is an embarrassment of riches from the artifact archives of science and technology: In 2015, the rare clocks and watches of London's prestigious Clockmakers' Museum, most dating from 1600 to 1850, were added. The hangarlike third floor, Flight, is a standout. Highlights there include a towering slice of a jumbo jet. The Mathematics gallery (second floor), one of the last projects overseen by the late architect Zaha Hadid, is full of lovely swooping forms inspired by the aerodynamic flow around its central object: an experimental Handley Page aircraft from 1929 that was only made possible by math (or as the English call it, "maths"). Of all the sections, Making the Modern World is the most consistently fascinating for its wealth of objects that helped our lives become so comfortable, but in the basement, kids seem to love guessing the function of the bygone household appliances in The Secret Life of the Home.

But not everything in the museum is enchanting. The gift shop (mostly mall-style toys) and guidebook disappoint. And when you've got the actual Model T (from 1916, in Making the Modern World) for free, you probably won't want to pay £11 for a gimmicky IMAX 3D cinema. None of the maps show you where to find the highlights, so I've done some of the legwork for you:

TOP DON'T-MISS EXHIBITS AT THE SCIENCE MUSEUM

○ "Puffing Billy" (1814), the world's oldest surviving steam locomotive, the first Daguerreotype camera from 1839, and the Leica M2 camera Nick Ut used in 1972 to take his iconic photos of the aftermath of a South Vietnamese strike on the village of Trang Bang. (Making the Modern World)

Though Prince Albert, consort to Queen Victoria, died a decade before Royal Albert Hall opened in 1871, it was a consummation of his work toward developing and protecting the arts, so it was named in his honor. The museum-and-research quarter of South Kensington that includes the Hall is nicknamed Albertopolis.

- A German V-2 rocket of the type that decimated many London neighborhoods in the late stages of World War II. These savage weapons claimed lives on both ends of their flights; prisoners of the Nazis assembled them. (Making the Modern World)
- A wooden telephone (1877) made by Alexander Graham Bell to show Queen Victoria how it worked. The earpiece was also the mouthpiece, so callers couldn't talk and listen at the same time. (Making the Modern World)
- A section of the first telegraph cable (1837), made even before the patent had been granted. The first message went between the station control rooms of Euston and Camden Town. It looks like a chunk of kindling; in the days before people realized rubber would be a better insulator, copper wires were threaded through a block of wood. (Information Age)
- The first sewing machine, brought to London in 1845 by the brother of its inventor, Elias Howe, to seduce investors. (Making the Modern World)
- The first attempts at toilet design by Thomas Crapper himself. (The Secret Life of the Home)
- 1969's *Apollo 10* command module. Between you and it, one of you has been to the moon. (Exploring Space)
- A porcelain bowl that was fused with sand and rocks in the 1945 atomic blast at Hiroshima. (Making the Modern World)
- A modified Vickers Vimy bomber, the first plane to cross the Atlantic without stopping. It was flown by Arthur Whitten Brown, who promptly became the first person to report jet lag. He called it something much less catchy: the "difficulty of adjustment to the sudden change in time."
- A complete De Havilland Comet, which was the first jetliner. (1952, Flight)

Exhibition Rd., SW7. www.sciencemuseum.org.uk. ⓒ **033/0058-0058.** Free admission, timed reservations recommended but not required. Daily 10am–6pm; last admission 5:15pm. Tube: South Kensington.

V&A ★★★ MUSEUM   If it was pretty, well-made, or valuable, the British Empire wanted to possess it. As a decorative arts repository, the V&A, or Victoria & Albert Museum, occupying a haughty High Victorian edifice (it was endowed by the proceeds from the first world's fair, the Great Exhibition of 1851), is about the eye candy of objects—not so much for paintings, but some—and if you're paying attention, it tells the story of mankind through the development of style and technique.

As for how to tour it, the ground floor, a jumbled grid of rooms, has lots of good stuff, but lots more bric-a-brac (Korean pots, 1,000-year-old rock crystal jugs from Egypt) that you'll probably walk past with polite but hasty appreciation. Rooms are arranged by country of origin or by medium (ironwork, tapestries, and the like) but you'll want to see the **20th Century** (rooms 74, 76; level 3), which surprises by including objects you may have once kept in your home (a Dyson vacuum cleaner, mobile phones); the U.K.'s only permanent **architecture** gallery (rooms 127–128a; level 4); the ever-popular **fashion**

Kensington & Knightsbridge

Fashion is just one of the decorative arts on display at the V&A.

gallery (room 40) for looks both historic and haute; and endless slices of **medieval stained glass** (rooms 83–84; level 3). Wherever you go, if you see a drawer beneath a display case, open it, because many treasures are stored out of the light.

TOP DON'T-MISS EXHIBITS AT THE V&A

○ The **Europe 1600–1815 galleries,** to the left as you enter, are bright, rich, and instructive. They're crammed with 1,100 precious objects including 300-year-old furniture, 18th-century court clothing that looks like it was made yesterday, and even an entire bedchamber from the 1600s. Stream the audio guide from www.vam.ac.uk/europeaudio (there's free Wi-Fi).

○ The seven **Raphael Cartoons** (room 48a), 500 years old in 2015, are probably the most priceless items. These giant paper paintings—yes, paper—were created by the hand of Raphael as templates for the weavers of his 10 tapestries for the Sistine Chapel. Before Queen Victoria moved them here, they hung for around 175 years in the purpose-built Cartoon Gallery at Hampton Court Palace (p. 205). The colors are fugitive, meaning they're fading: Christ's red robe, painted with plant-based madder lake, has turned white—his reflection in the water, painted with a different pigment, is still red. Look for the QR code that lets you explore the works layer by layer on your phone.

○ None of the sculptures in the sky-lit **Cast Court** (rooms 46 and 46a) are original. They're casts of the greatest hits in Renaissance art, and they crowd the room like a yard sale. They were put here in 1873 for the poor, who could never hope to see the real articles for themselves. Find Ghiberti's doors to the baptistery at Florence's San Giovanni, whose design kicked off the artistic frenzy of the Renaissance, and Michelangelo's *David,* floppy puppy feet and all; he was fitted with a fig leaf for royal visits. Depressingly, many of these replicas are now in better shape than the originals.

o Tipu Sultan of India hated imperialists. So, in the 1790s he commissioned an automaton of a tiger sinking its fangs into one. A crank on **Tippoo's Tiger** (room 41) activates a clockwork that makes an Englishman's hand flail while a hidden organ plays a death knell. To no avail; in the end, Tipu was killed by Europeans, and the English stole it as an ironic trophy. It has been a favorite since 1808, when it was part of the East India Company's trophy museum.

o The **Great Bed of Ware** (room 57), a 10×11-foot four-poster of carved oak that dates to about 1590, was once a tourist attraction at a country inn, renowned enough for Shakespeare to mention it in *Twelfth Night:* "big enough for the bed of Ware." As you admire it, consider that in those days, bed canopies were installed to protect sleepers from insects that might tumble out of thatched roofs and into mouths. Canopied beds, a mark of luxury today, were a sign of a humbler home requiring anti-insect measures. Nearby is James II's silver-embroidered wedding suit (1673, room 56).

o The **Ardabil carpet** (room 42), the world's oldest dated carpet (copies lay on the floors of 10 Downing St. and Hitler's Berlin office alike), is from 1539. To preserve its dyes, it's lit 10 minutes at a time on every half-hour.

o Implausibly well-preserved specimens of historic **fashion** (room 40), from pristine empire-waist dresses to mint-condition 18th-century silks.

o The **Hereford Screen** (1862, Ironworks balcony) is a liturgical riot by Gilbert Scott, the architect of the "Eros" (p. 146) and the St Pancras Renaissance (p. 143). It took 38 conservators 13 months to restore the 8-ton choir screen to its full golden, brassy Gothic Revival glory.

o The **Gilbert Collection** (rooms 70–73) of impossibly fine jewel boxes, cameos, silver, and mosaics was amassed by a rich enthusiast who originally gave them to LACMA in California, where he made his fortune. But in a museum-world scandal, he stripped them from it for not showing the whole collection at once. Despite that slap in the face, the V&A still displays only highlights.

o One volume of Da Vinci's legendary **notebooks** is on display in room 64 (Medieval and Renaissance).

o It's hard to forget the riotous figures and tilework of the **Ceramic Staircase** (1860s); originally, every staircase here was to look like this, but when the cost became apparent, even those excessive Victorians satisfied themselves with just one. To find it, turn left after coming through the Exhibition Road entrance.

o The second, third, and fourth levels have less space and therefore are more intuitive. Look for the **Theatre & Performance** collection (103–106b), which lends the spark of modern familiarity to the proceedings; you can see, for example, Ingrid Bergman's *Gaslight* dress by Irene, Fred Astaire's tux, Kylie Minogue's dressing room, and costumes from *The Lion King* and *Wicked*.

Questions about today's tours and how to find particular items will be referred to the information desk, which in turn may be referred to a search on the public website. Such is the sad reality of today's heavily touristed museum. That's why planning pays off: Download a map (vam.ac.uk/map) and you'll save £2. Also check to see what hot-ticket exhibitions are coming, many of them on topics that pander to a wide paying audience (David Bowie, Pink Floyd, and, in 2023, Coco Chanel) or are blatantly influenced by sponsors (historic underwear); £20 is a typical upcharge for an exhibition here. Free 1-hour tours are given at 10:30am (highlights), 12:30 (fashion), 1:30 (treasures of Europe), 2:30 (theater), and 3pm (Britain). Even the cafe (the world's first museum restaurant) is gorgeous; have a coffee in the extraordinary Gamble Room (1865–78), a visual feast in ceramic tile and enameled iron. Also visit the V&A's western exterior; scarred during the Blitz, the stonework was left unrepaired as a memorial.

Cromwell Rd., SW7. www.vam.ac.uk. ✆ **020/7942-2000.** Free admission. Sat–Thurs 10am–5:45pm; Fri 10am–10pm, with reduced gallery openings. Tube: South Kensington.

Other Kensington & Knightsbridge Attractions

Albert Memorial ★ LANDMARK   Albert, Queen Victoria's German-born husband (and, um, first cousin), was a passionate supporter of the arts who piloted Britain from one dazzling creative triumph to another. But when

he died suddenly of typhoid (some say Crohn's disease) in 1861 at age 42, the devastated queen abruptly withdrew from the gaiety and remained in mourning until her death in 1901, shaping the Victorian mentality. She arranged for this astounding spire—part bombast, part elegy—to be erected in 1872 opposite the concert hall Albert spearheaded. Some of its nearly 200 figures represent the continents and the sciences, and some, higher up, represent angels and virtues. It's Victorian high-mindedness in stone. At the center, as if on an altar, is Albert himself, gleaming in gold.

Kensington Gardens. www.royalparks.org.uk. Tube: South Kensington.

The Albert Memorial.

The Design Museum ★ MUSEUM   Relocated to a cavernous landmark modernist building in Kensington in 2016, the Design Museum is where you'll find the cool kids of current style and architecture waxing esoteric about their thought processes in themed exhibitions. The top-floor balcony celebrates everyday objects (typefaces, laptops) that have been designed well. In point of fact, it's more of a gallery than a museum, appealing more to designers than to scholars. Everything is imbued with an awareness of how design can improve the lives of the less fortunate, a notion that's at best Victorian and at worst consumerist, and through changing exhibitions, the curators occasionally appear to sell out (a 2017 show rhapsodized about Cartier wristwatches, another was about soccer). The shop has some interesting finds, as you might suspect.

224–238 Kensington High St., W8. www.designmuseum.org. ℂ **020/3862-5900.** Permanent collection free, exhibitions charge £10–£18. Sun–Thurs 10am–6pm; Fri–Sat 10am–9pm. Tube: High Street Kensington.

THE SOUTH BANK, SOUTHWARK & BOROUGH

Florence Nightingale Museum ★ MUSEUM   You probably don't know much about Florence Nightingale (1820–1910) now, but spend 45 minutes in this small and well-designed biographical museum (on the grounds of the hospital with which she worked) and you'll brim with newfound respect for this consequential person—as a founder of sensible nursing practices, as a leader who took no guff, and ultimately, as an all-around hard-core badass. It's broken into three sections, attractively presented and with kid-friendly elements: her headstrong youth, her fame-making work whipping the troop hospitals of the Crimean War into shape (another time events around Ukraine shaped the world), and her subsequent years of burned-out reclusiveness and ceaseless writing.

2 Lambeth Palace Rd., SE1. www.florence-nightingale.co.uk. ℂ **020/7620-0374.** Admission £10 adults, £8 seniors, £6 students, £5 children 15 and under. Wed–Sun 10am–5pm; last entry 4:30pm. Tube: Westminster, Waterloo, or Lambeth North.

Garden Museum ★ MUSEUM   Here, in a deconsecrated church (the tower, which you can climb, dates to 1377), you'll find artifacts and academic respect paid to the greatest gardeners of Britaindom, including John Tradescant the Elder, a green thumb and seed pioneer who himself was planted in the churchyard in 1638. You'll find an assortment of antique gardening implements, a collection of gardening-related art, plus a few curios such as an original 18th-century bronze season pass token for the Vauxhall Gardens—yes, only horticulture nerds need apply. The museum was set up in 1977 as a way to preserve the abandoned church of St Mary's, but—garden museum irony alert—no one thought to dig down. In 2016, workers discovered a vault containing a collapsing pile of 30 lead coffins topped with a rusted archbishop's miter cap—like your nightmare's nightmare. One of the corpses is Richard Bancroft, who oversaw creation of the King James Bible, and as many as five others are Archbishops of Canterbury, who were like England's popes. You can find the clear, sealed panel leading to their chamber in The Ark. There are other graves to see: Captain Bligh of *Bounty* fame is in the yard. A more cheerful fact: The roundabout outside, at Lambeth Bridge, is where Clark Griswold told his kids, "Big Ben! Parliament!" (You either know it or you don't.)

5 Lambeth Palace Rd., SE1. www.gardenmuseum.org.uk. ℗ **020/7401-8865.** Admission £14 adults, £11 seniors, £8 students, free for young people 17 and under. Church tower another £4. Daily 10am–5pm (but check ahead). Tube: Westminster, Waterloo, or Lambeth North.

Imperial War Museum London ★★ MUSEUM One of London's unexpectedly gripping museums has a deceptive name. It's not just for military buffs, and it's no gun-fondling armory, even if there is a Spitfire hanging from the rafters. Instead of merely showcasing heavy implements of death, which it does, this museum—the latest tenant of the commodious and palatial former mental hospital known as Bedlam—takes care to also convey the sensations, feelings, and motivations of soldiers and civilians caught in past

conflicts. It is ultimately not about weapons but a museum about *people* at war. In addition to easy-to-grasp background on major conflicts, the museum intelligently balances tanks and planes with storytelling that unravels propaganda. While some exhibits are perhaps oversimplified, the First World War Galleries are the most advanced, best-stocked, most comprehensible, and most moving you'll ever see on the topic, followed by another gut-punch segment on the Holocaust.

Lambeth Rd., SE1. www.iwm.org.uk. ℗ **020/7416-5000.** Free admission; timed reservations recommended but not required. Daily 10am–6pm; last admission 5:30pm. Tube: Lambeth North or Elephant & Castle.

The atrium of the Imperial War Museum.

London Eye ★ OBSERVATION WHEEL The Eye is now but a fading novelty, but when it was erected in 1999 as a temporary vantage point known as the Millennium Wheel, it became such a sensation—and a money-spinner—that it was made permanent. It rises above everything in this part of the city—at 135m/443 ft. high, it's 1½ times taller than the Statue of Liberty. The 30-minute ride above the Thames affords an unmatched and unobstructed

City & South Bank Attractions

Bank of England Museum **15**
The Charterhouse **12**
Dr Johnson's House **11**
Florence Nightingale Museum **6**
Garden Museum **5**
The Golden Hinde **19**
Guildhall & Roman
Amphitheatre **14**

Hayward Gallery **1**
HMS *Belfast* **22**
Hunterian Museum **9**
Imperial War Museum London **7**
The London Dungeon **3**
London Eye **2**
London Mithraeum **16**
The Monument **25**

The Old Operating Theatre
Museum & Herb Garret **20**
Sea Life London Aquarium **4**
Shakespeare's Globe **18**
Sir John Soane's Museum **8**
St Paul's Cathedral **13**
Tate Modern **17**
The Temple Church **10**
Tower Bridge Exhibition **23**
The Tower of London **24**
View from the Shard **21**
Whitechapel Gallery **26**

175

perspective on the prime tourist territory; there's no narration, but six tablets elucidate what's before you. On a clear day, you can see to Windsor, but even on an average day, the entire West End bows down before you. That's why you should either go as soon as you arrive in the city, to orient yourself, or on your last day in town (my choice), when you can appreciate what you've seen. Each of the 32 enclosed capsules, which accommodate up to 28 people (although there may be fewer with you), is climate-controlled and rotates so gradually that it's easy to forget you're moving—which means this ride will upset only the desperately height-averse. By the time you summit, you'll have true 360-degree views unobstructed by the

The London Eye offers fab views of Big Ben's tower across the Thames.

support frame. The ticket queue often looks positively wicked (book ahead if possible), but it moves quickly, chewing through 15,000 riders a day, 800 per revolution. The Shard (p. 180) is much taller (but costs much more). *Tip:* Booking online saves waiting in the first queue. The proprietors do everything they can to confuse you into paying more than you have to. Basically, a Standard timed ticket will do, although you still might have to wait in line and wind up behind schedule. You can pay up to £51 to wait in a shorter line at any time you choose ("Fast Track"). The Covid-19 pandemic forced the Eye to curtail its hours and close before sunset; check if hours have expanded again, because sundown is the best time to do this.

Riverside Building, County Hall, SE1. www.londoneye.com. ℂ **020/7967-8021.** £36 adults, £32.50 children 3–15; discounts for advance online bookings. Daily 11am–6pm. Tube: Waterloo or Westminster.

The Old Operating Theatre Museum & Herb Garret ★★ MUSEUM
In the mid-1800s, before general anesthesia, St Thomas' Hospital used the attic of a neighboring church as a space where surgeries, mostly amputations and other quick-hit procedures, could be conducted so that students could watch but other patients couldn't hear the agonized screams. When the hospital moved in 1862, the attic was abandoned, sealed away, and forgotten. It was considered lost until 1956, when an enterprising historian thought to look in the attic, and found the secret surgical stadium behind a wall. Creep up a tight, 52-step wooden spiral staircase (there's no lift) once used by the bell ringer and you'll find the theater, now the centerpiece of a ghoulish, but carefully educational, museum delving into medical methods of the early 1800s, from herbal remedies to leeches. Once a month on Saturdays (£12; book ahead),

you can even sit where the surgical students once did and imagine what it would have been like to watch some unlucky sod lose a leg without anesthetics. What a white-knuckle reminder that in the old days, medicine was less about science and more about soldiering on. Which you might also do; there are also no toilets here.

9a St Thomas St., SE1. www.oldoperatingtheatre.com. ☎ **020/7188-2679.** Admission £7.50 adults, £6 seniors and students, £4.50 young people 17 and under. Thurs–Sun 10:30am–5pm; last entry at 4:15pm. Tube: London Bridge.

Shakespeare's Globe ★ LANDMARK   A painstaking re-creation of an outdoor Elizabethan theater, it tends to bewitch fans of history and drama. Opened in 1997, the open-air "Wooden O" was made using only Elizabethan technology such as saws, pillars made from solid oak trees, 17,000 bundles of Norfolk water reed, and plaster panels mixed with goat's hair (the original recipe called for cow's hair, but the breed they needed is now extinct). The first Globe burned down in 1613, aged just 14, when a cannon fired during a performance of *Henry VIII* caused its thatched roof to catch fire; it took a special act of Parliament, plus plenty of hidden sprinkler systems, to permit the construction of this, the first thatched roof in London since the Great Fire. The original theater was the same size (and stood 180m/591 ft. to the southeast), but it crammed in 3,000 luckless souls. Today, just 1,600 are admitted

THE GREAT "lates"

When they are at full staffing levels, some attractions offer extended opening times for evening viewing in the main galleries. Often, extra inducements are tossed in, such as wine and sketch classes at the National Portrait Gallery or DJs at the V&A. Some major "Lates" events were suspended during the pandemic, but these are the ones that remain intact or are expected to return. They can really free up your daytime touring to include more sights:

ATTRACTION	LATE OPENING
British Library (p. 122)	Tuesday–Thursday to 8pm
British Museum (p. 126)	Friday to 8:30pm
Design Museum (p. 173)	Friday and Saturday to 9pm
London Zoo (p. 213)	Thursday and Friday to 10pm (selected nights)
National Gallery (p. 138)	Friday to 9pm
Natural History Museum (p. 165)	occasional Fridays to 9:30pm, occasional ticketed events such as silent discos
National Portrait Gallery (p. 142)	Friday to 9pm
Science Museum (p. 167)	Wednesday to 10pm (last of month); over-18s only)
Sir John Soane's Museum (p. 144)	once a month, announced online
Tate Modern (p. 179)	10pm closing last Friday of month
V&A Museum (p. 169)	Friday to 10pm
Whitechapel Gallery (p. 190)	Thursday and Friday to 9pm

An actor rides a hobbyhorse as part of the annual Harvest Festival at Shakespeare's Globe.

for performances. The Globe no longer opens its exhibition space to walk-ins, but particularly from April to October, it puts on a host of interesting **guided tours** (£17 adults, £10 children 15 and under; daily; reservations required) on topics including Shakespeare's Bankside, the ancient backstories of the plays that are running, and, of course, the attributes of this magnificent Wooden O itself.

21 New Globe Walk, SE1. www.shakespearesglobe.com. © **020/7401-9919.** Theater tours: daily 9:30am–5pm; check ahead for schedule changes. Tube: London Bridge.

Tate Modern ★★★ MUSEUM In 2000, Bankside's most reviled eyesore, a bleak power station—steely and cavernous, a basilica to the soulless grind of industry—was ingeniously converted into what is probably the world capital of contemporary art made since 1900. Its vast space is as integral to the tourist's London as the Quire of Westminster Abbey or the Dome of St Paul's. Enter via the ramp on the west side of the building (to the right if your back is to the river), and look for signs with QR codes: one lets you book a free ticket and one gets you a map (there's free Wi-Fi).

The mammoth **Turbine Hall,** cleared of machinery to form a meadowlike expanse of concrete, often hosts gargantuan works by major artists for its periodic Hyundai Commission (usually Oct–Mar). People of every background frolic on the cement as if it were a park. The Turbine Hall connects the **Natalie Bell Building** on the left, which contains the **collection** and whatever blockbuster **temporary exhibitions** are currently on (as much as £20 for those; book ahead), with a twisting 10-story tower on the right (the **Blavatnik Building,** named for a Soviet-born oligarch who gave cash), which stands above the power station's former oil tanks, now used as performance-and-video spaces (check online for what's on). The Blavatnik building is topped with an outdoor panoramic terrace (access was suspended during the pandemic).

Tate Modern's building is a star and will always merit a visit, but otherwise there are core problems that cause a majority of guests to wander the permanent collection like baffled ghosts. For one, its great works are too often rotated off display, so there's no guarantee of what you'll find, and the pieces that are on display have been criticized by many visitors as joyless or overly obtuse. You'll hear the Turbine Hall touted as a landmark, and it is, but its full use is seasonal and the commissions that go into it can take weeks to assemble, so there's a good chance you won't be able to enjoy that part of the experience on your visit. The explanatory signage throughout also tends to consist of pretentious art-underworld doubletalk, such as, "works gathered in this wing capture making as gesture, the trace of an action," whatever that means.

It may help you connect to the works if you take one of the daily free 45-minute guided tours at noon, 1pm, or 2pm (Level 2, Bell Building). One thing that doesn't miss is the surprising and well-stocked shop (on the lobby floor of the Blavatnik). Also carve out refreshment time: Kitchen and Bar on Level 6 (Bell; daily noon–6pm) is a city highlight: 30 first-come bar stools facing out over St Paul's and the Thames through floor-to-ceiling glass. You may not be able to rely on the art collection at Tate Modern, but the view from these cafe seats is always worth the trip.

Bankside, SE1. www.tate.org.uk/modern. ℂ **020/7887-8888.** Free admission. Daily 10am–6pm; 10pm closing on last Fri of month. Tube: Southwark.

View from the Shard ★ OBSERVATION DECK   In 2013 the Shard, one of the tallest buildings in Europe (but not even in the top 50 worldwide), added a pricey observation deck with timed tickets—sunset time slots sell out ahead of time, but if you come during the day, you can stay as long as you want—an advantage over the Eye. The jagged 306m/1,016 ft.-tall tower doesn't exactly fit in with its neighbors. Commerce is the theme, with staff members hustling you to purchase pricey green-screen souvenir photos, cocktails, or champagne. After airport-style security and two ear-poppingly fast elevator rides, you emerge 244m/800 feet up to some weird angel-like choir music and vertiginous floor-to-ceiling windows far, far above the city—so high that, after the initial impression, if you don't know London well, you're not likely to figure out most of what you see. A few levels up (stairs lead to those last three floors), there's a patio shielded at body-level from the elements, but you won't find seating. If the day turns cloudy, ask staff for a View Guarantee voucher that will allow you to return for free. If you have to choose, the London Eye is a more memorable experience than a £32 elevator ride.

Joiner St., SE1. www.theviewfromtheshard.com. ℂ **0844/499-7111.** Admission £32 adults, £25 children 4–15, no ticket required for kids 3 and under; slight discount for booking at least 4 days ahead. Hours change almost daily, so consult calendar online. Tube: London Bridge.

Other Bankside/Southwark Attractions

Brunel Museum ★ MUSEUM/HISTORIC SITE   Although the engineering contributions of Marc Brunel and his son Isambard Kingdom Brunel are commonly taken for granted, here they're given their due. With the help of a shield system they invented, these pioneers executed the first tunnel to be built under a navigable river. London's soft earth didn't make it easy, though—it took from 1825 to 1843. This redbrick building marked by a chimney was where steam engines pumped the seeping water out as diggers toiled. The tunnel, lined with arches and Doric capitals, was a commercial flop that deteriorated into a subterranean red-light district. It later found new purpose, however, as a part of the Overground Line, and it has gained new respect through this museum, which often creates special events to bring guests into the tunnel.

Railway Ave., SE16. www.brunel-museum.org.uk. ℂ **020/7231-3840.** Admission £6 adults, £4 seniors, students, and children. Thurs noon–6pm; Sat–Sun 11am–5pm. Tube: Rotherhithe.

The *Golden Hinde* ★ HISTORIC SHIP   Tucked into one of the few remaining slips that enabled ships to unload in Southwark (another is Hay's

Galleria, downstream by the HMS *Belfast* [see below], now a boutique shopping area) is a 1:1 replica of Sir Francis Drake's square-rigged Tudor galleon, which circumnavigated the world from 1577 to 1580. This 1973 version, which is so tiny you will forever feel pity for those old explorers, made its own circumnavigation in 1980. The schedule is full of events (rum tastings, author talks, sleepovers), so maximize your visit by coordinating it with one.

St Mary Overie Dock, Cathedral St., SE1. www.goldenhinde.co.uk. ℂ **020/7403-0123.** Admission £6 including audio guide. Daily 10am–5pm. Tube: London Bridge.

HMS *Belfast* ★ HISTORIC SHIP   It's as if the powerful 1938 warship, upon being retired from service in 1965, was motored straight to this dock and opened to visitors the next day. Nearly everything, down to the checked flooring and decaying cables, is exactly as it was, making the boat a fascinating snapshot of mid-20th-century maritime technology, and smart exhibits do a lot to make it come alive again. Authenticity also makes it a devil to navigate, especially if you have any bags with you—sorry, no cloakrooms, sailor. Getting around its labyrinth of decks, engine rooms, ladders, and hatches requires dexterity and a well-calibrated inner compass—it seems the Health and Safety rules that bedevil every aspect of British life do not apply here. You can roam as you wish, visiting every cubby of the ship from kitchen to bridge, touching nearly anything you want, while being thankful that it wasn't you who was chasing German cruisers (the *Belfast* sank the *Scharnhorst*) and backing up the D-Day invasion in this tough tin can. Admission includes an excellent audio guide, but privately, crew members tell me that they wish visitors would pause and ask them questions in person—there's so much more to point out to you.

Morgan's Lane, Tooley St., SE1. www.iwm.org.uk. ℂ **020/7940-6300.** Admission £23.60 adults, £21.25 seniors, £11.80 children 5–15; higher posted prices include a voluntary donation. Daily 10am–6pm; last admission 1 hr. before closing. Tube: London Bridge.

A Poignant Pocket Park

Little-known **Postman's Park** is beloved by those lucky enough to have stumbled across it. Hemmed in between buildings, its central feature is the moving **Watts Memorial,** a collection of plaques dedicated to ordinary people who died in acts of "heroic self-sacrifice." Have a seat on a bench and ponder John Clinton, 10, "who was drowned near London Bridge in trying to save a companion younger than himself" in July 1894. In 1893, William Freer Lucas tantalizingly "risked poison for himself rather than lessen any chance of saving a child's life and died." Alice Ayres saved three children from a burning house in 1885 "at the cost of her own young life." The commemorations mostly ceased in Edwardian times (poor Leigh Pitt squeaked in after saving a drowning child in 2009), making these forgotten faces obscure once again. (West side of St Martin's-Le-Grand between St Paul's Cathedral and the Barbican Centre; daily 8am–dusk; Tube: St Paul's or Barbican.)

THE CITY

Museum of London ★★★ MUSEUM   This repository's miraculous cache of rarities from everyday life would do credit to the greatest national museums of any land. The collection has been so successful that in December 2022, it closed its home of 46 years in preparation for an upgrade to a lavish new facility in the historic Smithfield General Market, by the Farringdon Underground stop, where it will reopen as The London Museum in 2025. For now, only its East London spinoff, Museum of London Docklands (p. 195), is open.

150 London Wall, EC2. www.museumoflondon.org.uk. © **020/7001-9844.** Free admission. Closed until 2025. Tube: Farringdon.

St Paul's Cathedral ★★★ HISTORIC SITE/CHURCH   The old St Paul's, with its magnificent spire, stood on this site for 600 years before it was claimed by 1666's Great Fire. It was so beloved that when Sir Christopher Wren was commissioned to rebuild London's greatest house of worship, he tried to outdo the original, devoting 40 years to the project and going one further by crowning it with a mighty dome—highly unusual for the time. It was also stark and plain, like the Catholics did their churches, not Gothic and complicated like the Protestants. My, how people talked.

St Paul's cost £750,000 to build, an astronomical sum in 1697 when the first section opened for worship, and now, it costs £3 million a year to run. Wren overspent so badly that decoration was curtailed; the Byzantine-style mosaics over the Quire weren't added until Queen Victoria thought the place needed spiffing up (and some purists are still complaining). Stained glass is still missing, but that just allows the sweep and arch of Wren's design to shine cleanly through. Many of us were introduced to the front steps by "Feed the Birds" in *Mary Poppins* and to the sanctuary by the wedding of Prince Charles and Lady Diana Spencer in 1981, but the pulpit also saw a sermon by Martin Luther King, Jr. in 1964 and Churchill's funeral the next year. Frustratingly, you're not allowed to take photos on your tour.

The **Great West Doors,** which are largely unused unless you're important, are 27m high (90 ft.) and on their original hinges; they're so well-hung that even an infirm vicar can swing them open. In 2005, the cathedral completed a £10.8-million cleaning program; a stone panel beside the doors was left filthy to show just how gloomy centuries of candles had made it in here. The **High Altar** has a canopy supported by single tree trunks that were hollowed out and carved, and its 15th-century crucifix and candlesticks require two men to lift. (They're nailed down, anyway. As one docent, a half-century veteran of Cathedral tours, lamented, "You'd be surprised what people try to steal.") Behind it is the **American Memorial Chapel** to the 28,000 American soldiers who died while based in England in World War II; in a glass case, one leaf of a 500-page book containing their names is turned each day. The **organ,** with 7,000 pipes, was regularly played by Mendelssohn and Handel, and the **lectern** is original. Give special admiration to the impossibly fine limewood

St Paul's Cathedral

carvings in the Quire by Grinling Gibbons—dark wood is original and lighter wood has been replaced or restored. Nearby, there's a monument to pretty-boy poet and cleric **John Donne** that still bears on its urn the scorch marks it suffered in Old St Paul's during the Great Fire (it was the only thing that survived the conflagration).

Eight central pillars support the entire weight of the wood-framed dome; Wren filled them with loose rubble. In 1925, engineers broke them open to find the debris had settled to the bottom, and they filled them again with liquid concrete. If you're fit, you can mount the 259 steps (each just an awkward 13cm/5 in. tall, but double-wide with some spots to catch your breath) to the circular **Whispering Gallery** (closed indefinitely), 30m/98 feet above the floor. Famously, its acoustics are so fine that you can turn your head and mutter something that can be understood on the opposite side, 33m/108 feet away. Climb higher (you've gone 378 steps now, and now the stairs get tight) to the **Stone Gallery,** an outdoor terrace just beneath the dome. Catch your breath, if you choose, for the final 152-step push to the **Golden Gallery**—you'll be scaling the inner skin of the dome, past ancient oriel windows and along tight metal stairs. There are three domes, in fact—the inner skin with the monochrome paintings by Sir James Thornhill, the leaden outside, and in between, a brick one that holds it all together. That's what you traverse—look sharp for ancient carved graffiti by tourists who preceded you in the 1700s, and look for the strips of metal installed by Benjamin Franklin himself when he brought his newfangled lightning protection system to the cathedral. It's safe, but it's not for those with vertigo or claustrophobia. The spectacular 360-degree city view from the top (85m/279 ft. up), at the base of the Ball and Lantern (you can't go up farther), is so beautiful it defies full appreciation. For more than 250 years, this was the tallest structure in a city that itself was atop the world.

If you miss the **Crypt,** you'll have missed a lot. In addition to memorials to the famous dead (such as Florence Nightingale and plenty of obscure war heroes), you'll find tombs, such as composer Sir Arthur Sullivan's ebullient bronze plate and the tombs of two of Britain's greatest military demigods: **Admiral Horatio Nelson** (whose body was preserved for the trip back to England by soaking in brandy and wine), and **Arthur, Duke of Wellington** (flanked by flags captured on the field of battle; they will hang there until they disintegrate). To the right of the OBE Chapel, in **Artists Corner,** you'll find the graves of the artists **J. M. W. Turner** and **Henry Moore,** plus, under a black slab by a window, **Christopher Wren** himself, who rests inside his masterpiece. "I build for eternity," he once said, and so far, so good: In 2010, the cathedral celebrated 300 years since its completion.

Volunteers, called "supers," lead a variety of free tours at various times between 11am and 3pm: 20-minute Highlights tours, 90-minute tours of the Crypt and Cathedral Floor, and short talks on the Geometric Staircase (to join any of those, ask when you arrive). You can also secure a 1-hour tour of the

The music sung during St Paul's services is hauntingly beautiful.

The Forgotten Colosseum

Guildhall, a magnificent stone structure originally completed in 1440 but heavily rebuilt time and again, was once where Londoners went to pay taxes but today is used as the City's most regal events space. Partly due to World War II's wrath, the collection at its **Guildhall Art Gallery** is perhaps second-rate (for this city), although its works depicting London can be interesting. But the real reason to come is in the cellar: the foundations of the eastern entrance of **London's Roman Amphitheatre**, 2,000 years old, which were discovered when the gallery was being built in 1987. Once the largest in Britannia, the amphitheater could hold some 7,000 specta-tors at a time when the entire population of London was only about 25,000. Slots carved into one of the rooms suggest there was once a trap door that could release wild animals to fight in the arena. Sometimes it's hard to believe the Romans trod the same streets as you, but here in the darkness deep underground, the bones of their abandoned plaything provide an eerie reminder. (Gresham St., EC2; www.guildhall.cityoflondon.gov.uk; ✆ 020/7332-1313; free admission except for exhibitions; monthly tours £10, booked online; daily 10am–4pm; Tube: Moorgate or St Paul's.)

high-level **Triforium** balcony, 141 steps up, for £10, but that must be booked along with your entry ticket. Listen closely, because the volunteers are the elder statesmen; many have been here for decades. Lest you forgot it's actually a cathedral, you can also worship here outside of sightseeing hours—for free (there's a service at 8am daily, but the Choral Evensong at 5pm on weekdays, after the tourists have gone, is atmospheric). When you're done inside, head just east to the **One New Change** shopping complex, where the free rooftop terrace has some spectacular close-up views of the dome—perfect for vacation snaps.

St Paul's Churchyard, EC4. www.stpauls.co.uk. ✆ **020/7246-8357**. Advance-purchase admission: £18 adults, £16 seniors and students 18+, £7.70 children 6–17, free for children 5 and under, family tickets £30.70–£43.70, all including a multimedia guide; walk-up prices £3 higher. Mon–Sat 10:30am–4:30pm, last entry 4pm; Sun open for worship only. Tube: St Paul's.

Tower Bridge Exhibition ★★ LANDMARK   It took 8 years and unprecedented spunk and ingenuity to build this iconic bridge, and you may wonder: How did such a distinctive monument survive the Blitz when everything around it got flattened? Simple: The Luftwaffe needed its proud towers as a visual landmark.

It's always free to walk across the bridge on your own, but visiting this museum is like getting two attractions in one. The first one satisfies sightseers who dream of going up in the famous neo-Gothic towers and crossing its two high-level observation walkways—once you've been inside, you'll never look at a photo of the bridge the same way again. In a portion of both high-level indoor crossings, a glass floor was installed so visitors can get giddy to the sight of the river 42m (138 ft.) below their feet—the floor is frosted so

This is Tower Bridge, not London Bridge, and it's an engineering marvel (as you'll learn in its museum—where you'll cross the upper level).

weirdos can't take upskirt photos from below. The second fascinating aspect (which you'll encounter by leaving the towers, walking along the bridge, and entering the machine room on the southern shore) delves into the steam-driven machinery that so impressed the world in 1894. The bridge's boilers had to be fed and tweaked 24 hours a day, and those Victorian mega machines are still there, in fine condition despite being retired in favor of electricity in 1976. A visit here is even more fun if it's timed with the raising of the spans, which is controlled by joystick from a cabin in the north tower—since lifts must be scheduled at least a day in advance, the website's "Bridge Lift Times" can always give you a head's up. At the turn of the last century, it was opened some 9,000 times a year to accommodate bustling river trade. Now that freight ships are too big for the Thames, it only raises about 1,000 times a year, mostly for pleasure craft. *Note:* Tickets are discounted if you also buy entry to the Monument (p. 192).

Tower Bridge (on the Tower of London side), SE1. www.towerbridge.org.uk. © **020/ 7403-3761.** Admission £11.40 adults, £8.60 seniors and students, £5.70 children 5–15. Daily 9:30am–6pm, last admission 5pm. Tube: Tower Hill or Tower Gateway DLR.

The Tower of London ★★★ MUSEUM/HISTORIC SITE   Every morning at 9am, a military guard escorts the keys to the Tower, and its huge wooden doors yawn open again for outsiders. It's the most famous castle in the world, a UNESCO World Heritage Site, and a symbol of not just London, but also of a millennium of English history. Less a tower than a fortified mini-town of stone and timber, its history could fill this book. Suffice it to say that

Tower of London

its oldest building, the four-cornered White Tower, went up in 1078, and the compound that grew around it has served as palace, prison, treasury, mint, armory, zoo, and, now, a lovingly maintained tourist attraction that no visitor should neglect. Exploring its sprawl should take between 3 and 5 hours.

The key to touring the Tower is to arrive close to opening, since intimidating queues can form by lunchtime for the Crown Jewels, located in the Waterloo Block at the north wall (farthest from the Thames), and the White Tower, in the center. Tickets are sold outside the battlements. Hit the Welcome Centre, just past the Ticket Office, and grab a copy of the free "Daily Programme," which runs down the times and locations of all the free talks, temporary exhibitions, and mini-performances. Plenty are offered—the Tower at times feels like a theme park with 1,000 years of history behind it. As soon as you're in, between the Middle and Byward towers, note the next time of the prime excursion: the 1-hour **Yeoman Warder Tour** (every 30 min.; from 10am Tues–Sat, 10:30am Sun–Mon; last tour 2 hrs. before close), led with theatrical aplomb by one of the Beefeaters—the nickname of the Yeoman Warders— who live in the Tower and preserve it. (There are about 100 Tower residents, including families, but only three of the 35 Beefeaters are female.) The tour (don't come later than 2pm if you want one) is engaging, but juvenile—expect bellowing and histrionics, each reciting an identical script with a gleeful fetish

A Beefeater leads a tour at the Tower of London.

for yarns about beheadings and torture. (In truth, you can count the people executed inside the Tower on your fingers and toes; it was considered an honor to be killed here, because it was private.) If you'd like your history delivered without vaudevillian shenanigans, head to the gift shop on the right after Middle Tower and grab an audio tour (£4), but do it early; headsets can run out. The official guidebooks (£5) here are pretty good, and they certainly help with orientation.

As you enter the **Crown Jewels** exhibition, you'll see archival film of the last time most of the jewels were officially used, at the coronation of Queen Elizabeth in 1952. After passing into a vault, visitors glide via people-movers past cases of glittering, downlit crowns, scepters, and orbs worn (awkwardly—they're 2.3kg/5 lb. each) by generations of British monarchs. Check out the legendary 105-carat Koh-I-Noor diamond, once the largest in the world, which is fixed to the temple of the **Queen Mother's Crown** (1937), along with 2,000 other diamonds; the Indian government has sought to get the stone back. The 530-carat Cullinan I, the world's largest cut diamond, tops the Sovereign's **Sceptre with the Cross** (1661). The **Imperial State Crown**— ringed with emeralds, the 170-carat Black Prince's ruby, and diamonds aplenty—is the one used in the annual State Opening of Parliament; the solid gold **St Edward's Crown** is for coronations. After those come candlesticks that could support the roof of your house, trumpets, swords, and the inevitable traffic jam around the 1m-wide (3-ft.) **Grand Punch Bowl** (1829), an elaborate riot of lions, cherubs, and unicorns that holds 144 bottles' worth and shows what it would look like if punch bowls could go insane. Because Oliver

Cromwell liquidated every royal artifact he could get his hands on, everything dates to after the Restoration (the 1660s or later). Clearly, the monarchy has more than made up for the loss.

The four-sided **White Tower** (completed in 1098) is the heart of the fortress, and for more than 200 years, it was the tallest structure in London. Touring its four cavernous levels requires much circuitous stair-climbing, but takes in a wide span of history, including a fine stone chapel, Norman-era fireplaces and toilets, the gleaming **Line of Kings** collection of the **Royal Armoury** (even small children can't help but notice the exaggerated codpiece of King Henry VIII's intricately etched suit from 1540), and some models depicting the Tower's evolution (it's been much altered, but the six smallest arched windows on the White Tower's south side are original to the 11th c.). Try to time your arrival on the top floor to take one of three daily tours (10:45am, 12:45, or 2:15pm) of the nearly 1,000-year-old **Chapel of St John.** After you're finished in here, you'll have an excellent overview of how the whole complex worked.

Once you've got those two areas under your belt, take your time exploring the rest. I suggest a stop in the brick **Beauchamp Tower** (pronounced *beech-um*, built in 1280), where important political prisoners were held and where you can still glimpse graffiti testifying to their suffering. In front of it on Tower Green is the circular glass memorial designating the **Scaffold Site,** where the unlucky few (including sitting queens Anne Boleyn and Lady Jane Grey) are said to have lost their heads. In reality, we don't know exactly where they were killed, but Queen Victoria wanted a commemorative site set, and because of the evident dangers of displeasing the monarch, this spot was chosen.

The **St Thomas's Tower,** from the 13th century, is closest to the Thames and re-creates King Edward's bedchamber with authentic materials. Beneath it, **Traitor's Gate,** once called Water Gate, originally was used to ferry prisoners in secret from the Thames. Torture was never a part of English law, but it happened here anyway, and the **Bloody Tower** was where some of the worst stuff went down. In truth, there were only 48 recorded cases of torture in the Tower, but that doesn't stop curators from devoting an entire room to a display

The Ravens, Forevermore

Ravens probably visited the Tower in the 1200s to feast on the dripping corpses of the executed, who were taken from Tower Hill (the public execution ground, near the present-day Tube stop) and hung outside the battlements as a warning. You've probably heard the legend that if the ravens leave the Tower, England will fall, but it's a modern superstition. Nevertheless, seven of the carnivorous birds are kept in cages north of Wakefield Tower; in 2018, one raven died of old age, but it has been replaced by a baby, Poppy. They are fed raw meat, blood-soaked cookies, and the occasional finger from a tourist dumb enough to get too close.

GREAT galleries

Hayward Gallery ★ Hidden on a back rampart of the vital nonprofit Southbank Centre, the Hayward hosts terrific blockbuster shows, which have included Ansel Adams, Roy Lichtenstein, 1920s surrealism, and a panorama of modern art from the African diaspora. Always modern, never staid, and back on London's art A List after a renovation completed in 2018—make an advance booking. It also takes itself quite seriously, which can be good for a laugh. Southbank Centre, Belvedere Rd., SE1. www.southbankcentre.co.uk. ℂ **020/3879-9555.** Charge for exhibitions £11–£20. Wed 11am–9pm; Thurs–Sat 11am–7pm; Sun 10am–6pm. Tube: Waterloo.

Saatchi Gallery ★ This landmark, the only resident in the three-story, 6,500-sq.-m (70,000-sq.-ft.) former Royal Military Asylum building (1801) in Chelsea, used to be unmissable for avant-garde contemporary art; now exhibitions are too often shills for luxury brands (Hermés, Rolls-Royce, Tiffany & Co.). Only commit if the current fare is a true artists' showcase. Duke of York Square, SW3. www.saatchigallery.com. ℂ **020/7811-3070.** Free admission, but advance booking recommended. Sat–Wed 10am–6pm; Thurs–Fri 10am–8pm. Tube: Sloane Square.

Whitechapel Gallery ★★ Since 1901, the Whitechapel has reliably led the development of new artistic movements. In 1939, it brought to Britain Picasso's newly painted *Guernica* as part of an exhibition protesting the then-current Spanish Civil War. Later it introduced Jackson Pollock's abstracts. There's always a challenging exhibition, talk, or screening going on. 77–82 Whitechapel Rd., E1. www.whitechapelgallery.org. ℂ **020/7522-7888.** Free admission. Tues–Wed and Fri–Sun 11am–6pm; Thurs 11am–9pm. Tube: Aldgate East.

of (mostly replica) torture devices. Don't forget to climb the ramparts for that classic photo of the Tower Bridge. Skip the Royal Fusiliers Regimental Museum, a dreary hodgepodge of military memorabilia.

Daily at 2:50pm, the guards parade outside the Waterloo Block to the Byward Tower. On Sundays, your admission ticket allows you to attend services at the **Chapel Royal of St Peter ad Vincula,** the Tower's church with a Tudor-era Spanish chestnut ceiling, at 9:15 or 11am; otherwise, the only way to get in, and to see the marble slab beneath which Boleyn and Grey's decapitated bodies were entombed, is with a Yeoman Warder Tour—salacious tales of gory fates are spun virtually on top of the graves of the people who suffered them, which by any measure is tacky. It's a shame the cheap histrionics of the interpretation strip this ancient Tower of so much depth and dignity.

Tower Hill, EC3. www.hrp.org.uk. ℂ **033/3320-6000.** Admission £29.90 adults 18–64, £24 seniors and students, £14.90 children 5–15; family tickets £52.20–£82.10. June–mid-Sept daily 9am–5:30pm; mid-Sept–May Tues–Sat 9am–5:30pm, Sun–Mon 10am–5:30pm; last admission 1 hr. before closing. Tube: Tower Hill or Tower Gateway DLR.

Other Attractions in the City

Bank of England Museum ★ MUSEUM The intermittently compelling tale of the B of E is recounted in appealingly patronizing but generous detail in a disused section of the complex. The exhibition is guarded like a fortress (you'll go through metal detectors) and accompanied by plenty of antiques from the vaults. There's a lot to soak up if you understand finance, but most people lose the plot pretty quickly. Along the way are some fun oddities, including an explanation of how the current polymer banknotes are made and reimbursement claims from families of *Titanic* victims. There's also lots of expensive swag, such as a primitive safe from 1700, heaps of silver treasures, and a gold bar so pure (1 part in 10,000 impure) that it was given to Queen Elizabeth as a coronation gift. Guess she didn't need it. It's also fun to watch monarchs age on the money over the years. The most popular exhibit is a 28-lb. standard gold bar, encased in a clear plastic box, that you're challenged to lift. The rest of the bank isn't open.

Threadneedle St., EC2. www.bankofengland.co.uk/museum. © **020/7601-5545.** Free admission. Mon–Fri 10am–5pm; last admission 4:30pm. Tube: Bank.

The Charterhouse ★★★ HISTORIC SITE Once you enter this once-powerful vestige of medieval England, opened in 2017 after being off limits since 1348, it's hard to believe you're still in modern London. These ancient collected quads and halls have been a monastery (brutally and gorily crushed by Henry VIII), mansion, school, hospital, home for the poor, and burial ground—it's still the last four, and in fact, you'll meet the skeleton of one longtime resident, a victim of the Black Plague in the 1300s, discovered in the digging for the new Elizabeth Line. A journey so winding makes for a hodge-podge of ancient things to amaze you: gardens and cobbled courtyards, slanted slots used by monks to receive food so they wouldn't have the disturbance of human contact, and a paneled Jacobean chapel (full of carvings of dogs and weapons, its patron's symbols) that miraculously survived the Blitz thanks to the protection of a mere wooden door that now hangs blackened on its hinges. The museum is free to see, but to truly get inside, you must be escorted. One of the 40 "Brothers" (even the women are called "Brothers") who have been lucky enough to be selected to retire here gives affectionate tours of what the last 700-odd years have left behind. On the afternoon tours, the smell of lunch still lingers in the great dining hall, for this time-stunned, one-of-a-kind hideaway is still in active use. On one tour I took, the Brother cocked his ear at the sound of church bells in the distance. "St Bartholomew's," he said. "The only set of bells to date from before the Dissolution. 1510, I think." At the Charterhouse, another miracle of survival, we can hear and see exactly what people did half a millennium ago.

Charterhouse Square, EC1. www.thecharterhouse.org. © **020/3818-8873.** Free admission. Standard tours £15 and Brothers' Tours £20 (both 11am and 2:15pm); book ahead. Tues–Sat 10:30am–4pm. Tube: Barbican or Farringdon.

Dr Johnson's House ★ HISTORIC HOME A rare surviving middle-class home from the 18th century (built in 1700), this slouching and brick-faced abode happens to be that of famous lexicographer Samuel Johnson, who lived here from 1748 to 1759. If you're hoping to learn a lot about him, you'll have to spring for a book in the gift shop. Little substance is provided in the house itself, which fortunately merits some mild interest on its own terms (the corkscrew latch on the front door, which prevented lock-picking from above, is an example). The rooftop garret in which Johnson and six helpers toiled to publish the first comprehensive English dictionary was burned out in the Blitz, ironically, by a barrel of burning ink that flew out of a bombed warehouse; you can still see some scorch marks on the ceiling timbers. Ink defined the house and nearly destroyed it, but it also saved it, because the printers who used the house in the intervening years boarded up the walls, preserving them. While you're here, pop round the corner to the wonderful Ye Olde Cheshire Cheese pub (p. 120). Dr Johnson sure liked to.

17 Gough Sq., EC4. www.drjohnsonshouse.org. ℂ **020/7353-3745.** Admission £8 adults, £7 seniors and students, £4 children 5–17, family ticket £20. Mon and Thurs–Sat 11am–5:40pm. Tube: Blackfriars.

London Mithraeum ★ RUINS   It's so beautifully produced that you won't realize until you're back out on the street how slight the whole thing was. In the middle 3rd century, Romans built a temple to Mithraism, a male-only religion now lost to time. The foundational ruins of the temple were lost, too, until 1954, when construction unearthed them. Moved twice since then, they're now displayed a few meters from where they started in what's now the sub-basement of 2017's Bloomberg London building. You're admitted by appointment in groups of around a dozen, shown a wall of some 600 Roman artifacts found here (and given a tablet, but not the time, to read the overly simplified captions for them all), then brought downstairs, where the recorded super-elocution of Joanna Lumley prepares you for the ruins themselves, which you finally see for 5 minutes in the last stage, the "experience." That's when you stand on a catwalk around the rocks and they're ingeniously lit with scrims of powerful light and you hear voices that simulate what a ceremony to Mithras might have been like. It's all just a theatrical new way to make a ruin interesting. In truth, we barely know a thing about what happened here. But it's presented with artistry, forethought, and a ton of money, and it's a rare tangible reminder of a history that goes back two millennia right where you stand.

12 Walbrook, EC4. londonmithraeum.com. Free admission. Reservations suggested. Tues–Sat 10am–6pm; Sun noon–5pm; first Thurs of month until 8pm. Tube: Bank or Cannon Street.

The Monument ★ LANDMARK   Back in 1677, it was the tallest thing (61m/200 ft.) in town and it made people gasp. Today, it's hemmed in by personality-free glass buildings. The Monument was erected to commemorate the destruction of the city by the Great Fire in 1666. Its height also represents the distance east from its base to the site of Thomas Farynor's bakery in Pudding Lane, where the conflagration began. There's only one thing to do in this fluted column of Portland stone: Climb it. The spiral staircase of 15cm (6-in.) steps, which has no landings, gradually narrows as it ascends to the outdoor observation platform. They'll tell you it's 311 steps to the top, but they're lying—it's 313, if you count the two steps before the box office. Check out the metal band snaking down the north side; it's a lightning rod, and it crosses along a Latin inscription blaming Catholics for starting the fire (the insult was chiseled off in 1831). Tickets are discounted in combo deals with the Tower Bridge Exhibition (p. 185). Go on a pleasant day (unless you'd like a good wind whipping) and be prepared to leave large bags downstairs.

Monument St. at Fish St. Hill, WC4. www.themonument.org.uk. ℂ **020/7403-3761.** Admission £5.80 adults, £4.40 seniors and students, £2.90 children 5–15. Cash only. Daily 9:30am–1pm and 2–6pm; last admission 30 min. before closing. Tube: Monument or Bank.

EAST LONDON & DOCKLANDS

The part of London east of the City encompasses many square miles and dozens of separate neighborhoods, but most visitors will only hear it referred to broadly as "East London." It starts around Shoreditch and Whitechapel and, as you go east, begins to incorporate rehabbed former industrial wastelands. **Docklands,** the area bordering the river, is rich in upscale condos and corporate offices. **Greenwich** is a gorgeous villagelike neighborhood on the southern bank of the Thames. And in Stratford, the biggest population center of East London, everything seems newly made, including the Queen Elizabeth Olympic Park.

Dennis Severs' House ★★★ MUSEUM This 1724 townhouse was dragged down by a declining neighborhood until 1979, when eccentric Californian Dennis Severs purchased it for a pittance, dressed it with antiques, and delighted the intelligentsia with this amusingly pretentious imagination odyssey—he called it "Still Life Drama." Other museums are unrealistically neat and cordoned off, but his house looks lived-in, so the past feels as real as it truly was. As Severs, who died in 1999, put it, "In this house it is not what you *see*, but what you have only just *missed* and are being asked to imagine." You could go during the day, but it's best for "Silent Night" (Fri evenings). As you approach, the shutters are drawn and a gas lamp burns. You're admitted by a manservant who speaks little. He motions you to explore the premises, silently and at your own pace. Suddenly, you're in the parlor of a prosperous merchant in the 1700s; the owners seem to be home but in the next room. Candles burn, a fire pops in the hearth, the smell of food wafts in the air, and a black cat dozes in the corner. Out on the street, you hear footsteps and hooves. Room by dusky room, you silently explore corners overflowing with the implements of everyday life. It's as if the residents were just there, leaving toys on the stairs, beds rumpled, mulled wine freshly spilled, tea growing cold. By the time you explore the attic, you'll have accompanied the house and its occupants through its decay into a collapsing slum. "Silent Night" is one of London's most invigorating diversions.

18 Folgate St., E1. www.dennissevershouse.co.uk. ℂ **020/7247-4013.** Silent Night (Fri evening) £20, Silent Visit (Sat–Sun afternoon) £15. Fri 5–9pm; Sat noon–9:30pm; Sun noon–4pm via timed entry. Reservations required. Tube: Liverpool Street.

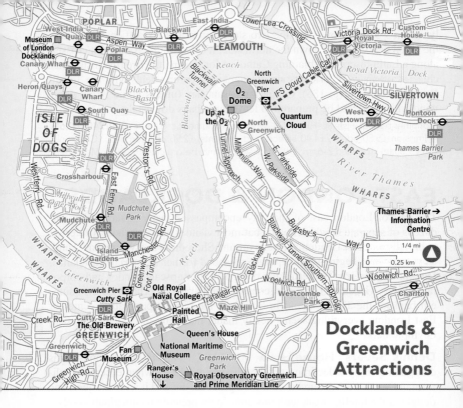

Docklands &
Greenwich
Attractions

Museum of the Home ★★ MUSEUM   This investigation of the home was installed in a place constructed for people who didn't have one: a U-shaped line of 14 dignified brick houses built in 1714 to house indigent ironworkers. Inside is a walk-through of the history of typical dwellings, which the museum calls **Rooms Through Time:** re-creations and sundry artifacts form abodes from the 1600s to the present, artfully arranged and explained with plenty of interactive diversions for kids (like squashing digital bedbugs). This under-appreciated institution, which opened in 1914 as the Geffrye Museum, explores all sorts of historical ephemera we rarely think about. What did mass-produced chairs look like in the 19th century? When did servants stop eating alongside their employers at the same table? How long did it take for mirrors to be inexpensive enough for average people to have one in their own house? Outside in **Gardens Through Time,** you'll see live plantings that mirror the popular botanical trends you'd have found in yards in the Tudor, Stuart, Georgian, and Victorian eras. Make sure to take a minute to unwind and inhale in the fragrant **Herb Garden,** in the northern-most cloister—it's one of London's most idyllic secret spaces. You can also visit the museum's restored almshouse, where charity cases were allowed to live back in the day. People in the past were so cruel to the poor! They blamed

Museum of London Docklands retells stories of the past with a range of family-friendly interactive exhibits.

them for their own poverty, left them to suffer without health care, and then blamed them for their own misery by calling them lazy! Good thing we're not so mean to poor people now.

136 Kingsland Rd., E2. www.museumofthehome.org.uk. ℰ **020/7739-9893.** Free admission. Tues–Sun 10am–5pm. Tube: Hoxton.

Museum of London Docklands ★ MUSEUM

Most of the city's museums would have you believe that London was always a genteel bastion of refined gentlemen. The real story lies in working men who shortened their own lives to put teacups into more privileged, manicured hands. Housed in a brick rum-and-coffee warehouse from 1804, the three-floor museum, strong on plain-speaking explanations, traces the history of working on the Thames. The most trenchant and effective section by far is the one that fully confesses and explains the sin of slavery, the profits of which powered London for centuries, yet which is rarely acknowledged with such depth at its museums. You'll also roam Sailortown, a creepy warren of quayside alleys, all shanties and low doorways, meant to evoke the area's early-19th-century underworld. Finally, the spotlight shifts to the harrowing Blitz, when the East End, taking the brunt of the Reich, was obliterated by fire from the sky and forced to reinvent itself as a corporate citadel. The whole circuit takes about 90 minutes because unlike the main Museum of London (which is closed until 2025 for a big move), there aren't very many rare artifacts to tarry over. There's also an interactive, river-themed play area for kids, Mudlarks (arrive close to opening to book free tickets), and plenty of places to eat overlooking the old hand-dug shipping dock.

No. 1 Warehouse, West India Quay, E14. www.museumoflondon.org.uk/docklands. **$020/7001-9844.** Free admission. Daily 10am–5pm; galleries close 4:40pm. Tube: West India Quay DLR or Canary Wharf.

Ragged School Museum ★ MUSEUM

The Victorians weren't very nice people. Although in 1883 as many as 60,000 London families lived in a single room, church-run schools still charged a penny a week and had a dress code, and the many kids who couldn't manage ended up on the street. Thomas Bernardo was headed for missionary work abroad when he realized East London kids needed him more than foreigners did; he took in the "ragged" children who couldn't even muster shoes, gave them an education, and made them his "home kids," feeding and nurturing them. From 1877 (when one in four children who lived around here died) to 1908, he used this canalside warehouse as a school—playground in the basement, classrooms (now re-created) up top—and he worked to help the most desperate kids emigrate for better lives. One in 11 Canadians can trace their ancestry to "home" children who went to ragged schools like this one. *Note:* The museum was recently closed for emergency refurbishment work. Check to see if it has reopened.

46–50 Copperfield Rd., E3. www.raggedschoolmuseum.org.uk. $ **020/8980-6405.** Free admission (suggested donation). Hours before refurbishment: Wed–Thurs 10am–5pm; first Sun of the month 2–5pm. Tube: Mile End or Limehouse DLR.

The Royal London Hospital Museum ★ MUSEUM

The Royal London Hospital has been central to London life since 1740, when it was established—supported by donations—to help the desperate condition of the poor. That history has put a lot of cool material in its hodgepodge archive, including letters by unfairly forgotten hero nurse Edith Cavell, forensic files from the Jack the Ripper case, a portion of George Washington's false teeth, and personal belongings of Joseph "The Elephant Man" Merrick (his bones are in a hospital archive), the sweet but luckless soul who lived in rooms on the premises until his death at age 27. You'll see it all, plus lots of skin-crawling, archaic medical instruments that will fascinate anyone who works in modern healthcare. *Note:* The museum closed indefinitely during the pandemic. Call to see if it has reopened.

St Augustine with St Philip's Church, Newark St., E1. www.bartshealth.nhs.uk. $ **020/7377-7608.** Free admission (suggested donation). Hours before pandemic closure: Tues–Fri 10am–4pm (closed 12:30–1pm). Tube: Whitechapel or Aldgate East.

Up at the O₂ ★★ TOUR

Built on a toxic peninsula wasteland on the Thames in the 1990s, the Millennium Dome was conceived as a showplace for what turned out to be a poorly attended turn-of-the-century exposition. It's supported by a dozen 100m-tall (328-ft.) yellow towers, one for each hour on the clock, in honor of the nearby Greenwich Prime Meridian—a preening and meaningless symbolism that cost £789 million, and then stood empty for half a decade. In 2007, however, it was finally reborn as the city's finest performance arena, with 20,000 seats (p. 275). Now, Londoners can stomp on it like they always wanted. Climbers, about 10 at a time, hook into a safety rigging system and follow a guide over a tensile fabric catwalk laid a few feet over the Dome's roof, to an observation platform at the zenith of the structure. There they pause for 15 minutes of photos of East London (the City is mostly hidden behind Canary Wharf's towers). Beneath them, humming like a ship at sea, is a Dome conquered. The excursion isn't for the height-averse—at your highest, you're 52m (171 ft.) above the ground—and it's not for big eaters or children either (the weight cutoff is 130kg/286 lb., and you have to be at least 8 years old). But it's also not scary, because you're tethered and the shoes they lend you grip well. If the weather's bad, you get matching jumpsuits like Ooompa-Loompas. The climb, which is more like a stroll up a steep hill, takes 45 minutes; the rest of the 90-minute experience consists of getting harnessed and psyched up.

Peninsula Sq., SE10. www.theO2.co.uk. ℂ **020/8463-2680.** Climbs £35–£40, depending on weekday/weekend/holiday/sunset/twilight. Minimum age 8, minimum height 1.2m/47 inches, maximum weight 130kg/286 lb. Daily 10 or 11am to 6–8:30pm, depending on season. Tube: North Greenwich or North Greenwich ferry.

Young V&A ★★ MUSEUM The awesome V&A Museum (p. 122) chronicles kid-dom through the ages at this location, pulling from a considerable archive of 33,000 toys, clothing, dollhouses, books, teddy bears, and games going back 400 years. Previously called the Museum of Childhood, the facility closed for major renovations in 2020 and is scheduled to reopen sometime in 2023. Its double-galleried glass-and-steel hall, which turned 150 in 2022, is itself an artifact; it began its life in South Kensington as the home of the nascent V&A collection but was re-erected here in the 1860s—the fish-scale mosaic floor was assembled by female prisoners, many of whom (in an ugly irony) were forbidden to see their own kids.

Cambridge Heath Rd., E2. www.vam.ac.uk/young. ℂ **020/7942-2000.** Free admission. Hours before the renovation: daily 10am–5:45pm. Tube: Bethnal Green.

Greenwich Attractions

Situated on a picturesque slope of the south bank of the Thames, Greenwich once was home to Greenwich Palace, where both Henry VIII and Elizabeth I were born. The last part of the palace to be constructed, the **Queen's House** (1616, Inigo Jones, p. 201), still stands, but most of the grounds were rebuilt in the late Georgian period as the equally palatial Royal Hospital, a convalescence haven for disabled and veteran sailors now known as the **Old Royal Naval College** (p. 117). High on the hill, in Greenwich Park, is the **Royal Observatory** (p. 202), and between them stands the **National Maritime Museum** (p. 198). Many of these treasures are owned by the state, so most entrance fees are waived; you can play the whole day without paying more than a few pounds. Most tourists come to get a photo straddling the **Prime Meridian,** the line that slices through the observatory and marks zero degrees longitude. Stop by the **Discover Greenwich visitor center,** alongside the *Cutty Sark,* for background information and to pick up a walking tour from the **Greenwich Tour Guides Association** (www.greenwichtours.co.uk; ℰ **0757/577-2298**). The Meridian Line tour is at 12:15pm. Tours cost £10 and last about 90 minutes.

Cutty Sark ★★ HISTORIC SHIP   The only clipper ship left in the world was launched in 1869; by the end of its 52-year career, it had traveled the equivalent of to the moon and back, carrying cargos including tea, wool, and furniture. By the sunset of its sailing life, it was a decrepit old thing, renamed *Ferreira,* having survived hurricanes in America and the loss of its mast in Cape Town. It was eventually dry-docked in Greenwich to show off for tourists, but worse indignities were yet to come: A 2007 fire twisted its iron frame and devastated its hull planking (fortunately, sails, masts, prow, figurehead, and deckhouses had been safely stored for a restoration). As you tour its hold, climbing stairs and weaving across decks (and banging your head on low thresholds), note that the white-painted framework you see is original, while the grey is new. Restoration provided an opportunity for the present lavish presentation: Today, it's as gorgeous as when Britain dominated the seas, and instead of floating in the Thames, it floats 3.6m (11 ft.) over a dry dock skirted by a glass canopy. At the end of a full ship tour, visitors can peep beneath the streamlined brassed keel. It's a slight cheat, because the hull originally was coated with Muntz metal, bitumen, and felt, but hey, it looks incredible. The ship will never be speedy again, but it's never looked hotter. Now you can also safely climb up its rigging partway on a tethered **Rig Climb** (up to £41, entry ticket included). If you're also entering the Royal Observatory (p. 202), buy a Royal Museums Day Pass combo and save a few pounds.

King William Walk, SE10. www.rmg.co.uk/cuttysark. ℰ **020/8312-6608.** Admission £16 adults, £10 students, £8 children 4–15. Daily 10am–5pm; last admission 4:15pm. Tube: Cutty Sark DLR, Greenwich river ferry, or Greenwich National Rail.

The Fan Museum ★ MUSEUM   This is as niche as museums get, but it's classy and it truly has the best of what it claims to honor—some 4,000 artful specimens, many of them precious, going back a millennium. Ladies are always fainting in English literature for a reason: In the centuries before air-conditioning, corsets severely restricted breathing and flames generated constant heat, so these tools were often the only things that helped fabric-swaddled women remain conscious. This charming collection of fans hosts regular exhibitions of the foldable lifesavers, such as collections of Christmas-themed imagery, Biblical themes, and so on.

12 Crooms Hill, SE10. www.thefanmuseum.org.uk. ℰ **020/8305-1441.** Admission £5 adults, £3 seniors and students 7–16. Wed–Sat 10am–5pm; last admission 4:30pm. Tube: Cutty Sark DLR, Greenwich river ferry, or Greenwich National Rail.

The National Maritime Museum ★★ MUSEUM   Don't be put off by the topic: The world's largest maritime museum is extraordinarily kid-friendly,

In Greenwich, visitors get a close-up view of the distinct shape of the hull that made the *Cutty Sark* such a speedy icon of world trade.

Appraising ship models at the free National Maritime Museum.

brimming with buzzy toys such as a giant play area that looks like a world map. So it's not as, ahem, dry as most would expect. Because so much of Britain's history from the 17th to 20th centuries was transacted via the high seas, there's a lot of meat. The facility has an endless supply of Smithsonian-worthy artifacts that would do any museum proud. In 2018, it expanded with some excellent galleries: In Polar Worlds, you see artifacts recovered from several ill-fated exploration attempts and hear by video from an Inuit man who explains how he survives the cold (the secret, surprisingly, is not wearing much clothing). Pacific Encounters comes to terms with British influence (islanders say missionaries were both "the coming of the light" and "one of the straightforward colonization tools"), and you'll see Fijian tattooing tools and a cannon thrown overboard from Captain James Cook's HMS *Endeavor* in 1770 to keep from sinking in the Great Barrier Reef; it was brought up 199 years later. The museum's crown jewels, ghoulishly, are probably the blood-stained breeches and bullet-punctured topcoat that Admiral Lord Nelson wore on the day he took his fatal shot (in a gallery devoted to the man). Also excellent is the Atlantic Worlds display, which plumbs the British role in the slave trade. The museum also presents the oft-ignored viewpoint that through the East India Company, England looted India—in fact, the English word *looted* has Hindi origins. It's not all so gloomy, though; there are big set pieces such as figureheads, models, antique instruments, entire wooden vessels, and a dark room just for J. M. W Turner's masterpiece *The Battle of Trafalgar* (1822–1824). Weekends are full of free kids' events (storytelling, treasure hunts) that bring suburban London families pouring into the gates, and the fun Greenwich Market is running nearby then, too.

Romney Rd., Greenwich, SE10. www.nmm.ac.uk. ✆ 020/8858-4422. Free admission. Daily 10am–5pm. Tube: Cutty Sark DLR, Greenwich river ferry, or Greenwich National Rail.

Old Royal Naval College ★ HISTORIC SITE/LANDMARK   This 1696 neoclassical complex, primarily the work of Christopher Wren, is mostly used by a university but offers two main sights: the Painted Hall and the Royal Chapel. The **Painted Hall** (daily 10am–5pm; £12.50 for a ticket good all year, £7.50 seniors and students; £5 first Sun of each month), fresh off an £8.5-million conservation completed in 2019, is adorned with 40,000 square feet of truly gob-smacking paintings by Sir James Thornhill that took nearly 2 decades (1707–26) to complete. It was the setting for the funeral of Admiral Nelson, but it may never have looked more glorious than today, following the removal of years of candle grime and crusty food splatters from rowdy pensioners' banquets. The **Royal Chapel,** in the Greek Revival style, is the work of James Stuart. If the ORNC's stately symmetry rings a bell, that's because it was used as a stand-in for Paris in the movie musical *Les Misérables*. It's also where you'll find the **Old Brewery** (p. 117), with plenty of garden space where you can kick back with very stiff pints.

Greenwich, SE10. www.ornc.org. ✆ 020/8269-4747. Free admission. Grounds daily 8am–11pm; buildings daily 10am–5pm; Royal Chapel open Sun 11am for worship and Mon 7:30pm for Choral Evensong. Tube: Cutty Sark DLR, Greenwich river ferry, or Greenwich National Rail.

The Queen's House ★ HISTORIC HOME   Viewed from the river and framed by the newer Old Royal Naval College, the Queen's House enjoys as elegant a setting a building could wish for. Inigo Jones took 22 years to come up with a Palladian-style summer retreat for Charles I's wife, Henrietta Maria, and his daring style set new trends in architecture that we still follow today. It was completed only in 1638—just before the Civil Wars cut both Charles and his schemes off at the head, and Henrietta scurried off to France. The house now serves as a picturesque setting for paintings, most notably *The Armada Portrait of Elizabeth I* (supposedly commissioned for Sir Francis Drake in 1588) in the Queen's Presence Chamber. Elizabeth was born in Greenwich Palace, which once stood on these grounds, and the artwork was acquired for £10.3 million in 2016. The nautilus-shaped Tulip staircase, plus other rooms, are considered to be haunted by an unknown specter, so have a camera ready.

Romney Rd., SE10. www.rmg.co.uk. ✆ 020/8312-6565. Free admission including multimedia tour. Daily 10am–5pm; last entry 4:15pm. Tube: Cutty Sark DLR, Greenwich river ferry, or Greenwich National Rail.

The Ranger's House ★ HISTORIC HOME   Although Ranger's House, on the western edge of Greenwich Park, is open only in the warm months, that's all right, because most people don't want to go in. They make a pilgrimage these days because it's used as the exterior of the Bridgerton family's

5

EXPLORING LONDON | East London & Docklands

manse on the television series *Bridgerton*. The stuff inside (the priceless art collection of a German-born baron of South African diamond mines) is sumptuous indeed, but poorly signed and explained, and none of his collection originated from the house anyway, which has a not-very-scintillating history. Chesterfield Walk, Blackheath, SE10. www.english-heritage.org.uk. ✆ **020/8294-2548.** £10 adult, £9 senior, £6 kids 5–17; reservations recommended. May–Oct Wed–Sun 11am–4pm. Tube: Cutty Sark DLR, Greenwich National Rail, or Blackheath National Rail.

The Royal Observatory ★ HISTORIC SITE/MUSEUM   Commanding a terrific view from the hill in Greenwich Park, with the towers of Canary Wharf spread out in its lap, the observatory is yet another creation of Christopher Wren (from 1675), and the place from which all time zones emanate. Historically the Empire's most important site for celestial observation, it now houses significant relics of star-peeping, but the paid areas aren't worth the money. Most of the good stuff is free, including a small Astronomy Centre and an exhibition on the challenges of marking time. If you pay for admission, your money only buys you an unremarkable ceiling-projection planetarium and the sparsely furnished, borderline-interesting Flamsteed House by Wren, which has a collection of 18th-century clocks once used to crack the mystery of measuring longitude (an advance that ushered the English Empire to worldwide dominance). Most people plunk down admission because it also buys access to the Meridian Courtyard. The Prime Meridian, located at precisely 0° longitude (the equator is 0° latitude), crosses through the grounds, and hordes of coach tourists pay to wait an hour for an Instagram moment of straddling the line with a foot in two hemispheres at once—but the secret is they don't have to. The line continues down the wall on the walkway north of the courtyard, where the Meridian is free and there's never a wait. In the old days, the red Time Ball fell precisely at 1pm daily so that the city could synchronize its clocks; it still rises at 12:55pm and drops 5 minutes later. You could set your watch by it, but technically, you already do. If you're also visiting the *Cutty Sark* (p. 198), buy a Royal Museums Day Pass combo to save a few pounds, but overall, the ticket structure is needlessly complicated. Greenwich Park, Greenwich, SE10. www.rmg.co.uk. ✆ **020/8312-6565.** Free admission for most of grounds. Flamsteed House and Meridian Courtyard: Admission £16 adults, £10 students, £8 children 4–15. Daily 10am–5pm; last admission 4:15pm. Tube: Cutty Sark DLR, Greenwich river ferry, or Greenwich National Rail.

OUTER LONDON

Dulwich Picture Gallery ★★ MUSEUM   A 15-minute train ride from Victoria and an 8-minute walk lands you in a pretty, villagelike enclave of South London, where a leafy stroll acclimates one to contemplation and appreciation. Here you'll find one of the world's most vital collections of old master paintings of the 1600s and 1700s, kept in just a few rooms. Magnanimous donors made it England's first public gallery (opened 1817), designed

Small but peerlessly curated, the skylight-lit Dulwich Picture Gallery debuted in 1817 as the first purpose-built public art gallery in England. It established a model for open-door museums that benefits everyday people around the world today.

with a surplus of light by Sir John Soane (who also left us his own cramped museum; p. 144). A visit is almost indescribably serene, the better to stare into the Cheshire Cat face of one of its star masterpieces, Rembrandt's *A Girl at a Window*—how did he capture her bemusedly frank expression? A handheld video tour unspools fascinating backstories of a few works you might otherwise pass by, such as the portrait of young Venetia Stanley, which exists because she was discovered dead in bed and her distraught husband summoned Van Dyck to capture her beautiful corpse. Twist ending: Her beloved might have poisoned her. The airy cafe is reasonably priced.

Gallery Rd., Dulwich Village, SE21. www.dulwichpicturegallery.org.uk. © **020/8693-5254.** Admission £16.50 adults, £8 seniors and students, free for young people 17 and under; special exhibitions cost more. Tues–Sun 10am–5pm; last entry 4:30pm. National Rail: West Dulwich Station.

Eltham Palace and Gardens ★ HISTORIC HOME

Eltham (*ell*-tum) was once a palace on the level of importance with Hampton Court or Greenwich—Henry VIII was a boy here. Time was not kind to the grounds, though, and by the 1920s, Stephen and Virginia Courtauld, a wealthy couple with no children, bought the Tudor ruin to rebuild into an ocean liner–inspired mansion for entertaining their movie-industry friends. The guided tour provides a delightful peek into the eccentricity and insularity of the wealthy—while it worships their entertaining skills, the evidence uncomfortably suggests they were simply awful people. Stephen was prone to sulking in public, and their obnoxious pet lemur, Mah-Jongg, had a thing for biting friends—in fact, it bit one guest, an Arctic explorer, so badly an artery was severed, which postponed his exploration by 3 months. (Note Jonggy's likeness carved into various architectural details.) Most country houses drive home stiff Georgian elegance, but Eltham is about the excesses of Art Deco living and a capsule of Britain between the wars. After they tore down some irreplaceable sections that might have had Tudor origin, the Courtaulds lived here only 11 years. The surrounding moat and 19 acres of greenery and gardens, however, still feel like they must have 400 years ago.

Court Yard, Eltham, Greenwich, SE9. www.english-heritage.org.uk. © **020/8294-2548.** Admission £16 adults, £14.30 seniors and students, £9.60 children 5–17; posted prices are higher and include voluntary donation. Apr–Oct daily 10am–5pm; Nov–Mar Sat–Sun 10am–4pm. National Rail: Eltham from Charing Cross.

The Freud Museum ★ HISTORIC HOME

In a hilly Hampstead neighborhood of spacious brick-faced homes, Sigmund Freud, having just fled the Nazis, spent the last year of his life here. His daughter Anna, herself a noted figure in psychoanalysis, lived on in the same house until her own death in 1982. Sigmund's study and library, which came from the doctor's famed offices at Berggasse 19, Vienna, were left precisely as they were on the day he died—which he did on a couch, of course.

20 Maresfield Gardens, NW3. www.freud.org.uk. © **020/7435-2002.** Admission £14 adults, £12 seniors, £9 students 12–16, free for children 11 and under. Wed–Thurs and Sat–Sun 10:30am–5pm. Tube: Hampstead.

Hampton Court Palace ★★ PALACE A 35-minute commuter train ride from the center of town, Hampton Court *looks* like the ideal palace because it *defined* the ideal. The rambling redbrick mansion was a center for royal life from 1525 to 1737, its forest of chimneys standing regally in 24 hectares (59 acres) of achingly pretty riverside gardens, now painstakingly restored to their 1702 appearance. Some people come seeking vibrations left by Henry VIII during the 811 days he spent here (yes, that's all; he had more than 60 houses, partly because his court devoured so much food it kept exhausting local resources). Others come because they've seen it on TV in *Bridgerton* as Queen Charlotte's abode (but in real life, she favored Buckingham Palace). The Crown still stocks precious art in many of the 70 public rooms, which start out Tudor and end up Georgian. It can take a whole day to see properly.

Historic reenactors at Hampton Court Palace.

The inflexibly programmed audio guide, which follows a handful of themed trails (Young Henry VIII's Story, Henry VIII's Apartments, and so on), is free, but it harps endlessly on the same old stories about King Henry's wives; if you're looking for deeper explanations, research beforehand. What you're told panders to Tudor scandals because curators apparently think it makes history more interesting. On a surface level it does, but ultimately, it reduces this famous location to little more than a stereotypical set of a tawdry bygone play. The staff can't even adequately describe the paintings on the walls because the Royal Collection, which loans them, keeps switching their locations at a whim. Days are full of live events, which may include reenactments of gossipy events by costumed actors; traditional cooking using bygone methods in the **Tudor Kitchens** (a popular stop); bizarre spoken-word performances in the hammer-beamed **Great Hall;** or ghost tours. Whatever you do, don't neglect the 26.7-hectare (66-acre) **gardens**—regally planted with historical accuracy (topiaries, sculpted yews, 300-year-old trees), they're half the reason to visit. Make time to lose yourself in the Northern Gardens' 500-year-old shrubbery **Maze,** installed by William III; kids giggle their way through to the middle of this leafy labyrinth. The well-mannered **South Garden** has the Great Vine, the oldest and largest vine in the world, planted in 1768; its black grapes are sold in the gift shop in early September. Wear sturdy shoes because the grounds are cobbled. Seeing this

TAKE THE thames TO HAMPTON OR KEW

From April to September daily, you can take **London River Services** (www.thamesriverboats.co.uk; *℗* **020/7930-2062;** £22 adults, £12 children 5–15) all the way from Westminster in central London to Hampton Court, the way Henry VIII did on his barges. It can be a commitment of 3 hours, however, with a change at Richmond on weekdays, and tides sometimes play such havoc with schedules that you may arrive too late to see much. Because of tides, if you want to tour the palace you will probably have to take the train the other way. Trains go twice an hour from Waterloo, take 35 minutes, and let you off across the river from the Palace: much easier.

consumes at least half a day, if I had to choose between it and Windsor (p. 323), I'd choose Windsor.

East Molesey, Surrey. www.hrp.org.uk. *℗* **084/4482-7777.** Admission £26.10 adults, £20.90 seniors, £13 children 5–15; family tickets £45.60–£71.70. Sept–June Wed–Sun 10am–5:30pm; July–Aug daily 10am–5:30pm; last admission 4:30pm. Check ahead for unexpected closures. National Rail: Hampton Court from Waterloo Station.

Royal Botanic Gardens, Kew ★★ PARK/GARDEN   The 121-hectare (300-acre) gardens, with many expansive lawns, earned a spot on the UNESCO list of World Heritage Sites in 2003. As you'd expect, the glasshouses are world-class—there are 2,000 varieties of plants, many descended from specimens collected in the earliest days of international sea trade. Of the seven conservatories, the domed **Palm House,** built from 1844 to 1848 and jungle-warm, is probably the world's most recognizable greenhouse, while the **Temperate House** is the world's largest glasshouse containing the world's largest indoor plant (the 17.7m-tall/58-ft. Chilean wine-palm, planted in 1843—and that's not a typo). In 2018 it completed a £41-million restoration, and it's full of some 1,500 species of incredible plants, some once thought lost, like the *Dombeya mauritiana,* and some, like the *Encephalartos woodii* cycad, extinct in the wild. Other attractions at Kew include a bamboo garden, a waterlily pond, **Treetop Walkway** (a tree-themed path 118 steps high in the branches), and, it must be said, a heartwarmingly charming village outside the gates. The gardeners are champs; in 1986, they coaxed a bloom from a portea that hadn't flowered in 160 years. Kew's contributions to botanical science are ongoing since 1759, but not mired in the past; it also provides a free app that lets you scan labels to learn more and find blooms. Unless you're a fevered horticulturalist, however, it will ultimately feel like a park you have to pay for—and pay a lot, at that. Also be aware that many of the goodies clamp down in winter (including Kew Palace, included in the price, p. 208), so this is best in the summer.

Kew, Richmond, Surrey. www.kew.org. *℗* **020/8332-5655.** Admission Feb–Oct: £15–£19.50 adults, £14–£17.50 seniors, £8.30–£9 young people 16–29, £5 children 4–15; Nov–Jan: £11–£13.50 adults, £10–£12 seniors, £6–£6.50 young people 16–29, £4 children 4–15; lower prices are for advance booking. Daily 10am–7pm (closes between 4–6pm in fall and 3pm in winter); last entry 1 hr. before closing. Tube: Kew Gardens.

Warner Bros. Studio Tour London—The Making of Harry Potter ★★★ MUSEUM London's most popular family outing deserves the acclaim; it's as gripping as the fine museums can be. On the very lot where the eight movies of history's most successful film franchise were shot, it seems that every set, prop, prosthetic, wig, and wand—and I mean every last thing—was lovingly saved for this polished, informative, and exhaustive walk-though feast. You could spend hours grazing the bounty, from the students' Great Hall to Dumbledore's roost to Dolores Umbridge's den to the actual Diagon Alley to the massive Gringotts Wizarding Bank lobby. There's not much filler. The biggest mistake people make here is arriving too late in the day, so book your entry time for around opening time and you'll have time to wander. Even if you care nothing about the movies, you will be blown away by the craftsmanship of items that got barely 2 seconds of screen time. The finale, an astounding 1:24 scale model of Hogwarts Castle embedded with 2,500 fiber optic lights, is 15m (50 ft.) across and takes up an arena-size room, lit to simulate day and night. Midway through the tour, in an outdoor area containing 4 Privet Dr. and the actual Knight Bus, you'll find one of the only places on Earth where you can taste Butterbeer and Butterbeer ice cream. And you won't *believe* the gift shop. Easy 15-minute trains (don't get on one that takes 40 min.) go three times an hour from Euston Station—but not, fans sigh, from Platform 9¾ at King's Cross, where London's official Harry Potter shop is. Wait just outside the Watford Junction station for the shuttle bus.

Warner Bros. Studios Leavesden, Aerodrome Way, Leavesden, Hertfordshire. www.wbstudiotour.co.uk. © **0345/084-0900.** Admission from £45 adults, £37 children 5–15, free for children 4 and under, £148 family of 4. Round-trip train ticket £10–£20. Reservations required. Daily 8:30am–10pm in summer and 9:30am–6pm in winter; check calendar ahead. First tours 9–10am, last tours 2:30–6:30pm depending on day. National Rail: Watford Junction, then a return shuttle bus (included in admission) that meets trains.

Other Outer London Attractions

Fuller's Brewery Tours ★ FACTORY TOUR Beer has been made at Griffin Brewery, this Thameside property in West London, since the 1600s, and Fuller's has been in charge of the brewing since 1845. Now this steampunk-feeling brick complex supplies some 380 pubs with its products, particularly its popular London Pride. They refuse to move to cheaper digs because a new water supply would change the flavor. Its tour is professional and engaging, more educational than bacchanalian—these people are passionate about their heritage. Free samples once you're done!

Chiswick Lane South. www.fullersbrewery.co.uk/brewery-tours. © **020/8996-2662.** Tours £25. Tues–Thurs and Sat hourly 11am–3pm; Fri hourly 11am–4pm; Sun hourly 1–3pm. No one under age 18 admitted. Reservations required. Tube: Turnham Green, then a 20-min. walk.

Home of Charles Darwin—Down House ★★ HISTORIC HOME Charles Darwin made one of history's most important voyages, but once back in England, he barely left his home here in the idyllic parish village of Downe. Upstairs you'll find out about the man and his life (did you know the scientist who theorized about mutation married his own first cousin?), and downstairs, guided by an audio tour narrated by Sir David Attenborough, you'll explore his study, his greenhouse, and his enchanting garden of lawns and breezy fields. No wonder Darwin never left again. There are two charming country pubs to enjoy while you wait for the bus back; your Oyster card will get you here.

Luxted Rd., Downe, Kent. www.english-heritage.org.uk. ✆ **01689/859-119.** Admission £14.80 adults, £13.30 seniors, £8.90 children 5–17; posted prices are higher and include voluntary donation. Mar–Oct daily 10am–5pm; Nov–Feb Sat–Sun 10am–4pm. National Rail: Bromley South, then bus no. 122 and 7-min. walk.

Horniman Museum ★ MUSEUM   A rich Victorian dilettante collected crazy stuff from all over the world, and rather than let it gather dust, he built a museum in South London. This repository of some 350,000 items has since blossomed into a wild educational ride, with something for everyone, particularly children. To wit: a cherished collection of 7,000 musical instruments (Boosey & Hawkes, once the U.K.'s largest instrument maker, donated its archive) and a huge range of items regarding anthropology (masks, puppets, folk art) and natural history (stuffed creatures galore). There's even a modest aquarium, a cafe, and some gorgeous gardened grounds on a hill with a panorama of London 10km (6 miles) north.

100 London Rd., Forest Hill. www.horniman.ac.uk. ✆ **020/8699-1872.** Free admission. Daily 10am–5:30pm; last entry to Butterfly House 3:30pm. Tube: Forest Hill Overground.

Kenwood ★★ HISTORIC HOME   Bask in a country-house high without leaving the city. Kenwood is a sublime 18th-century job by Robert Adam with a sigh-inducing southern view across Hampstead Heath, from within the green embrace of 112 acres. Inside, the walls are hung with paintings that would be the envy of the National Gallery, including Vermeer's *The Guitar Player,* a John Singer Sargent, and a Rembrandt self-portrait. The title character of the 2014 film *Belle* was raised by Lord Mansfield in this house, and the film was shot here. There's no better place to enjoy an English summer than on its acres of lawns or alongside its ornamental pond.

Hampstead Lane, NW3. www.english-heritage.org.uk. ✆ **020/8348-1286.** Free admission, guided tours £17.20 adults, £15.50 seniors and students, £10.30 children. House: daily 10am–5pm (summer until 6pm); grounds: daily 8am–dusk. Tube: Archway or Golders Green, then bus no. 210.

Kew Palace and Queen Charlotte's Cottage ★ PALACE   Remember George III? He's the dilettante ruler who, during his reign from 1760 to 1820, lost the American colonies and went crazy from suspected porphyria: See the movie *The Madness of King George* for the tragic tale. Kew Palace is where he spent his childhood and later went insane, and you can tour a piece of his vanished palace, restored with scientific exactitude. It's only the size of a standard manor house and lacks interpretation except for some ill-advised histrionic audio enactments that no one pauses to endure. Across Kew

Gardens, the little Queen Charlotte's Cottage is an imitation of a humble village home. Its Picnic Room is painted with vines across its vaulted ceiling—work attributed to King George's daughter, Princess Elizabeth. In late April, the cottage, which is at Kew's southwest end, is surrounded by bluebells in bloom.

Royal Botanic Gardens, Kew, Richmond. www.hrp.org.uk. © **020/8332-5655.** Included in Kew Gardens admission: Admission Feb–Oct: £15–£19.50 adults, £14–£17.50 seniors, £8.30–£9 young people 16–29, £5 children 15 and under; Nov–Jan: £11–£13.50 adults, £10–£12 seniors, £6–£6.50 young people 16–29, £4 children 15 and under; lower prices are for advance booking. Kew Palace: Apr–Sept 11am–4pm; closed Oct–Mar. Cottage: Apr–Sept Sat–Sun and bank holidays 11:30am–3:20pm. Tube: Kew Gardens.

Mandir ★ TEMPLE The breathtakingly pretty, many-pinnacled Mandir in northwest London is the largest Hindu temple outside of India. This fabulous concoction was completed in 1995, after some 5,500 tons of Italian Carrara marble and Bulgarian limestone were carved in India and assembled by volunteers. Its dome was built without using steel or lead. The interior is as white and lavishly detailed as a doily—it's apt to amaze even people generally unimpressed by such virtuosity. Tourists are welcome—try to be there to witness the musical wick-lighting Arti ceremony at 11:45am. If you're entering, shorts or skirts must fall at least to the knee (although ankle-length is preferable and sarongs are available to borrow); visitors must also remove their shoes.

105–119 Brentfield Rd., NW10. https://londonmandir.baps.org. © **020/8965-2651.** Free admission. Daily 9am–6pm. Tube: Wembley Park, then bus no. 206, or Stonebridge Park, then bus no. 112.

Thames Barrier Visitor Centre ★ LANDMARK/MUSEUM People forget that London floods. Parliament has been under water, and in 1953, surges killed 307 people in the U.K. At least, London *used* to flood. The Thames Barrier is the city's primary defense against it, comprising ten 20m (66-ft.) steel-and-concrete gates that can be raised to block the 520m (1706-ft.) span of the river in just 10 minutes. And it's doing it a lot more lately now that sea levels are rising and severe rain events are increasing—there's a big question about whether a more advanced shield will be needed soon. Most of the time you can't see the gates, which rest on the riverbed, but the piers that raise and lower them are always visible, strung across the river like a row of mini–Sydney Opera Houses. The Information Centre is now only open to groups, but you can still admire the barrier from shore.

1 Unity Way, Woolwich, SE18. www.gov.uk/guidance/the-thames-barrier. National Rail: Woolwich Dockyard or Charlton.

Wimbledon Lawn Tennis Museum ★★ MUSEUM Most of us can't get into the tournament (see "Netting Wimbledon Tickets," p. 211), and there's an 11-year waiting list to become a member of the All England Lawn Tennis & Croquet Club, the official name of Wimbledon. But for us, there's still something worth seeing the rest of the year. The museum is like a Hall of

An ornate entryway to the Mandir, a Hindu temple.

Netting Wimbledon Tickets

It's easy watching the Wimbledon Championships on TV for 2 weeks in late June and early July, but seeing it in person is a trickier matter. High hotel prices are just the beginning. Because tickets for the final matches go to VIPs, you're more likely to catch famous players during the early rounds, when the club's 19 grass courts are all in use. For the price of a "ground pass" (£18–£27) you can get roaming access to all but three courts (surcharges of £30–£180 are levied for Centre, No. 1, and No. 2 courts, and those tickets are distributed by lottery the previous summer). Around 6,000 ground passes are distributed each morning starting at 7:30am, so arrive many hours before that (by 5:30am at the latest) to camp in Wimbledon Park, Church Road side (no large luggage allowed). If you snag one, you'll probably be inside by noon, before matches begin. You can wander around to your heart's content, drinking Pimm's Cup and eating strawberries and cream, and watching matches on giant screens,

but you'll still need to get into the three most important courts. You can try by online ballot, but that closes in December. Meanwhile, Ticketmaster (and no one else; www.ticketmaster.co.uk) may release several hundred tickets for Centre Court and Court 3 the day before play. Another clever way to get in is to bum tickets off people as they get tired and leave for the day; just don't offer money—the organizers hate that because they sell unused tickets, too, for charity. Those are resold after 3pm to those already on the grounds (£5–£10). On weekdays and rainy days, your chances of getting unfilled seats for the best courts are better, because people are working or huddling indoors. And after 5pm, ground-pass rates dip to, at most, £18, which isn't such a bad deal because matches continue until 9pm. It's all ridiculously complicated—the English love complicated admission schemes—so check ahead on www.wimbledon.com to ensure rules remain the same.

Fame, with an emphasis of course on Wimbledon, with artifacts going back to 1555. The climax, most times of year, is the hallowed room shimmering with the silver men's "Challenge-Cup" and women's "Challenge-Plate," which are the actual Championships trophies inscribed with every winner's name. There is no other museum in the world where a ghostly video apparition of John McEnroe appears in a locker room to vent about opponents. (He comes in peace. No need to duck.) Tennis fans should absolutely spring for the tour of the grounds, too, which is truly all-access, including entry into the Competitors' Complex reserved for players, a photo op in the press conference room where they meet the media, and the all-important Centre Court, where finals are always played, and always on grass. The guides are fantastic and challenge you to stump them.

Church Rd., SW19. www.wimbledon.com/museum. © **020/8946-6131.** Museum admission £13 adults, £11 seniors and students, £8 children 5–16. Museum with tour: £25 adults, £21 seniors and students, £15 children 5–16 (one free child for each paying adult). Apr–Sept daily 10am–5:30pm; Oct–Mar daily 10am–5pm. Tube: Southfields, then 15-min. walk or bus no. 493; or National Rail from Waterloo to Wimbledon Station, then bus no. 493.

OVERRATED ATTRACTIONS

In every city, you invariably find attractions that are heavily publicized but, once seen, are revealed to be time poorly spent. London provides a variety of overpriced pursuits catering to people who are ignorant of its treasures—there's even an attraction by the London Eye about the movie *Shrek,* which needless to say you can safely skip. Take our advice: These are overhyped.

ArcelorMittal Orbit OBSERVATION TOWER   This 114.5m-tall (376-ft.) vertical scribble, a failing publicity exercise by a steel concern, has observation decks at 76m (249 ft.) and 80m (262 ft.), but it barely matters when there's not much to look at. It originally overlooked the Olympics, but with the torch and the games gone, it now peers into a stadium many miles from town. So tragic have attendance numbers been that in 2016 it desperately added a 40-second tube slide, the world's longest and tallest—narrow enough to bonk your head and fast enough to shatter your phone—that drops from one of the observation levels, wrapping around the structure 12 times. They put a helmet and elbow pads on you, tuck your feet into a cubby at the end of a mat, and send you screaming. Claustrophobes need not apply. On Saturdays, it offers an abseil thrill from 80m/262 feet high (www.wireandsky.co.uk; ✆ **020/3198-0407;** Apr–Oct; £95; reservations recommended; minimum age 14, maximum weight 120kg/264 lb.). Wear a jacket because it gets windy in the exposed areas. And no, it doesn't orbit.

Queen Elizabeth Olympic Park, E20. www.arcelormittalorbit.com. ✆ **0333/800-8099.** Admission £17.50 adults, £15.50 seniors and students, £12.50 children 3–16; tower without slide £12.50 adults, £10.50 seniors and students, £7.50 children 3–16; slight discount when booked online. Slide restricted to people taller than 4'2"/1.3m. Mon–Fri 11am–5pm; Sat–Sun 10am–6pm; slide opens 30 min. after tower opening; last admission 30 min. before closing. Tube: Stratford.

The Household Cavalry Museum MUSEUM   Along Whitehall, where guards try mightily to ignore buffoonish tourists who try to get them to crack a smile, this tiny museum pays soporific tribute to the martial ceremonies of the King's Life Guard. You might see troopers groom horses through a glass partition or regard cases of uniforms and regalia with glazed eyes, but—nothing against these dedicated marchers—you won't get much back on your investment. On the hour, mounted dutymen change, and at 11am, the Life Guard changes, but you can see those outside for free.

Horse Guards, Whitehall, SW1. www.householdcavalrymuseum.co.uk. ✆ **020/7930-3070.** Admission £10 adults, £8 seniors and children 5–16. Apr–Oct daily 10am–6pm; Nov–Mar daily 10am–5pm; last entry 45 min before closing. Tube: Embankment.

IFS Cloud Cable Car OBSERVATION GONDOLA   Opened for the Olympics as a Thames crossing between the ExCeL convention center and the O₂ dome, it's an enclosed, 10-person gondola with (barely audible) recorded commentary that shuttles between two places most tourists never go. It's too far from the City to be a panoramic substitute for the Eye or the Shard. Don't waste money on the packages that include champagne or "VIP Fast Track" access. The ride takes 5–10 minutes. It costs what a Tube ride does, and you can use Oyster.

Edmund Halley Way, E10, or Royal Docks side 27 Western Gateway, E16. https://tfl.gov.uk. © **0843/222-1234.** One-way fare £6 adults, £3 children; using Oyster card: £5 adults, £2.50 children (journeys do not count toward daily fare caps). Mon–Thurs 7am–10pm, Fri 7am–11pm, Sat 8am–11pm, Sun 9am–10pm; in winter, closed at 9pm Sun–Thurs. Tube: North Greenwich or Royal Victoria DLR.

The London Dungeon ATTRACTION   Avoid it like the plague. This sophomoric gross-out, with locations in 10 cities, sops up overflow from the London Eye. Costumed actors bray at you as you're led through darkness from set to set, each representing a period of English history as a 13-year-old boy might define them. The climax is a pair of indoor carnival rides. If you dread being picked on by bad stand-up comics, you're going to hate this place. Booking ahead may not save you having to queue. If you can't resist, at least bundle it with a ticket on the London Eye for a discount.

County Hall, Westminster Bridge Rd., SE1. www.thedungeons.com. © **020/7967-8023.** Admission from £31 adults, £25 children 5–15; slightly cheaper online. Times change but roughly daily 10am–5pm. Tube: Westminster or Waterloo.

The London Zoo ZOO   Yes, it has an esteemed history going back to 1828 as a menagerie for members of the Zoological Society of London. It's just that it's ultimately only a zoo, and a smallish one at that, with few large animals. Sumatran tigers, baby penguins, and a newly renovated monkey aviary are not enough to justify the high ticket price, especially for first-time London visitors who could be exploring the city instead.

Outer Circle Rd., Regent's Park, NW1. www.zsl.org. © **0344/225-1826.** Admission £26.50–£35.50 depending on when you buy and when you visit. Daily 10am to 4–6pm, depending on the month. Tube: Camden Town, then bus no. 274.

Madame Tussauds ATTRACTION   Have you ever heard of Mo Salah? Little Mix? Deepika Padukone? If your answer is no, you won't get much joy out of this ferociously priced, miserably crowded wax trap. The execution of its doppelgangers, which you can usually touch, is generally superb—you'll never get this close to the real Tom Hardy without consequences. But the focus of this world-famous waxworks is either on British celebrities or on *Star Wars* and Marvel characters. A 5-minute, Disney-esque ride, "The Spirit of London," invokes every conceivable London stereotype, from the Artful Dodger to plague victims. As you glide through, you'll suddenly wonder if you're the real dummy here.

Marylebone Rd., W1. www.madame-tussauds.com/london. © **020/7487-0351.** Admission based on time of year and time of day, peaks at £37 adults, £33.50 children 3–15; slight discounts online. Daily 9am to 4–6pm, depending on the week, slightly longer Sat–Sun and holidays. Tours continue at least 45 min. past posted closing time. Tube: Baker Street.

ritual ABUSE

I'm only telling you this because I love you: **Changing the Guard,** sometimes called Guard Mounting, is an underwhelming use of your time, even if admission is free. Arrive at Buckingham Palace at least 45 minutes before the 11am ceremony (10am Sun) if you don't want to face the backs of other tourists. A marching band advances from Birdcage Walk (often, playing themes from *Star Wars, West Side Story,* or ABBA—so much for traditional English customs), then members of the King's Life Guard—two if the king's away, three or four if he's in—do a change around their sentry boxes behind a heavy fence. And that's it, give or take additional prancing. It takes place Monday, Wednesday, Friday, and Sunday, and it gets canceled in heavy rain (Tube: St James's Park, Victoria, or Green Park).

Guards patrol all day, without crowds, at both Buckingham Palace and at Horse Guards Arch on Whitehall (which does its own, uncrowded change daily at 11am, or 10am Sun). Or park yourself at **Wellington Barracks,** just east of the palace along Birdcage Walk, by 11am, and catch the Inspection of the Guard that happens before the same guards march over to the palace for the main event. Then use the day's golden hours for something less touristy.

Ceremony of the Keys at the Tower of London (www.hrp.org.uk; Tube: Tower Hill, or Tower Gateway DLR) is held every night at 9:53pm as the Yeomen Warders lock up the Tower of London. It's been a routine for more than 700 years—not even German bombs canceled it. But it's an awful lot of work for not much payoff: You must enter the Tower at 9:30pm (several hours after closing time, so you can't combine it with a day's visit) and leave around 10:05pm, even though the whole show takes less than 7 minutes—plus, photos aren't allowed. As for the event, the Chief Yeoman Warder approaches the heavy wooden gate with keys and a lantern, is asked "Halt, who comes there?," passes muster, and locks up the gates to a bugle call. The end. If you want to see that, apply for tickets online (admission is free), with a nightly maximum of six places April to October. Spots are released on the first working day of each month for the following month.

Sea Life London Aquarium AQUARIUM   Sure, it's fun to see sharks under your feet and penguins on a faux floe. But sorry, Charlie, the truth is there is nothing here you can't see at other fish zoos. There are more than three dozen other locations worldwide by Sea Life, the McDonald's of fish tanks, and this one feels as cramped as a 16th-century galleon.

County Hall, Westminster Bridge Rd., SE1. www.sealifelondon.co.uk. © **0871/663-1678.** Admission £31 adults, £28 children 3–15, free for children 2 and under; discount online. Times change but roughly daily 10am to 4–5pm; last admission 1 hr. before closing. Tube: Waterloo or Westminster.

The Sherlock Holmes Museum ATTRACTION   Set up a house as if it were really the home of a fictional character, prop up some shabby mannequins, and then charge tourists to see it. That's the scheme and it works so well there's often a line.

221b Baker St., NW1. www.sherlock-holmes.co.uk. © **020/7224-3688.** Admission £16 adults, £14 seniors, £11 children 6–15. Daily 9:30am–6pm. Tube: Baker Street.

OUTDOOR LONDON

Buildings come and go, but London's open spaces have remained unchanged for centuries—they're the city's oldest places. There are often official walks and tours scheduled, so check websites to see what's coming.

Epping Forest ★★★ PARK/GARDEN   Mostly because its soil is unsuitable for farming, for a millennium this remained a semi-virgin woodland—it's the best place to get a feel for what Britain was like before humans denuded its land. It's the largest open space in London, 6,000 acres, 12 miles long by 2½ miles wide, and it contains a universe of diversity—650 plant species, 80 ponds where waterfowl splash, and even some 1,500 species of fungi. Getting lost in the woods is feasible, but not likely, because it stretches in a single direction. Henry VII built a timber-framed hunting lodge in 1542 that was inherited by his daughter Elizabeth and, astoundingly, still stands: **Queen Elizabeth's Hunting Lodge** (reach that via the Chingford rail station).

Rangers Rd., Chingford, E4. www.cityoflondon.gov.uk/eppingforest. ⓒ **020/8529-6681.** Free admission. Daily 6am–dusk. Lodge: daily 10am–5pm. Tube: Snaresbrook or Wood Street. National Rail: Chingford.

The Green Park ★★ PARK/GARDEN   The area south of Mayfair between Hyde Park and St James's Park was once a burial ground for lepers, but now is a simple expanse of meadows and light copses of trees. It doesn't

---

FAMOUS graves

London's top tombs don't just belong to royalty. Visit these historic area cemeteries for a tranquil day out and to say hello to some major figures.

Bunhill Fields (Tube: Old Street): *The Pilgrim's Progress*'s **John Bunyan,** poet **William Blake,** author **Daniel Defoe**

Golders Green Crematorium (Tube: Golders Green): Ashes of writers **Bram Stoker, Doris Lessing,** and **Seán O'Casey;** musician **Keith Moon;** dancer **Anna Pavlova;** actor **Peter Sellers; Sigmund Freud**

Highgate Cemetery (Tube: Archway; p. 216): **Karl Marx,** pop star **George Michael**

Kensal Green Cemetery (Tube: Kensal Green, and National Rail Kensal Green): Writers **Terence Rattigan, Anthony Trollope, Harold Pinter, Wilkie Collins,**

J. G. Ballard, William Makepeace Thackeray; engineers **Marc Isambard Brunel** and **Isambard Kingdom Brunel**

Royal Hospital Chelsea (Tube: Sloane Square): **Margaret Thatcher**

St Mary's Church, Battersea (Clapham Junction National Rail): Lapsed rebel **Benedict Arnold** (his crypt is now used as a kindergarten)

St Mary Magdalen Roman Catholic Church Mortlake (Mortlake National Rail): adventurer **Sir Richard Burton** (under a tent made of Carrara marble)

St Nicholas Church, Chiswick (Tube: Stamford Brook): Artists **William Hogarth** and **James McNeill Whistler**

St Nicholas Church, Deptford Green (Deptford National Rail): Writer **Christopher Marlowe**

have much to offer except pastoral views, and most visitors find themselves crossing it instead of dawdling in it, although its springtime flower beds (which bloom brightest Mar–Apr) are marvelous. Don't sit in one of those picturesque striped deck chairs unless you've got a few quid to pay as rent.

Piccadilly, SW1. www.royalparks.org.uk. *℗* **030/0061-2350.** Free admission. Daily 24 hr. Tube: Green Park.

Greenwich Park ★★ PARK/GARDEN The top of its clean-swept main hill offers one of the more marvelous views in London (of the river and the Canary Wharf district), and the world-famous **Royal Observatory** (p. 202), commissioned in 1675 by Charles II, serves as the intersection point for the Prime Meridian, making it the center of Greenwich Mean Time. Decently sized (74 hectares/183 acres), it was once a deer preserve maintained for royal amusement; a herd of them still have 5 hectares (13 acres) at their disposal. It's been a Royal Park since the 15th century, although the boundary wasn't formally defined until the early 1600s when James I erected a brick wall around it, much of which still survives. Most people combine a visit here with the many other museums of Greenwich (p. 197).

Greenwich Park, SE10. www.royalparks.org.uk. *℗* **030/0061-2000.** Free admission. Daily 6am–9pm. National Rail: Greenwich or Maze Hill, or Cutty Sark DLR or Greenwich ferry.

Hampstead Heath ★★★ PARK/GARDEN Some 7 million visitors a year come to the 320-hectare (791-acre) Heath, in northwest London, to walk on the grass, get enveloped by thick woods, and take in the view from the magnificent Pergola, a beguiling overgrown Edwardian garden and a true London secret. The Heath is a perennial locale for aimless strolls and (it must be confessed, George Michael) furtive trysts. The Heath has several sublime places to rest, including **Kenwood House** (p. 208), a sumptuous neoclassical home dating from 1640 and redesigned in the 18th century; and the inviting and woody pub **The Spaniards Inn** (Spaniards Rd. at Spaniards End, NW3; www.thespaniardshampstead.co.uk; *℗* **020/8731-8406**). The Heath's hilltop is another favored lookout point. The Heath isn't considered a park by locals, but a green space. The difference is irrelevant. It's transporting.

www.cityoflondon.gov.uk/hampstead. *℗* **020/7332-3505.** Daily 7:30am–dusk. Tube: Hampstead or Hampstead Heath Overground.

Highgate Cemetery ★★★ CEMETERY/HISTORIC SITE For fans of spooky stuff and of history, this grand but decaying necropolis has no equal. The two-section, 37-acre cemetery was opened in 1839 to serve a booming city. Time passed, though, and the classical stone carvings and mausoleum terraces, once paragons of Victorian memorial architecture and design, succumbed to neglect and vandalism. They now quietly crack, crumble, and molder beneath ivy and gnarled branches. Self-guided tours of the East Cemetery, where you'll find Karl Marx and authors Douglas Adams and George Eliot among the 170,000 lives here, have been possible for a while, but only

WORKERS OF ALL LANDS

UNITE

KARL MARX

JENNY VON WESTPHALEN,
THE BELOVED WIFE OF
KARL MARX.
BORN 12TH FEBRUARY 1814.
DIED 2ND DECEMBER 1881.

AND KARL MARX.
BORN MAY 5TH 1818, DIED MARCH 14TH 1883.

AND HARRY LONGUET.
THEIR GRANDSON
BORN JULY 4TH 1878, DIED MARCH 20TH 1883.

AND HELENA DEMUTH.
BORN JANUARY 1ST 1823. DIED NOVEMBER 4TH 1890.

AND ELEANOR MARX, DAUGHTER OF KARL MARX
BORN JANUARY 16TH 1856, DIED MARCH 31ST 1898.

THE PHILOSOPHERS HAVE ONLY
INTERPRETED THE WORLD IN
VARIOUS WAYS THE POINT
HOWEVER IS TO CHANGE IT

In 1883, Karl Marx was buried in his wife's grave off a side path at the evocative Victorian necropolis called Highgate Cemetery. His ceremony was attended by only 13 people. But in 1956, admirers moved the couple to a more prominent spot under a bold new memorial.

in 2021 did the deeply atmospheric West Cemetery begin allowing visitors again. There, among the moss and gloom of jumbled memorials, you'll find actor Jean Simmons, artist Lucian Freud, and singer George Michael. The 70-min. guided tour (£15 adults, £8 children 8–17; daily 11:30am, 12:30pm, and 2pm; reservations recommended) is unforgettable—it takes you through locked areas such as the shadowy tunnel of mausoleums of Egyptian Row and into the chilling Terrace Catacombs, where you'll stand in near darkness alongside actual coffins from the Victorian age. *Warning:* Wear sturdy shoes and stay on paths because it's frightfully easy to tumble into concealed open vaults and become a permanent resident.

Swain's Lane, N6. https://highgatecemetery.org. ✆ **020/8340-1834.** Self-guided visit £10 adults, £6 children 8–17; tours another £5. Daily 10am–5pm (until 4pm Nov–Feb). Tube: Archway.

Hyde Park & Kensington Gardens ★★★ PARK/GARDEN   Bordered by Mayfair, Bayswater, and Kensington, these two conjoined areas are

---

THE watery park

Sure, everybody knows about London's famous green spaces, but there's one recreation area, stretching from London's northwest to its east through gentrified lanes and industrial wasteland alike, that few tourists are told about. It's **The Regent's Canal,** which threads from Paddington through Camden, Islington, and East London before joining with the Thames (26m/86 ft. lower) just before Canary Wharf. It was completed in 1820 to link with canals all the way to Birmingham and feed the city's massive seagoing trade. In those days, barges were animal-drawn and the districts along the waterway were rat-infested and perilous, but today, it's one of the frontiers for development. Many of the horse tracks are leafy promenades, shadowy warehouses have become expensive loft condos. A new development north of King's Cross station is revealing even more glories. Along the shore, you'll pass docks where houseboat barges tie up; their owners can be found topside, making conversation with passersby. The most popular segment is probably the crescent just north of the Regent's Park. Set in a former icehouse, the **London Canal Museum** (12–13 New Wharf Rd., N1; www.canalmuseum.org.uk; ✆ **020/7713-0836;** admission £6, free audio tour on its website; Wed–Sun 10am–4:30pm; Tube: King's Cross St Pancras) is devoted to the waterway and operates tours of its towpath and boat tours of the Islington Tunnel, which stretches for 1.2km (¾ mile) under the streets. April to early November, **London Waterbus** (www.londonwaterbus.com; ✆ **020/7482-2550**), **Walker's Quay** (www.walkersquay.com; ✆ **020/7485-4433**), and **Jason's Trip** (www.jasons.co.uk; no phone) ferry riders in longboats through the 82m (270-ft.) Maida Hill Tunnel and the glorious villas that line the canal between Little Venice (Tube: Warwick Ave.) and Camden's markets (Tube: Camden Town). Ferries run in either direction, year-round; a ride costs around £17.50 for adults, £9 seniors and children 3–15. There are no tourist boats that currently ferry riders east of the locks at Camden.

the largest park in the middle of the city. Hyde Park is home to a meandering lake called the Serpentine, the famous **Speakers' Corner** (p. 161), and the **Diana Memorial Fountain,** a graceful, O-shaped fountain that undulates down a gentle slope. The most famous promenade is Rotten Row, probably a corruption of "Route de Roi," or King's Way, which was laid out by William III as his private road to town; it runs along the southern edge of the park from Hyde Park Corner. Kensington Gardens, which flows seamlessly from Hyde Park, only opened to plebes like us in 1851, and it hasn't yet shed its country-manor quality. You'll also find the **Serpentine Galleries** (west of W. Carriage Dr. and north of Alexandra Gate; www.serpentinegalleries.org; ✆ **020/7402-6075;** free admission and free audio guide through the Bloomberg Connects app; Tues–Sun 10am–6pm; Tube: South Kensington), a venue popular for its modern art exhibitions and its excellent art bookshop. Each summer (mid-June to Oct), a leading architect creates a fanciful pavilion there. Volunteers sometimes run guided tours of the park's quirks; check the bulletin boards at each park entrance to see if one is upcoming. Borrow a Santander Cycle and cruise around this giant green playground, and don't forget to look for Sir George Frampton's marvelous bronze statue of Peter Pan (1912) near the west shore of the Long Water.

Hyde Park, W2. www.royalparks.org.uk. ✆ **0300/061-2000.** Free admission. Daily 5am–midnight. Tube: Hyde Park Corner, Marble Arch, or Lancaster Gate.

Queen Elizabeth Olympic Park ★ PARK/GARDEN A dearth of trees and a usually bracing wind make this feel a lot like a theme park in which all of the attractions were torn down. Locals mostly love it because they remember when it was an industrial wasteland. The Pringle-shaped Aquatics Centre and Velopark make for striking architecture, but this park is mostly of interest if you want to see the place you saw on TV—yet the torch is gone, the stadium has been downgraded for a soccer team, and the ArcelorMittal Orbit tower (p. 212) is ultimately pointless. If you take the Underground there, Stratford station dumps into a mall (one of the nicest in the city); go up one level to exit.

Stratford, E20. www.queenelizabetholympicpark.co.uk. ✆ **020/3288-1800.** Free admission. Daily 24 hr. Tube: Stratford.

The Regent's Park ★★★ PARK/GARDEN It's the people's park (195 hectares/487 acres), best for sunning, strolling grassy expanses—it can take a half-hour to cross it—and darting into the bohemian neighborhoods that fringe it. Once a hunting ground, it was very nearly turned into a development for the buddies of the Prince Regent (later King George IV), but only a few of the private terrace homes were built. You will notice Winfield House, on 5 hectares (12 acres) near the western border of the park, which has the largest garden in London after the king's; the American ambassador lives there—surprised? The most breathtaking entrance is from the south through John Nash's elegant Park Crescent development from the 1820s, by the Regent's Park and

An aerial view of Queen Mary's Garden in the Regent's Park.

Great Portland Street Tube stations. North of the park, just over the Regent's Canal and Prince Albert Road, **Primrose Hill Park** (Tube: Chalk Farm or Camden Town) affords a panorama of the city from 62m (203 ft.) high.

The Regent's Park, NW1. www.royalparks.gov.uk. ✆ **030/0061-2300.** Free admission. Daily 5am–9pm. Tube: Baker Street, Great Portland Street, or Regent's Park.

Richmond Park ★★★ PARK/GARDEN   The biggest and wildest park, if you have the time, is 30 minutes from Waterloo station, in Richmond, which was once a distinct village but has been absorbed and yuppified by the greater city. It's more than a park—it's a habitat: 2,500 deliriously green acres brimming with herds of deer (since the 1600s!), 144 species of birds, and 11 of Britain's 17 bat species. Beeline to the Isabella Plantation, a 40-acre woodland garden, in May for a nearly pyrotechnic display of pink rhododendrons and azaleas. The visitor center is by the square in front of Pembroke Lodge, a Georgian mansion. Even if you don't have time to explore the whole park (no one does), you can follow the footpath on the south bank of the Thames for miles, starting by Richmond's waterside pubs and carrying on past ancient oaks (some nearly 800 years old) until you're ready to double back for a second pint.

Richmond-upon-Thames. www.royalparks.org.uk and www.visitrichmond.co.uk. ✆ **0300/061-2200.** Free admission. Daily 7am–7:30pm. Tube or National Rail: Richmond.

St James's Park ★ PARK/GARDEN   The easternmost segment of the contiguous quartet of parks that runs east from Kensington Gardens, it was laid out by James I in 1603 and Buckingham Palace redeveloped it a century

The deer that roam Richmond Park are descended from the ones introduced by Charles I in 1637. Keep your distance—they're wild.

later. Its little pond, St James's Park Lake, hosts ducks and other waterfowl. The Russian ambassador made a gift of pelicans to the park in 1667; a few still call it home, and are fed their 13kg (28 lb.) of whiting daily at 2:30pm at the Duck Island Cottage (during the pandemic, feedings were done in private). The park has a fine view of Buckingham Palace's front facade, where royal couples smooch on balconies (but live in a section of the building you can't see). The real draw is people-watching; a cross-section of all London passes through here. It's not a place for picnics or ball throwing, and there's little in the way of amenities or activities—unless you count voyeurism, and why wouldn't you?

The Mall, SW1. www.royalparks.org.uk. ℭ **0300/061-2350.** Free admission. Daily 5am–midnight. Tube: St James's Park.

Victoria Park ★★ PARK/GARDEN   This was the largest and finest open space in East London when it opened in 1845, the capital's first public park. Bordered by canals and divided in two by Grove Road, it covers an area of just under 87 hectares (220 acres) and contains two lakes, formal gardens, sports facilities, and a bandstand. Other notable features include a Grade II–listed 1862 drinking fountain and two arches from the pre-1831 London Bridge—now turned into benches. In summer, big music events come here. The park also forms the central section of the **Jubilee Greenway Walk,** a route marked out in 2009 with glass paving slabs in honor of Queen Elizabeth's Diamond Jubilee (in 2012), and stretching for exactly 60km (37 miles)—1 kilometer for each year of her reign—from Buckingham Palace to the Olympic Park.

Grove Rd., E3. www.towerhamlets.gov.uk/victoriapark. ℭ **020/7364-7971.** Free admission. Daily 7am–dusk. Tube: Mile End/Overground, Hackney Wick, or Homerton.

Walking Tours

The best ones are led by government-accredited "Blue Badge" professionals who go through a rigorous historical training program, so always look for a Blue Badge (or, sometimes, Green Badge) guide—there are more than 500 in town, and their trade group has a website, **www.guidelondon.org.uk**, that can matchmake them to your interests and schedule. Plenty of other qualified operators cater to custom business (many only cater to groups), but these will let you join individually. Also check that online compendium of day tours, **Viator** (www.viator.com). Tours around Bankside are conducted by **Shakespeare's Globe** (p. 177) from April through October.

Brit Movie Tours ★★   Most city tour companies try their hand at Harry Potter now, but this outfit specializes in movies, filming locations, and cinema history and hews in on entertainment icons like Bridget Jones, Doctor Who, *Downton Abbey,* and *Killing Eve*—its excursion about romantic comedies like *Love Actually* and *Notting Hill* is a particular hoot.

www.britmovietours.com. ℭ **0844/247-1007.** Walking tours around £12–£30 adults and £10–£21 children 15 and under.

City of London Walks ★★ The government that oversees the Square Mile of the oldest part of London gives written and performance-based exams to the experts who lead its excellent tours, which have been running since 1983. The experience is less casual and denser with facts than what London Walks (see below) generally provides, and group sizes tend to be smaller, too. The pandemic pruned the menu substantially, but the list should recover; expect topics like a Thames river walk, tours of Smithfield Market, and Dickens. No need to book; just turn up at the starting point because tours go rain or shine. Between May and October, the City of London Guide Lecturers Association also runs a few themed **Garden Walks** in the City, including historic gardens, the hidden gardens of the legal quarters, and the atmospheric Bunhill Burial Ground (schedule and reservations: www.citygardenwalks.com; £12).

City Information Centre, St Paul's Churchyard, EC4. www.cityoflondonguides.com. Tours £12–£17 via eventbrite.co.uk. Early morning or midday hours. Tube: St Paul's.

The Classic Tour ★ If you don't have all day, this summer-only, 75-minute whirlwind of the major sites gives you as much style as possible in a limited window of time: You ride on a modified double-decker 1960s Routemaster bus—for decades the standard for commuting Londoners—as a somewhat hammy guide gives you the quick lowdown on everything you pass, from Buckingham Palace to the famous Tower Bridge (which you'll cross).

www.theclassictour.com. ✆ **0844/318-7655.** Tours £24 adults, £18 seniors and students, £16 children 5–15. One or two tours daily in summer.

Dotmaker Tours ★★ Dotmaker's clever weekend (mostly) walks delve into offbeat topics such as chimneys, tunnels, where geniuses have discovered inspiration, where the city dumps its rubbish, and the seats of London's power brokers. One tour is designed around taking moments to people-watch and observe the rhythms of the town.

www.dotmakertours.co.uk. ✆ **07985/464-314.** Tours generally £20. Most tours Sat–Sun; reservations required.

Eating London Tours ★★ I recommend the 3½-hour, stuff-yourself-silly walking romp through some of the greatest victuals in the East End. You'll get to try tastings of flavors that are truly East End and not faked for tourists, from fish and chips to Brick Lane curry to Beigel Bake salt beef to a pint in an old-fashioned pub—all while getting a solid lay of the land from an entertaining guide. It also does a more expensive evening tour of Soho (£109; no kids on that one). Locations vary.

www.eatingeurope.com. info@eatingeurope.com. Text WhatsApp: ✆ **+31-658/95-6001,** or 215/688-5571 in U.S. Tours £79–£89 adults, £50–£69 ages 13–17, £50–£55 ages 4–12.

FlipsideLondon Tours ★★★ Clever people lead clever tour concepts that explore the underbelly of Soho from several angles, from gangster yarns to David Bowie haunts to The Clash landmarks.

www.flipsidelondontours.com. Tours £16. Fri–Sat. Reservations recommended but not required.

Footprints of London ★★★ For creative walks that aren't from canned scripts, tour with the truly passionate, accredited guides with a depth of knowledge who both own and operate this company; they come up with topics that are much more diverse and surprising than rivals': Art Deco in the West End, ghost signs on the sides of buildings, great paintings of London, Agatha Christie's Kensington, and even an exploration of spy hangouts. Great stuff! Have a look to see what they've concocted for when you visit.

www.footprintsoflondon.com. Tours £12 adults, £9 seniors and students. Reservations recommended but not required.

Free Tours by Foot ★ Okay, so it's not supposed to be totally free. At the end, you're supposed to pay what you feel it was worth. Fortunately, that means guides work hard for your approval, so these tours are highly rated. There are four to six choices (from Harry Potter to World War II to street graffiti) every day, so giving up £10 or £15 in thanks should not be too difficult.

www.freetoursbyfoot.com/london-tours. Tours mostly by donation. Reserve online.

Greenwich Guided Walks ★ Like London, Greenwich operates its own official tours with carefully vetted guides. There is usually at least one basic 90-minute tour daily from the Greenwich Tourist Information Centre (Discover Greenwich) that takes in the main sights plus the Royal Observatory and the Meridian Line. No booking is required.

www.greenwichtours.co.uk. ℂ **07575/772-298.** Tours £12 adults, £10 seniors and students, £5 kids 6 and older. Tube: Cutty Sark DLR.

Karl Marx Walking Tour ★★ It's often forgotten that Karl Marx fled Prussia and lived in the U.K. for nearly 40 years, where dire conditions shaped everything he wrote, taught, and thought about revolution and the rights of man. The world changed because of what Marx did in London. This excursion, fine for beginning economists, runs you past the landmarks of his life, many of which are still standing (such as the Dean Street slum where one of his children died of malnutrition—and he lost three others, too), and culminates at the British Museum, where he studied but you can run off and explore. The guide who created the tour in 2012, Mick Brooks, passed in 2021 from Covid-19, but his acolytes continue his edifying legacy.

www.marxwalks.com. ℂ **077/2252-3629.** Tours £10. Sun 11am–1pm. Reservations required.

London Walks ★★ Undoubtedly one of the city's premier tourist services, London Walks's tour list is inspiring. Although the Covid-19 pandemic trimmed its sails somewhat and reduced its output, on weekdays there can still be more than a dozen choices from Oscar Wilde to Harry Potter, and it takes care to match true experts to each topic. And on weekends, nearly 25, which means that if you ever find yourself with a few hours to kill, you can always find instant occupation. Every tour (most are £15) departs from a Tube stop, and none require reservations, which makes arrangements easy. On weekends, it unfurls a fun list of specialty themes (like a history of horses in the capital or tracking infamous East London murder twins The Krays). The marquee tour is probably "Jack the Ripper," which heads out to the streets of Whitechapel and, in the pursuit of ghoulish entertainment, employs considerably more grotesquerie than uncontested facts. Many of the group's other walks are more informative, including guided tours of the British Museum and Tate Modern. Other topics can supply authoritative tours on lesser-visited areas such as Hampstead village or the "Little Venice" near the Regent's Canal, places few other touring companies touch. Tours are 2 hours; prices and locations vary.

www.walks.com. ℰ **020/7624-3978.** Tours from £15 adults, £10 seniors/students, £5 kids 8–15.

Look Up London ★★★ Guide Katie Wignall started this thriving entrant in the field in 2015. She now employs several Blue Badge guides, who lead a slate of witty weekend tours ("The Feminist Jack the Ripper Tour," "Sordid Soho," "Bankside Behaving Badly") with quality and professionalism. Wignall also augments her tours with lively content on Instagram (@Look_UpLondon), YouTube (LookUpLondon), and through affordable downloadable history books, which help you get to know her fun-loving, groovy-librarian vibe before committing.

https://lookup.london. katie@lookup.london. Walking tours around £20. Sat–Sun.

Take Walks ★★★ This company operates in several cities worldwide, but in London, it shines via special access and innovative offerings that make for an intelligent replacement for tour buses. These include the exploration of Parliament, which goes into spaces most groups can't. It also sells passes that let you jump in on any of its scheduled tours and "London in a Day," a guided tour that takes care of admission to Westminster Abbey and the Tower of London (and you'll skip the entry lines), a Thames boat ride linking them, and the Changing the Guard.

www.takewalks.com/london-tours. ℰ **888/683-8670** in U.S., or 170/296-7516 in U.K. Tours £19–£129.

Tour for Muggles ★★ This well-assembled tour dispenses reams of Harry Potter trivia, from the books to the movies and locations from the movies. Groups of 20 start near the Monument Tube stop and wind up near Borough Market (p. 105). Because so much London history is folded in, there's enough for non-Potterheads. Book online. Tours are 2 hours.

www.tourformuggles.com. ℰ **020/4548-3535.** Tours £17 adults, £15 children 11 and under. No tours Mon. Tube: Monument.

Unseen Tours ★★★ London is more than kings and queens, art, and canned tall tales. See it from a raw angle, and plumb its modern issues, on a walk guided by someone who has experienced homelessness here. Walks go on four different routes—around Brick Lane, Covent Garden, London Bridge, and Soho. Tours last 2 hours; locations vary.

https://unseentours.org.uk. enquiries@sockmobevents.org.uk. Tours £15.

Escorted Tours

There are many reasons to avoid hop-on, hop-off bus tours. First, they're expensive. Also, after 10 minutes of rolling down the streets in these hit-or-miss tourist-processing machines, everything you've seen will blend into a miasma of antiquity. Third, these tours are like playing Russian roulette, because your experience depends on the skill and brains of your guide and/or the quality of the amplification system, over which you have no control. Fourth, gridlock.

Day tickets may come with a free walking tour (Changing the Guard, Jack the Ripper) and a hop-on, hop-off pass for the river shuttle boat (although some report that paying customers may crowd out passholders like you). Unfortunately, both of those perks must often be used during the same 24-hour period of the bus ticket's validity, demolishing their usefulness. Because tickets are sometimes given a time stamp that begins your validity period, don't print out any vouchers until the moment you're ready to use them.

HOP-ON, HOP-OFF

These get you there but won't include attraction tickets. Although many advertise "24-hour" tickets, keep in mind they generally only run between around 9am and 5pm.If you're thinking of using these because they'll take care of transportation for you, think again. The city's public transportation is much quicker, more frequent, and obviously far cheaper.

We do not recommend **Tootbus,** which used to be known as **The Original Tour London Sightseeing.** It attempts to allow customers to track the next vehicle with an app that, in our experience, is not accurate.

Big Bus Tours ★   Like its competition, it offers a few circuitous routes. There are three in this case, although two of them (Red and Blue) are most useful for city overviews, and narration is frequently prerecorded with filler music (it's live on Red, recorded on Blue, and broken more than should be acceptable) with out-of-date information. It doesn't matter at which of the 45-odd stops you get on, but because drivers often change at Green Park on Piccadilly, you can avoid that wait by starting there. Most people get on at Marble Arch, Regent Street south of Piccadilly Circus, Charing Cross Road north of Trafalgar Square, or under the South Bank Lion at Westminster Bridge. Prices can be a few pounds higher if you don't book ahead.

48 Buckingham Palace Rd., SW1. www.bigbustours.com. ✆ **020/7808-6753.** 24-hr. tours £37 adults, £28 children 5–15 (cheapest price is online); walk-up prices slightly higher.

Golden Tours Open Top Bus Tours ★   Golden Tours is one of the big machines in town, offering every permutation of bus tour and day-trip excursion you can imagine. None are particularly special, but they get the job done at low-ish prices, which means crowds. Its main product is a system of three routes, although the cheapest tickets limit the routes you can use. Its Classic

Tour covers most of the core city including South Kensington. Sold separately, its London Express Tour forgoes South Ken to get a circuit done in 2 hours, but is the only line with a live narrator. Commensurate with the lower prices, buses can be shabby. The same company also runs 2-hour bike tours (www.goldentours.com; £29 adults, £23 children 10–17, no children under age 10).

11a Charing Cross Rd., WC2; 156 Cromwell Rd., SW7; and 4 Fountain Sq., 123–151 Buckingham Palace Rd., SW1. www.hoponhopoffplus.com. ℰ **020/7630-2040** in U.K., and 800/509-2507 in North America. One-day tickets from £34 adults, £14 children 5–15, £76 for family of 2 adults and 2 children. Daily 10am–5pm.

RIVER AND AIR TOURS

You can choose between the narrated City Cruises tourist circuit or the similar-looking Thames Clipper "River Bus" (p. 361), now branded as Uber Boat, that commuting Londoners themselves use. I think Clippers are better: They have no narrators but they do have snack bars, Oyster card payment capability (unfortunately, the fare does not count toward your daily price capping), and a lot more options for places to get on and off.

City Cruises ★★★   When you take a standard trip on these generously glass-sided and -topped boats, live narrators point out details of interest. The Red Rover ticket allows you to hop on and off all day, which is a novel way to sightsee. Boats, which have cafe-bars, depart every 40 min., generally between 9am and 9pm, from four piers: Westminster, London Eye, the Tower, and Greenwich, which cover a lot of areas tourists like seeing. Using it to get to Greenwich and back costs a few pounds more than the un-narrated Clipper ferry service does for the same route.

www.cityexperiences.com. ℰ **020/774-0400.** Tours £14.25 single, £18.65 return. 24-hr. passes: £21 adults, £13.75 children 5–15, £42.25 for 2 adults and 3 children; 10% online discount. Does not accept Oyster cards.

London Eye River Cruise ★★   It's river tourism on speed, but it may suit a tight schedule: This scenic whirlwind takes just 40 minutes with a live narrator. It goes round-trip from London Eye pier, has a top deck (something the commuter ferries don't), and can be packaged with tickets to the Eye (prepare for crowds), but ultimately, it's less of a value than other choices because you can't get off to explore.

www.londoneye.com. ℰ **020/7967-8021.** Tours £14 adults, £11 children 3–15; slight discount for booking ahead online. Does not accept Oyster cards.

The London Helicopter ★   Six-seated choppers take off from Battersea and supply an epic bird's-eye view of the city, following the Thames to Canary Wharf, back to Hammersmith, and returning to Battersea in 12 to 18 minutes (the "Taste of London" route doesn't go west of the heliport but it gets the major sights in). Your pilot is pressed uncomfortably into double duty as a guide, dispensing dubious information such as dating the *Cutty Sark* 300 years before its actual construction. Never mind; the view is the thing, and it's an unbeatable view. You'll see the Shard from above, the ligature of countless rail lines binding the city together, and flights at 11:30am will spy Changing the Guard in the distance at Buckingham Palace. There are two seats in the front at the dashboard and four in a row along the back, so on shared flights, those two middle passengers get a bad view for the same money.

London Battersea Heliport, The Pod Building, Bridges Court, Battersea, SW11. www.thelondonhelicopter.com. *©* **020/7887-2626.** Tours £200–£300 per seat. Daylight hours only. Tube: Clapham Junction.

Thames RIB Experience ★

Touristy to the core and annoying to everyone except passengers, this outfit loads groups of about a dozen in semi-inflatable RIB speedboats with 740-horsepower engines and flits downriver to Canary Wharf, around the O_2, or Greenwich, from three far-flung piers. Try in vain to make a lasting memory of Canary Wharf flying past, your eyes blurry from estuary spray. Tours are 50 to 75 min. Its competition, offering similar thrills: **Thames Rockets** (www.thamesrockets.com; *©* **020/7928-8933;** £42–£57), which goes from close to the London Eye and from a pier near the Tower of London to Canary Wharf; and **Thamesjet** (www.cityexperiences.com; *©* **020/7740-0400;** £42).

Victoria Embankment (weekends, also from Tower Pier and North Greenwich), WC2. www.thamesribexperience.com. *©* **020/3245-1177.** Tours £30–£57 adults, £26.50–£41 children 15 and under; prices depend on tour length; max. 12 passengers per boat. Tube: Embankment or Charing Cross, Tower Hill, or North Greenwich.

LONDON SHOPPING

Blame Elizabeth I. Sure, the old girl loved her baubles and gold-embroidered bodices, but her biggest contribution to English consumerism was defeating the Spanish Armada. That established England as the dominant player on the high seas, which opened channels of international trade, and soon the Thames was more jammed with bounty than the parking lot at the mall on Christmas Eve. Ever since then, London has had a hankering for the finer things. Grease up your credit card!

Stores across the city generally open at 9 or 10am daily and close at 7 or 8pm, although boutiques may close at 6pm and the department stores and Oxford Street shops are often open as late as 9pm. On Sunday, relatively new terrain for British shopping, 11am or noon to 6pm is common (although arcane laws mean some stores won't make a sale until noon); very few places stay open past then. Expect crowds on weekends, when people pour into town from the countryside.

THE GREAT SHOPPING STREETS

Appropriately for a city obsessed with class, London's prime shopping streets aren't usually defined so much by what they sell as by how much you'll spend to bring home their booty. Most of these streets run a website listing which stores they host.

The Arcades of Piccadilly & Old Bond Street

Tube: Green Park. There are several iron-framed, skylighted "arcades" (many shops closed Sun), built by 19th-century blue bloods for shopping along these streets in any weather. The best include the longest one, Burlington Arcade, a block-long parallel to Old Bond Street at Piccadilly (watches, cashmere, handbags, Ladurée macarons); the Royal Arcade, south of Burlington Gardens (antiques, shoes, watches, and Budd Shirtmakers, in residence since the arcade's 1910 opening); and Piccadilly Arcade, across from Burlington Arcade (men's tailoring; it leads to Jermyn St. [see below], a harbor for haberdashery). burlingtonarcade.com; https://royalarcade.london; piccadilly-arcade.com.

Carnaby Street

Tube: Oxford Circus or Piccadilly Circus. Soho's famous street used to be for the mod crowd, but today its trendsetting looks are mostly found on Memory Lane. Instead, expect mainstream sporty choices such as North Face and Vans. Better for browsing is **Kingly Court,** a former timber warehouse converted into a mini-mall for 21-odd restaurants, cafes, and bars. carnaby.co.uk. Soho: www.thisissoho.co.uk.

The Burlington Arcade.

Cecil Court

Tube: Leicester Square. Distinguished by original glazed-tile Victorian storefronts, Cecil Court (it and St Martin's Court just north are said to have inspired Harry Potter's Diagon Alley) was once the cradle of British cinema, but today it's a holdout of the antiquarian book trade that used to dominate Charing Cross Road. Favorites are Marchpane, at 16, a trove of vintage children's literature; Storey's for antique maps at 1 and 3; and Travis & Emery, at 17, specializing in music and books about music. www.cecilcourt.co.uk.

Coal Drops Yard

Tube: King's Cross St Pancras. The former freight-and-gas wasteland of Somers Town, north of King's Cross station, is in the latter stages of a major transformation, and major tech giants are gathering their offices in it. The brick arches and viaducts of the former horse stalls and coal warehouses (the Coal Drops Yard) are reborn as one of the most successful revitalizations of the city's industrial Victorian past, full of carefully chosen shops (often, unique twists on known designers and brands), pop-up boutiques, and buzzy restaurants for sophisticated urbanites with ready cash. www.coaldropsyard.com.

Jermyn Street

Tube: Piccadilly Circus or Green Park. The quintessential street for the natty man for more than a century. Try Harvie & Hudson, Hilditch & Key (since 1899), Hawes & Curtis, and mahogany-lined Turnbull & Asser (1895)—dresser of Chaplin, Churchill, Charles, Ronald Reagan, William, Harry, and James Bond. There's also a growing number of shoemakers, such as Tricker's, which tend to be better as you move toward St James's Street. It connects to Piccadilly via Princes Arcade, which is also strong on shoes. www.jermynstreet.net.

King's Road

Tube: Sloane Square or South Kensington. The Chelsea avenue where affluent "Sloaneys" spend is where you go to dream—increasingly, about what King's Road used to be. Most of the unique stores have been elbowed aside by the same new names, but you'll find a few independent boutiques, high-end mommy wear, and some designer furnishings. The cafes on Sloane Square remain prime for watching rich kids. www.kingsroadchelsea.london.

Lamb's Conduit Street

Tube: Russell Square. This Bloomsbury lane is the ideal respite after a trip to the British Museum, with dapper men's shoes (Grenson, since 1866), hip young clothing names (Folk, Oliver Spencer), two Victorian pubs, a wine bar (Noble Rot; p. 82), the well-loved restaurant Honey & Co. (p. 77), which moved here in 2022—and no corporate chains.

New Bond Street

Tube: Bond Street or Green Park. The ultimate high-end purchasing pantheon runs from Oxford Street to Piccadilly, partly as Old Bond Street. Every account-draining trinket maker has a presence, including Sotheby's, Van Cleef & Arpels, Harry Winston, Chopard, and Boucheron. A short walk west, **South Molton Street** continues the luxury, but at a half-step down in expense. Check out Browns (p. 241), which gave Alexander McQueen and John Galliano early validation. www.bondstreet.co.uk.

Oxford Street

Tube: Marble Arch, Bond Street, or Oxford Circus. The onetime king of London shopping streets is on the downswing. Once anchored by worthy department stores, Oxford Street over the last 15 years has been undermined by major closures, and now the thoroughfare supports only a few stragglers (like Selfridges and Marks & Spencer), international "fast fashion" (Bershka, Uniqlo, H&M, Primark), some weird corporate players (IKEA), and a lot of empty storefronts and filler. Destination clothing shops and bookstores were replaced by fly-by-night businesses such as the American candy shops (American Sweet Dreams, Candy Surprise, and so on) that have aroused legal suspicion by never seeming to have customers in them. There's been a movement to pedestrianize nearly half a mile of this avenue, but so far the plan has hit snags. For the most part, the shopping action has moved to smaller boutiques—and online. www.oxfordstreet.co.uk.

Redchurch Street

Tube: Shoreditch High Street. This 6-block Shoreditch stretch, once rammed with cabinetmakers, today is at the forefront for stylists. The 150-year-old menswear brand Sunspel opened its first retail shop here; Labour & Wait (p. 249) vends desirable kitchen toys; and the late Terence Conran's super-chic hotel/restaurant/cafe complex Boundary, including the cafe Albion, seals the deal for scenesters. Around the corner, **Boxpark,** a hipster mall comprising five dozen rehabbed shipping containers, hosts both emerging names and slumming corporate brands, while **Cheshire Street** is ideal for vintage discoveries.

Seven Dials

Tube: Covent Garden. The pandemic dimmed the party somewhat, but every lane around Covent Garden still has boutique shopping appeal. Check out **Neal Street** for shoes, **Long Acre** for big clothing stores, and **Floral Street** for designers. www.sevendials.co.uk; www.coventgardenlondonuk.com.

Sloane Street

Tube: Knightsbridge. Offshore millionaires come here to feast at the top of the consumerist food chain: Bulgari, Valentino, Miu Miu, Prada, Chanel, and everything else haute and showy. And no farther than you can throw a choco-late truffle, Harvey Nichols and Harrods. www.sloanestreet.co.uk.

THE SHOPPING PALACES

Fortnum & Mason ★★★   So venerable is this vendor, which began life in 1707 as the candlemaker to Queen Anne, that in 1922 archaeologist How-ard Carter used empty F&M boxes to tote home the treasures of King Tut's tomb. The quintessentially British, modestly sized department store, which has a focus on gourmet foods, is renowned for its glamorous food hampers. These were first distributed in the days before World War I, when soldiers' families were responsible for feeding their men on the field. Picnic sets now come with bone china and can cost £300, but you can also pack your own. For the full experience, which will leave your heirs with no inheritance, head to the first floor to peruse its famous wicker hampers, which you can then fill with goodies from the ground-floor Food Hall and have shipped. Select from a cornucopia of such tongue-teasing triumphs as jarred black truffles and fresh Blue Stilton cheese in ceramic pots. In addition to a huge selection of truffles, sauces, and pickles, F&M makes its own "parlour ice" (ice creams), stocks countless types of honey in the comb and "royal game pie" (loaves of seasonal game meats layered with cheese), and presents varieties of tea that will sur-pass your understanding of the topic. Most wares are available in small, pack-able sizes but you can content yourself, as most do, with a wander through the carpeted upper-floor departments, which are lit by chandelier, serenaded by classical music, and illuminated by a lotus-like atrium skylight. The fragrance department smells like a rose garden. High tea can be taken in the Tea Salon, since 1926 among the city's most sumptuous (reservations ℂ **020/7734-8040**), while lunching ladies can be found in the excellent corner brasserie called 45 Jermyn St., which in 2015 replaced the Fountain Restaurant after its 6-decade run. When the clock strikes the hour over the store's Piccadilly entrance, two modern mechanical representations of Mr. Fortnum and Mr. Mason emerge, bow to each other approvingly, and return to business inside.

An entrance to Fortnum & Mason, a foodie department store renowned for its elegant picnic hampers.

181 Piccadilly, W1. www.fortnumandmason.com. © **020/7734-8040.** Tube: Green Park or Piccadilly Circus.

Harrods ★   Now owned by the Qatari royal family's financiers, a miraculous holdover from the golden age of shopping has been retooled into a bombastic mall appealing largely to free-spending out-of-towners. Few London-born people bother with it, yet it thrives, proof of just how awash with foreign fortunes the city truly is. Its thronged but terrific Food Hall rooms are a glut of exorbitantly priced meats and cheeses, its ornate seven-floor facade emblazoned like a Christmas tree after dark, its jewelry hall attended by robotic staff plying the husbands of spoiled wives with champagne until they give in. But much floor space, where too-loud rock music blares nonstop, is devoted either to brands you'd find for a third of the price at your local mall or to One-Percenter nonsense such as £150,000 sculptures. The artificial environment, from the overpriced razzmatazz to the clerks wearing straw hats, would be more authentic at Disneyland than in London of old. In the souvenir "emporium" on the second floor (£37 for Harrods gusset bags; £21 mugs; teddy bears aplenty), I sense the air has been pumped with the same scent you smell at Disney wherever the company wants to coax customers into purchasing (a trick called "olfactory coding"). Of the many escalator banks, the most interesting is the uproarious Egyptian-themed one at the store's center. If you crave a real British department store, visit Fortnum & Mason or Selfridges; if you want to be flabbergasted by the pompous excesses of the jet set, Harrods is the overly shellacked circus for you, but don't be fooled into thinking it's something traditional. 87–135 Brompton Rd., SW1. www.harrods.com. ✆ **020/7730-1234.** Tube: Knightsbridge.

Harvey Nichols ★   The shallow anti-heroines Patsy and Edina of *Absolutely Fabulous* spoke of it with the same breathless reverence most people reserve for deities. You'll need the income of a god to afford a single thread of Harvey Nick's women's and men's fashions, and although the British-owned store isn't as popular as it used to be—it's been here since the 1880s—a stroll through this eight-floor spendthrift's heaven is entertaining. Note the lunching ladies on display in the fifth-floor restaurant—think of it as a zoo for old money. 109–125 Knightsbridge, SW1. www.harveynichols.com. ✆ **020/7235-5000.** Tube: Knightsbridge.

John Lewis ★★   Everyone English knows that if you want a sound deal, you go here, where there's a price guarantee; it employs an army of people to scout for the lowest prices in the area, which it matches. That may sound like the gimmick of a low-rent wannabe, but John Lewis, established in 1864, is in fact a respected cooperative owned by its employees. Still, times are changing and it's slowing down. In recent years, the company has investigated turning part of its Oxford Street flagship into offices. Art fans shouldn't miss the building's eastern face, upon which is mounted an abstract cast-aluminum sculpture, *The Winged Figure* (1960), by one of the most important artists of the 20th century, Dame Barbara Hepworth, whose work is in the Tate Britain (p. 151). Oxford St. at Holles St. www.johnlewis.com/oxfordstreet. ✆ **020/7629-7711.** Tube: Oxford Circus.

Liberty ★★   Founded in 1875, Liberty made its name (and earned some mockery) as an importer of Asian art and as a major proponent of Art Nouveau style and of dresses that freed ladies from the tyranny of corsets. Now its focus is distinctly British. The timber-and-plaster wing looks Tudor, but it is actually a 1924 revival constructed from the salvaged timbers of two ships, HMS *Impregnable* and HMS *Hindustan;* the length of the latter ship equals the building's length along Great Marlborough Street. The store's stationery and scarf selections are deservedly celebrated, as are its fabrics (many of which are designed in-house or only available briefly), and the beauty hall is one of

At Liberty, an in-house design team crafts beautiful bespoke fabrics.

FACING PAGE: The bronze Queen of Time clock has welcomed shoppers from high on the facade of Selfridges since 1931.

the best. The soft wooden spaces are creaky and seductive, while the staff service is so obsequious it evokes a bygone era. 210–220 Regent St., W1. www. liberty.co.uk. ℭ **020/7734-1234.** Tube: Oxford Circus.

Marks & Spencer ★★★   The beloved M&S is the country's favorite mid-level department store for good-looking clothing staples. Its own-brand looks, once shoddy and ill-fitting, have been re-envisioned as affordable riffs on well-tailored fashions, and it sells the go-to suit for many a young man starting out in life. M&S is particularly beloved for its underwear, and its bathrobes are preternaturally soft. But its crowning achievement is its giant **food halls** ★★★ (usually tucked underneath the store but sometimes a stand-alone shop called **Simply Food**), which sell an astonishing array of prepared meals, soups and sandwiches, and well-selected yet inexpensive wines. M&S is a national middle-class treasure. Flagship: 458 Oxford St., W1. www.marksand spencer.co.uk. ℭ **020/7935-7954.** Tube: Marble Arch.

Selfridges ★★★   Selfridges fills the real-life role in London life that many tourists think Harrods does; aside from Harrods' olive drab sacks, no shopping bag speaks louder about your shopping preferences than a canary yellow screamer from Selfridges. It's unquestionably the better of the two stores, since it's not merely a sprawling sensory treat, but also sells items you'd actually buy. Since its 1909 opening by Harry Gordon Selfridge, an immoderate American marketing genius from Marshall Field's in Chicago (the building was designed by Daniel Burnham, of Manhattan's Flatiron Building fame), Selfridges has pioneered many department store practices. Placing the perfumes near the front door, filling its 27 ground-floor windows with consumerist fantasias, coining the phrase "the customer is always right"—all Selfridges inventions. Some one million products are for sale, and the beauty department is Europe's largest. The thicket of food counters on the ground floor gets busy at lunchtime, and the rest of the store is just as popular at other times; some 17 million visits are recorded each year. Selfridges has traded in history, too; the first public demonstration of television was held on the first floor in 1925, and 3 years later, the store sold the world's first TV set. During much of the Blitz, Churchill's transatlantic conversations with FDR were encoded via a scrambler stashed in the cellar. The store's popularity got a goose thanks to the series *Mr. Selfridge,* with Jeremy Piven barking his way through the title role, which gives the store the soapy treatment. 400 Oxford St., W1. www.selfridges.com. ℭ **0800/123-400** (U.K.) or 113/369-8040 (overseas). Tube: Bond Street or Marble Arch.

RECOMMENDED STORES

For a city world-famous for shopping, where people from around the world arrive with one fat wallet and leave with 10 stuffed suitcases, there's no way to give proper celebratory due to everything that is wonderful and for sale. Some stores, though, are so original and site-specific that they can sweeten the experience of being in London, even if you don't buy a thing.

Art & Antiques

Blue Mantle ★   For dream renovations back home, the largest antique fireplace showroom in the world salvages the good stuff with warm English touches when developers knock down classic buildings—which is happening more than we like. 306–312 Old Kent Rd., SE1. www.bluemantle.co.uk. ✆ **020/7703-7437.** Tube: Borough.

Camden Passage ★★   Plenty of tourists swing through the booths, so bargains aren't always easy to come by. Still, shimmering examples of china, silverware, cocktail shakers, military medals, coins, and countless other hand-me-downs overflow the cases. Despite the name, it's in Islington. Off Upper St., N1. www.camdenpassageislington.co.uk. Market on Wed, Sat, smaller one Sun. Tube: Angel.

Grays ★★   Not the place to go if you're looking for the lowest deal (it's in Mayfair), but it's definitely a source for variety. Some 100 vendors, many experts registered in the official antiques societies, are split among two buildings, selling everything from Victorian jewelry to toys to strange bric-a-brac and collectible silverware. Weekdays are best. Head into the basement of the Mews building to see the River Tyburn, which was buried by 18th-century redevelopment but now feeds into Grays' goldfish trough. Grays is closed on weekends. 58 Davies St., W1. www.graysantiques.com. ✆ **020/7629-7034.** Tube: Bond Street.

LASSCo ★★   From stained glass to paneling and faucets to wood flooring, you'll get an incredible selection of fittings and furniture rescued from museums, churches, pubs, and homes at LASSCo (the London Architectural Salvage and Supply Company). It's closed on weekends. 41 Maltby St., SE1. www.lassco.co.uk. ✆ **020/7394-8061.** Tube: Bermondsey. Also at Brunswick House: 30 Wandsworth Rd., SW8. ✆ **020/7394-2100.** Tube: Vauxhall.

The Best Museum Shops

Many London museums are free, which means they must get creative about making money in other ways. Some of their gift shops would be worth a visit even if there weren't priceless exhibits attached. All can be accessed for free.

The British Library (p. 123): Literary totes, toys, and tomes

Churchill War Rooms (p. 148): World War II posters, postcards, and novelties

The Design Museum (p. 173): Selection of clever gadgets and conversation pieces actually better than the museum itself

London Transport Museum (p. 136): Tube-themed bags, clothes, reproduction posters; items made from the same fabric ("moquette") as Underground seats; plus, a big selection of train toys and books

Tate Modern (p. 179): Gifts, books about art and London, prints, and the Tate Edit line of slick homewares

The V&A (p. 169): Gorgeous fabrics, handbags, jewelry, stationery, and design glass—a mega-emporium of good taste

Books

The territorial nature of copyrights means that many books that are for sale in London won't be in print back home. Take time to trawl the dwindling used-book stores along **Charing Cross Road** and **Cecil Court** (p. 230), which runs to St Martin's Lane. The major art museums are strong on titles in their respective disciplines, especially **Tate Modern** (p. 179) and the **National Portrait Gallery** (p. 138). Performing artists turn to the scripts and theatrical ephemera at the **National Theatre** (Southbank, SE1; shop.nationaltheatre. org.uk; ℰ **020/7452-3456;** Tube: Waterloo) and **Samuel French** (Balcony Bar at the Royal Court Theatre, Sloane Square; www.royalcourttheatre.com; ℰ **020/7565-5024;** Tube: Sloane Square).

Daunt Books ★★ Lined with oak galleries and lit by a long, central skylight, Daunt prides itself on its travel collection, which is located down a groaning wooden staircase. Everything is arranged by the country it's about—Third Reich histories under Germany, Tolstoy under Russia. It's no slouch in the general interest categories, either. Clerks seem to know what will interest the vaguest browser, and the cashier's desk is always piled with choice curiosities. There are other locations around the city. 83 Marylebone High St., W1. www. dauntbooks.co.uk. ℰ **020/7224-2295.** Tube: Baker Street.

Travel specialist Daunt Books.

Foyles ★★ In business since 1903, this institution's huge inventory of 200,000 titles straddles both popular and specialty topics. There are small outlets at Waterloo Station and the Royal Festival Hall on Southbank, but this beloved HQ is more like a theme park for readers, full of talks, events, and signings. 107 Charing Cross Rd., WC2. www.foyles.co.uk. ℰ **020/7437-5660.** Tube: Tottenham Court Road.

Gay's the Word ★ Most English-speaking cities have lost their niche LGBTQ bookstores to Amazon and apathy, but London still has this venerable specialist, trading since 1979. 66 Marchmont St., WC1. www.gaystheword.co.uk. ℰ **020/7278-7654.** Tube: Russell Square.

Hatchards ★★ Although the Duke of Wellington and Jane Austen have been counted among its customers, Hatchards, the oldest bookseller in the city (1797), is noted for its signed first editions, as well as for its famous shoplift-ers: An 18-year-old Noël Coward was apprehended as he stuffed a suitcase full of books. (Characteristically, he talked his way out of trouble.) It has been trading since 1801 at its current location, which means it was selling books before Hardy, Dickens, or the Brontës were writing them. Virginia Woolf wrote about it, too, in *Mrs Dalloway.* 187 Piccadilly, W1. www.hatchards.co.uk. © **020/7439-9921.** Tube: Piccadilly Circus.

Housmans Booksellers ★ London supports a vibrant protest community—don't forget this is where Karl Marx fashioned his views that changed the world—and since 1945, the city's preeminent store for radical books has been Housmans. You're not going to find most of the stuff here published back home. Wednesdays at 7pm, an author speaks. 5 Caledonian Rd., N1. www.housmans.com. © **020/7837-4473.** Tube: King's Cross St Pancras.

Persephone Books ★ Persephone rediscovers and reprints works by forgotten mid-20th-century writers, most of them female—it was responsible for reintroducing *Miss Pettigrew Lives for a Day,* which then became a movie. The shop, on a street brimming with other boutiques, is charming. 59 Lamb's Conduit St., WC1. www.persephonebooks.co.uk. © **020/7242-9292.** Tube: Russell Square.

Stanfords ★★★ Marvelous since 1853, Stanfords trades in globe-trotting goodness, from guides to narratives to fiction with a worldview. There are reams of maps for purchase, especially for walking trails across Britain, and tons of travel-themed gifts. Times forced it to leave its glorious Long Acre flagship building in 2019, but it's still kicking and still superlative. 7 Mercer Walk. www.stanfords.co.uk. © **020/7836-1321.** Tube: Covent Garden.

Waterstones ★★★ In a location opened in 1936 as Simpson's clothiers—the Art Deco model for Grace Brothers in the saucy Britcom *Are You Being*

The expansive children's book section at Waterstones Piccadilly.

The Royal Warrant

When you're snooping around the refined shops of St James's or Mayfair, keep an eye out for a royal crest near the store's sign. That insignia is a seal of approval—its presence means that the business counts a member of the royal family as a customer and has done so for at least 5 years. A lion and a unicorn were selected to represent the sovereign. The Duke of Edinburgh got his rifles from Holland & Holland, est. 1835. To earn the plumed crest Charles used when he was Prince of Wales, stores had to go the extra mile and abide by a sustainable environmental policy. Once a business wins one—about 800 have done it, from chandeliers to elevator repair—it's uncommon to see it withdrawn (to its eternal humiliation, Harrods lost its seal in 2000, and Rigby & Peller, which had made Queen Elizabeth's bras since 1960, was ejected in 2018 after its owner wrote a memoir that revealed too much). Which hotel received the queen's preference? The Goring (p. 57), which earned its warrant in 2013. More great retailers: **Anderson & Sheppard** (Charles's clothing), **Corney & Barrow** (wine), **Charles Martell & Sons** (cheese), and **Dewar's** (which was Queen Elizabeth's quaff). To learn which companies supply the Windsors, search the current warrant holders at www.royalwarrant.org.

Served? (the show's creator was a clerk)—this branch of the giant chain is now Europe's largest bookshop. Even if Waterstones is a Big Gorilla of bookselling, it handles the stewardship of that dubious title with dignity; there are six sweeping floors, an enormous London section, plenty of easy chairs for freeloaders, and scads of discount offers. The top floor's panoramic cafe, 5th View, hops after work and into the evening. The Bloomsbury location at 82 Gower Street, WC1 (Tube: Goodge Street), once the famous bookstore called Dillons, benefits from its location by University College London. That outlet is particularly rich in history, nonfiction, and biography titles. 203 Piccadilly. www.waterstones.com. *(C)* **020/7851-2400.** Tube: Piccadilly Circus.

Clothing, Shoes & Accessories

The clothes you find in the U.K. will not be the same as in major stores elsewhere. Different markets, different tastes, different inventories. Sizes are probably different than at home, too, so make sure to consult a conversion chart.

Albam ★★   Unusually, this men's boutique seeks out well-constructed, honest clothing (most made in the U.K.), but doesn't mark it up by insane factors. Although its prices are similar to those of high-casual chain stores, the store has a following among guys because its clothing lasts so long. 23 Beak St., W1. www.albamclothing.com. *(C)* **020/3157-7000.** Tube: Piccadilly Circus or Oxford Circus.

Arket ★★   Scandinavian-simple and ethically sourced, it aims a little higher in style and substance than its corporate cousin, H&M. This clean-and-casual newcomer does homewares, too. 224 Regent St., W1. www.arket.com. *(C)* **020/3402-9150.** Tube: Oxford Circus. Also at 27–29 Long Acre, WC2. Tube: Covent Garden.

Article ★★ Everything a young urbanite needs to keep up: premium casual menswear from around the world, beautiful homewares from Scandinavia, great-looking bags and sunglasses. 150a Commercial St., E1. www.article-london.com. ℭ **020/7377-8558.** Tube: Shoreditch High Street. Also at Arch S3, Hawley Wharf, Water Lane, NW1. Tube: Camden Town.

Atika ★★ Once called Blitz, Atika has crowned itself Europe's largest vintage shop, a boast I cannot authenticate, but it's true that within its 6,000 square feet, you'll be spoilt for choice. 55–59 Hanbury St., E1. www.atikalondon.co.uk. ℭ **020/7377-0730.** Tube: Shoreditch High Street.

Beyond Retro ★★ A one-stop shop for classic items (jeans, jackets, boots, and other casuals), it's a haunt of the poor and stylish, who can put together an off-margin look without overdrawing. 110–112 Cheshire St., E2. www.beyondretro.com. ℭ **020/7729-9001.** Tube: Shoreditch High Street or Whitechapel. Also at 19-21 Argyll St., W1. Tube: Oxford Circus.

Blackhorse Lane Atelier ★ If you can't afford to cut a new suit on Savile Row, how about some bespoke jeans? Lifelong experts in the fabric industry set out to create the perfect manufacturer of custom jeans that are crafted from sustainable denims. Every step of the process is immaculately overseen (they even plant their own indigo in a garden nearby), and although the results aren't cheap (nudging £300), they'll fit your body perfectly and last for years. Unit 32, Lower Stable St.,Coal Drops Yard, N1. www.blackhorselane.com. ℭ **020/3746-8303.** Tube: King's Cross St Pancras.

Browns ★★ Some 100 designers, all of them for higher-end purchasers, fill these five connected shops at the top of Mayfair. Since 1970, it's been a marketplace for upscale women, but increasingly, it's pitching to a younger and more casual set. 23–27 S. Molton St., W1. www.brownsfashion.com. ℭ **020/7514-0016.** Tube: Bond Street.

Burberry Factory Outlet ★ Although its East London location is charmless, light on menswear, and somewhat laborious to reach, it's worth it for overstock prices that dip 30% to 70% lower than what's on sale in the brand's high-end stores—still expensive, but a lot less than the usual damage. 29–31 Chatham Place, E9. ℭ **020/8328-4287.** Tube/National Rail: Hackney Central.

Cordings ★★ Britain's top manufacturer of Wellington boots, which were invented for the first Duke of Wellington, can be found at this well-heeled and very English emporium of field clothing, suits, waistcoats, tweeds, and knitwear that cost a pretty pound. It has traded here since 1877. 19 Piccadilly, W1. www.cordings.co.uk. ℭ **020/7734-0830.** Closed Sun. Tube: Piccadilly Circus.

Diverse ★ Diverse spotlights white-hot labels, many of which go on to greatness. Clothes tend toward arty, clientele tends toward obsessive. 148 Fortress Rd., NW5. www.diverseclothing.com. ℭ **020/7813-7425.** Tube: Tufnell Park.

Dover Street Market ★   A high-minded multi-designer concept, heavy on pretentious industrial architecture, is supported by couture fused with multimedia art installations. 18–22 Haymarket, SW1. www.doverstreetmarket.com. ⓒ **020/7518-0680.** Tube: Piccadilly Circus.

The Goodhood Store ★★   Consummately East End, the clothing and "life store" products sold in this popular, half-serious two-story emporium are all about what it means to feel cool. Don a faux-vintage T-shirt printed with inscrutable gibberish, carry home a "The Masses Are Asses" mug for your latte, and stock up on the latest on-trend grooming products. Independent, self-knowing—but it only *looks* secondhand. 151 Curtain Rd., EC2. www.goodhood store.com. ⓒ **020/7729-3600.** Tube: Old Street.

Herbert Johnson ★★   This hatter, in business since 1889, made Indiana Jones' famous fedora, called The Poet Hat, for Steven Spielberg in 1980. That's so awesome, not much more needs to be said, except that it can make a cool hat for you, too. In the Swaine store, 7 Piccadilly Arcade, SW1. www.herbert johnson.co.uk. ⓒ **020/7409-7277.** Closed Sun. Tube: Green Park or Piccadilly Circus.

Irregular Choice ★★★   Shoe fans, you will not believe these. They are the heels of a fabulous, take-no-prisoners, drag queen anime disco goddess. They are one-of-a-kind parties for your little piggies. I cannot be held responsible if you blow your rent in this shop. 35 Carnaby St., W1. www.irregularchoice. com/carnaby-store. ⓒ **020/7494-4811.** Tube: Oxford Circus.

Jack Wills ★★   "Fabulously British," it brags, but these looks still come off a bit like American Eagle Goes to Eton. It aims for a sporty prep school look with rugby shirts, tweeds, cute striped trunks, and brightly hued jumpers. Jack Wills has expanded internationally, but here's the three-story flagship. 136 Long Acre, WC2. www.jackwills.com. ⓒ **020/7240-8946.** Tube: Leicester Square.

James Smith & Sons ★★★   This shop out of time, hung from the outside with old-style high Victorian lettering, is rattling the rafters inside with handmade umbrellas and walking sticks. That's all it makes, as it has done methodically since 1830, so you can imagine the wonders: handles of hazelnut wood, ebony, buffalo horn, and antler, from £25 to more than £300. Clerks can also fashion a box so you can get your purchase onto the plane. Hazlewood House, 53 New Oxford St., WC1. www.james-smith.co.uk. ⓒ **020/7836-4731.** Tube: Holborn or Tottenham Court Road.

Levisons ★★   In an old storefront with the vintage smell of bygone closets, find early-era men's jackets and suits you could only locate in England—Harris tweeds, school uniforms, tailored peacoats. The stock changes weekly. In fact, all of Cheshire Street hosts multiple boutiques for unusual vintage finds. 1 Cheshire St., E2. www.levisons.co.uk. ⓒ **020/3609-2224.** Tube: Shoreditch High Street.

Few souvenirs are more British than fine handcrafted umbrellas and walking sticks from James Smith & Sons.

Lock & Co. ★   Exquisitely crafted classic British hats (Panamas and bowlers, for men, women, and kids, too) are made by this hatter dating to 1765. Their hats have been favored by Wilde, Churchill, Charles, Oddjob from *Goldfinger,* and even the late queen—it tailors the inside of her crowns. 6 St James's St., SW1. www.lockhatters.co.uk. ✆ **020/7930-8874.** Closed Sun. Tube: Green Park.

Mango ★   Take the cream of high fashion and make it accessible for the typical English young woman—that's the formula at this slightly upmarket label, which does well when you want your look to be colorful, casual, and maybe even beachy. 229–235 Oxford St., W1. mango.com. ✆ **020/7534-3505.** Tube: Oxford Circus. Also at 8–12 Neal St., WC2. ✆ **020/7240-2935.** Tube: Covent Garden.

The Mercantile ★★   Founder Debra McCann, sorting through the work of some 150 international designers for her long-running and relaxed boutique, knows how to select looks that are appealing to women, fashion-forward enough to be original but wearable, and relatively easy on the wallet. That's why she's been succeeding at this since 2012. 17a Lamb St., E1. themercantile london.com. ✆ **020/7377-8926.** Tube: Shoreditch High Street or Liverpool Street.

Misan ★★ If you sew, uncover a wealth of unique fabrics at this well-regarded Soho showcase and stock up on beautiful stuff you won't find imported at home. 4 Berwick St., W1. misan.co.uk. *℃* **020/3556-9806.** Closed Sun. Tube: Piccadilly Circus.

Monsoon ★ One of the favored High Street brands for women, Monsoon's outfits are for independent dressers who favor bright hues and aren't afraid of a few embellishments. It also does good evening wear. 19 Marylebone High St., W1. monsoon.co.uk. *℃* **020/7486-4138.** Tube: Bond Street.

New Look ★★ Another reliable and very successful High Street chain, New Look does a huge amount of cute casual wear fashionably and cheaply. Its specialty is women's clothes, but it does a few men's as well, and it captures trends without going overboard. Victoria Place Shopping Centre, SW1. www.newlook.co.uk. *℃* **020/7802-9768.** Tube: Victoria.

Nick Tentis ★ This London-born men's designer (favored by Eddie Redmayne and Martin Freeman) revitalizes the Savile Row neighborhood's fusty looks with ready-to-wear suits in youthful, Mod-culture cuts and modern, sometimes daring, fabrics. 37 Savile Row, W1. www.nicktentis.com. *℃* **020/7287-1966.** Tube: Piccadilly Circus or Oxford Circus.

Office ★★ The H&M of footwear rips off designer styles cheaply but effectively. Office's major competition **Schuh,** found around town, mostly stocks other brands (although it has its own sub-line). 190 Oxford St. and 47 Oxford St., W1. www.office.co.uk. *℃* **020/7379-1896.** Tube: Oxford Circus or Tottenham Court Road.

Philip Treacy ★★ If you're invited to Ascot, it would be churlish not to be seen in one of Philip Treacy's world-famous designs in *haute couture* hats, bonnets, or fascinators. If you're not, you're welcome to go home with a £1,200 white elephant. 69 Elizabeth St., SW1. www.philiptreacy.co.uk. *℃* **020/7730-3992.** Closed Sun. Tube: Victoria or Sloane Square.

Primark ★★★ The most intense, most crowded, most rewarding store on Oxford Street roils with young families stuffing baskets with cheap-as-chips outfits, shoes, luggage, and outrageously lowballed accessories. Unfortunately, we're also talking about a clientele that discards garments wherever they want, staff that

A Philip Treacy hat makes an unforgettable fashion statement.

WHAT CAN I bring home?

Although you should always claim edibles when you pass through Customs, very few things will be confiscated. Most stuff, including baked goods, honeys, vinegars, condiments, roasted coffee, teas, candy bars, crisps, pickles, and homemade dishes are good to go. And Cadbury chocolate! Stores can't export the British-made version to the U.S. now, so grab all you can! Always check your country's requirements, but these things are certain to make the inspector dog's nose twitch:

- Meat and anything containing meat, be it dried, canned, or bouillon.
- Fresh fruit and vegetables.
- Runny cheeses, but not firm ones (rule of thumb: If you have to keep it chilled, leave it behind).
- Rice. As if you would import rice.
- Plants, soil, wood, and seeds (non-edible). Ask the nursery whether you need paperwork, because many varieties are permitted. And be warned that officers in Australia respond to wood like it's kryptonite.

deals with the rubble using big push brooms, no washrooms, long lines at checkout, and products that won't last a year. But the bargains! Oh, the bargains—most stuff is less than £10, and £1 deals are common. You just can't help leaving with sacksful. "The devil wears Primark," mutter the snobs. 213 Oxford St., W1. www.primark.co.uk. ℂ **020/7495-0420.** Tube: Marble Arch. Also at 14–18 Oxford St., W1. ℂ **020/7580-5510.** Tube: Tottenham Court Road.

River Island ★★ A queen among Britain's popular, affordable women's fast fashion brands, River Island is headquartered in West London and designs most of its wares in-house. Dresses are affordable, shoes are cool, leather jackets well-cut, and there's a kid's line. In 2013, Rihanna tried her hand at formulating a collection for the brand. Police had to restrain the crowd. The course of fashion did not change. 473 Oxford St. (ℂ **0844/826-9835**), 207–213 Oxford St. (ℂ **0844/847-2666**), W1. www.riverisland.com. Tube: Marble Arch.

Rokit ★★ Because it's been cool for longer than many of its competitors have been in business, Rokit has a following. Probably the largest collection in the city, it sells retro and vintage threads, shoes, and accessories that are funky and hipster-prone, from 1950s industrial uniforms to tracksuits. 42 Shelton St., WC2. www.rokit.co.uk. ℂ **020/7836-6547.** Tube: Covent Garden. Also in Whitechapel (101 and 107 Brick Lane, E1; ℂ **020/7375-3864;** Tube: Shoreditch High Street) and Camden (225 Camden High St., NW1; ℂ **020/7267-3046;** Tube: Camden Town).

Vivienne Westwood Worlds End ★ For a few years in the 1970s, Vivienne Westwood's shop was the coolest place on the planet. The clock at this guerilla boutique still runs backward, but London's punk heyday is long over. Never mind the bargains—her Anglomania label is a fashion history itself, but it's not cheap. Still, the fanciful couture inventions, flowing with fabric, are outlandish enough to enchant. 430 Kings Rd., SW10. www.worldsendshop.co.uk. ℂ **020/7352-6551.** Closed Sun. Tube: Fulham Broadway.

Food

Don't neglect the many fine foodie markets (p. 100) or the food halls of the shopping palaces (earlier in this chapter). *One warning:* Don't buy tea from a touristy shop. It'll be old and awful. You have a rare chance to patronize world-famous purveyors like **Twinings** (below) or **Fortnum & Mason** (p. 232), so plunder them instead.

Berry Bros. & Rudd ★★ If you think you don't have the need for a wine shop on your vacation, then you haven't been inside this delicately wood-paneled institution, which has traded from this very shop since 1698. It's true that its most devoted clients tend to be exclusive (notice the royal warrants), but the staff still knows how to cater to anyone's budget and even pours single servings on premises. 63 Pall Mall, SW1. www.bbr.com. ℰ **020/7318-2075.** Closed Sun–Mon. Tube: Green Park.

Biscuiteers ★★★ Adorable, edible souvenirs that people love: whimsical, hand-iced cookies depicting London icons. Drop by its cute location in a Belgravia mews and pair them with tea or a glass of fizz at its prosecco bar. It also runs 2-hour classes on how to decorate cookies. 14–15 Eccleston Yards, 21 Eccleston Place, SW1. www.biscuiteers.com. ℰ **020/3954-6650.** Tube: Victoria.

Charbonnel et Walker ★★ This is chocolate fit for a queen, and I can prove it: It earned Elizabeth's royal warrant while she was alive, declaring it her favorite. Charbonnel has been meticulously preparing high-end confections since 1875 right here, in one of London's most exclusive shopping arcades. One The Royal Arcade, 28 Bond St., W1. www.charbonnel.co.uk. ℰ **020/7318-2075.** Tube: Green Park.

Dark Sugars Cocoa House ★★ Sublime handmade chocolates and truffles (gin and lime, stem ginger and honey, and more) sourced from a family farm in Ghana are the addictive wares at this Brick Lane success story. The golden "pearl" orbs containing smooth hazelnut nougat are delicate and divine, and the shop makes incredible hot chocolates, piled with chocolate shavings that melt into the cup—try it with chili—and even vegan versions. 141 Brick Lane, E1. www.darksugars.co.uk. Tube: Shoreditch High Street. Also at 9 Nelson Rd., SW19, in Greenwich. Tube: Cutty Sark.

Twinings ★★ Does this tea boutique rely on tourist traffic? Definitely. But it's still steeped in tradition, having taken over from a coffee shop in this narrow, portrait-lined location in 1706. Here you can sample, taste, mix-and-match, and savor the leaf in all its varieties—or just peruse its little tea museum. 216 Strand, WC2. www.twinings.co.uk. ℰ **020/7353-3511.** Tube: Temple.

Health & Beauty

Boots ★ Something like 80% of fragrance sales in the U.K. are conducted at this chain, and its endless 3-for-2 promotions almost always include something worth taking home. Makeup costs a few pounds less than at most other stores. It's authentically British, too—its founder, John Campbell Boot, the second Baron Trent, has his picture in the National Portrait Gallery. Multiple locations. www.boots.co.uk.

Floris ★★★   In 1730, when this perfumery was established in this building using the dowry of young Juan Famenias Floris' bride, carrying a pleasant scent beneath your nose was crucial for drowning out the stink of the 18th-century city. Later on, Queen Victoria obtained her aromas here, Oscar Wilde favored the Malmaison Carnation variety, and Marilyn Monroe ordered some Rose Geranium (still sold) to be delivered to her at the Beverly Hills Hotel. Everything is historic; the shop's Spanish mahogany cabinets were purchased at the Great Exhibition of 1852 and there's a small Floris museum in back. You can hire them to create a bespoke fragrance to suit your own tastes, but that requires at least three meetings with you to get the details right. 89 Jermyn St., SW1. www.florislondon.com. ✆ **0330/134-0180.** Tube: Covent Garden.

Neal's Yard Remedies ★★★   At the forefront of Britain's powerful green consumer goods movement, this shop supplies beauty aids, holistic treatments, massage oils, and even make-your-own-cosmetics ingredients, all cruelty-free, clear of toxins, and naturally formulated. Its products—London's answer to the New York beauty boutique Kiehl's—are respected for their quality. 15 Neal's Yard, W1. www.nealsyardremedies.com. ✆ **020/7379-7222.** Tube: Covent Garden.

Penhaligon's ★★★   I don't enjoy the mental image of King Charles lighting a Lily of the Valley candle and anointing his body with English Fern eau de toilette, but the fact is that Penhaligon's, established in 1870, is listed as an official supplier of "toilet requisites" to Charles, so it may be happening right now. The company hand-squeezes and custom designs its own fragrances for both men and women—generally floral-based and gentle—and sidelines in luxury shaving and grooming products. Another picturesque

Humidorable

Cigars are big business in London, and not just because the city was once the capital of the world tobacco trade. Many wealthy visitors from Arab countries are not permitted to drink alcohol by dint of their religion but they may enjoy a fine stogie, so most finer hotels offer humidors as well as cocktail bars. Dating to 1787, **James J. Fox** claims to be the oldest cigar merchant in the world, and its pedigree is peerless: Oscar Wilde indulged himself here, and Winston Churchill slouched in its weary brown leather armchair while he tasted the Coronas. Come to inhale the rich, musky aroma, to select one of its fine bowl pipes, or even to smoke—the city's public smoking ban does not apply here. (19 St James's St., SW1. www.jjfox.co.uk. ✆ **020/7930-3787.** Tube: Green Park.)

Penhaligon's fragrances: England-created since 1870.

location is at 16–17 Burlington Arcade (Tube: Green Park). 41 Wellington St., WC2. www.penhaligons.co.uk. ☎ **020/7629-1416.** Tube: Covent Garden.

Housewares

Conran Shop ★★   Gorgeous, contemporary, smartly selected pieces made Conran's name in housewares; its flagship store is a master class in elegant urban furnishings and desirable home accessories. Its building is just as worthy: the 1911 Art Nouveau headquarters of the Michelin Tire Company, coated with decorative tiles of the era's racing cars and the Michelin Man (aka Bibendum). The newer location in Marylebone, however, is more convenient (55 Marylebone High St., W1; ☎ **020/7723-2223;** Tube: Baker Street). 81 Fulham Rd., SW3. www.conranshop.co.uk. ☎ **020/7589-7401.** Tube: South Kensington.

Heal's ★★   A stalwart since 1810, but not stuffy like one, Heal's (like Liberty; p. 234) was instrumental in forwarding the Arts and Crafts movement in England. Its furniture and housewares, which are usually defined by chic, up-to-date shapes, have proven so influential that in 1978 it donated its archive to the Victoria & Albert Museum. The kitchen department is popular. 196 Tottenham Court Rd., W1. www.heals.com. ☎ **020/7636-1666.** Tube: Goodge Street.

Labour and Wait ★★ The most expensive dustpan you'll ever own will be the envy of dirt everywhere. This store's gorgeously designed kitchenware, bathroom items, gardening tools, and stationery—from vintage enamel to new sculptural metalwork—will put some chic into your chores. Even its location, an emerald-tiled former pub, is functionally fabulous, and its neighbors along Redchurch Street, selling clothes and interior items, are just as stylish. 85 Redchurch St., E2. www.labourandwait.co.uk. ✆ **020/7729-6253.** Closed Mon. Tube: Shoreditch High Street.

Stationery

Choosing Keeping ★★ Truly beautiful stationery, gorgeous wrapping paper, artisan-made notebooks and sketchbooks, nib pens—this tidy boutique's throwback ethos, which appeals to anyone who loves a desk filled with quality things, celebrates the vibrancy of Victoriana. 21 Tower St., WC2. www.choosingkeeping.com. ✆ **020/7613-3842.** Closed Mon. Tube: Leicester Square.

Present and Correct ★ Well-designed, midcentury-modern wares for an organized and impeccably stylish desk. Even the Italian staplers and Japanese erasers ("made of natural rubber, for superior error removal") look like

Natty housewares await at the carefully curated Labour and Wait.

they've been approved by a museum curator when in fact, the owner was once a graphic designer for *Monocle*. 23 Arlington Way, EC2. www.presentandcorrect. com. ⓒ **020/7278-2460.** Closed Sun–Mon. Tube: Angel.

Ryman Stationery ★ If you're into office supplies (admit it—it's time to come out of the supply closet), the ubiquitous chain, which makes an appearance on almost every busy U.K. shopping street, is a good place to stock up on hard-to-find English-size A4 paper, clamp binders (not common in the U.S.), and convenient "box files" (also absent from other countries' stationers), available in a spectrum of sprightly colors. Multiple locations. www. ryman.co.uk.

Smythson of Bond Street ★★★ In addition to a line of leather journals, organizers, and handbags, this firm, founded in 1887, does stationery impeccably. The late Queen Elizabeth II, a one-woman thank-you note industry, bought her paper here. The cotton-fiber content is probably higher than in your bedsheets. 131–132 New Bond St., W1. www.smythson.com. ⓒ **020/3535-8009.** Closed Sun. Tube: Bond Street or Oxford Circus.

Toys

Hamleys ★★★ Remote-control helicopters in your hair, magicians at your elbow, rugrats at your knees. This high-octane toy store is run by a gaggle of cheerful young floor staff, themselves kids at heart, who giddily demonstrate the latest toys. The experience will send you into sensory overload. Seven floors are stuffed with amusements—the fifth floor is nothing but sweets. Depending on when you go, there may be free pirate face painting, a caricaturist, or even a beach party. It's one of the world's few department stores devoted just to children, and the only must-see toy store in London—even if you don't have kids. 188–196 Regent St., W1. www. hamleys.com. ⓒ **0871/704-1977.** Tube: Oxford Circus.

Peppa Pig at Hamleys.

The Harry Potter Shop at Platform 9¾ ★ On the western flank of King's Cross station, from which the storied Hogwarts Express is said to depart, there's an always-busy boutique where Warner Bros. cashes in on Pottermania. London has many imitators that sell off-brand wizardly gear, but this is the only official store, offering much of the same J.K. Rowling-approved stuff you can find at the Wizarding World in Universal's theme parks: wands, school gear, collectibles, and even a carbonated version of Butterbeer that isn't sold in theme parks. Out front, you can pose for a souvenir photo (£10–£20) as you appear to push a luggage cart through a brick wall to the legendary Platform 9¾—staff will throw a scarf on you and then fluff it when the shutter snaps to simulate racing speed. That cheesy photo op gets busy, so if that's why you're going, you're warned to come at least an hour before closing to get a place in the queue. Unfortunately, the train to the actual Harry Potter sets (p. 207) leaves from a different station, Euston, which is a 15-minute walk west. King's Cross Station, N1. www.harrypottershop.co.uk. Mon–Sat 8am–8pm; Sun 9am–8pm. Tube: King's Cross St Pancras.

LONDON'S GREATEST MARKETS

Unfortunately, with the inexorable spread of megastores, outdoor markets that have been feeding central Londoners since the Dark Ages are finding themselves extinguished. The following markets soldier on. Not every market sells something you can take home, unless you count memories: For example, the Columbia Road Flower Market (Sun at 8am; Tube: Old Street), is an Eden for English blooms, which get cheaper around 2pm, near closing time. Borough Market, which is fully described on p. 105, is all about prepared foods or things you can't get past Customs. Whether

Market Hours
Unless otherwise noted, markets are mostly outdoors and generally kick off around 8 or 9am and start packing up around 3pm.

for gourmets, tourists, or locals, markets are a front-row seat to the ongoing opera of everyday life, and a taste of London as it once was.

Berwick Street Market ★

Berwick St. around Broadwick St. Daily 9am–6pm except Sun. Tube: Piccadilly Circus.

Good for: The last daily street market in the West End, dating to the crowded days of the 1840s, is now being art directed by developers. Gone are the Cockney calls, in are the overpriced baked goods and Apple Pay—convenient, but false. I only mention it because it's historic.

Also check out: The gourmand-pleasing specialty shops lining the route.

Brick Lane Markets ★★★

Brick Lane at Buxton St. www.sundayupmarket.co.uk. ✆ **020/7770-6028.** Tube: Shoreditch High Street.

Good for: The Vintage Market (Thurs–Sun, clothes), Backyard Market (Sat–Sun, crafts), Boiler House (Sat–Sun, food), and Tea Rooms (Sat–Sun, antiques). As you can see, Sundays are a banner day: UpMarket for trendy fashions, antiques, food stalls, and Spitalfields Market (p. 255) are also in full swing.

Also check out: The Beigel Bake (p. 109) for London's version of a bagel.

Brixton Market ★

Electric Ave. at Pope's Rd. brixtonmarket.net. Mon–Sat. Tube: Brixton.

Good for: Global produce, spices, halal meats, music from soul to reggae and hip-hop. Don't expect something grand; expect a real immigrant community.

Also check out: Brixton Village (brixtonvillage.com), stalls selling African and Caribbean clothes, foods, and housewares. Check its calendar for the theme of the day.

Camden Markets ★★

Camden High St. at Buck St. www.camdenlock.net. Daily (Sat–Sun busiest). Tube: Camden Town.

Good for: A rambling warren of 700 stalls for vintage wear, sunglasses, leather, goth gear, and fast foods, partly in a canal-side setting, and favored by

Camden Markets are a top source for vintage and classic-styled wear, including hats.

tourists. Between the Lock Market, the Market Hall, the Horse Stables, and Camden Lock Village across the street, the crowds are utterly exhausting.

Also check out: Stables Market, on the other side of the railway off Chalk Farm Road, sells vintage clothes, antiques, and pop culture knickknacks, and it's where you'll find a beehive hairdo–bedecked statue of Amy Winehouse, who died in Camden in 2011; Electric Market (on Camden High St.) is an indoor fair of vinyl, programs, and film posters (Sat) and retro and punk clothes (Sun).

Chapel Market ★

Penton St., Islington. Tues–Sun. Tube: Angel.

Good for: Cheese, dumplings, meat pies, toiletries—a real catch-all working-class market that actually feeds workaday Londoners.

Also check out: The antithesis of a market, the gleaming Angel Central mall dominates the eastern end of the street; it's New London versus Old London.

Greenwich Markets ★★

11a Greenwich Market. www.greenwichmarketlondon.com. Daily 10am–5:30pm (Sat–Sun best). Tube: Cutty Sark DLR or Greenwich National Rail.

Good for: Antiques, crafts, jewelry, books, honeys, breads, and cakes under a historic market roof.

Also check out: The truffles, ice creams, and gifts at popular chocolatier Dark Sugars (p. 246), on Nelson Road at the Market's south end.

Leadenhall Market ★★

Gracechurch St., EC3. www.leadenhallmarket.co.uk. Space open 24 hr., businesses keep own hours. Tube: Monument.

Good for: The shops are high end and the cafes always packed with suited City workers, but what a locale! The glorious wrought-iron-and-glass canopy (1882), once shelter for a meat market, is an architectural treasure. In the first Harry Potter film, this is where The Leaky Cauldron is found. The original heart of Roman London is also under your feet.

Also check out: The Monument (p. 192), two streets away.

Portobello Road Market ★

www.portobelloroad.co.uk. ☏ **020/7727-7684.** Mon–Wed 9am–6pm; Thurs 9am–1pm; Fri–Sat 9am–7pm. Best on Sat. Tube: Notting Hill Gate or Westbourne Park.

Good for: Antiques, hot foods, jewelry, vintage clothes, tourist tat by the ton. Overcrowded and overrated, but thanks to the movies, it's not going anywhere.

Also check out: The packed pubs along the route; the galleries and antiques shops in the storefronts, where prices can be better than at the stalls.

When London hosted the Olympics in 2012, the marathon was routed through the magnificent Leadenhall Market. The market dates to the 1300s.

When you see a price in England, that's the full price. Tax is always included.

That tax is usually charged at a rate of 20%. It's called VAT (Value-Added Tax), and it goes to enviable programs such as national health care, so that British citizens who get sick don't have to go bankrupt to get well.

Tourists used to have the option of stopping by a VAT desk at the airport with their goodies-stuffed luggage to claim some of that money back on major souvenir purchases, but that privilege as we knew it is over. Brexit ended it.

As this book went to press, the U.K. government was devising a new digital system for getting a rebate on the VAT you paid. Until the new system is in force, the only way to claim some of the tax money back is to have a purchase mailed directly to an address outside the U.K., and only if the store participates in VAT refunds (and many don't).

To check on how that works and on whether the replacement VAT refund scheme has launched, look for updated information at www.gov.uk/tax-on-shopping/taxfree-shopping

Queen's Market ★

Green St. at Queen's Rd. www.newham.gov.uk. ⓒ **020/8475-8971.** Tues and Thurs–Sat 9am–6pm. Tube: Upton Park.

Good for: 80 stalls and 60 local stores for ingredients from Asia, Africa, Russia, the Caribbean, and elsewhere; international clothes and rugs. Although it's not very posh, it is very Everyday London. Sunday is a quieter day.

Also check out: Its defenders' website, www.friendsofqueensmarket.org.uk, which has argued their market is half as expensive as Walmart.

Southbank Centre Book Market ★★

Southbank under the Waterloo Bridge. Daily noon–7pm in good weather. Tube: Waterloo.

Good for: Tables of used books, maps, lithographs, and wood engravings. Small, but the setting is its own destination.

Also check out: Lower Marsh Market (www.lowermarshmarket.co.uk) on Lower Marsh between Westminster Bridge and Baylis roads (south of Waterloo station), a classic produce market.

Spitalfields Market ★★

Commercial St. between Brushfield St. and Lamb St. www.oldspitalfieldsmarket.com. Daily. Tube: Liverpool Street.

Good for: Prepared world food, handmade housewares, jewelry, vintage posters. It's the most gentrified market in town, and especially on Saturdays, there are one-of-a-kind clothing items. Sit-down restaurants surround it. The market's success was a linchpin in East London's revitalization.

Also check out: Visit the Style Market for fashions on Saturday afternoons.

6 | Walthamstow Market ★

Walthamstow Market St. Tues–Sat. Tube: Walthamstow.

Good for: 450 non-touristy stalls selling everything from knockoff clothes to junky food to Chinese-made batteries—it's the longest market street in Europe, and it's been going since 1885.

Also check out: You may not have the energy to see much else in this multicultural neighborhood—the market itself is a kilometer (about half a mile) long.

LONDON NIGHTLIFE

Let no one tell you that London tucks itself into bed early. Perhaps that was true in your grandfather's day—not now. The Tube may shut down after midnight on weeknights, but now the main lines go all night on weekends, so for the intrepid, the entertainment can rollick until morning. With hundreds of theaters, nightclubs, cinemas, and bars, London offers more on a single night than many cities muster in an entire year.

That said, London's nights aren't perfect. The city's prevailing liquor laws force places to often unceremoniously evict their clientele in mid-toast. Whereas in Spain, Greece, and New York, the night rarely begins before 1am, that's usually when floors are being mopped at many spots. If you require just one more cocktail to close the deal, a very few clubs will serve until 3am, and they come and go; ask your new friends at the bar which after-hours place is the cool one right now. Where the Night Tube doesn't go, the Night Bus system (p. 359) does, but it's a buzzkill to end a festive night of drinking with your legs crossed on an infrequent and slow-moving bus.

GETTING THE SCOOP Complete listings information for entertainment is published Saturdays in the London papers, but you don't have to wait until you arrive. Excellent online sources for things to do include **Londonist.com** and **TimeOut.com/London**.

THEATER

If you leave London without seeing at least one stage show, then you'll have missed one of this city's pillars: This is where Shakespeare defined great writing and Gilbert and Sullivan shaped modern musical theater. The great work continues to this day, and if you doubt it, look at the lists of Oscar, Emmy, and Tony winners from the past decade.

Whenever you hear the phrase "West End" in relation to shows, think of the term as describing the 60-odd top-tier theaters in the middle of town. These are the shows that most tourists flock to see, but that doesn't mean they're always the best—the West End is increasingly clogged with mediocre dramas propped up by

Hollywood names and by so-called "jukebox" musicals that are intentionally simplified so tourists who don't speak English can have fun.

Many West End shows begin their lives at companies found elsewhere in town at "Off West End" or "Fringe" stages. We name some of the best ones here. For challenging work mounted by producers intent on taking artistic risks, look to them. Many of them have designed and built facilities expressly for pumping out fresh projects. The stars perform here, too—all at prices that are half what you'd shell out for a West End show created by committee.

It's easy to make a night of it. Most theaters have a bar, and even Off West End companies might have their own mid- to high-end restaurants so you can pre-show on the doorstep.

Curtain times range from 7 to 8pm for evening shows, with most starting at 7:30pm; matinees start anywhere between 2 and 4pm. Every theater is different, so check your ticket. Most shows are closed, or "dark," on Sundays, but some of the family-oriented crowd-pleasers may go dark on Monday or Tuesday instead.

Theater Tickets for Less

Even at full price, West End shows cost dramatically less than Broadway's. Considering £30 tickets are typical even for musicals, you can actually afford to see a few. If you are desperate to see a specific show, book tickets directly with the production before you leave home to ensure you won't be left out. Check the **Society of London Theatre,** or SOLT (www.officiallondontheatre.co.uk), the trade association for theater owners and producers (established in 1908), for a season rundown and discounts. Keep in mind that many other websites will deliver you to third parties who charge a premium of as much as 20% for your booking. Only use that method if you'd be heartbroken to miss a particular show. It's perfectly normal to be charged a booking fee and/or a "restoration fee" (that goes to the city's ancient theater buildings) of a few pounds.

The free app **TodayTix** handles "**rush tickets**" (a daily allotment of low-cost tickets) for dozens of shows. Each show has different rules, but most of their rush seats cost around £25 each and begin selling at 10am on the days when they're available. If worrying about rush seat timing is too much for you, TodayTix also sells advance tickets for fair prices. (See box, below, for more tips.)

Many theaters post steep **student discounts,** but distribution methods vary—students are advised to check the websites of the major theaters and sign up ahead of time. And bring your student ID, or you will be denied.

Given a lead time of a few days or weeks, anyone can find some discounts on TodayTix or **LoveTheatre.com** (click "Special Offers.")

On the day of the show, **TKTS** (south side of Leicester Square; www.tkts. co.uk; Mon–Sat 10:30am–6pm, Sun noon–4:30pm; Tube: Leicester Square), operated by SOLT, has same-day seats for as much as half off—the best stuff is sold in the first hour of the booth's opening. Take note that unlike the TKTS booths in New York City's Times Square, London's booth sells its seats early in the day and does not remain open right until showtime. While the white-hot

saving ON THE STAGE

Apart from using TKTS, how can you save on a show?

- **Use the TodayTix app to find cheap same-day "rush" seats.** "Day seats," or "rush seats," are a daily allotment of cheap seats. Only a few theaters require you to queue in person anymore—you'll need to have a quick trigger finger on the TodayTix app, which handles the majority of shows.
- **Matinees are often cheaper than evening shows.** Unfortunately, they also cut into your daylight touring time.
- **Ask about standing room tickets and "day seats."** Many theaters sell standing room tickets (£15–£20).

- **Buy at the box office** to avoid paying booking fees. This method is increasingly falling out of favor, though.
- **In one of the older theaters, you can often settle for a restricted-view seat.** You may have to crane your neck to see around the edge of a balcony or a pillar, but you'll be in the room. They cost about a third of top-price seats. **Theatre monkey.com** posts theater-specific ratings, and **AViewFromMySeat. com** posts actual crowdsourced photos taken from seats in many houses—use it to determine whether a cheap seat is worth it.

Theater

tickets won't be found here, about 80% of West End shows are—TKTS posts a list of going deals (but no show descriptions) on its website so you can know if it's worth the visit. Certain machinelike shows (*The Phantom of the Opera*, *Mamma Mia!*, *Wicked*) seemingly never die and can always be relied upon.

The West End is dotted with closet-size stalls hawking tickets to major shows and concerts. Don't deal with them. They are for audiences who simply *must* get tickets to their chosen show regardless of the fees—as high as 25% over cost. Before you give your money to any of these outfits, check the directory of the self-policing **Society of Ticket Agents and Retailers** (www.star. org.uk; ✆ **01904/234-737**) to find out who is reputable. Scalpers, called **touts** here, routinely issue counterfeit tickets or abscond with your cash. Some sightseeing discount cards also brag about discounts, but their deals are mostly for the longest-running, touristy shows and they don't save you nearly as much as TKTS would—only around £20 off the top price.

London's Landmark Performance Places

ABBA Voyage ★★★ In 2022, the members of the '70s Swedish supergroup created a new concert show at their own custom-built arena in East London, where computer-generated "ABBA-tars" of their younger selves jam to the band's greatest hits in a party atmosphere. It's a technological wonder, it's a nonstop feat of cutting-edge lighting and staging, and it's a thousand times more fun than it sounds. *Warning:* The DLR stop outside gets swamped after performances; walk 20 minutes to Stratford instead. ABBA Arena, Pudding Mill Lane, E15. https://abbavoyage.com. Shows Thurs–Mon. Tube: Pudding Mill Lane DLR (arrival) and Stratford or Hackney Wick (departure).

The Barbican Centre ★★   In the 1950s, earnest but misguided city leaders turned their attentions toward redeveloping a bombed-out crater. The end result was a forbidding mixed-use concrete complex that took more than 20 years to finish. They optimistically planned for lively crowds by adding Europe's largest arts and conference center, too, with a concert hall, two theaters, three cinemas, and two galleries, and now they're the best thing about the place—and one of the best things about London arts in general. You can't always find something going on in all of its venues, and even when things are rocking full-tilt, the bunkered Barbican is so windswept it makes *Blade Runner* look like Candy Land, but what does play here is rarely dull. It's nearly impossible to classify the Barbican's fare, since it hosts a wide range of the world's great orchestras (including the London Symphony Orchestra and the BBC Symphony Orchestra), singers, and composers, plus a handful of banner festivals each year, particularly in the realm of contemporary music and experimental theater. Some of the most prestigious international touring theatrical productions come here, so always check what's on. Its cinemas also screen films fresh from major festival triumphs. Silk St., EC2. www.barbican.org.uk. ✆ **020/7638-8891.** Tube: Barbican.

The Bridge Theatre ★   In late 2017, a major new venue opened near City Hall. The bridge in the name is none other than Tower Bridge, the southern foot of which is just outside the door, making for a sublime nighttime view as you emerge after a show. This venue places an emphasis on well-produced new work and is unquestionably A-list, attracting heavy-hitters Ben Whishaw and Simon Russell Beale in *Julius Caesar*, Laura Linney in *My Name Is Lucy Barton*, and in 2022, Ralph Fiennes in a premiere of a new play by David Hare. Not shabby! 3 Potters Fields Park, SE1. www.bridgetheatre.co.uk. ✆ **0333/320-0051.** Tube: London Bridge.

The Bush Theatre ★★★   The Bush, which since 1972 has showcased a formidable output from a diverse group of new writers, started as a pub theater. In 2011, thanks to a lifesaving campaign that rallied support from the likes of Judi Dench and Daniel Radcliffe, it got its own complex in a disused Victorian library. 7 Uxbridge Rd., W12. www.bushtheatre.co.uk. ✆ **020/8743-5050.** Tube: Shepherds Bush.

Donmar Warehouse ★★★   This 250-seat house mounts mostly limited runs of vividly reconceived shows, both new work and revivals. Past coups for this comfortably converted brewery warehouse include the *Cabaret* revival that introduced Alan Cumming to the world, as well as appearances by world-class performers such as Ian McKellen and Nicole Kidman. You can usually find standing room or cheap student tickets; check its website for the rules for the current show. 41 Earlham St., WC2. www.donmarwarehouse.com. ✆ **020/3282-3808.** Tube: Covent Garden.

Menier Chocolate Factory ★★   In an intimate setting among exposed beams and cast-iron columns, a converted you-know-what from the 1870s is

where some of the city's hottest musical revivals have been mounted. Its

Sunday in the Park with George and *A Little Night Music* transferred to the West End and later to Broadway. This company, which also does non-musical plays, is one of the few to do Sunday shows; it's dark on Mondays. 51–53 Southwark St., SE1. www.menierchocolatefactory.com. ℂ **020/7378-1713.** Tube: London Bridge.

Old Vic ★ There's always something worthwhile at the Old Vic, which draws celebrities like, to take a recent few, Vanessa Redgrave, Kim Cattrall, Sally Field, Bill Pullman, and *The Crown* couple Claire Foy and Matt Smith acting together again; acting legend Glenda Jackson was even coaxed back on stage here after a quarter century in Parliament. The place is known for mounting meat-and-potatoes drama—stuff actors love to sink their teeth into—as well as lively fare such as the musical *Groundhog Day,* which it exported to Broadway. The 200-year-old building was once the home of the National Theatre, under the artistic direction of Laurence Olivier, before that organization built its own digs on the Thames in 1976. The not-for-profit house it left behind is pulling bigger crowds than ever, and its annual production of *A Christmas Carol* is an institution of its own. The Cut at Waterloo Rd., SE1. www.oldvictheatre.com. ℂ **0844/871-7628.** Tube: Waterloo or Southwark.

Royal Court Theatre ★★ The preeminent writer's theater (it also hosts the Samuel French theater bookshop), the Royal Court has fought censorship and unveiled international brilliance for so long that it's now a preeminent actor's theater as well. On the east side of jaunty Sloane Square, it devotes a hefty portion of its schedule to important premieres by the likes of Bruce Norris and Caryl Churchill and performances from fierce actors. Among the plays it gave the world are *Look Back in Anger, The Rocky Horror Picture Show* (in its upstairs studio theater), George Bernard Shaw's *Major Barbara* and *Heartbreak House,* and Jez Butterworth's *The Ferryman.* Sloane Square, SW1. www. royalcourttheatre.com. ℂ **020/7565-5000.** Tube: Sloane Square.

Royal National Theatre ★★★ The government-subsidized powerhouse people simply call the National is the country's, and possibly the world's, most noted showpiece for top-flight drama and classical acting. Laurence Olivier was its first director, and the tradition of world-class performances has been unerring: Judi Dench, Ralph Fiennes, Anthony Hopkins, Olivia Colman, and Benedict Cumberbatch have been regulars, plus every other British actor you have ever respected. In recent years, the National has broadcast screenings of its live performances to cinemas around the world and even into homes, earning it wider acclaim than ever. The National always mounts a diverse repertoire of works in its three permanent theaters, spanning Shakespeare to classic musicals (the *Oklahoma!* that made Hugh Jackman a star) to emotional spectacles (*War Horse* began here) to world premieres of well-made plays by the world's best playwrights. The brutalist riverside complex is a pleasure to spend time in, with several pre-show places to eat, caffeinate, or tipple on picnic benches facing the Thames outside the Understudy, its craft beer bar. The fascinating (and free) Sherling High-Level Walkway allows anyone off

You'll find several star-making shows with high production values happening simultaneously at the riverfront National Theatre complex.

the street to watch the activity backstage; there's even a periscope so kids can peer over railings into the scenery shops. To find that, head down the eastern-side road toward the Dorfman, go inside, and take the lift to the second level. As the people's theater, the National's pricing is populist. On Fridays at 1pm on its website, a bevy of £20 "Friday Rush" seats (nationaltheatre.org.uk/fridayrush) are released for the coming weeks' shows. Check the calendar for the 75-minute tours (£10–£15) showing off the inner workings or costume department, or shop in the lobby bookstore, a performing arts nirvana. South Bank, SE1. www.nationaltheatre.org.uk. © **020/7452-3000.** Tube: Waterloo.

Sadler's Wells ★   Sadler's Wells has been a part of the fabric of London life for so long (since 1683) that its current two-house home, dating to 1998, is actually the sixth. You can turn to this Islington establishment to catch some of the world's greatest companies in movement- or rhythm-based performances that transcend language. Its specialties are ballet (Matthew Bourne is a frequent guest artist), contemporary dance, and daring opera, although it dabbles in musicals as well. It also programs the Peacock Theatre on Portugal Street near the Holborn Tube. Rosebery Ave., EC1. www.sadlerswells.com. © **020/7863-8000.** Tube: Angel.

Shakespeare's Globe ★★   This reconstruction of an Elizabethan theater on the Thames (see p. 177 for architectural details) is a serious concern that attracts the finest classically trained performers, thanks partly to its founding artistic director (1995–2005), Oscar-winning actor Mark Rylance. The tone for quality that he set is maintained today—in 2017, the artistic director was fired, in part, for the anachronistic sin of using artificial lighting—although it can be startlingly progressive as well, as its female-performed *King Lear* proved. Groundling ("Yard") tickets to stand for the show have been £5 since the 1990s. The season at the open-air Globe is spring through fall, but in a 340-seat Jacobean indoor theater, the Sam Wanamaker (named in honor of the American actor who fought to reconstruct the Globe), there's something happening year-round. The smaller, candle-lit Wanamaker premiered Rylance in *Farinelli and the King,* which went to Broadway in 2017. 21 New Globe Walk, Bankside, SE1. www.shakespearesglobe.com. ℭ **020/7401-9919.** Season: Apr–Oct. Tube: Southwark or Mansion House.

Southbank Centre ★★★   Like the Barbican, this is a bleak, canvas-colored slab architects don't know quite how to fix. It was conceived as a postwar pick-me-up for a creativity-starved city, but age was not kind; despite a peerless Thames location, it's a forbidding architectural scowl, looking more like a pile of sidewalk curbs than an artistic capital. It's perkier on the inside, however. An ever-interesting hodgepodge of some 1,000 programs a year go down at its three concert venues, as well as in its huge central hall, which has a cafe and is open to everybody. Dance, film, classical and contemporary music, and the London Jazz Festival fill the bill, which is prolific if self-important. Don't miss the Undercroft, the hideous concrete negative space under the building along the Thames. When the Centre went up, this area was thought to be useless, so skateboarders and street artists claimed the

THE QUIRKS OF LONDON theatergoing

London theater can be a strange experience for outsiders:

- Programs are not free; they cost from £4 (for plays) to £6 (for musicals). Big productions may only sell a glossy souvenir brochure, for £7 to £10.
- What North American theaters call "orchestra" seats, London houses call the "stalls." And instead of a "mezzanine," they have a "Dress Circle," and above that, "Upper Circle" or "Royal Circle." If there happens to be a third, topmost level, that is the "balcony," or sometimes, the "gallery." And because many theaters were constructed in a class-obsessed era, there may be a separate street entrance for each area.
- The break between acts is called an "interval," not "intermission."
- The big snack? Ice cream, sold by ushers (or "attendants").

- Most theaters allow you to preorder drinks and snacks before the show so you can pick them up with little waiting during the interval. Some even let you do it digitally from your mobile phone.
- During the bows, many musicals add a celebratory mini medley of the songs, and it's the only part of the show that you're allowed to video with your smartphone.
- Older theaters are required to deploy the "fire curtain," which seals the stage from the auditorium in the event of flames, once during every performance. It's usually done discreetly during the interval.
- Leave big bags at the hotel, not just because of security (they will be searched), but also because these old seats can be knee-knockers. And ladies, cover your knees, because in the Circles, they will likely be at head-level of the person sitting in front of you.

architectural mistake. Landlords have tried to evict them for shops, but too late—the skaters proved too beloved. Belvedere Rd., SE1. www.southbankcentre. co.uk. ℂ **020/3879-9555.** Tube: Waterloo.

London's Great Smaller Theaters

Almeida Theatre ★★   The inviting Almeida, which has its own contemporary pub, is gaining esteem by bounds. It regularly unveils new work by the likes of Jeremy O. Harris and *The Crown* auteur Peter Morgan, and its performers include the likes of Juliet Stevenson, Vanessa Redgrave, Saoirse Ronan, and Matt Smith. It also sticks to its guns, mounting intelligent and politically poignant plays (some new, some unfairly forgotten) without much regard for pushback. It has added *Ink, King Charles III,* and *American Psycho–The Musical* to the canon. Almeida St. off Upper St., N1. www.almeida.co.uk. ℂ **020/7359-4404.** Tube: Angel.

The Coronet Theatre ★   This place was built as a small variety house in 1898, but for most of the 20th century it was a cinema—this is where Hugh Grant's character wistfully attended a space movie starring his estranged girlfriend (Julia Roberts) in *Notting Hill.* Now it's one of the up-and-coming Fringe theaters, specializing in international work. 103 Notting Hill Gate, W11. www.thecoronettheatre.com. ℂ **020/3642-6606.** Tube: Notting Hill Gate.

Hackney Empire ★   One of London's greatest and most ornate old houses (1901) was where, once upon a time, you could catch Charlie Chaplin as a vaudeville act. The ever-changing slate still presents the best of variety, but now with a multicultural twist that serves the community: kids' shows, opera, Christmas pantomime, hip-hop drama, and concerts. 291 Mare St., E8. www.hackneyempire.co.uk. ℂ **020/8985-2424.** Tube: Hackney Central Overground.

The Hackney Empire (1901), once a music hall, hosts a pioneering slate of live performances, many of them by new voices and young artists, that change nearly nightly.

Lyric Hammersmith ★ It may look like a fusty Victorian jewel-box theater, but inside, you'll find spectacular stuff—a mix of multimedia-based works, avant-garde experiments, and an annual Christmas show to write home about. Its kids' fare is its bread and butter. Lyric Square, King St., S6. www.lyric. co.uk. ✆ **020/8741-6850.** Tube: Hammersmith.

Roundhouse ★★ Located in a rehabbed 1846 locomotive shed, the Roundhouse picks up on the maverick spirit of neighboring Camden with a frisky, fast-changing lineup of innovative musical dramas and spectaculars, many of them given a crowd-pleasing, dance-inflected, shock-to-the-system twist. In the 1960s, it was one of London's most important stages, particularly for counterculture concerts. In more recent seasons, you're just as likely to see one-off comedy events, poetry slams, or concerts. Chalk Farm Rd., NW1. www. roundhouse.org.uk. ✆ **030/0678-9222.** Tube: Chalk Farm.

Soho Theatre ★ The Soho functions like a one-building arts festival; it casts a wide net in looking for the latest voices in theater, comedy, A-list drag, and cabaret. On weekend days, come for kids' shows. Its Theatre Bar is a fine hangout even sans tickets. 21 Dean St., W1. www.sohotheatre.com. ✆ **020/7478-0100.** Tube: Tottenham Court Road.

The Unicorn Theatre ★ A children's theater that caters to kids without suffering from a debilitating case of preciousness, the Unicorn runs at least two productions, one for each of its theater spaces. Some are script-based and some sensory-based for younger kids and kids with autism. Many are designed to expose kids to other cultures, places, and classic stories. If only every city had a kids' facility as lush. 147 Tooley St., SE1. www.unicorntheatre.com. ✆ **020/7645-0560.** Tube: London Bridge.

Young Vic ★ Spry and defiant, this company programs a mixed bag of jar-ring plays, conversational touchstones (*Yerma*), edgy musicals (Daniel Fish's so-called "Sexy *Oklahoma!*," *The Scottsboro Boys*), and affordable opera, then stands back and hopes for frisson. It often achieves it, and if it fails, it doesn't dally long, since it has three theaters (seating 500, 160, and 80) to fill. There's nearly always something high-quality and new-to-you to plumb here. 66 The Cut, SE1. www.youngvic.org. ✆ **020/7922-2922.** Tube: Waterloo or Southwark.

Pub Theaters

For something easy, cheap (under £15), and daring, try pub theaters. In the early 1970s, this new form of alternative theater swept London. Often just a tatty back room where you can bring your beer from the scruffy front bar, they're where some of the city's most affordable, idiosyncratic, neighborly stuff is found—which is why they launched so many megastar actors to fame. And if you don't like the play, it won't be hard to find a drink to make it seem better.

The Etcetera Theatre ★★ Odd, challenging fare (sometimes several different shows a night) in a very small black box. 265 Camden High St., NW1. www.etcetheatre.com. ✆ **020/7482-4857.** Tube: Camden Town.

If you're in London at the end of the year, see a pantomime, or panto—it's a rambunctious, hilarious holiday tradition. Pictured: a comedy version of *Beowulf* at the King's Head.

Hen & Chickens ★   Frequent comedy bookings as well as strong writing are presented by the resident company, Unrestricted View. 109 St Paul's Rd., N1. www.henandchickens.com. ☎ **020/7354-8246.** Tube: Highbury & Islington.

The King's Head ★★★   Alums include Kenneth Branagh, Clive Owen, Joanna Lumley, Ben Kingsley, Juliet Stevenson, Hugh Grant, and John Hurt in their younger, braver, poorer days. In 2020, it finally graduated to its own space on the same block. 115 Upper St., N1. www.kingsheadtheatre.com. ☎ **020/7226-8561.** Tube: Angel.

Old Red Lion ★   The very pubby ORL hires its 60-seat space to a variety of aspiring producers and hosts the occasional comedy night. 418 St John St., EC1. www.oldredliontheatre.co.uk. ☎ **0333/012-4963.** Tube: Angel.

White Bear Theatre ★   Oscar nominee Emily Watson is an alum of this space, which has made a specialty of reviving forgotten plays. Its pub, here since 1780, has a spacious back garden. 138 Kennington Park Rd., SW11. www.whitebeartheatre.co.uk. ☎ **0333/012-4963.** Tube: Kennington.

OPERA

Opera can be a budget-breaker. Frugal travelers should try the street singers who perform daily at the **Covent Garden Piazza** (Tube: Covent Garden). That's not a joke: Performers are auditioned before being awarded buskers' licenses, so the caliber is high. Also check to see if there's a touring opera putting down stakes at Sadler's Wells (p. 262) or the Barbican (p. 260). Of course, nothing compares to these institutions:

English National Opera ★★   With the Royal Opera entrenched as the country's premium company, the ENO at the gorgeous London Coliseum (built in 1904) is the progressive one that angles for younger audiences. Tightening purse strings have made it slimmer and more crowd-pleasing; its 2016 revival of Glenn Close in *Sunset Boulevard* went to Broadway. The slate consists of both progressive choices and classics: A season usually includes one world premiere, a few revivals, and two new collaborations. Tickets start at just £10 plus £2.25 booking fee—although bear in mind that the balcony, where those cheapest seats are located, is distant indeed. More ways to find affordable seats are listed at www.eno.org/your-visit/ways-to-save-offers. St Martin's Lane, WC2. www.eno.org. ✆ **020/7845-9300.** Season: Sept–Apr. Tube: Leicester Square.

Royal Opera House ★★   Opera fans don't need to be reminded of the role the ROH plays on the world scene, but outsiders might be surprised at how inviting and attractive its terrace and cafe are. The main house, which is shared by the Royal Opera (conducted by Antonio Pappano until 2024) and the equally prestigious Royal Ballet (now past its 70th year here and now directed by Kevin O'Hare), is supplemented with two smaller spaces for chamber opera and studio dance. Surtitles appear on little screens or monitors. Happily, 40% of the tickets cost £40 or less—Friday Rush tickets, which can commonly cost around £12, appear online under Ticket Deals on Fridays at 1pm and you have move quickly. Daytime tours are available, too, for back-stage, the set and costume workshops, and its 2,256-seat, horseshoe-shaped auditorium (✆ **020/7304-4000;** £12–£16; 75 min.; recommended for kids 6 and over; must reserve days or weeks ahead with the online calendar). Bow St., Covent Garden, WC2. www.roh.org.uk. ✆ **020/7304-4000.** Tube: Covent Garden.

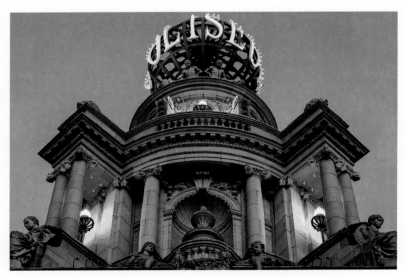

Architect Frank Matcham's Free Baroque tower and rotating globe (1904) atop the London Coliseum, the largest theater in the West End.

DANCE PERFORMANCE

London's dance scene has yet to achieve the vibrancy of New York's or Germany's, but that's not to say there's nothing to see; it's just that some of the best terpsichorean productions are put on by visiting companies, not by Londoners. The first thing to do is check the schedules at the Barbican (p. 260), Roundhouse (p. 265), Sadler's Wells (p. 262), and Southbank Centre (p. 263), which present a cornucopia of performance genres. The country's largest company, **Royal Ballet ★★**, shares space with the Royal Opera (above). The adventurous **English National Ballet ★** tours Britain much of the time but finds itself in London often (www.ballet.org.uk; ℂ **020/7581-1245**), especially for its December *Nutcracker.*

The Place ★★★ (17 Duke's Rd., WC1; www.theplace.org.uk; ℂ **020/7121-1100;** Tube: Euston) is known for contemporary dance—specifically, as the 25-year home of the Richard Alston Dance Company, until 2020—and the host venue of some 100 companies a year from around the world. The lucky tenant of a gleaming translucent building by the same team that designed the Tate Modern, **Trinity Laban ★** (Creekside, Greenwich, SW8; www.trinitylaban.ac.uk; ℂ **020/8691-8600;** Cutty Sark DLR or Greenwich National Rail) puts on a mixed bill of works from around the world and by up-and-comers from its conservatory.

CLASSICAL MUSIC

Cadogan Hall ★   With 900 seats, this onetime Christian Scientist church (built 1907 in the Byzantine Revival style) is now the home of the Royal Philharmonic Orchestra and, in summer, the BBC Proms, which books it during the summer for its chamber music as a supplement to its concerts at Royal Albert Hall. 5 Sloane Terrace, SW1. www.cadoganhall.com. ℂ **020/7730-4500.** Tube: Sloane Square.

King's Place ★★   If you find yourself bored in London, it's not King's Place's fault. The relatively new development behind King's Cross (it shares a building with *The Guardian*) has become a versatile, exciting venue, with spaces for multiple galleries, chamber groups, choirs, and orchestras. Comedy, folk music, jazz, interviews with world notables—surprises abound. 90 York Way, N1. www.kingsplace.co.uk. ℂ **020/7520-1490.** Tube: King's Cross St Pancras.

Royal Albert Hall ★★★   Imposing, ornate, and adored by music lovers worldwide, the RAH is one of the few performance arenas on earth where, once they have performed there, artists can truly claim to have made it. During the summer, the storied BBC Promenade Concerts (the Proms) fill this historic, 5,200-seat circular hall with classical music, but the rest of the year, the space books a hodgepodge of movies with live music in concert (the house organ is 21m/69 ft. tall and has 10,000 pipes), arena-style musicals, regular engagements by Cirque du Soleil, tours—even tennis matches. See p. 167 for tour information. Kensington Gore, SW7. www.royalalberthall.com. ℂ **0845/401-5034.** Tube: South Kensington.

A wide array of performances is booked into Royal Albert Hall (1871), from world-class musicians to Cirque du Soleil, and daytime tours are offered.

St Martin-in-the-Fields ★★★ Right in the thick of Trafalgar Square, this handsome church's evening candlelight concerts and lunchtime performances are London traditions. It's non-fussy with clean acoustics. Trafalgar Square, WC2. www.smitf.org. ✆ **020/7766-1136.** Tube: Charing Cross or Leicester Square.

Wigmore Hall ★★ Opened in 1901 as a recital hall for the Bechstein piano showroom that was next door, it was seized (along with the company) as enemy property in World War I. A nasty start, but in time performers came to include Ravel, Saint-Saëns, Britten, and Artur Rubinstein. Today this intimate space, noted for chamber music and for a bombastic Arts and Crafts cupola over the stage, is known for ideal acoustics and a roster of some 450 concerts, mostly classical, each year. Some nights, there's free music in the bar. 36 Wigmore St., W1. www.wigmore-hall.org.uk. ✆ **020/7935-2141.** Tube: Bond St.

THE MUSIC SCENE

Just as many of London's live music venues don't draw a heavy line between the genres they present, no rigid division exists between gig venues and dance venues; in fact, many spaces switch from live music to dance in a single evening. That's one of the things that makes the city's nightlife so vibrant, but it's also why it's important to check programming in advance. Students can often get discounts on entry—as if you needed any more proof that education is valued in England. Bring your ID—under 18s aren't usually admitted.

Live Music, Including Jazz, Pop, Folk & Rock

Dozens of theaters and arenas in town book concerts by recognizable names, but it would be fruitless to list them since they're almost all rented by promoters and don't always have something going on. The better advice is to stay on top of who's playing by checking *Time Out* (www.timeout.com/london) or *New*

PRINCE CHARLES CINEMA: THE WORLD'S silliest MOVIE THEATER?

The family-friendly "Sing-a-Long-a" *The Sound of Music*, a silly participatory screening of the 1965 classic, was born in 1999 at the eccentric **Prince Charles Cinema** (7 Leicester Place; www.princecharlescinema.com; ℂ 020/7494-3654; Tube: Leicester Square) and swept the world thereafter. Participants—some of whom arrive dressed as Nazis and nuns, without regard to gender—receive a "magic moment" bag with edelweiss, curtain swatches, and a party popper to deploy at the moment of Maria and the Captain's kiss. It does frequent movie marathons (Harry Potter, *Lord of the Rings*). It also supplies a rare chance to view curated 70mm projections of seminal cinematic masterpieces such as *Lawrence of Arabia, 2001: A Space Odyssey*, or, um, *Die Hard*. On other nights, it's an all-night Disney musical pajama party. Or a *Labyrinth* Masquerade Ball. Or a *Murder, She Wrote* "solve-along." And on Friday nights, campier favorites are given the call-and-response treatment, *The Greatest Showman, Grease, Moulin Rouge*, and *Dirty Dancing* among them.

Musical Express (NME; www.nme.com). Since big shows sell out months in advance, the best recourse is to book ahead via **See Tickets** (www.seetickets.com; ℂ 087/1220-0260); **Ticketweb** (www.ticketweb.co.uk; ℂ 0333/321-9990); or the latter's partner **Ticketmaster** (www.ticketmaster.co.uk; ℂ 0333/321-9999), all of which levy fees but let you buy from abroad. Also visit **SouthbankLondon.com** to see what's playing in all the South Bank venues.

All London venues have moved almost exclusively to online booking. I give you the phone numbers when I have them, but if you use them, beware that you're most likely to connect with the void of a voicemail box that's never checked.

The 100 Club ★★   Many decades have passed since this was a prime hangout for U.S. servicemen homesick for the jazzy sounds of Glenn Miller (who died serving in the U.K., you'll remember) and his colleagues. In 1976, after passing through an R&B and jazz period that had Louis Armstrong puckering up for audiences, it sponsored the world's first punk festival, and bands like the Sex Pistols—unsigned at the time—took the stage. This battered red-walled basement institution with good sightlines and expensive drinks still can't decide which era to honor, so it careens among punk, swing, R&B, jazz, and up-and-coming bands—but it never has lost the respect of the musicians' community. 100 Oxford St., W1. www.the100club.co.uk. ℂ 020/7636-0933. Cover £10–£21, 25% discounts often available in advance. Music starts around 8:30pm. Tube: Tottenham Court Road.

The Camden Assembly ★   When it was known as Barfly, this dark, intimate bar/performance space in Camden was the launch pad for a thousand indie bands, some of which actually ended up soaring (Coldplay, Blur, and the like). Today it offers a good mix of club nights and concerts for students, musicians, and old-time locals. Gentrification has tamed the overzealous moshers. When the bands wrap up, a house DJ spins for a few more hours while the audience chills. 49 Chalk Farm Rd., NW1. www.camdenassembly.com. ℂ 020/7424-0800. Cover under £10. Tube: Chalk Farm.

The Crazy Coqs ★★ The stylish 1920s-style room is petite but classy, making it a romantic setting for music, cabaret, and the occasional magic act, all accompanied by potent cocktails. It's part of the accessibly elegant Brasserie Zédel (p. 89) complex north of Piccadilly Circus. 20 Sherwood St., W1. www.brasseriezedel.com. ℂ **020/7734-4888.** Tickets £20–£35. Reservations required. Performances usually 7pm. Tube: Piccadilly Circus.

Dublin Castle ★ Any bar that proclaims itself the birthplace of the 1970s and '80s ditty band Madness would not, on the surface, seem to be a place you'd want to enter without prior insobriety. But it has street cred—it was the first bar in London to win a late liquor license from the government, so it became an important nightspot, and its legendary status was sealed in 1980 when AC/DC singer Bon Scott drank himself to death here. Really no more than a threadbare, greenish pub with a teeny backroom stage, it hosts acts struggling to make it—and a few (Blur, for one, and Madness, for two) that actually have, including the impromptu June 2022 reunion of the original members of Kate Bush's 1970s touring band. On weekends, late-night DJs spin. 94 Parkway, NW1. www.thedublincastle.com. ℂ **020/7485-1773.** Cover £6–£15. Tube: Camden Town.

Electric Ballroom ★★ One of those dicey, utilitarian halls (ca. 1938) that never loses the lingering smell of old beer, the Electric Ballroom has hosted the likes of Sid Vicious, The Clash, Prince, and U2. Steel yourself for a steady roster of punk, goth, industrial, glam, hardcore, metal, and other sensory abusers (like British pro wrestling and Kiefer Sutherland's band). Their aficionados could hardly inflict more architectural damage to the

Another raucous evening at the Electric Ballroom.

premises than what's already been done by the ravages of time and benign neglect. The divine Ultimate Power club event is all power ballads, all night long. 184 Camden High St., NW1. www.electricballroom.co.uk. ⓒ **020/7485-9007.** Cover: live music £15–£20, club nights £8–£28. Tube: Camden Town.

The Garage ★★ This 600-person concert space (once a billiard hall for teetotalers) has enough cred as a modern choice for indie and rock that Harry Styles chose it for a surprise gig in 2017. Overpriced drinks in cans, intimate but loud; you know the drill. There's an all-day bar, too, but upstairs is better: **The Grace**, capacity of around 150, has a late license to serve alcohol till the wee hours (2am Mon–Thurs, 4am Fri–Sat) and tends to host grown-up gigs by singer-songwriters (over the years, Jeff Buckley, Sondre Lerche, and others). 20–22 Highbury Corner, N5. https://thegarage.london. ⓒ **020/7619-6720.** Tube and National Rail: Highbury & Islington.

Green Note ★★ This welcoming vegetarian cafe/bar books acoustic live gigs, from folk to jazz, roots to singer-songwriters. Softened by pillows and upholstered seating, it's a laid-back scene with no dancing. You can eat in the front room (tapas at sensible prices, no meat, all organic) and hear the music, or a cover charge will let you swing into the bar in the back room just for the show. 106 Parkway, NW1. www.greennote.co.uk. ⓒ **020/7485-9899.** Cover £2–£18. Opens 7pm. Tube: Camden Town.

Jazz After Dark ★ Trios, funk, and soul singers, all packed on a tiny stage (so tiny, it's wise to book a table). Amy Winehouse used to come—it's said she applied for a job but they gave her a gig instead. Who knows how true that is, but the cellar vibe is why visitors manage to overlook the grumpy owner and weak drinks. You know it's no good—but dammit, it has a certain charm. Much of its longevity is owed to the fact it serves later than most Soho pubs do. 9 Greek St., W1. www.jazzafterdark.co.uk. ⓒ **020/7734-0545.** Cover: live music £15. Until 2am. Tube: Tottenham Court Road.

Jazz Café ★★★ A prime Camden venue for "names" keeps the music going nightly until 2am, usually in the form of acts (jazz, bluesy vocalists, noisy crap) seen up close. Converted from a bank and renovated with Deco touches in 2016, it has both cabaret tables and an upstairs gallery with food. In the past, there have been occasional club nights for EDM or Cuban dancing, so check the schedule. 5 Parkway, NW1. www.thejazzcafelondon.com. ⓒ **020/7485-6834.** Cover: live music £10–£14. Until 3am Sat–Sun. Tube: Camden Town.

Koko ★★★ Some time ago, Koko stopped being a mere joint for gigs and became an institution. It began its creative life in 1900 as the Camden Hippodrome and saw performances by Ellen Terry and Charlie Chaplin. By the 1970s and '80s, though, as it crumbled, its role as a global fixture was cemented when it rose as an epicenter for pop—the Eurythmics, Boy George, and Wham! all played their earliest gigs here, and it's where Madonna made her U.K. debut. The name Koko brings respect, so when, amid the pandemic, its run-down building caught fire and nearly faced destruction from melted metal and water damage, you could almost hear the collective scream of horror from the music world. The close call prompted promoters to lavish Koko with all the love it's worth. In 2022, it came roaring back with a refurbishment befitting such an icon, adding an incredible rooftop terrace, a quirky bar in its crowning dome, a new performance space in the fly space of the old theater, a speakeasy, a recording studio, a multimedia broadcast space, a shop, and a late-night pizzeria. None other than Arcade Fire opened the venue anew, and Koko also regularly sells out its weekend club nights. The grubby old court jester now wears the vestments of a monarch. 1a Camden Rd., NW1. www.koko. uk.com. ℂ **087/0432-5527.** Cover £14–£35, student discounts before midnight. Tube: Mornington Crescent.

The Piano Works ★★ A live band takes written requests while you eat, drink, and dance on a small dance floor, while its side room, **SingEasy** (https://SingEasy.bar), invites with an intimate, piano-and-mic cabaret vibe and sing-along theme nights. The best is Musical Theatre Brunch Party on Saturdays, when servers, many of them West End performers, join in as they tote bottomless mimosas and prosecco. Yes, of *course* someone will belt "Defying Gravity." There's a second Piano Works location at Farringdon (113–117 Farringdon Rd., WC1; Tube: Farringdon) without the theater kids. 47 Whitcomb St., WC2. https://pianoworks.bar/venues/tpw-west-end. ℂ **020/7889-1966.** Cover £5–£20. Closes at 3am (West End) and 2am (Farringdon). Tube: Piccadilly Circus.

PizzaExpress Live ★★ Unlikely as it may seem, this so-so restaurant chain holds lunchtime and night concerts in jazz clubs at three of its locations—and unlike its food, they're widely respected. The cellar **PizzaExpress Jazz Club** in Soho (10 Dean St., W1; ℂ **020/7439-4962;** Tube: Tottenham Court Rd.) has seen acts such as Jamie Cullum, Norah Jones, and Roy Haynes. There's an upscale supper club for cabaret and talks at the **Pheasantry** in Chelsea (152 Kings Rd., SW3; Tube: Sloane Square), and the recently added PizzaExpress Live (99 High Holborn, WC1; Tube: Holborn) centers on acoustic, jazz, and vocals. www.pizzaexpresslive.com. Cover: live music £15–£65.

PowerHaus ★★ After 1973, when it started as a dance hall in a former industrial space by Camden Lock, Dingwalls (as it was named then) evolved into an ever-popular house of rock, folk, and acoustic guitar. It was special for granting audiences (which usually number no more than 500) the dignity of sitting at tables to enjoy the music, and performers responded: The Sex Pistols, the Ramones, and Blondie in its U.K. debut were all artists who made the pilgrimage. In 2020, Dingwalls changed ownership and, because of a legal claim to the original name, became PowerHaus, a home for contemporary music—yet still the musical monuments come. The legendary Van Morrison came out of solitude to open it in 2021. Choose from a loft-like bar, a terrace bar, and one overlooking the Regent's Canal, where pub food is served all day. Middle Yard, NW1. www.powerhauscamden.com. Daily 11am–3am. Tickets generally handled through Ticketmaster.co.uk. Tube: Camden Town.

Ronnie Scott's Jazz Club ★   Since the 1960s, when it was first recommended in Frommer's, Ronnie Scott's has been London's standard bearer for stylish, American-style jazz, and it honors a long tradition of pairing visiting U.S. greats with local acts. But the old dive got ritzy—after a £2.1-million renovation, the 255-seater began charging prices in the £55 range. Still, it's true that the club draws names, including John Legend, Patti Austin, Van Morrison, Tom Waits, Cleo Laine, Chaka Khan, and George Clinton, and it's also true that, like its landmark neon sign promises, it's open until 3am, which is rare in these parts. 47 Frith St., W1. www.ronniescotts.co.uk. 📞 **020/7439-0747.** Kids 14–18 only permitted before midnight. Tube: Leicester Square.

Scala ★★   When it was a cinema, Stanley Kubrick got it shut down for screening *A Clockwork Orange* without permission. Good thing he did, or this 1920 theater might not have been reborn as a pleasing place to catch an acoustic or lyrical band. Its three levels give nearly everyone a good view of the stage, fostering a sense of intimacy appropriate to its (standing) capacity of around 1,000 people. A warren of rooms confuses the drunk ones and conceals the shy ones. Weekdays, Scala hosts gigs by indie bands, and weekends, it turns to club nights (the long-running Face Down, every first Fri, is rock). 275 Pentonville Rd., N1. www.scala.co.uk. 📞 **020/7833-2022.** Cover: £11–£30. Tube: King's Cross St Pancras.

The Water Rats ★★   If you're not a headbanger, the modest singer-songwriters here may appeal more than Camden's squalling sets. Once it was a pub known as the Pindar of Wakefield; Bob Dylan made his U.K. debut on its back room stage in 1962, Oasis braved London audiences for the first time here in 1994, and Katy Perry played it before arenas—and returned for a nostalgia gig in 2017. The food should be rebuffed. 328 Grays Inn Rd., WC1. www.thewaterratsvenue.london. 📞 **020/7209-8747.** Cover from £12 for several bands. Until midnight Mon–Fri, 1am Sat–Sun. Tube: King's Cross St Pancras.

Major Venues

If you want to get into the big-name gigs, you have to book ahead, before you arrive. Grittier, midsize venues, mostly repurposed century-old music halls, include **Bush Hall** (www.bushhallmusic.co.uk); the **O₂ Academy Brixton** (www.O2academybrixton.co.uk), good for metal and alt-rock; the **O₂ Academy Islington** (www.O2academyislington.co.uk); the Art Deco **Eventim Apollo** in Hammersmith (www.eventimapollo.com); the **O₂ Empire Shepherds Bush** (www.O2shepherdsbushempire.co.uk); and the **Electric Ballroom** and **Koko** (see above). The most massive venues—where your favorite artist will look like a tiny, bouncing smudge on the far side of an ocean of sweaty fans—include the **London Stadium** (www.london-stadium.com), originally the main Olympics stadium but now an occasional concert venue. Tours of that, open daily 10am to 3pm, cost £19 adults, £11 kids 5 to 15, when booked ahead online. Finally, there's **OVO Arena Wembley** (www.ovoarena. co.uk), the site of many an epic concert through its incarnations over the years.

THE illuminated RIVER

In London, even the river views have been taught to perform. In 2021, private donors sank more than £31 million into a project called The Illuminated River, which lights up the bridges in central London, from Lambeth to St Paul's, with an atmospheric and slow-changing light show by New York–based artist Leo Villareal. It's not the kind of display that prances and dazzles, but one that changes gradually over the hours, inviting you to stop, pay attention to the slow-rolling sequence, and come away with a sense of beauty and gratitude that someone cared enough to bring beauty to your nighttime promenade.

The O₂ The £789-million boondoggle on the Thames in East London is a dome 10 times the volume of St Paul's. It's where gargantuan acts from Dolly to Gaga to Kylie to Monty Python appear, packing in their own religious followings, in a 20,000-place arena (ladies, there are 550 toilets for you, too) fringed by a mall for food and clubs. Michael Jackson was in rehearsal for a concert series for the O₂ when he died. For those not keen to see their favorite artist reduced to a speck on a distant platform, there's O₂'s "intimate" performance space, **Indigo at the O₂** (*© 020/8463-2700*), although even that is still plenty big, with 2,800 places. An acoustically superior, contemporary room, it has four bars, and attracts major comics and talent (the late Prince, Black Eyed Peas) and more than a little boxing. If you aren't carrying a ticket for a show, there's not much to do there except eat at chains—there are no retail stores—but if you need something more jolting, you can climb above it, at the **Up at the O₂** roof-walking attraction (p. 196). Thames Clippers (p. 361) docks here, too. Peninsula Square, London, SE10. www.theo2.co.uk. *© 020/8463-2000.* Tube and ferry: North Greenwich.

Clubs

The city's dance scene, being embedded in the style scene, is various and shifting, and by the time you read this, the variety will have shifted again. Spaces are discovered, celebrated, and then redeveloped in the space of a few short years. The social distancing demands of Covid-19 crippled the club scene and caused some popular venues to seek other uses, and nightlife is still trying to recover. Aside from club nights at the venues listed above (see "Live Music," p. 269), the best source for tips on parties you stand a chance of getting into is *Time Out* (www.timeout.com/london/clubs). The clubs around Shoreditch, Old Street, and King's Cross were until recently the markers of cool, but both gentrification and development have squeezed some of the scene northeast to Dalston, which makes getting home in the middle of the night expensive—freelance cabbies charge double. Covers nudge toward £20. Most other places in this section are accessible to the Night Tube.

The king of clubs remains **Fabric** (77a Charterhouse St., EC1; www.fabric london.com; *© 020/7336-8898;* Tube: Farringdon or Barbican), a former butchery that sets a world standard. Its all-weekend parties (from Sat 10pm 'til the cock crows on Mon) are engineered to drill teeth-chattering bass frequencies into the souls of those who dare to submit. Buy early to pay as little as £10. The City is not lost to the nerds yet; the pedigreed managers of **XOYO** (32–37 Cowper St., EC2; www.xoyo.co.uk; ✆ **020/7729-5959;** Tube: Old Street) turned a former printworks into a stripped-down sound tank, and succeeded. The **Ministry of Sound** (103 Gaunt St., SE1; www.ministryofsound. com; ✆ **020/7740-8600;** Tube: Elephant & Castle), which began spinning in 1991, when cavernous and humanity-stuffed dance spaces were the vogue, is known around the planet for its top-notch sound system, upper-crust DJs, and extreme cover charges in the low £30s if you wait until the door.

93 Feet East (150 Brick Lane, E1; www.93feeteast.co.uk; ✆ **020/7770-6006;** Tube: Liverpool Street or Shoreditch High Street) was one of the first pioneers to reclaim disused industrial space in Spitalfields for the hipsters; it mounts a mix of experimental electronic music, live bands, club nights, and day parties. World-class DJs head to **Phonox** (418 Brixton Rd., SW9; www. phonox.co.uk; ✆ **020/7095-9411;** Tube: Brixton), which starts as a bar but opens into an all-night event. It's so carefully produced that smartphone use is banned on the dance floor. Otherwise, wander Dalston and its environs for cutting-edge venues and basement clubs. Huge windows overlooking a decommissioned gasworks make partying memorable at the vast **Oval Space** (29–32 The Oval, E2; www.ovalspace.co.uk; ✆ **020/7183-4422;** Cambridge Heath National Rail), with its eclectic programming of alternative and progressive music. In 2019, it was the first venue to have a plastic-free club night. Its **Pickle Factory**, nearby, is more intimate, attracting cult dance names. The **Dalston Superstore** (117 Kingsland High St., E8; www.dalstonsuperstore. com; ✆ **020/7254-2273;** Dalston Kingsland Overground) is a pansexual party mix of DJs, disco, and ravey go-go boys.

COMEDY CLUBS

London's comedy scene is dominated by Edinburgh's. Each August in the Scottish capital, seemingly all of Britain attends the city's famous festival season, where sharp minds vie for awards, audiences, and perversely, that shiniest of brass rings, a major London booking. The rest of the year, it seems that half the stages in town are either helping artists groom material for Edinburgh (June and July schedules are packed with new shows) or cashing in on past successes in Scotland. The fevered competition has created a comedy scene that has less in common with the stand-and-discuss neuroses of New York clubs and more to do with brittle high concepts. You may miss a few local references, but you're sure to appreciate the wit. All comedy venues serve food and alcohol (so kids 17 and under may not be allowed), and tickets are almost always under £10 unless it's a big name or a very central location. Main shows are usually at 7:30 or 8pm. The tiny **Angel Comedy Club** (2 Camden Walk, N1; www.angelcomedy.co.uk; no phone; Tube: Angel), even though it's in the back of the Camden Head pub, is (legit) one of the best places in town to catch smart up-and-comers, and it's (legit) free to enter; just get there by 7pm on weekends (shows start daily at 8pm; no parties larger than 4 people) to avoid being shut out. It's on the upswing and, as a consequence, added a second space nearby, which it named The Bill Murray. The cluttered, 60-seat **Canal Café Theatre** (The Bridge House, Delamere Terrace, W2; www.canalcafetheatre.com; ℂ **020/7289-6054;** Tube: Warwick Avenue) puts on a dozen shows a week; its biggest draw is "NewsRevue" (www.newsrevue. com; runs Thurs–Sat), a weekly send-up of current events running since 1979, which gives it a Guinness World Record for longest-running live comedy show. The 400-seat **Comedy Store** (1a Oxendon St., SW1; www.thecomedy store.co.uk; ℂ **0844/871-7699;** £18–£25; Tube: Leicester Square or Piccadilly Circus) was created in 1979 in imitation of clubs popular in New York; it launched both Eddie Izzard and Jennifer Saunders. Today it presents improv on Sunday and mainstream stand-up sets the other nights of the week. In a former wood warehouse 20 minutes from the center of town, **Pleasance Theatre Islington** (Carpenters Mews, North Rd., N7; www.pleasance.co.uk; ℂ **020/7609-1800;** Tube: Caledonian Road) has stronger ties than most venues have to Edinburgh; it operates the Scottish festival's chief comedy hub, and it starts previewing entrants in the spring for as little as £5.

CINEMA

Major movie premieres attended by major movie stars are routinely held at a handful of giant cinemas around Leicester Square. Chief among them is the **Odeon Luxe** (24–26 Leicester Square, WC2; www.odeon.co.uk; ℂ **087/1224-4007;** Tube: Leicester Square), opened in 1937 and intensely renovated in 2018 to replace the traditional setup with push-button recliners and top-form audio systems. It's the largest cinema in the country. **The Odeon Luxe West End** is an overflow house of 168 seats in a soundproofed box in the basement of the Londoner hotel, on the south side of Leicester Square. But tickets for Leicester Square theaters can cost over £20 at peak times (it's cheaper in the afternoon). The **Everyman** cinema chain (www.everymancinema.com; 14 locations around London) serves food and drink and schedules a mix of new films, revivals, and live broadcast events. Because so many handsome old cinemas have survived around town, movie-going can still feel like an event. In most theaters, you can enjoy a beer and even select your seats when you buy your ticket—London was doing that long before America was.

BFI Southbank ★★★   The programming of the British Film Institute (BFI)—a world leader in film restoration, preservation, and exhibition—is mind-bogglingly broad and savvy, from classics to mainstream to historic— more than 1,000 titles a year. On a single day, its three screens might unspool a retrospective of Indian director Satyajit Ray, Alfred Hitchcock's *Dial M for Murder* in 3D, a mid-20th-century series from the largely forgotten Boulting brothers, and outdoor screenings of Gothic monster schlock. As the country's preeminent archive and exhibitor, it also programs plenty of talks, special previews, and the occasional free screening. The on-premises **Mediatheque**

is a free video arcade for on-demand viewing of the BFI archive, including tons of titles you'd never see abroad because of rights issues. The shop stocks an incomparable list of rare DVDs, including many treasures the BFI has restored and re-released, such as Charlie Chaplin's early Keystone and Mutual films, and war-era British propaganda films, which you can only find here. There are also two popular bars, one in the lobby and one on the water. Belvedere Rd., South Bank, SE1. https://whatson.bfi.org.uk. ℂ **020/7255-1444.** Tube: Waterloo.

The BFI is a riverfront complex of cinemas, research libraries, chic bars, and restaurants.

The Electric Cinema ★★★ It's one of the world's great screens: Leather seats are softer and deeper than anything you have at home, and each one is equipped with a footstool, table, and a wine basket—it's a luxurious, romantic way to pass a few hours. The bar in the back of the house sells everything from crudités to booze, and downstairs is a barrel-roofed diner. Meanwhile, films, which change daily, hop between first-run and well-received art house movies—nothing too obscure. Shockingly, this place stood derelict from 1993 to 2001, and only a fierce campaign saved it. Now it's run by the exclusive Soho House, which opened a private club here and replaced some seats with bookable beds and sofas. Its outpost in Shoreditch is a new build and not so richly historic. 191 Portobello Rd., W11. www.electriccinema.co.uk. ℂ **020/7908-9696.** Tube: Ladbroke Grove or Notting Hill Gate.

Phoenix Cinema ★ Thought to be the oldest purpose-built cinema in the U.K., the Phoenix was constructed as the Premier Electric Theatre in 1910; by 1985, despite its handsome Edwardian barrel-vault ceiling, it was nose-to-nose with the wrecker's ball until fans (including director Mike Leigh) rallied. It screens an immense range of films from across eras and borders, plus frequent transmissions of live theater. It also has a liquor license. 52 High Rd., East Finchley, N2. www.phoenixcinema.co.uk. ℂ **020/8444-6789.** Tube: East Finchley.

COCKTAIL LOUNGES

The cocktailing in London is so spectacular that you could happily remain tipsy for your entire stay—if only most bars didn't kick everyone out before midnight. You'll find some of the best and most famous hotel bars on earth here, be it **The American Bar** at the Savoy (p. 51), or the bar said to have inspired James Bond's beverage choice at **Dukes** (p. 55), or **Donovan Bar** at Brown's Hotel (p. 62), which combines long tradition (this space has been serving since the 1830s, and Victoria used to have tea in the adjoining paneled room) with modern sophistication. The atmospheric **Trader Vic's** tiki bar (22 Park Lane, W1; https://tradervicslondon.com; ℭ **020/7208-4113;** Tube: Hyde Park Corner), in the basement of the Hilton, has been pouring potent rum drinks, preparing Polynesian-style dishes, and entertaining the likes of Kylie Minogue and Brando and Prince Harry since 1963, qualifying it as the oldest Trader Vic's that's still operating in its original location.

But there are plenty of other bars playing at a modern world-class level. Some critics have called **Lyaness** (https://lyaness.com; ℭ **020/3747-1063;** Tube: Blackfriars or Southwark), facing St Paul's Cathedral across the river in the Sea Containers hotel (p. 66), the best bar in the world. That's also been said about the Italian-themed **Bar Termini** (http://bar-termini-soho.com; ℭ **078/6094-5018;** Tube: Leicester Square) and the moody **Swift** (www.bar swift.com; ℭ **020/7437-7820;** Tube: Leicester Square), which are just doors away from each other at 7 and 12 Old Compton St., W1, respectively. Swift also opened a second location in Shoreditch (91–93 Great Eastern St., EC2; Tube: Old Street). **The Gibson** (44 Old St., ECI; https://thegibsonbar.com; ℭ **020/7608-2774;** Tube: Old Street), an Edwardian-era fantasia by modern back-of-the-bar geniuses, renovates classic cocktails with wild ingredients such as lion's mane mushrooms and marshmallow tea.

You don't have to take your imbibing so seriously, though. First, there are fun bars atop skyscrapers with a view (see "Tall Orders," p. 108). London has also fallen in love with theme bars about London itself. My favorite is **Cahoots** (13 Kingly Court, W1; www.cahoots-london.com; ℭ **020/7352-6200;** Tube: Oxford Circus), a cocktail bar themed to the London

Solve codes to get your cocktail at The Bletchley.

Underground. In the 1940s. Probably during the Blitz. It's amusingly detailed (the menu is a newspaper, there are announcements in the toilets), and sometimes there's live swing music. Book ahead, and if possible, get a seat in the Tube carriage. Or remain in the wartime period at **The Bletchley** (459 King's Rd., SW10; www.thebletchley.co.uk; ℰ **020/3488-1678;** closed Sun–Mon; Tube: Gloucester Road), a World War II codebreaker–themed joint where you have to solve the clues to get your quaff and every recipe is unique to you.

There are eight locations of the Victoriana/steampunk "experience" bar **Mr Fogg's** (www.mr-foggs.com) around central London, and all of them are meticulously detailed evocations of the various haunts of a fictional explorer named Phileas J. Fogg, who has a complex backstory that informs each space a little differently. Gin, 19th-century-inspired cocktails, and British food are served in rococo and arcane settings of antique furniture, scientific collections, and sepia-toned decor Jules Verne might have loved, drawing tourists and parties alike who are always having a grand time of it. Probably my favorite is **Mr Fogg's Society of Exploration** (1a Bedford St., WC2; Mon–Fri 4:01pm–12:01am, Sat 1:01pm–12:01am, Sun 4:01–11:01pm; Tube: Charing Cross), which is set apart by a giant, handmade cocktail-making contraption that mixes Negronis on command. You can't get much more touristy than that, unless it's at **The Cauldron** (5d Stoke Newington Rd., N16; www.thecauldron.io; ℰ **011/7456-2442;** closed Mon–Tues; Tube: Dalston Kingsland Overground), a Harry Potter–themed (but for legal reasons, only ostensibly) potions laboratory where guests don robes, wave wands, learn to mix smoking drinks, and conjure beer from a tap in a magical tree. It even does a wizardy afternoon tea.

GAY & LESBIAN

London's gay and lesbian scene is retrenching in the face of development. In 2015 came the unthinkable closure of Camden's half-century-old drag landmark The Black Cap, and several important Soho bars including Madame Jojo's and Molly Moggs have been forced out or have been sold. Nevertheless, the city still has one of the most varied scenes in the world. The music seems to crank a few notches louder when the jolly and outrageous **Pride London** (www.prideinlondon.org) season rolls along, in early summer.

Daily gay-oriented pursuits have traditionally been centered around Soho, where the bars and clubs take on a festive, anyone-is-welcome flair, and after work, guys spill into the streets. But as a mark of a truly integrated city, now nearly every neighborhood has its own pubs and gay nights. Where you spend an evening depends on your proclivities and willingness to commute. At most places, there aren't usually cover charges unless an event or show is on, when they're about £5 at bars and £11 for clubs. Lesbians who want to go out at night must usually plan a little because most girls' events take the form of weekly scheduled nights in bars that might cater to other niches during the rest of the week.

The weekly **Boyz** (www.boyz.co.uk) and **QX Magazine** (www.qxmagazine. com) publish schedules that favor club events. *Time Out* also has a weekly "Gay and Lesbian" section that dwells more on clubbing than on well-rounded pursuits, and **Nonchalant** (www.nonchalantmagazine.com) is a lesbian publication that dips into London nightlife and lifestyle stories alike.

There are many smaller venues, but these standouts in every flavor are welcoming to tourists and will provide a good overview of the culture.

Comptons ★★   This old two-level pub (built in 1890 as The Swiss Hotel) wears the tatty garb of a bygone saloon but it's one of Soho's most beloved hangouts for men who are out of their bubble-gum years. **Admiral Duncan,** across the street, and the **Duke of Wellington** ("Duke of Welly's"), where Old Compton Street T-bones into Wardour Street a few steps west, cater to the same professional age group. 51–53 Old Compton St., W1. www.comptonsofsoho. co.uk. ✆ **020/7096-5470.** Tube: Piccadilly Circus.

Bethnal Green Working Men's Club ★★   Serving drag, quiz nights, and cabaret hosted by an unmoored Mariah Carey spoof performer—the straight-friendly hipster roster is louche and camp (check the theme ahead of time) but reliably messy. 42–44 Pollard Row, E2. www.workersplaytime.net. ✆ **020/7739-7170.** Cover £10. Tube: Bethnal Green.

Eagle ★   No longer sullied by the dank cruise bar status it once shared with other Eagles worldwide, it's been brightened up and scrubbed down, and now it's a club with a beer garden that's more about celebrating queerness than worshipping leather. Sunday night's Horse Meat Disco is long-running, fun, and welcoming. 349 Kennington Lane, SE11. www.eaglelondon.com. ✆ **020/7793-0903.** Wed–Sun. Tube: Vauxhall.

G-A-Y ★★   It's about partying, cruising, and dancing. The main event is the Saturday night club at Heaven, near Charing Cross Station. No other dance club in Europe, gay or straight, comes close to attracting such a pantheon of legendary live performances: Kylie, the Spice Girls, Adele, Bjork, and, of course, Madge, all made pilgrimages here and have been known to return impromptu. Every night, G-A-Y also runs a light pre-show hangout, G-A-Y Bar, where a twink crowd steeps in cheery Europop and watches videos on the plasma screens. And you can imagine the vibe at its G-A-Y Late venue, which goes until 3am. **Club:** Heaven, Under the Arches, Villiers St., WC2. Tube: Charing Cross or Embankment. **Bar:** 30 Old Compton St., W1. www.g-a-y.co.uk. ✆ **020/7494-2756.** Tube: Leicester Square. **Late:** 5 Goslett Yard, W1. ✆ **020/7734-9858.** Tube: Tottenham Court Road.

The Glory ★★   This pleasingly shabby corner pub in the East End is the modern evolution of London's iconic club kid scene and is known for its unabashedly queer acts and genre-pushing drag (queens, kings, and gender-fluids alike), with a basement disco and regular shows of many stripes. It's far less interested in safe, commercial performances than some other drag spots

where you might bring a supportive mother. 281 Kingsland Rd., E2. www.the
glory.co. ℂ **020/7684-0794.** Tube: Haggerston Overground.

Ku Bar ★★ A manageably sized, young-skewing, three-level lounge is the
place you go when you don't want a scene but you wouldn't mind being
served by shirtless boys. It has a later license: until 3am Monday to Saturday.
30 Lisle and 25 Frith sts., WC2. www.ku-bar.co.uk. ℂ **020/7437-4303.** Tube: Leicester
Square.

Royal Vauxhall Tavern ★★★ A 2013 biography revealed that Diana,
Princess of Wales, once secretly attended this gay drag landmark dressed as a
man. Two years later, it became the first U.K. building to gain protection for
its status as an LGBTQ landmark. Inside, anything still goes. Whether it's
club nights, cabaret nights, drag nights, or just dancing, when the party's
thumping, this little brick building from the 1860s literally leaks dance-floor
fog. 372 Kennington Lane, SE11. www.vauxhalltavern.com. ℂ **020/7820-1222.** Tube:
Vauxhall.

She Soho ★ She's one of London's only 7-days-a-week lesbian bars and,
given that there aren't too many part-time girl bars, either, it attracts a wide
spectrum of types—even tagalong men. 23a Old Compton St., W1. www.she-soho.
com. ℂ **020/7437-4303.** Tube: Piccadilly Circus.

The Two Brewers ★★ As drag rises in global popularity, the role of this
casual, friendly High Street pub as a major hub for mainstream acts has like-
wise strengthened. All the big British names, including the first *RuPaul's
Drag Race UK* winner The Vivienne, tend to pass through. 114 Clapham High
St., SW4. www.the2brewers.com. ℂ **020/7819-9539.** Tube: Clapham Common.

The Yard ★★ On weekends, all the cute jock types are here, cramming
the courtyard-like duplex space. Weekdays, it's more subdued and a place for
the after-work crowd, but it's always straight-friendly. Developers are licking
their chops over the space. 57 Rupert St., W1. www.yardbar.co.uk. ℂ **020/7437-
2652.** Tube: Piccadilly Circus.

WALKING TOURS OF LONDON

Paying for a bus tour might seem smart in principle, but you'll glimpse monuments only briefly and hear only one or two eye-glazing facts about them as you whiz past. No coach tour convinces you that the things you're seeing are quite real, or allows you to mull over what's before you, or lets you breathe in the atmosphere. Get close to London. Don't pass it. Touch it—so that it can touch you.

WALKING TOUR 1: WESTMINSTER, WHITEHALL & TRAFALGAR SQUARE

START:	**Westminster Tube station**
FINISH:	**Trafalgar Square**
TIME:	**Allow 60 minutes, not including time spent in attractions**
BEST TIME:	**Be at the starting line just before noon to hear Big Ben deliver its longest chime of the day**
WORST TIME:	**After working hours, when energy drains out of the area**

When most people hear the word "London," this is the area they picture: the Houses of Parliament, the wash of the Thames, the gong of Big Ben, and the Georgian facade of No. 10 Downing St. Kings and queens, prime ministers and executioners, despots and assassins—this is where they converged to shape a millennium of events, at the command center for England and the British Empire. History buffs, lace up.

---

1 Westminster Tube Station

The best train to take here is the Jubilee line, which was added at great expense in 1999. The station's concrete-grey, 36m-deep (118-ft.) cavern, ascended by escalators from the Jubilee's platforms, is one of the city's finest newer spaces, providing a modern-day analog to the majestic space of Westminster Abbey nearby. Portcullis House, where many MPs (Members of Parliament) keep offices, is overhead.

2 Victoria Embankment at Westminster Bridge

Once you're outside, you'll see the River Thames. If you stood here in 1858, in the midst of what came to be known as The Great Stink, you'd have choked on the fumes rising from the fetid effluvia floating in the river below. Until then, the city had no sewers to speak of—only pipes that dumped into the water. The solution was the Victoria Embankment, a daring engineering project, completed in 1870, that saved engineers from having to dig up the whole city. They simply built a new riverbank, laid sewers along it, paired that with new Underground railway tracks, and topped the unattractive additions with a garden and a road. Destructive, but effective—how Victorian.

Today, the Embankment has benches that are raised to allow a good view of the water, and it's dotted with triumphant statuary like Boudicca in her bladed chariot, which you can also see from here. This tribal queen rose up against the Romans; she failed politically but, as you see, succeeded aesthetically.

The London Eye, spinning on the opposite bank, had a tricky birth in 1999; it was constructed lying flat over the river, resting on pontoons, and then it was laboriously hoisted upright and into place. The mock-baroque building behind it is County Hall—it looks old, but it only dates to the early 20th century—which was once the seat of the London city government.

At the bridge's opposite landing, you can see the South Bank Lion. Weighing 14 tons, 3.6m (12 ft.) tall, and as eager-eyed and floppy-pawed

The Victoria Embankment, a historic engineering feat, is a place for gardens, strolling, and glorious Thames views.

Walking Tour 1: Westminster, Whitehall & Trafalgar Square

0 | 1/4 mi
0 | 0.25 km

Stairs

"Take a Break" stop

Covent Garden Market

Leicester Sq.

Leicester Square

Waterloo Bridge

Piccadilly Circus

Piccadilly Circus

Piccadilly

National Portrait Gallery

National Gallery

finish here ★ 15

14

Charing Cross

Charing Cross Station

Cleopatra's Needle

Embankment

Jermyn St.

Trafalgar Square

13

Embankment Pier

Craven St.

Northumberland Ave.

Whitehall Pl.

Hungerford Bridge

St James's Square

Pall Mall

Carlton House Terr.

ST JAMES'S

The Mall

Craig's Ct.

Whitehall

Horse Guards Ave.

Horseguards Ave.

St.James's Palace

ST JAMES'S PARK

Horse Guards Parade

11

12

River Thames

St James's Park Lake

10 Downing Street

10

Downing St.

Victoria Embankment

8

King Charles St.

9

start here ★ 1

Westminster

2

Westminster Millennium Pier

Birdcage Walk

7

Parliament Square

4

Westminster Bridge

Tothill St.

5

3

Houses of Parliament

6

Millbank

Victoria St.

WESTMINSTER

Westminster Abbey

Monck St.

Marsham St.

Smith Square

Lambeth Pier

Horseferry Rd.

Lambeth Palace Rd.

Regency St.

Page St.

Lambeth Bridge

Millbank

1 Westminster Tube Station
2 Victoria Embankment at Westminster Bridge
3 The Palace of Westminster
4 Parliament Square
5 St Margaret's Church
6 Westminster Abbey
7 Birdcage Walk
8 St James's Park
9 The Cenotaph
10 Downing Street
11 Horse Guards
12 The Banqueting House
The Sherlock Holmes
13 Statue of Charles I
14 Nelson's Column & Trafalgar Square
15 North Trafalgar Square

as a puppy, he was carved in 1837 by the Coade Stone Factory, which once stood where County Hall stands today. Made of a durable, synthetic ceramic stone formulated by a mother-daughter team, the lion stood proudly for over a century, painted red, atop the Red Lion Brewery that was located past the London Eye. Blitz bomb damage destroyed his roost, but at the request of King George VI, he was saved and placed just feet from his birthplace.

Go back into Westminster station, head down the corridor, and turn left before the set of four stairs. Leave the station via Exit 3, marked Houses of Parliament.

3 The Palace of Westminster

You're now standing under the iconic Elizabeth Tower of the Houses of Parliament, once called St Stephen's Tower but renamed in 2012 in honor of QE2's Diamond Jubilee. This is as close as you can get to it—it stands in a restricted area. Look up: Assorted crowns, kings, and crests are carved into the facade. These buildings may look like they're from the Gothic period, but in fact they date to 1859, when they rose from the ashes of the old Parliament House, destroyed by a nightmarish fire in 1834. Big Ben, the name of the largest of four bells inside (2.7m/9 ft. in diameter, 13 tons), was named for the portly commissioner of works who oversaw its installation. (There's actually a bigger bell in town: Great Paul at St Paul's is 2 tons heavier.) Each side of the Clock Tower's four faces is 6.9m (23 ft.) long. Since 1923, the very earliest days of wireless, the BBC has broadcast the 16-note prelude (called "Westminster Quarters" and replicated in doorbells around the world) of Big Ben before its news

Few panoramas are as iconic as that of Big Ben's tower and the Palace of Westminster.

summaries. Thanks to a crack that developed in the 1860s, the bell is now slightly off from its original note—E above middle C. This Big Ben is truly a ringer; the first Big Ben actually cracked within 3 months after being struck by bad hammers. A slightly smaller version was recast by the Whitechapel Bell Foundry which, 107 years earlier, made America's Liberty Bell, which also cracked. Apparently, that happened a lot to big bells and it didn't affect business. But what cracked bells couldn't kill, gentrification did: After 450 years of bell-making and 250 years in Whitechapel, the foundry finally shuttered forever in May 2017.

This plot of land has been used by royals since 1050, when Edward the Confessor built a palace here, away from the hubbub of the walled city. Kings ceased living on this block as of Henry VIII, when nearby Whitehall became his main London pad, followed in later reigns by St James's and, currently, Buckingham palaces. But Parliament's land is nationally owned, so technically it meets in Westminster Palace.

Head away from the river to:

4 Parliament Square

The heavy metal bars on the spiked fence that distances you from this building are not there out of mere paranoia; as far back as the thwarted Gunpowder Plot of 1605, the Houses of Parliament have been a target for would-be revolutionaries. Prime Minister Spencer Perceval was fatally shot on the steps of the House of Commons by a former convict on May 11, 1812, and in the Blitz, the buildings were smashed on more than a dozen occasions, including one (May 10, 1941) that caused the near-total destruction of the House of Commons.

The section of the Houses that juts into the yards, behind the statue of Oliver Cromwell, is Westminster Hall, from 1097, one of the only survivors from the 1834 fire. Charles I, Sir Thomas More, and Guy Fawkes were all condemned to death in the Hall. Big Ben's tower completed a renovation in 2022; the entire Parliament complex is due for its own refurbishment starting in 2025.

For more on visiting the **Houses of Parliament,** see p. 146.

Turn left and walk in front of the Houses of Parliament. Use the first crosswalk to your right, heading toward the church. At the far side of the church, enter the gate to see:

5 St Margaret's Church

The little side church by Westminster Abbey (p. 153), the one with the four sundials on its tower, is the Church of Saint Margaret, dating to the early 1500s and much changed over the years. Sir Walter Raleigh, who was executed outside the Palace of Westminster, is buried inside, and both the poet Milton and Winston Churchill married their wives here.

You can see the statues of Parliament Square better from here. Probably the most famous one is that of American president Abraham Lincoln, at the western end; it's a copy of one in Chicago by Augustus Saint-Gaudens. During the anti-capitalist protests of 2000, the statue of Winston Churchill that stands here received a temporary Mohawk made of grassy turf. This square has always attracted well-intentioned goofs: In 1868, the world's first traffic light was erected here. Gas powered, it blew up.

Follow the footpath to the front of:

6 Westminster Abbey

The lawn beside the abbey—yes, the one you just walked across—is in fact a disused graveyard. In a city this old, you simply can't avoid treading on final resting places. There are an unknown number of plague pits scattered through the city, into which thousands of victims were hastily dumped to avoid the spread of disease, and several city parks likely had the germ of their beginnings, so to speak, as potter's fields—group graves for paupers.

Although most of the Abbey is in the Early English style, the stern western towers above you now were the 18th-century work of Nicholas Hawksmoor, a protégé of Christopher Wren. Hawksmoor's designs are famous for emphasizing the forbidding, angry side of God; some critics accuse him of using architecture to frighten people into piety. Most of the time the people who use this main entrance in an official capacity do so in a crown, a gown, or a coffin. For more on visiting **Westminster Abbey,** see p. 153.

If you peer down Broad Sanctuary, which becomes Victoria Street, you can see the Italianate tower of Westminster Cathedral, the primary Roman Catholic cathedral of England. Good news, Catholics: The English don't execute you anymore!

Cross the street to your right (Broad Sanctuary), and cross again. You should be a block west of Parliament Square on Storey's Gate now. Walk straight until you find yourself at the corner of St James's Park. You're at:

7 Birdcage Walk

You've just walked past a variety of government offices; the proximity to the Houses of Parliament has appealed to paper-pushers for centuries. The military has a presence here, too. The road that heads to the left, Birdcage Walk, leads to the front of Buckingham Palace. Halfway down, you'll find the Wellington Barracks, the headquarters of the Guards Division, where a battalion of one of the king's five regiments of foot guards (Grenadier, Coldstream, Scots, Irish, and Welsh) bunks down. There's also a small, curio-packed Guards Museum (www.theguardsmuseum. com; © **020/7414-3271;** daily 10am–4pm; £8), where you learn that their tall "busby" helmets are made of Canadian brown bearskin. Who knew?

Storey's Gate, the street you just walked, was named for the keeper of Charles II's aviary. Birdcage Walk, the street you're now on, was named after a royal aviary that stood in St James's Park; until 1928, only the Hereditary Royal Falconer was permitted to drive on Birdcage Walk. The park continues its tradition of hosting bird menageries; the pond is a haven for ducks and geese, and a small flock of pelicans has been in

FACING PAGE: Though hardly a saint, King Henry VIII gets a stained-glass window in Westminster Abbey for being a founder of the Church of England (but he's buried at Windsor).

288

residence since the 1600s. They are fed fresh fish daily at 2:30pm (during the pandemic, it happens out of view).

Cross Birdcage Walk and walk 1 block up Horse Guards Road, passing the Treasury Building on your right, until you reach Clive Steps at King Charles Street on the right. On your left, peek into:

8 St James's Park

See if you can spot the lake in the park. The body of water was originally a formal canal belonging to St James's Palace, the official royal residence from the burning of Whitehall in 1698 to the time Victoria moved into Buckingham Palace in 1837. The old canal was prim and straight in the French style and outfitted with gondolas, a gift of the Doge of Venice. In winter, as Samuel Pepys described in the 1600s, it would freeze over, and people would frolic upon it using skates made of bone. It was later sculpted into something calculated to appear more random and thus more English. St James's Palace, which is not open to the public, is located on the north (far) side of the park. You might be able to make out a rustic-looking shack just inside the park. That's Duck Island Cottage, built in 1840 as a dwelling for the bird keeper. Not shabby for a servant's quarters.

You'd think that if London were under attack from flying bombers that you'd be much safer if you were a little farther from the Houses of Parliament. Yet in the basement of the sturdy 1907 Treasury Building, Britain's leaders orchestrated their country's "finest hour." Unbeknownst to the world, it was the hideout of Winston Churchill and his cabinet, known as

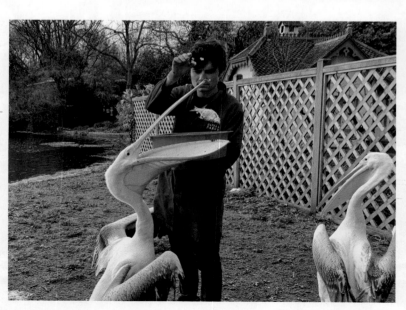

Pelicans have lived in St James's Park for over 400 years. They were originally a gift from a Russian ambassador.

the Cabinet War Rooms. Famously, but hardly wisely, that daredevil Churchill went onto the roof of the building so he could watch one of Goering's air raids slam the city. The cellar, preserved down to its typing pool and pushpins, is now the **Churchill War Rooms** (p. 148), a superlative museum paying homage to the bulldoggy prime minister.

Who is Robert Clive, the cutlass-wielding subject of this statue on the steps? He was the general who helped the East India Company conquer India and Bengal, partly through a series of underhanded bribes, thus delivering the region into the control of the British Empire for nearly 2 centuries. Don't be too hard on this hardened colonialist; the opium-addicted fellow committed suicide by stabbing himself with a penknife.

Walk down King Charles Street and through the arches at the end. You are now on Parliament Street. Look into the center of it. The somber stone column in the traffic island is:

9 The Cenotaph

The Cenotaph (from the Greek words for "empty" and "tomb") is a simple but elegiac memorial to those killed in the two World Wars and later conflicts. A 1919 plaster parade prop that was made permanent in stone by Edwin Lutyens the next year, it was executed with inconceivable restraint when you consider that nearly a million British subjects died in the Great War alone. Its inscription to the "Glorious Dead," coined by Rudyard Kipling, is repeated on other memorials in Commonwealth nations; the Cenotaphs in Auckland, New Zealand, and in London, Canada, are replicas. Uniformed servicemen and -women will always salute it as they pass, and on the Sunday closest to November 11, Britain's Remembrance Day, the sovereign lays the first wreath while other members of the Royal Family observe from the balcony of the Foreign Office. You may see flowers around it, or possibly silk poppies, the national symbol of remembrance.

Walk left up Parliament Street, which becomes Whitehall. In about 30m (98 ft.) on the left, you reach a black fence with glass lanterns. Look inside the gates. This is:

10 Downing Street

On the right, by the tree and tough to make out, is No. 10, the official home of the prime minister. It's famous for its lion's head knocker—although to be frank, if you have to knock, you aren't welcome. Once, you could walk around in there, but Margaret Thatcher made many enemies, so you'll have to make do with peering down the lane through metal bars. Such security was a long time coming. In 1842, a lunatic shot and killed the secretary to the prime minister, mistaking him for the big man; and in 1912, suffragette Emmeline Pankhurst and friends pelted the house with stones, breaking four windows, in one of many acts of civil disobedience in the fight for voting rights for women. If sentries prevent you from approaching, then the prime minister might be on the move. Prepare for the black gates to burst open, spew forth an armada of cars, and watch the prime minister's Jaguar blast onto Whitehall as if fleeing a bank heist.

The lane was laid out by George Downing, the second man to graduate from Harvard University in America and by all accounts a shady individual, a turncoat, and a slumlord. He's one of history's great scoundrels; his underhanded dealings resulted in Dutch-held Manhattan being swiped by the British and the slave trade multiplying in the Colonies. Strange that the most important street in British politics should bear his name.

Downing built No. 10 (then, no. 5) as part of a row of terraced houses in the late 1600s, fully intending for it to fall apart after a few years (instead of actually laying bricks, he just painted on lines with mortar). Yet George II had his eye on the house, and he kicked out a man with the tantalizing name of Mr. Chicken—further information about him, to our eternal despair, is lost to the mists of time—to give it as a gift to the first prime minister, Robert Walpole, in 1730. Walpole insisted that the house be used by future First Lords of the Treasury, his official capacity. He also connected it to a grand home behind it on Horse Guards, now nicknamed The House at the Back—this deceptive Georgian facade actually conceals 160 rooms. No. 10 is also connected with nos. 11 and 12, and it's even linked to Buckingham Palace and Q-Whitehall, a sprawling war bunker, by long underground tunnels. Many prime ministers elected to live in their own homes, using No. 10 for meetings, but not William Pitt, who moved in upon becoming prime minister at the virtually pubescent age of 24 in 1783. He lived here for more than 20 years, longer than any other prime minister, until his death at 46. Whitehall became a slum in the mid-1800s, and the house fell out of fashion, but then it served as the nerve center for the two World Wars and became indispensable to the British spirit. You can see the original front door, now replaced by a stronger one, on display at the Churchill Museum at the Churchill War Rooms (p. 148), two stops back.

A little up Whitehall from Downing Street, look for the bronze monument to "The Women of World War II," which depicts no women, but rather their uniforms and hats, hanging on pegs as if they'd been put away after a job well done. The implication of this 6.6m-tall (22-ft.) tableau is, of course, that the women went back to the kitchen after briefly filling a more robust societal role. This sly bit of statuary-as-commentary was unveiled by Queen Elizabeth in 2005. Some 80% of the cost of the memorial was raised by a baroness who won money on ITV's *Who Wants to Be a Millionaire?*

Continue up Whitehall, past the monumental government buildings. In about 60m (200 ft.), you will reach another black gate broken by two stone guardhouses. Head inside the yard to view:

11 Horse Guards

Built in the Palladian style between 1750 and 1758 on a former jousting field of Whitehall Palace, the Horse Guards is the official (but little-used) entrance to the grounds of St James's Palace and Buckingham Palace. Two mounted cavalry troops are posted in the guardhouses every day from 10am to 4pm, and they're changed hourly. At 11am Monday to Saturday and 10am Sunday, the guard on duty is relieved by a dozen members who march in from The Mall behind, accompanied (when the king is in town) by a trumpeter, a standard bearer, and an officer. Don't try to crack up guards with your shenanigans. You'll look boorish and rude—and they still won't react.

If you think the clock tower arch looks small, you're right. Its designer made it that way so that its proportions would match the rest of the building. Walk through the clock tower arch to reach the graveled Horse Guards Parade, the city's largest non-park gathering space, which you may recognize as the setting for volleyball during the 2012 Olympic Games.

Return from the yard to Whitehall. Across the street you'll see:

12 The Banqueting House

Built by Inigo Jones, this is not a home but it is the last remaining portion of the great Whitehall Palace. The Banqueting House closed to tourists in 2020.

Inside is a bombastic ceiling by Rubens depicting the king as a god. That vainglorious posture, and the king's grabs for more power, led to the gory event that happened on this spot on January 30, 1649. If you were standing here then, you would have been in the crowd that watched King Charles I mount the scaffold (wearing two shirts so that he wouldn't shiver—he was no true god, after all), place his head on the block, and be decapitated, delivering the country to a military dictatorship led by Oliver Cromwell. When the executioner held the head aloft, one witness said there was a queasy silence, followed by "such a groan by the thousands then present, as I never heard before and I desire I may never hear again." Charles I was buried privately at Windsor, not at Westminster Abbey, to avoid more unpleasant scenes. If you want to see what poor Charles looked like alive, hang on for the next stop. The regicide was somewhat for naught; by 1660, the country grew weary of its leadership and Charles I's son, the hedonistic spendthrift Charles II, was back on daddy's throne. In revenge, the second Charles chose the Banqueting House as the site for his restoration party, and then had the nerve to show up late. England was royal again—and how.

Continue up Whitehall. Take the next right, Great Scotland Yard (the corner of Scotland Place was the "visitor's entrance" of the Ministry of Magic in the Harry Potter movies), and then cross Northumberland Avenue, veer slightly left, and head into Craven Passage.

The Sherlock Holmes 🍺

Time for a pint and maybe some traditional English pub grub, so head to **The Sherlock Holmes** (10–11 Northumberland St.). In 1957, a collection of Arthur Conan Doyle memorabilia was assembled as a tourist attraction for the huge Festival of Britain that gave London the Southbank Centre, and it became the centerpiece of this pub. It's nowhere near 221b Baker St., but it has a roof garden and a terrace.

Return to Northumberland Avenue and turn right. When you reach Trafalgar Square, cross the street so you're in the oval traffic island.

13 Statue of Charles I

That this bronze statue stands here is a miracle. It's of Charles I, pre-headectomy, and is a precious Carolinian original from 1633. When the king was beheaded in 1649, the Royal Family was deposed (permanently, so people thought). The owner of this statue was commanded to destroy it, but he was clever enough to bury it instead. A man named Rivet, a scrapper

Stop for a pint at the Sherlock Holmes pub near Charing Cross.

by both trade and character, made a tidy fortune selling knives and forks that he pretended were made from its metal, but after the Restoration, the statue was dug up and placed here, in about 1675. By then, his customers were too tired to demand refunds. All that happened even before Trafalgar Square existed (the zone was, as an equestrian statue suggests, used as stables). Charles wasn't a tall man, and boosting him with a horse went some way toward making the luckless fellow seem imposing. Someone stole his sword in 1867, and he went into hiding again during the Blitz, but otherwise, this is one of the oldest things in this part of London that remains in its original place. Its pedestal, unloved and weathered, could use a restoration, too.

This is a good spot, free of traffic and obstructions, to survey your surroundings and take some photos. Look back down Whitehall, from where you just came, and you'll see Big Ben's tower. To the right, the vista through Admiralty Arch concludes in the distance with the grand Victoria Memorial and Buckingham Palace. Important buildings for two Commonwealth nations stand astride Trafalgar Square: Canada House to the left (west) and South Africa House to the right (east; its country's name is inscribed in Afrikaans as Suid-Afrika).

Cross again so that you're on the south side of:

14 Nelson's Column & Trafalgar Square

Why is Lord Nelson atop that column? Money. The admiral sacrificed his life in 1805 to defeat Napoleon Bonaparte's naval aspirations at the Battle of Trafalgar, thus securing Britain's dominance over the oceans—and pumping untold wealth into London. In the late 1800s, lightning struck Lord Nelson—or at any rate his statue—damaging his left arm. It took until 2006 for the city to finally eliminate the bronze bands that held him together, repairing him with the same Craigleith sandstone with which he was constructed in 1843. During the work, they realized that the monument is actually 4.8m (16 ft.) shorter than guidebooks had been claiming for generations—it's 51m (167 ft.) from the street to the crown of Nelson's hat. The man himself is 5.5m (18 ft.) tall. The column's base is lined with four bronze reliefs that were said to be cast using metal from French cannon captured at the battle that each one depicts. All are guarded by four huge lions (installed in 1867), the mascots of the square, by Queen Victoria's favorite painter, Edwin Landseer. You might think such animals don't belong here, but in the 1950s, under their noses, archaeologists found prehistoric deposits with remains of rhinos, elephants, hippos, and yes, cave lions. Landseer was onto something.

Edwin Lutyens, who did the Cenotaph (p. 291), also designed the plaza's two fountains (from 1845 originals), which were ostensibly for beautification but conveniently prevented citizens from gathering in numbers. Trafalgar Square has long been the setting for demonstrations that turned from complaint to unrestful, such as infamous riots over poll taxes and unemployment. The English gather here for happy things, too, as they did for the announcement of V-E Day (May 8, 1945), and as they still do for festivals and free summer performances. In the southeast corner, you'll see a stone booth big enough for a single person, built in 1926. Once a closet for a phone that was used to summon backup, now it's used mostly to store chemicals for the fountains.

Nelson's Column in Trafalgar Square.

You may have heard about Trafalgar Square's famous pigeons. So where are they? Banished for overactive excretion. Until the early 1990s, the square swarmed with them—the fluttering flock was estimated to peak at 35,000—and vendors made a living from selling bird feed to tourists. Eventually, the GLC, London's government, grew tired of shoveling streaky poo off the statues and decided to return the square to its original function as a great public space to edify its great museum, the National Gallery. They began feeding the pigeons themselves first thing in the morning, and then hired a team of hawks (from the superhero-sounding Hawkforce, tended by a leather-gloved keeper) to patrol the square. The flock learned to chow down and then clear out for the day; anyone who feeds the birds is subject to a £500 fine.

15 North Trafalgar Square

At night when landmarks are picked out by lights, the views down White-hall are sublime. Most of the statues dotting the square are of forgotten military men and nobles: James II (1686; in front of the National Gallery) is finely crafted, but he looks ridiculous, pointing limply in those Roman robes. He was deposed in the Glorious Revolution just 2 years after the statue was cast. It used to stand outside the Banqueting House; for years, detractors joked he was pointing in the direction he planned to flee. (And yes, that's George Washington, who wrested the Colonies from the Crown, standing nearby. Feelings are no longer hard—he was a gift from Virginia in 1921. Urban legend has it the pedestal contains a layer of Virginia earth so he can be said to remain on American soil.) The north-western plinth of Trafalgar Square was designed for an equestrian statue of its own, but money ran out and it stood empty from 1841. More than 150 years later, the naked spot was named the Fourth Plinth and filled by works commissioned by a subversive panel of top artists. Sculptures show for 12 to 18 months, and they get the city talking. Marc Quinn's *Alison Lapper Pregnant* (2005) depicted a snow-white, nude woman born with limb deformities and heavy with child, and *Hahn/Cock* (2013) was Katharina Fritsch's two-story, ultramarine rooster, a sly send-up of the pompous military iconography elsewhere in the square. In late 2022, the coveted spot was taken by Oxford professor Samson Kambalu's sculpture of Baptist pastor John Chilembwe, a Black African who defied British colonial oppression in Malawi in 1914 by wearing a hat in front of white people—and was later killed for impertinence. In 2024, it will make way for Teresa Margolles' white box comprised of slowly degrad-ing plaster life masks of the faces of 850 transgender people.

Along the north terrace, by the Café on the Square, look for the Impe-rial Standards of Length, which were set into the wall in 1876 and moved in 2003 when the central stairs were installed. They are the literal yard-sticks against which all other British yardsticks are measured, showing inches, feet, and yards, plus mostly obsolete measures such as links, chains, perches, and poles.

And now, reward yourself with a visit to the loo, left of the stairs, and a spot of tea in the cafe. Or, if you crave some more substantial victuals, head over to the street east of the square to St Martin-in-the-Fields church, finished in 1724. Its combination of spire and classical portico was controversial at the time, but today, it pleases people of all persua-sions with its excellent Café in the Crypt (p. 91). And, of course, two of the city's greatest museums, the National Gallery (p. 138) and the National Portrait Gallery (p. 142), share the same block and tower above you now.

WALKING TOUR 2: **ST PAUL'S & SOUTHWARK**

START:	**St Paul's Tube station**
FINISH:	**The George Inn, near London Bridge Tube station**
TIME:	**2 hours, not including restaurant breaks or attractions**
BEST TIMES:	**Weekend days in good weather, when the area is abuzz; Borough Market is most vital from Thursday to Saturday**
WORST TIMES:	**After dark, when cobbled streets are too dark to see well**

It was the best of advertisements, it was the worst of advertisements. Charles Dickens' novels, largely social protests wearing the cloak of entertainment, made readers feel as if they'd traveled to London when they never left their own armchairs. Trouble is, the city that Dickens has primed visitors to expect—the foggy, coal-smudged metropolis teeming with pickpockets and virtuous orphans—is nowhere to be found. Partly thanks to Dickens' work, London reformed itself. On this tour, you'll explore what's left of its darker side—from the libertine London of Shakespeare's day to the desperate one Dickens sought to solve with his pen. Along the way, you'll enjoy gourmet food and a beer on the Thames, which conceals a body count of its own.

1 St Paul's Tube Station

If you just took the Central Line here, you rode what was once called the Central Railway. In the first 75 years of the Underground, train lines were independently owned, and separate tickets were required each time a passenger changed trains. Fares were cumbersome, calculated according to the distance traveled and the class of carriage chosen. When the Central Railway held its grand opening in 1900, in the presence of American wit Mark Twain (who lived in London at the time), it soared above its competitors by dint of several innovations, the most important of which was that anyone could ride as far as they wanted on a flat fare. The so-called "Twopenny Tube," which had one class of carriage like today's Tube trains, was a sensation. Gilbert and Sullivan, swept along, amended a line in their operetta *Patience* from a reference to the threepenny bus to "the very delectable, highly respectable Twopenny Tube." The Central Railway helped democratize public transit and accelerated expansion into the suburbs—even if authorities eventually went back to the old format of charging passengers by distance. The St Paul's station opened on July 30, 1900, as Post Office station—the city's main post office was then across the street (hence the name of Postman's Park just north; p. 181).

Exit the St Paul's Underground station and turn left, toward:

2 Panyer Alley

Panyer Alley, where you're standing, was named for the basket makers, or panyers, who once traded here. Look for a plaque on the wall depicting a child sitting on a basket. This plaque, the so-called Panyer Stone, is dated "August the 27, 1688," and reads, "When you have sought / the citty round / yet still this is / the highest ground." The artists behind this stone surely knew that Ludgate is not the highest point in the City; that's Cornhill, which is about 30cm (12 in.) higher. But the sign has been here so long that it would quite literally be a crime to take it down.

Head left, toward St Paul's, and make a right through the pedestrian alley, Paternoster Row, to Paternoster Square. Go through the ornate arch at the far left:

3 St Paul's Cathedral

The area you've just walked through, Paternoster Row, ranks among the most sacred in London. There have been major houses of worship on the plot of St Paul's as far back as 604, and for centuries these narrow surrounding streets have teemed with ecclesiastical scribes and clergy, as well as untold hordes of supplicants desperate for a handout from the merciful church. Paternoster Row was later known as the center of literary London, first for its publishers—who replaced the scribes—and later for its book market. This is where Shakespeare bought the historical texts that inspired him to write his plays. Yet what you'll see today is modern; even the 23m-tall (75-ft.) column in Paternoster Square was created to appear older than it is. Why would planners permit the wholesale demolition of such a rich heritage? They didn't. This was Ground Zero of the Blitz in 1940. The Germans, recognizing that the destruction of St Paul's would demoralize the nation, focused their power on it, and the spillover devastated everything around it. Every firefighter was called to the cathedral, saving it at the expense of just about everything else.

The ornate stone archway that you pass through, however, is a true antique. It's Temple Gate, one of eight ancient gateways to The City of London, which originally stood where Strand becomes Fleet Street from 1672. Charles Dickens described it in *Bleak House* as "a leaden-headed old obstruction." It was dismantled in 1878 and was destined for a dump somewhere when a visionary stepped in and brought the stones home. After spending more than a century in the hinterland of his family's Hertfordshire estate (and being spared the Blitz), the gate, possibly designed by Christopher Wren, was restored and re-erected here in 2004. The seven other gates, including Aldgate and Moorgate, were all lost over time.

In front of the cathedral (you might know the steps from "Feed the Birds" in *Mary Poppins*), a statue of Queen Anne, who ruled England when St Paul's was completed, looks down Ludgate Hill. In attendance are ladies symbolizing England, France, Ireland, and North America, which she considered her subjects. The statue is an 1886 copy of the 1712 original, which (like Temple Gate once did) now resides, in scabby condition, in the countryside.

Herbert Mason's iconic photograph of St Paul's dome, snapped during the mighty conflagration that engulfed London after air raids on December 29 and 30, 1940, was taken from Ludgate Hill. Next time you see that picture, note that it's lit by firelight. To take a photo that feels nearly as good, follow the main road, St Paul's Churchyard, down the length of the

Walking Tour 2: St Paul's & Southwark

1 St Paul's Tube Station
2 Panyer Alley
3 St Paul's Cathedral
4 St Paul's Churchyard
5 Peter's Hill/Sermon Lane
6 Millennium Bridge
7 Bankside
8 Southwark Bridge

The Anchor
9 Clink Street
10 Borough Market
11 Southwark Cathedral
12 Nancy's Steps
13 London Bridge
14 Pool of London
15 The George Inn

"Take a Break" stop

Queen Anne was hostile to dissenters of the church, and a flattering statue of her was placed at St Paul's Cathedral in 1714, shortly before she died at age 49.

cathedral, cross the street called New Change, and enter 22 Cannon Street Gardens, where a smooth-rimmed reflecting pool helps you line up drop-dead romantic images of the world-famous dome. For more on visiting St Paul's, see p. 183.

Return toward the cathedral along the busy street called:

4 St Paul's Churchyard

At the crossing below the dome, go over the street. Now's a good time to duck into the City of London Information Centre, located inside the origami-style, wing-roofed building, and stock up on free tourist brochures and timetables. It also runs daily guided walks on many afternoons. Covid-19 forced it to restrict opening hours to Friday and Saturday, but check current opening times by visiting www.cityoflondon.gov.uk/things-to-do/city-information-centre.

If you don't need information, turn left. If you do use the office, when you come out again, turn right. After the patch of grass, turn right again. You can see down Peter's Hill to a white pedestrian bridge over the river. Stroll down:

5 Peter's Hill/Sermon Lane

On the right is the Firefighters National Memorial, which depicts a young man gesturing wildly toward St Paul's as two others grapple desperately with a hose. It's impossible to exaggerate the devastation caused by the Blitz, both in property and in lives. The superheated firestorms created damage greater in area than those of the Great Fire of 1666. More than

Designed by Sir Christopher Wren and completed in 1711, the majestic St Paul's Cathedral became a national icon. It was saved from destruction during the Blitz, and today modern buildings surround it.

20,000 people were killed, and 1.4 million left homeless. The names of some 1,000 victims, all volunteer firefighters defeated by the wild blaze and collapsing buildings, are inscribed on the octagonal base. Winston Churchill dubbed this monument "The Heroes with Grimy Faces." For their families, the survival of St Paul's Cathedral amid utter devastation remains a testament to their sacrifice. Keep going toward the river.

Go onto the:

6 Millennium Bridge

You're now on the steel, pedestrian-only Millennium Bridge, the central city's first new crossing over the Thames since the Tower Bridge in 1894. Its design, which features side-located suspension cables that sag about six times shallower than a conventional suspension bridge's supports do, was a little too advanced for its own good. When the bridge opened in 2000, it was discovered that the shifting weight of pedestrians caused it to sway, and people had to grasp the rails for support. (At the start of *Harry Potter and the Half-Blood Prince,* Death Eaters attack the bridge and make it wobble—that scene was an inside joke for Londoners.) Engineers closed the 325m (1,066-ft.) span, poured in another £5.2 million to solve the issue, and reopened it in 2002. Now locals (and visitors) love it because it has transformed accessibility to the river's southern bank. It's still not perfect—it's plagued by joggers with little regard for idle strollers—but crossing the river here, in view of many of the city's landmarks, young and old, makes for some stirring photos.

Straight ahead is the monumental Tate Modern (p. 179), signaled by its factory-like "campanile" smokestack, which from 1952 to 1981 belched exhaust from the Bankside Power Station. Energy has been a fundamental part of the district's character for generations. The power station replaced an earlier one that dusted everything near it with a coating of soot, and that plant, too, supplanted a foul gasworks. Before that, the district was the domain of a legion of coal merchants who shuttled their filthy wares around town in shallow boats. These "lightermen" worked from docks that lined the entire southern shore, where land was cheaper than it was in the City on the northern side. The building you see before you is a direct descendant of the way of life that prevailed on the bank in the 1700s.

How deep is the Thames? The river fluctuates greatly with tides (so it's dangerous for swimming—in fact, that's illegal between Putney and the Thames Barrier), but depending on when you measure

Millennium Bridge links the City with Bankside.

around here, it's generally 8.9m (29 ft.) deep at highest tide and 1.8m (6 ft.) at low tide. The Thames' moodiness is the main reason Southwark, the side of the river where the Tate Modern sits, was written off for so many centuries. Until medieval times, the low-lying southern bank was boggy and mostly uninhabitable, so it was instead thought of as part of Surrey, the county south of London. Londoners made use of the water-logged land by turning it into gardens for secret trysts and fish farms (the Pike Garden, or Pye Garden, stood pretty much in front of you around the Tate's eastern flank). It wasn't until the latter part of the 1700s that people figured out how to drain the water and settle the area fully. Southwark was where you went for a rowdy time—that is, until the Puritans quashed the fun in 1642.

Before you completely cross the river, turn back for a stupendous view of St Paul's Dome symmetrically rising from the center of the bridge.

Once you're on the opposite bank, with the river in front of you, turn right. Stand mid-way between the cluster of houses and the building with the thatched roof. You're on:

7 Bankside

This river promenade also continues west, past the Tate Modern, to the London Eye and the Houses of Parliament. In *Four Weddings and a Funeral,* when Hugh Grant told Andie MacDowell he loved her (in the words of David Cassidy), he did it farther along this walkway by the National Film Theatre, the building now known as the BFI. There's no better place to stroll, people-watch, and appreciate the sweep of the city.

As late as the 1960s, much of the path you're on, which at this place is called Bankside, was a vehicular street bearing two-way traffic, as it had been since the 1600s. Each building on the street owned rights to the docks or water-stairs on the river opposite it, so tenants were usually people who needed access to the water, such as ferrymen or sailors. The four-story white house at the left of the blind Cardinal Cap Alley, no. 49, was built around 1710 on the foundations of a pub, the Cardinal's Cap, which itself was built in 1547 to entertain the people who came to Southwark to carouse. No. 49 was home to successive generations of coal merchants, but not, as its plaque purports, to Sir Christopher Wren as he built St Paul's. Wren did live nearby, but in a building that was torn down when the power station needed land. This plaque hung on that vanished home, but was appropriated by a D.I.Y. revisionist in the mid–20th century. No. 49 has received its own biography, *The House by the Thames* by Gillian Tindall.

To the left is Shakespeare's Globe (p. 177), a theater that made a premature exit in its own era, only to be rebuilt in ours. The circular Globe's stage is even at the same compass point as the 1599 original's. Interestingly, the city's theatrical life was centered here from about 1587 to 1642, when it was illegal to operate a theater in the City proper. Once the laws relaxed, the entertainment venues moved back into town, where they've been ever since.

The near-exact replica of the Shakespeare-era Globe is both a museum and a working theatre.

Southwark was the Tudor version of a multiplex, and the biggest blockbuster was bear-baiting—the spectacle of vicious dogs let loose upon tethered bears. Even Henry VIII and Elizabeth I were huge fans; he had a bear pit installed at Whitehall Palace, and she barred Parliament from banning the pursuit on Sundays. One and a half blocks past the Globe, squeeze between modern buildings down an alley called Bear Gardens to find a small courtyard, three-quarters of the way down the street. That's the rough location of the Davies Amphitheatre, one of the most popular bear pits. Samuel Pepys wrote in his diary in 1666 of attending one such slaughter where he "saw some good sport of the bull's tossing the dogs—one into the very boxes. But it is a very rude and nasty pleasure."

Under a modern office building in the next street, Rose Alley, lie the foundations of another theater known to have premiered plays by Shakespeare, the Rose. It lasted from 1587 to about 1606. The Swan stood nearby, too, although we may never find the footprint. The Rose's footprint gave us vital clues about what Elizabethan theaters looked like—architects also studied sketches made of it by a Dutch tourist in 1596. (Are you sketching your trip?)

Historians think they know where the original Globe stood. If you'd like to see it, head down Bear Gardens (between two modern buildings) one block to Park Street, turn left and go under the bridge, and just after it, past the buildings on the right, you'll find slightly red cobbles showing locations of fragments archaeologists found in 1989. Not very suggestive, is it? In 1949, it was even drearier. It lay behind the gate of the decrepit Anchor Brewery, and when American actor Sam Wanamaker (father of Zoë, who played Madam Hooch in the Harry Potter movies) dropped by to pay pilgrimage, the indignity of the meager plaque (still there) so enraged him that he resolved to rebuild the Globe as a living home for England's great theatrical tradition—which is what came to pass, albeit 4 years after his 1993 death. Oscar-winning actor Mark Rylance was its first artistic director, serving for a decade.

Continue along the river, keeping it to your left. You'll go through a pedestrian tunnel under:

8 Southwark Bridge

On the wall of the tunnel, you'll see illustrations of skaters and revelers at the bygone "Frost Fairs" that, starting in 1564, were regularly held on the icy Thames. No matter how many winters you spend in London, you'll never see the Thames freeze over. But back then, they had the London Bridge, a few hundred yards downstream. Its 19 arches were so narrow, and its supports so thick, that the river's flow became sluggish, allowing water (and the outhouse filth that churned within it) to freeze. By contrast, during outgoing tides the rush was so fierce that boats capsized and passengers (few of whom knew how to swim, given the filth) drowned. When the bridge was dismantled in 1814, the Frost Fairs melted into history.

Take a look underneath Southwark Bridge where it meets the shore. You can still discern the remains of some water-stairs, dating to before the construction of the first bridge here in 1819. Back then, getting across the river usually required boatmen, the taxi drivers of their day. Ferrymen would court business by shouting destinations to theatergoers after their plays: "Eastward ho!" or "Westward ho!"

In 1912, this bridge's central 72m (236-ft.) span was the largest ever attempted in cast iron.

The Anchor 🍺

Few pubs are more lively than the **Anchor** (p. 112), situated where Bankside meets the railway viaduct. The riverside patio is open in good weather; otherwise, the interior is charming. This pub was once controlled, as nearly all pubs once were, by a brewery; it was Barclay Perkins, located just behind it from 1790 until about 1980. Even before that, it was a fixture; in 1666, Samuel Pepys watched the Great Fire rage from here before coming to his senses and hurrying across the river to rescue his possessions from his home in Seething Lane, near the Tower of London. In the 1950s, the Anchor was considered a slum and nearly was demolished.

After the Anchor, the path jogs inland. Take the first left onto:

9 Clink Street

Pass under the railway arch. In a few moments, you've gone from Elizabethan Southwark (theaters, bear-baiting) to Georgian Southwark (coal merchants, breweries). Now you're in Victorian Southwark, a claustrophobic underworld teeming with fetid-smelling industry and river rats. You can almost hear distant reverberations on this narrow wharfside street. If you called the sensation Dickensian, you wouldn't be wrong. When the writer was 12 years old, his father was thrown into a debtor's prison near where you're standing, off the Borough High Street.

Prisons were something of a cottage industry for the area; the Clink Street Prison stood here from 1127, when the Bishop of Winchester built it as a lockup for his Winchester Palace, until 1780, when the anti-Catholic Gordon Riots saw the dismal hole destroyed. Although the Clink gave its name as slang to all prisons that came after it, no one knows for sure how it got the name itself—Flemish or Middle English words for latch are likely the origin. Suffice to say it was awful—and so is the "museum" here that purports to tell its story. Avoid it.

In the 1800s, warehousing goods instead of people became this street's stock-in-trade. You'll still see hints of the street's past maritime uses, from wooden loft doors to cranes used to hoist crates into upper floors. Today, these spaces house media companies and architects. During the week, you'll see professionals in their fashionable clothes, strutting in their Italian shoes across pavers that until recently were the original rounded cobbles. On weekends, you'll follow a current of tourists.

The latter Bishops of Winchester were not nice guys. Henry II (1133–89) gave them control of this neighborhood, and because it was outside the jurisdiction of the city, they could pretty much get away with whatever they wanted to. Principally, they cultivated countless brothels and skimmed the profits for themselves—which is how Southwark got its rep as a den of vice. Anyone who annoyed them (heretics, troublemakers) wound up in the Clink, where no one was likely to find them again. As you continue down Clink Street, past the modern building with the rounded grid of windows, on your right you'll see all that's left of the Bishops' palace: a fragment of old stone wall, dating to the 1300s, with a round panel of stone tracery at the top. That tracery once held a rose window, which lit the palace's great hall. This fragment was forgotten behind a wall until a warehouse fire exposed it again. Double back to Stoney Street.

Turn down Stoney Street and walk under the railway. On your left, you'll see:

10 Borough Market

Stop at the frilly grey portico.

The mood of the neighborhood has changed drastically again. To your left, behind the portico, is Borough Market, a fantasy for the tongue (described in gastronomic detail on p. 105) and the oldest fruit and vegetable market in the city. A market has been held around here since A.D. 43, when Roman soldiers noted passing a market on their way to sack the City. More reliable records date it to 1014, when it served the denizens on the old London Bridge, the city's only river crossing. The cream-grey portico is not original to this place; it's the cast-iron Flower Hall of

Covent Garden, rescued when the Royal Opera House was renovated in 2003. If it seems to blend seamlessly, it's because it was made around the same time as the rest of the Borough Market structure (1859–60). You are standing very near the spot, outside the Wheatsheaf pub, where police guns swiftly put an end to a ghastly Saturday night terrorist attack by knife-wielding attackers in June 2017.

The market is best known for gourmet supplies. Park Street, which runs into Stoney Street, looks as quaint as a movie-set version of old England; in fact, it was used in *Harry Potter and the Prisoner of Azkaban,* and no. 7a was the entrance of The Leaky Cauldron. The market itself has appeared in films including *Howard's End* and *Bridget Jones's Diary.* The city's first railway, a 6.4km (4-mile) run to Greenwich, plowed its route .8km (½ mile) east of here in 1836. Even after tunneling technology improved, railway tycoons kept barricading thriving neighborhoods with massive brick viaducts, cutting them off from each other and creating slums, all because it was cheaper than digging. On your tour, you have crossed under a number of railway viaducts built that way, and shortly, you'll see how narrowly one of England's most historic churches averted its own destruction.

Enter the market to the right of the portico and walk straight. Cross the next street and enter the brick arch marked Green Market. Before you is:

11 Southwark Cathedral

(If for some reason the Green Market arch is closed, turn left down railway-covered Bedale Street until you see a church appear on your right.)

Before you stands the oldest Gothic church in the city, and the oldest building in Southwark. In Roman times, it was the site of a villa. You'll see its tower appear in every medieval drawing of the city. Its Christian chapter was begun by the daughter of a ferryman in the 7th century; it was rebuilt in the 850s and again 300 years later. There was once a monastery and a chapel in this yard, where office workers now lunch on gourmet items from Borough Market, but those came and went, too. Southwark teemed with the poor, with factory workers, and with grubby river men. One such blue-collar child was John Harvard, one of nine kids of a man who owned a tavern and butcher shop just northeast of here. John was baptized in this church in the early 1600s, but when he grew up and became a minister, he fled this slum for the Massachusetts Bay Colony, where Harvard University was later named for him. In time this place was limping along as a humble parish church called St Saviour's and dissolving into dilapidation. The rerouting of London Bridge Road sheared away several small chapels, and in 1863, the rumbling railway forced its way alongside the yard. But by 1905, its fortunes reversed when it was elevated to a cathedral, and now it's so well cared for that it's hard to discern its true age and sordid past.

In Chaucer's *The Canterbury Tales,* a motley group of pilgrims set off from the Tabard, a tavern (once located in today's Talbot Yard) near Southwark Cathedral (pictured here).

The cathedral has some beautiful painted monuments, including one of England's oldest wooden effigies (1280). Shakespeare's brother Edmond was buried here in 1607, as was Philip Henslowe, who built the Rose theater, in an unmarked grave. Other worthwhile sights include Edwardian stained-glass tributes to the Bard's plays, the Harvard Chapel with masonry from the Norman period, and some of the original ceiling bosses, carved in 1469 and saved when things got bad. How bad? During Elizabeth I's reign, the retro-choir (the part behind the altar) was walled off and rented to a baker. Later on, vestrymen discovered the baker was also raising swine in there. Yes, inside the church. Things were rough.

Keeping the cathedral on your right, walk toward the Thames on Montague Close, which bends right to follow the north side of the cathedral. Just before the overpass, look left for:

12 Nancy's Steps

These are popularly held to be the location, in the Dickens novel *Oliver Twist*, where Noah Claypole eavesdrops on a conversation that leads to Nancy's murder by Bill Sikes. In the book, those steps faced the Thames; in fact, these steps are a rare surviving remnant of the New London Bridge, built here in 1821 as a replacement for the 600-year-old, overcrowded London Bridge. (The steps that Dickens wrote about were sold in 1968 to an American oilman. Locals superciliously quip he was duped, but, in fact, he knew exactly what he was doing and preserved what the English wouldn't. He had most of the New London Bridge shipped, stone by stone, to Lake Havasu, Arizona, to form a tourist attraction, and there it remains today, standing near a marina on a desert lake.) These steps were left behind and attached to the existing London Bridge, a featureless 1973 replacement.

Just so you know, the modern London Bridge was not the source of the nursery rhyme "London Bridge Is Falling Down"—that either referred to the burning of a wooden version in 1013, during a skirmish between Danes and Norwegians; or to Henry III's "fair lady" Queen Eleanor, who skimmed the tolls of the medieval bridge for her own purse, leaving its maintenance in a parlous state.

Climb the stairs to the road above. You're now on:

13 London Bridge

At the top of the stairs, you'll see a pedestal topped by a dragon, the symbol of the city, holding London's crest. You'll see these dragons at several of the city's medieval borders. About 30m (98 ft.) east of here, under modern buildings, is where you would have entered the Stone Gateway, the entry to the disaster-prone medieval London Bridge. For more than 3 centuries, tar-dipped heads of executed criminals were impaled on pikes and stuck atop the Gateway as a vivid warning to would-be ne'er-do-wells.

Turn to the right to use the crosswalk. Go to the opposite side of the street and walk onto London Bridge, over the river. Don't cross the river—just enjoy the view of the:

14 Pool of London

This section of the Thames between London Bridge and the Tower Bridge is known as the Pool of London. It may be quiet now, but for nearly 2,000 years, it was the heart of international trade. So many goods passed through here that warehouses along the southern bank became known as "London's Larder." The water was so overcrowded with boats that developers kept having to carve new basins throughout East London where vessels could pull in and unload (you can see the mini-lakes forming a honeycomb of waterways on the maps), but ships eventually became so giant that now they have to unload downstream, closer to the sea. The part of river in front of you, parallel to this bridge, is where the medieval London Bridge stood.

Across the river from the Tower, you'll just make out an egg-shaped glass building on a riverside open space. From 2002 to 2022, that was London's City Hall, designed by Norman Foster (who also did the Millennium Bridge) to be ergonomic, with a huge spiral staircase curling around its atrium and "smart" windows that open on hot days. Just like a politician, it has no edge and you can't tell if it's coming or going. Now the city's offices are way out at the Royal Docks in East London, near London City Airport, but the riverside open space they left behind, Potters Fields Park, will be where you can take some of the best possible photographs of the Tower Bridge.

Turn around and keep London Bridge to your back, keeping on the left side of the road. This street becomes Borough High Street. You will pass under a railway arch. Just after you pass Southwark Street forking off to the right, look for "The George" sign. It marks:

15 The George Inn

Because the London Bridge was the only crossing to the city from the south for so many centuries, this area became the equivalent of a train depot, and it was dotted with inns, stables, coach yards, and pubs. Everyone going to or coming from southern England or Europe stopped here, often spending the night before pushing into the shoulder-to-shoulder crowds of London Bridge. If you've ever read *The Canterbury Tales,* you'll recall that in 1386, the pilgrims began their journey to the shrine of Thomas à Becket from the Tabard Inn. Until 1873, that was located a short walk farther down Borough High Street, on the left. The George, described on p. 113, is the last survivor from this bustling coaching era. Although the wooden building, which once encircled the entire yard, dates to 1677, the inn was here for at least another 130 years before that, if not longer. We know it was typical of the time because John Stow, in *A Survey of London* (1598), termed it "a common hostelry for travelers." A drink here makes a fitting end to your journey through time. Look up and you'll see the jagged glass spire of the Shard (p. 180), one of Europe's tallest buildings, peering down as you sit where people have lifted beer for nearly half a millennium.

WALKING TOUR 3: SOHO & ST GILES: POP, SHOP & MARX

START:	**Oxford Circus Tube station**
FINISH:	**British Museum**
TIME:	**2 hours, not including shopping or restaurant breaks**
BEST TIMES:	**Weekdays, when Berwick Street's market is on and Oxford Street is slightly less crowded**
WORST TIMES:	**Evening rush hour, when Oxford Circus Tube stop is positively rammed, and after dark, when stores and the museum close**

All churched out? London is more than stories about dead queens and bloody uprisings. It's always been cosmopolitan, too, and the flash point for trends that ripple out to the rest of the world. Songs first sung at the clubs of Soho soon caused toes to tap on the other side of the planet, and fashion trends born on Carnaby Street in the '60s remain internationally iconic all these years later. Bring along your credit cards as we roam some of the city's best shopping streets and touch upon a few leftovers from London's recent past, including forgotten air-raid shelters and the settings for some good, old-fashioned sex scandals. This is the London you found out about from the radio and the runways, not from your social studies teacher.

1 Oxford Circus

Leave the Tube station using Exit 2. Position yourself out of the fray.

You are in the thick of mile-long **Regent Street,** which to the right is punctuated by the witches-hat steeple of All Souls Church and to the left curves toward Piccadilly Circus. When the Prince Regent, later George IV, was planning his new pet project, Regent's Park, he decided he also wanted a road to connect his house to it. He chose this particular location because, in his mind, it would provide a suitable demarcation line between the gentry of Mayfair, to the west, and the rabble of the traders who lived in Soho, to the east. George tapped John Nash to do the job, completed in 1825. Originally, the sidewalks were covered by stone colonnades, but when those attracted prostitutes, they were removed, and most of the original buildings were later rebuilt—the only Nash original is now All Souls. Even if most of the facades you see now mask more modern buildings, few streets in London impart such a sweeping, uplifting feeling, though few are also as congested with the hoi polloi George would have spurned.

The other avenue intersecting before you is Oxford Street, following the same line as a Roman road. George's class-centered definition of the landscape has more or less held: The exclusive shops of Oxford Street still lie west of Regent Street, and the downmarket stores tend to be east of it. Having a presence on Oxford Street is considered crucial for brands with mass appeal.

The famous intersection known as Oxford Circus.

Head right, east on Oxford Street. You will pass Argyll Street on the right. When you pass Ramillies Street, prepare to stop in front of:

2 Marks & Spencer

London has a love-hate relationship with Oxford Street. People come here to shop by the thousands, but they often despair of the crush of the experience. Charles Dickens, Jr., described the street thusly in 1888: "It ought to be the finest thoroughfare in the world. As a matter of fact it is not by any means, and though it is, like all the other thoroughfares, improving, it still contains many houses which even in a third-rate street would be considered mean." We're only going to walk down a sample of Oxford Street. It's usually so crowded, that's as much as you can probably handle if you're keeping one eye on this book.

Marks & Spencer (p. 236), or M&S, dates to 1894 and is the favored British department store for staples. Perhaps proof of its appeal is that the chain can afford to run two giant frontages on Oxford Street; its flagship store is remarkably near here, between Bond Street and Marble Arch Tube stations. Its Food Halls (at this store, in the cellar) are well known as an ideal place to pick up prepared foods, sandwiches, and inexpensive but well-selected wines.

Turn right at Poland Street, walk 1 block, and turn right again onto Great Marlborough Street. Soon on your right, at nos. 19–21, you'll see a stout white building. That's the:

3 Great Marlborough Street Magistrate's Court

Charles Dickens worked here as a reporter just before hitting it big as a novelist, and a variety of other big names appeared before the judges here, including the Marquess of Queensbury (defending himself from

Walking Tour 3: Soho & St Giles: Pop, Shop & Marx

British Museum
Russell Square
Montague Pl.
Montague St.
Southampton Row
Bloomsbury St.
Bedford Ave.
Bedford Square
Gt. Russell St.
Store St.
Coptic St.
Museum St.
Bloomsbury Way
High Holborn
New Oxford St.
St. Giles High St.
Tottenham Court Rd.
Charing Cross Rd.
Shaftesbury Ave.
Monmouth St.
Long Acre
Bow St.
Covent Garden Market
COVENT GARDEN
Leicester Sq.
Gerrard St.
Greek St.
Frith St.
Dean St.
Denmark St.
Soho Square
Bateman St.
Old Compton St.
St. Peter St.
Wardour St.
Berwick St.
Poland St.
Lexington St.
Golden
Beak St.
Kingly St.
Carnaby St.
Regent St.
Conduit St.
Maddox St.
Gt. Marlborough St.
Marshall St.
Brewer St.
Broadwick St.
SOHO
Oxford St.
Ramillies Pl.
Margaret St.
Gt. Titchfield St.
Gt. Portland St.
Regent St.
Langham St.
Mortimer St.
Wells St.
Eastcastle St.
Berners St.
Berners Mews
Newman St.
Rathbone Pl.
Rathbone St.
Percy St.
Windmill St.
Hanway St.
Whitehead St.
Goodge St.
Charlotte St.
Cleveland St.
Goodge St.
Tottenham St.
Chenies St.
Foley St.
New Cavendish St.
Howland St.
Oxford Circus

start here
finish here
Take a Break stop

1. Oxford Circus
2. Marks & Spencer
3. Great Marlborough Street Magistrate's Court
4. Foubert's Court
5. Carnaby Street
6. Kingly Court
7. John Snow Pub
8. Berwick Street
9. Berwick Street Market
10. Brewer Street
11. Old Compton Street
12. Frith Street
13. The Dog & Duck
14. Denmark Street
15. St Giles
16. Shaftesbury Theatre
17. The British Museum

0   1/8 mi
0   100 meters

Oscar Wilde's libel charge). When this neighborhood turned bohemian in the Swinging '60s, the court began trying a string of drug charges against the likes of Mick Jagger, Johnny Rotten, Keith Richards, Francis Bacon, and, curiously (and coming full circle), the guy who wrote the musical *Oliver!*, Lionel Bart. It's now a hotel, but I suggest you go inside briefly, because much of the old judicial fittings were left intact. You can have a cocktail in one of the old jail cells—now converted into private booths—or even peek into a restaurant slotted into the authoritative Number One court, which still has its witness stand, bench, wood paneling, and vaulted glass ceiling.

Beyond the Courthouse Hotel on the left, you'll see a Tudor-style building of black beams and white plaster. This is Liberty (p. 234), famous for its haute fabrics. It's also famous for its building—it was made in 1924 using wood recycled from junked ships.

Great Marlborough Street runs into Regent Street. Turn left there and walk the short distance to:

4 Foubert's Court

Times have been better on Regent Street. Walmart-style box stores in the suburbs have put the screws on the destination shops of the city, and this avenue has seen long-termers lose their sizzle. Dickins & Jones, a department store at the corner you just turned, closed its doors in 2006 after nearly 170 years, and the same old shopping mall brands have been moving in.

Two doors farther from Foubert's Court, though, at nos. 188–196, is a well-loved holdover from the street's glory days. It's Hamleys (p. 250), one of the largest toy stores in the world. Some 5 million customers pour through its doors every year, but since the sales force is famous for putting on a nonstop show on every floor, it's understandable if many of those customers come to gawp and not to buy. If you go into Hamleys, when and if you come out again, turn right and go back to Foubert's Court.

Walk down the very short Foubert's Court for 1 block; you'll see "Carnaby" on a metal arch. Go under it and head 1 block. Go right, and now you'll see a larger arch on:

5 Carnaby Street

Yes, those obnoxious arches proclaim your location with a self-promotion that proves this street is no longer the super-cool, forward-trending street of the kids in the know. It's more of a mall with an edge. The days of Swinging London, when men could cruise from store to store trying on hip-hugging black trousers and frilly shirts, are behind it. *Time* magazine spilled the secret of Carnaby Street in 1966, and by the 1970s, it was pedestrianized as a shopping street, making hipness a matter of retrospect.

Just after you cross Ganton Street, where Broadwick Street hits Carnaby Street, duck into the passageway on the right:

6 Kingly Court

Clever entrepreneurs led Carnaby Street's rebirth with this development, a lively gathering of bars and restaurants in a former timber warehouse.

More than 20 restaurants and shops fill the Kingly Court food hub near Carnaby Street.

Slip out the back door of Kingly Court, opposite its front door, and hang a left on Kingly Street. No. 9 was the Bag 'O Nails pub, where future Wings-mates Paul McCartney and Linda Eastman first clapped eyes on each other—and also where in 1961 John Profumo met Christine Keeler, kicking off the Profumo Affair, a notorious national security scandal. It's also where Fleetwood Mac's John McVie proposed to Christine. (The free audio touring app Carnaby Echoes dives into the music history of the neighborhood.)

Return to Kingly Court. Retrace your steps out of it, cross Carnaby Street, and head down Broadwick Street. You'll stop around:

John Snow Pub 🍺
So grateful were Dr. Snow's neighbors that they renamed their pub for him, albeit a century later. It stands at no. 39, at Lexington Street, on the site of his practice. Raise a pint in his honor here, as we read the words of Dr. Snow himself: "I feel it my duty to endeavor to convince you of the physical evils sustained to your health by using intoxicating liquors even in the greatest moderation." (Oops.)

Continue on Broadwick Street to:

7 Berwick Street
In the mid-1800s, this block was a foul slum. French, Greek, and Italian immigrants fled hard times and revolutions by cramming into these tight streets, and by the 1850s, cholera was storming through the overstuffed city. An 1854 outbreak killed 500 people in barely 10 days. Common

wisdom at the time held that the disease was spread through the air—a reasonable conclusion, given how terrible the sewage-smeared city smelled—but a local anesthetist, John Snow (for whom the pub you just visited was named) had a different theory. Suspecting polluted water was the cause, he got permission to inspect the public pump at Broad Street, now Broadwick Street (in the block before Berwick St.) and found that it was being contaminated with sewage leaking from no. 40, at the corner of Broadwick and Poland streets. The saga was retold in the book *The Ghost Map* by Steven Johnson, and in 2015 the site of no. 40 was dug up to build this new building.

When you reach Berwick Street, look left. Think of this location as the modern-day Abbey Road. It's where, in 1995, Oasis photographed the cover of *(What's the Story) Morning Glory?,* one of the seminal CDs of the age. The photographer shot from farther down the street, aiming south, toward where you're standing. (Noel Gallagher, with characteristic tact, said he thought the album cover was "s**t.")

And here's another slice of rock history: One miniblock farther down Broadwick Street at no. 7, the corner shop covered in striking rust-colored tiles (now Sounds of the Universe record store, a local landmark for world music) was the Bricklayers Arms pub. Brian Jones auditioned the Rolling Stones here in 1962, and they held formative rehearsals upstairs. The word "Soho" is probably derived from a hunting cry used when this area was parkland—it's nice to see that some folks around here are still on the hunt.

Turn south on Berwick Street. Walk down it to:

8 Berwick Street Market

This is the vestige of the last great weekday market in the center of the city—it's been in operation at least since the 1840s (vestry records indicate some illicit trading was going on as far back as 1778). London's first publicly available grapefruit was sold here in 1890. Now that the produce sellers have been mostly elbowed aside for gourmet nibbles, the market again caters to those with exotic, expensive tastes.

Pass over Peter Street and under Maurice House, going under the crossover and winding up on:

9 Brewer Street

From the late 1700s to the 1950s, it was impossible for a single gentleman to pass unpropositioned through Soho. A 1959 act chased the open salesmanship indoors, to be replaced by drinking joints where men could buy lap time with a lady, and by the 1970s, even those were forced to seek a lower profile. By law, today's displays are not permitted to titillate, complying with the British reputation (inaccurate in my book) for sexual modesty.

It was in this fleshy carnival that Laura Henderson bought a theater near Great Windmill and Archer streets (across the intersection from no.

20, where Karl Marx's *The Communist Manifesto* was commissioned in 1847, by the way). She got around indecency laws by ensuring that the performers in her naughty entertainment, the Revudeville, never moved a muscle. Famously, her Windmill Theatre never closed, not even during the Blitz. You might have seen it in the film *Mrs Henderson Presents* (2005). By the 1950s, Soho was a den of gang warfare and prostitution, full of craftsmen of every sort—costumers, ostrich feather trimmers, gun makers—until the Conservative government re-zoned the neighborhoods to admit offices, and the old ways were priced out.

Go left to Wardour Street, make a right and then a quick left. You'll be at the head of:

10 Old Compton Street

First, note the church of St Anne's, a few yards down Wardour Street, on the left. It was built in 1685, possibly by Wren (which ones weren't?), 2.5m (8 ft.) higher than the street because it went on top of a graveyard for 60,000 bodies (until 1853, when burials stopped, the neighborhood reeked from it). Everything save the church's tower was creamed by the Nazis.

Walk down Old Compton Street, Soho's de facto main street, which is busy round the clock and a center of gay life. No. 54 is the Admiral Duncan, where Dylan Thomas once drank (then again, where didn't he?). It was here, in 1999, that Nazi sympathizer David Copeland planted a bomb stuffed with 500 nails, which killed three people and injured many more. Copeland, an obvious madman, also bombed the South Asian population of Brick Lane and Black people in Brixton, but his only fatalities were here.

On the corner of Dean Street, look right. Down the block on the left, at no. 49, is the French House, more commonly called the French Pub. During World War II, it was the drinking haunt of Charles de Gaulle; here the exiled leader formed the Free French government and army. The street beyond the French House is Shaftesbury Avenue, the famous theatrical thoroughfare; many of the side streets between Old Compton and Shaftesbury contain the stage doors for the major playhouses, where famous actors report to work. Now look left, north up Dean Street. In no. 28, Karl Marx dwelled in abject poverty with his wife and several kids, but no running water or toilet. Three of his kids died while he was in residence in Soho in the early 1850s, and he had to borrow £2 for a coffin for one baby. No wonder he thought Marxism would be better.

Turn left at:

11 Frith Street

Bar Italia, the stylish cafe at no. 22, is a nightlife landmark of its own (p. 90). Upstairs is where, in 1925, John Logie Baird privately tested a homemade invention he called "noctovision," using his grocer's delivery boy as a test subject. The next year, he unveiled an improved model for the science nerds of the Royal Institution upstairs in this building. (Unsatisfied, he made another attempt in 1928 that involved hooking up a fresh human eyeball he'd rushed by taxicab from Charing Cross

Old Compton Street has been one of London's most buzzing roads since the mid–18th century. It's also a major party place come nightfall (and before).

Ophthalmic Hospital. It created a mess.) Baird's system, which used a spinning disc, was eventually discarded, but it debuted ahead of American Philo T. Farnsworth's more famous electronic version. Within a decade, the BBC was broadcasting "television"—its new name—regularly. In the 1940s, Baird invented the first color picture tube.

Walk up three doors. For 10 months starting in September 1764, the 8-year-old Mozart lived with his father and sister at a house at no. 20 (the building was replaced in 1858). While he was in London, the prodigy amused King George III, wrote his first two symphonies, and befriended fellow composer J. C. Bach, who mentored him. By the 1800s, Soho's Wardour Street was the violin-making center of Europe. Music history of another kind happened at no. 47, which in 1969 hosted the first public performance of The Who's *Tommy*, and then Jimi Hendrix's last performance, in 1970.

The Dog & Duck 🍺

You should totally stop at another pub now. I mean, how often are you in London? This one, at 18 Bateman Street, is a beauty, rich with Victorian tilework and mahogany paneling. If it puts you in a literary frame of mind, perhaps you're sensing vibrations. It was a favorite of George Orwell's—he toasted with absinthe here when he learned he'd sold *Animal Farm* to a publisher.

Turn right into Bateman Street (pub behind you), go 1 block, then left at Greek Street. Take the first right, the alley of Manette Street, and continue to Charing Cross Road. Cross using the crosswalk on your left and keep going straight along Denmark Street.

12 Denmark Street

Look up, and you'll see the 35-story Centre Point development. Built in 1964 with government concessions, it was kept empty for years by its greedy owner, Harry Hyams, partly to hold out for astronomical rents and partly to get off the tax hook even as the city struggled through a crisis of homelessness. In 1974, a hundred squatters occupied it to make a point. The charity Centrepoint, which started in the basement of St Anne's Church in Soho and grew into a force, derisively took its name from the waste.

Denmark Street, recently decimated by Elizabeth Line construction and lined with a now-paltry scattering of specialists in musical instruments, is just a hundred yards long, but it's dense with stories. This is London's version of New York's Tin Pan Alley—a nucleus for the British popular music industry. At no. 4, the Rolling Stones recorded their first album at Regent Sounds Studios (now The Alley Cat Club). On the roof of no. 20, Bernie Taupin wrote the lyric for "Your Song" (1970), his first hit with Elton John, during a break from work, which is why the words reference sitting on a roof. Charlie Chaplin wrote the tune of the iconic "Smile" in 2 hours on this street. David Bowie, The Kinks, Jimi Hendrix, Bob Marley, the Sex Pistols, and Black Sabbath all had countless formative moments—buying guitars, hiring bands, recording albums—along Denmark Street. It's all in the past now.

Keep following this road. It hangs slightly right, then is renamed St Giles High Street.

13 St Giles

You are standing in the worst slum in London. In the middle 1800s, the census counted more than 50,000 paupers within a few hundred squalid square feet. One eight-room house was stuffed with 107 luckless souls. People called poor neighborhoods "rookeries" because inhabitants were packed, shoeless and shivering, into single rooms like birds in nests. This is the London of *Oliver Twist*'s Fagin and his haggard gang of orphan pickpockets, of William Hogarth's "Gin Lane" prints warning of the villainy of drink among the destitute, including kids. This is the lawless labyrinth teeming with penniless immigrants, sex workers, drug addicts, thieves, and rats. This spot is so far gone that in World War II, even Hitler didn't bother to bomb it.

Except it's not. Not anymore. The new toybox-colorful development by Renzo Piano tells you nothing of the depravity that shocked and reformed the heartlessness of English society. Most of the remnants of poverty were bulldozed aside by development, as happens in our age. But the church on the right, St Giles-in-the-Fields, has origins back to Saxon times (1101); this one was built in the 1730s because the architectural integrity of the previous one had been compromised by the huge number of plague victims buried all around it. The interior is fairly standard as churches go, but note The Angel pub (on St Giles High Street) just past it.

Until the late 1700s, St Giles was the last church on the wagon route from Newgate Prison to the gallows at the village of Tyburn a mile away (now near Marble Arch). The convoys of doomed criminals rolled as many as eight times a year, and it was the equivalent of a major sporting event. Thousands of people would line the route to watch the condemned be dispatched to their maker, and as they passed taverns, they would be offered one last draught of ale. The pub that stood here (in the past, called The Bowl) is recorded as being where many prisoners drank their last beer on this mortal plane. The phrase "on the wagon" may stem from this grisly ritual.

Continue straight to the Shaftesbury Theatre.

14 Shaftesbury Theatre

The Shaftesbury was built in 1911 as the New Prince's Theatre, and it has been one of the most important independent houses ever since. In 1923, the sibling dance team of Fred and Adele Astaire cemented their international stardom with *Stop Flirting*; Prince Edward, future abdicator and a man fatefully obsessed with Americans, attended almost nightly. Adele was soon swept off her feet by a duke, leaving Fred with the (then) unlikely prospect of finding a career alone. We know how all that turned out. Other past tenants: Peter O'Toole, Anthony Hopkins, the London premieres of *Pal Joey* (1954), *How to Succeed in Business Without Really*

The imposing facade of the Shaftesbury Theater (1911).

Trying (1963), *Hair* (1968), *Follies* (1987), *Rent* (1998), and *Hairspray* (2007).

Two short blocks later, you'll be where Museum Street and Drury Lane both cross High Holborn (the road you're on). Turn left onto Museum Street. In 3 blocks, one of them pedestrianized, you will find yourself standing before the world-famous British Museum (fully explained on p. 126).

15 The British Museum

When it received its charter from George II, in 1753, the idea was revolutionary: A museum not owned by either the king or a church, free for the masses to use, and dedicated to the advancement of a broad range of disciplines. It was called the National Museum, and as you've just learned, at the time, acres of slums roiled just outside its doorstep. But, in a miracle of liberal-leaning benevolence, the country was determined to improve itself. Even the filthy souls who inhabited mid-19th-century Soho and St Giles were welcomed here. And now, so are you.

DAY TRIPS FROM LONDON

You've flown all the way to England. It would be a shame to miss seeing some of the sights that make it special—the rolling countryside, the stately mansions, the ageless villages built on slow-flowing rivers. An excursion enriches you with two experiences for the price of one: You'll taste everyday English life while you immerse yourself in world-famous landmarks.

Britain has comprehensive transport, but it's not quick as mercury. Because of traffic and a dearth of superhighways, you can expect a 48km (30-mile) trip to take an hour, so a spot that's 129 to 161km (80–100 miles) each way, such as Stonehenge or Bath, will require you to rise at dawn if you want to buy yourself much touring time at all. Going by bus is often less expensive than by rail, but the inefficient journey will involve narrow roads.

The tourist offices listed will be able, for a fee (£4–£5, plus 10% of the room rate), to hook you up with a bed for the night, should you decide that you'd rather not trek back to London right away. You can find lots more information at **Visit England** (www.visit england.com) and **Visit Britain** (www.visitbritain.com).

For in-depth coverage of everything outside of London, bring a copy of *Frommer's England & Scotland*. For casual day-trippers, though, here's what you need to know to dash out of the city and see the best of these destinations.

WINDSOR & ETON

Buckingham Palace is a mere *pied-à-terre*. The Windsors actually prefer this great castle, which dominates the skyline of town like a cloud of stone. Windsor Castle (32km/20 miles west of London) has been the home of the Royal Family for some 900 years, far longer than anything in London. Queen Victoria is buried in the backyard (although they don't phrase it quite that way). Despite the inevitable crowds, this is unmissable.

Essentials

GETTING THERE   The price difference between transport options is negligible. Riding the rails is quicker, so it's got the edge. **Trains** (www.nationalrail.co.uk; ✆ **03457/48-49-50,** or 020/7278-5240 from overseas; 38–56 min.; £12–£24) go directly from Waterloo station to Windsor & Eton Riverside or from Paddington to Windsor & Eton Central with a change at Slough. Both Windsor stations are a 3-minute walk from the castle. Trains requiring no changes leave twice an hour; trains requiring a change leave a little more frequently. Or take coach 702 by **Green Line** (www.reading-buses.co.uk/greenline; ✆ **0118/959-4000;** 1 hr. 45 min.; £13 single before noon, £7 single after noon. Nos. 700, 701, or 702 leave from Hyde Park Corner or Victoria Coach Station, south of Victoria Station.

VISITOR INFORMATION Stop by **Windsor Guildhall** (High St.; www.windsor.gov.uk; ✆ **01753/743-900;** Wed–Sun 10am–4pm). From there (or www.windsorwalks.co.uk), you can be referred to Blue Badge guides for **town walks.**

TOURS The most appealing way to see the area is by **boat,** departing from Windsor Promenade, Barry Avenue, for a 40-minute round-trip with fine views of the castle. Tours are operated by **French Brothers,** Clewer Boathouse, Clewer Court Rd., Windsor (www.frenchbrothers.co.uk; ✆ **01753/851-900;** 40-min. trip at 10am £11 adults, £10 seniors, £7.35 children 3–13, cheaper online; 2-hr. trip in afternoon £18.75 adults, £17.25 seniors, £12.50 children 3–13).

Exploring Windsor

Legoland Windsor (www.legoland.co.uk; ✆ **0871/222-2001;** £32–£62 seniors and children 3–15, cheaper in advance online; Mar–Oct), 2 miles from town, has top-notch rides catering to small children and some impressive Lego constructions. The Green Line 702 and 703 coach from London goes there, as do shuttles from Windsor's railway stations. The tourist office sells discounted tickets for late-afternoon entry.

Windsor Castle ★★ You may have had your fill of palaces in London proper, but you haven't seen the best. A fortress and a royal home for more than 900 years, it was expanded by each successive monarch who dwelled in it—more battlements for the warlike ones, more finery for the aesthetes. The resulting sprawl, which dominates the town from nearly every angle, was Queen Elizabeth's favorite residence—she spent lots of time here in her final years (although she died in Scotland)—and its history is richer than that of Buckingham Palace.

The castle's **State Apartments** are sumptuous enough to be daunting, and a tour through them—available unless there's a state visit—includes entrance to some mind-bogglingly historic rooms. Around a million people file through every year, so sharpen your elbows.

State Apartments, Windsor Castle.

The palace has a cache of priceless furniture (some of it solid silver), paintings, ephemera (look for the bullet that killed Lord Nelson, sealed in a locket), and weaponry, all of which, frustratingly, the audio guide, signage, and souvenir book do little to describe, so the only recourse is to pepper staff with questions. In 1992, one-fifth of the castle area was engulfed by an accidental fire; Elizabeth recounted her despair over that, plus the breakup of two of her children's marriages, in her now-famous "annus horribilis" Christmas speech to the nation, and much effort and funding went into returning everything to the way it was before. In fact, Elizabeth originally opened Buckingham Palace to visitors to fund the restoration.

St George's Hall, one of the repaired areas, is the monarch's chosen room for banquets. Kids love **Queen Mary's Doll's House,** a preposterously extravagant toy built for the allegedly grown-up Queen Mary in the 1920s with working electricity, elevators, plumbing, specially written library books, and other details so extravagant they're borderline offensive. From October to March, the tour also includes the **Semi-State Rooms,** George IV's private area, considered by many to be among the best-preserved Georgian interiors in England. In August and September, you can climb the **Round Tower** for views, and sometimes in January and midsummer, the castle's ancient **Great Kitchen** is open. There's also a **Changing the Guard** ceremony at 11am (Mon–Sat, but alternate days Aug–Mar; check the website). **St George's Chapel** (closed Sun), a delicately vaulted Gothic spectacle opened by Henry VIII, is his final resting place and that of ten other monarchs, including Elizabeth II's father (George VI) and Elizabeth herself. Elizabeth II's mother (the Queen Mum) and sister (Princess Margaret) are with them in a side chapel; Prince Philip arrived here in 2021. It's also where Prince Harry married Meghan Markle in 2018.

The castle is the superstar here, but supporting roles are played by the succinctly named **Great Park** adjoining it, and the 4.8km (3-mile) pin-straight **Long Walk** that culminates with an equestrian statue of George III. **Frogmore,** open a pitiful few days in the summer, is the house where Victoria and Albert share their mausoleum. Just south of the castle is the **Guildhall,** where then-Prince Charles and Camilla Parker-Bowles had a quiet civil marriage ceremony in April 2005; it's no St Paul's, where in 1981 Charles wed his first wife, what's-her-name, but it is also the work of Christopher Wren (note its delicate arches). The building was apparently designed without the center columns, which made councilors nervous; Wren threw up some columns but left them an inch shy of the ceiling, just to prove that his architecture was sound.

Castle Hill. www.royalcollection.org.uk. ℭ **0303/123-7304.** Admission £26.50 adults (Sat £28.50), £17.50 young people 18–24 (Sat £18.50), £14.50 children 5–17 and people with disabilities (Sat £15.50), free for children 4 and under, all including multimedia guide device rental; cheaper if the State Apartments are closed. Mar–Oct Thurs–Mon 10am–5:15pm, last admission 4pm; Nov–Feb Thurs–Mon daily 10am–4:15pm, last admission 3pm. Closed for special events or when the royal family is in residence. National Rail: Windsor Central or Windsor & Eton Riverside.

Eton College ★   A 15-minute walk over a footbridge on the Thames (narrow at this western remove), you're in a world served by snooty stationers and haberdashers. Eton is probably the most exclusive boys' school on Earth. Princes Harry and William are alums, known as Old Etonians, as are kings and princes from around the world. There's a museum in its wine cellars—and the fact this school has a wine cellar tells you what kind of rich these kids are. Be nice to them. They're tomorrow's dictators.

Keats Lane, Eton, Windsor. www.etoncollege.com/Visits.aspx. ℭ **01753/370-611** or email admissions@etoncollege.org.uk. Admission £10. 90-min. tours May–early Sept, Fri at 2 and 4pm. Reservations required.

BATH

Easily roamed on foot, Bath, about 161km (100 miles) west of London, is revered as a splendid example of Georgian architecture—to tourists, Bath is resolutely stuck in that past. The pleasing sandstone hue of its buildings set against the slate-grey British sky, the assiduously planned symmetry of its streets, the newfound popularity brought to it by its *Bridgerton* locations, the illusion that Jane Austen (who lived here in 1800–1805) is taking tea within one of its 18th-century Palladian town houses—Bath's magic comes from its consistent and regal design. No wonder the upper crust of the 1700s found it so fashionable, and no wonder their descendants have not dared to alter it. And no wonder UNESCO inscribed it as a World Heritage Site—a rarity for an entire city.

Essentials

GETTING THERE   The fastest **trains** (www.nationalrail.co.uk; ℭ **08457/ 48-49-50;** 90 min., twice an hour; £40 return with advance purchase) leave from Paddington and let you off in Bath Spa, an ugly section of town about 5

In winter, steam rises from the Roman Baths in Bath.

minutes' walk from the good stuff. Because buses take twice as long, I don't recommend buses by National Express (www.nationalexpress.com; ⓒ **08705/ 80-80-80;** 3 hr.; £9 single). Most of the major tour bus companies (see box on p. 339) come here, combining it with Stonehenge (p. 340) for about £75.

VISITOR INFORMATION   Visit Bath/Bath Tourist Information Centre (Bridgwater House, 2 Terrace Walk; www.visitbath.co.uk; ⓒ **01225/614- 420;** closed for the pandemic but usually open daily; tourism@bathtourism. co.uk)

TOURS   Since 1934, the mayor's office has furnished professionally guided, free 2-hr. **Walking Tours of Bath** (www.bathguides.org.uk; Sun–Fri 10:30am and 2pm, Sat 10:30am; May–Aug also Tues and Thurs 6pm). Meet outside the Roman Baths near Bath Abbey; no reservation required.

Exploring Bath

Begin your tour of Georgian Bath at **Queen Square** for some of the famous streets laid out by John Wood the Elder (1704–1754). Walk up to the **Circus,** three Palladian crescents (a row of attached houses built on a curve) arranged in a circle, with 524 different carved emblems above the doors. His son designed the **Royal Crescent,** an elegant half-moon row of townhouses.

Robert Adam put up **Pulteney Bridge,** a shop-lined crossing of the River Avon, in 1773, just as a similar bridge in the same medieval style, London Bridge, was crumbling.

Roman Baths ★★★   The Romans (ca. A.D. 60) were the first to recognize the tourism potential of the natural hot springs, which bubble at a rate of 250,000 gallons a day. Springs were redeveloped or rebored every few centuries; the current buildings are mostly from the 1800s, but Roman artifacts are occasionally found, and the restoration and accompanying museum are excellent. The Victorians mounted a proud colonnade around the excavation, and water has long been drawn in the adjoining Pump Room; you can drink a glass of the sulfuric stuff if you like, or settle down for a pricey lunch in neoclassical style. It's been the done thing in Bath since your great-great-great-grandma was in bloomers.

Bath Abbey Church Yard, Stall St. www.romanbaths.co.uk. ⓒ **01225/477-785.** Admission £25.50–£27.50 adults, £24.50–£26.50 seniors and students, £18–£20 children 6–18, discounts for online bookings; higher prices are for weekends. June–late July daily 9am–6pm; late July–Aug daily 9am–10pm; Sept–Oct and Mar–June daily 9am–5pm; Nov–Feb daily 9:30am–5pm; last entry 1 hr. before closing.

Fashion Museum & Assembly Rooms ★★   The grand **Assembly Rooms,** designed by the younger John Wood and completed in 1771, once played host to dances, recitals, and tea parties. Damaged in World War II, the elegant rooms have been restored and look much as they did when Jane Austen and Thomas Gainsborough attended events here. Housed in the same building, the **Fashion Museum** offers audio tours through the history of fashion from the 16th century to the present day through some 165 dressed mannequins. Exhibits change every 6 months. There's also a "Corsets and Crinolines" display where enthusiastic visitors can experience the masochism of period garments.

Bennett St. www.fashionmuseum.co.uk. ⓒ **01225/477-789.** Assembly Rooms: free admission. Fashion Museum admission: £10 adults, £9 students and seniors, £7.75 children 6–18. Tues–Sun 10am–5pm; last entry 4pm. Open on bank holiday Mon.

Jane Austen Centre ★   This small homage to Britain's favorite 19th-century writer isn't in her house, but Miss Austen did live up the hill (at no. 25) for a few months in 1805. Exhibits and a video convey a sense of what life was like when Austen lived in Bath between 1801 and 1806. Ladies can also learn the esoteric skill of using a fan to attract an admirer. Wholesome, corny fun. Allow at least 45 minutes. The tearoom is worth a visit (see "Taking Tea in Bath," below).

40 Gay St. www.janeausten.co.uk. ⓒ **01225/443-000.** Admission £12.50 adults, £11.50 seniors, £10.50 students, £5.50 children 6–16; £35 family ticket. Sun–Fri 10am–5pm; Sat 10am–5:30pm.

No. 1 Royal Crescent ★★   First-time visitors are blown away by the sweep and elegance of the Royal Crescent, a dazzling 30-house development

People still live in the Royal Crescent, a curving row of townhouses that ranks as one of Bath's most regal examples of Georgian architecture. No. 1 Royal Crescent is a beautifully furnished museum that shows how 18th-century residents used the house.

that took some 8 years to complete, from 1767 to 1775. Its first house, which absorbed the old servants' quarters in a massive restoration that religiously presents daily life in those days, is worth a swing-by if you want the full Regency effect.

1 Royal Crescent. www.no1royalcrescent.org.uk. ✆ **01225/428-126.** Admission £11 adults, £10 students and seniors, £5.50 children 5–15, family ticket £24. Tues–Sun 10am–5:30pm; last admission 4:30pm.

OXFORD

Whereas the face of London, 92km (57 miles) east, has been forcibly reshaped by the pressures of war, disaster, and commerce, Oxford was made stronger by them. When plague killed townspeople, the colleges snapped up their houses, and when the Reformation cleaned out the churches, the colleges took their land, too. Academies used the extra space to carve out some of the most beautiful college buildings in the world. Here, the reverence for education borders on the ecclesiastical. Yet Oxford is no cloister; it's a decidedly modern city—thriving, sophisticated, and busy.

Essentials

GETTING THERE   The least expensive, easiest method is by coach, because companies compete for students with regular buses rolling round the clock. The so-called **Oxford Tube** bus (www.oxfordtube.com; ✆ **01865/772-250;** 100 min. with no traffic; £12 adults, £11 seniors over 60 or students age 16–26, £4 children 5–15; with Wi-Fi and power sockets) leaves every 10–20 min. at all hours. It picks passengers up near the Tube stations at Marble Arch, Victoria, Notting Hill Gate, and Baker Street. Give rush hours wide berth. **Trains** (www.nationalrail.co.uk; ✆ **08457/48-49-50;** 1 hr.; £15–£27 single with advance purchase) go from Paddington or Marylebone stations to Oxford, sometimes via Reading.

VISITOR INFORMATION Experience Oxfordshire (www.experience oxfordshire.org; *✆* **01865/686-441**) offers daily walking tours (10:30am and 1pm most days) using accredited guides; reservations required. You can download free maps of the city from Visit Britain (www.visitbritain.com).

TOURS The Information Centre offers excellent **theme tours** on topics such as "Harry Potter Highlights," "C.S. Lewis and J.R.R. Tolkien," and *Inspector Morse*; book ahead through Experience Oxfordshire. **Oxford River Cruises** (www.oxfordrivercruises.com; *✆* **01865/987-147**) runs several boat tours along the River Thames; the tranquil 50-minute Oxford Experience (cheaper online: £16 adults, £10 children 14 and under; reservations suggested) is popular. **City Sightseeing** runs hop-on, hop-off bus tours with prerecorded audio (https://city-sightseeing.com; *✆* **01789/299-123;** from £17; 10am–6pm daily).

Exploring Oxford

Wandering Oxford's cobbled streets and ducking into its colleges to soak up their hidden loveliness makes for a happy afternoon, particularly for fans of architecture. Many of the most iconic building clusters in this city of 140,000 (30,000 of whom are students) are collected together in the center of town. Oxford, like Cambridge (p. 336), comprises individual colleges that feed off a central university system. Each of the 39 colleges has its own campus, tradition, character, and disciplines—and each has finicky hours, so always check ahead before planning a day. Unfortunately, many close their grassy inner sanctums to visitors. During the school terms (mid-Jan to mid-Mar, late Apr to mid-June, Oct to early Dec), some university buildings required for study (libraries, residence halls) are closed to the public, or only open on Saturdays. At all times of year, watch out for zooming bicyclists; an unwritten law appears to grant them ownership of the city.

To get the most out of Oxford, poke around, looking inside cloisters and above rooftops. The doors between the inner and outer quadrangles of **Balliol College** (Broad St. and St Giles; www.balliol.ox.ac.uk; *✆* **01865/27-77-77;** £3 adults, £1 seniors and students; daily 10am–5pm) still bear scorch marks from where Bloody Mary burned two Protestants alive for refusing to recant. Viewpoints are popular attractions in Oxford: The 22m (72-ft.) rectangular **Carfax Tower** (£3 adults, £2 children 15 and under; Apr–Sept daily 10am–5:30pm, Oct–Mar daily 10am–4:30pm) is the last remaining chunk of the 13th-century St Martin's Church; it has only 99 steps, so it's not too taxing. It's located by the crossroads of the city center. Other popular panoramas are from the octagonal cupola above Sir Christopher Wren's **Sheldonian Theatre** (Broad St.; www.sheldonian.ox.ac.uk; *✆* **01865/277-299;** £4, £8 with guided tour; hours change daily with many closings, so check ahead, but opening tends to be at 10am). Perhaps the top view is from the **University Church of St Mary the Virgin** (www.university-church.ox.ac.uk; *✆* **01865/279-113;** £5; Mon–Sat 9:30am–5pm, Sun noon–5pm, last tower admission 30 min. before closing).

Christ Church college's dining hall was an inspiration for the one in the Harry Potter films and books.

The Ashmolean Museum ★★ Offering more than just a pretty facade, the Ashmolean was founded way back in 1683, literally before anyone knew what the word "museum" meant. It houses an important hodgepodge of antiquities and art on par with (but on a smaller scale than) the British Museum, including a lantern carried by Guy Fawkes during the foiled Gunpowder Plot; the Anglo-Saxon Alfred Jewel of gold, enamel, and rock crystal; a Stradivarius violin; and assorted Old Masters paintings. Oh, and you know, minor stuff by Raphael and Michelangelo.

Beaumont St. at St Giles. www.ashmolean.org. ℂ **01865/278-000.** Free admission. Daily 10am–5pm. Closed Dec 24–26.

Christ Church ★★★ The largest, most beautiful, and most popular college to visit looms large in children's literature: It was copied for Hogwarts School in the Harry Potter films, and it was where Lewis Carroll (aka mathematician Charles Dodgson) befriended the little girl for whom he wrote *Alice in Wonderland.* The college chapel, which dates from the 12th century, also serves as Oxford Cathedral for the local diocese. Bowler-hatted "custodians" still patrol the pristine lawns, and Christ Church Meadow, still grazed by cattle, is a delightful place to watch punters on the rivers Isis and Cherwell. Just being here makes you feel smarter.

St Aldate's. www.chch.ox.ac.uk. ⓒ **01865/276-492.** Tours £16.80 adults, £15 seniors, students, and children 5–17, free for children 4 and under; slight discount for advance online purchase. Mon–Sat 9am–5pm; Sun 2–5pm; last admission 4:30pm. Closed for week around Christmas and New Year's.

Magdalen College ★★ Pronounced "*Maud*-lin," it is one of the largest and most peaceful colleges here; its tower is the city's highest point, and its chapel is carved with breathtaking detail. Its site has a virtual tour to prep you on your explorations. Retired U.S. Supreme Court justice Stephen Breyer attended.

High St. www.magd.ox.ac.uk. ⓒ **01865/276-000.** Admission £8 adults, £7 seniors, students, and children. July–Sept daily noon–7pm; Oct–June daily 1–6pm or dusk (whichever is earlier). Closed for a week around Christmas and New Year's.

Old Bodleian Library ★★ The main research library in a town that made its name in research, "the Bod" opened in 1602 and has been burrowing under the streets of Oxford, trying to find new places to store its multiplying collection (11 million tomes and counting) ever since. See it by tour. The round **Radcliffe Camera** ("Rad Cam"; open via guided tours at the Bodleian) was built in the 1740s to house scientific books. It stands on the north side of Radcliffe Square.

Catte St. visit.bodleian.ox.ac.uk. ⓒ **01865/287-400.** Admission £2.50, Divinity School only; 30-min. Library tour £9, 60-min. Library tour £12, 90-min. Library tour including Radcliffe Camera £18. Reservations suggested; check current tour times online. Mon–Fri 9am–5pm; Sat 9am–4:30pm; Sun 11am–5pm. Closed for week around Christmas and New Year's.

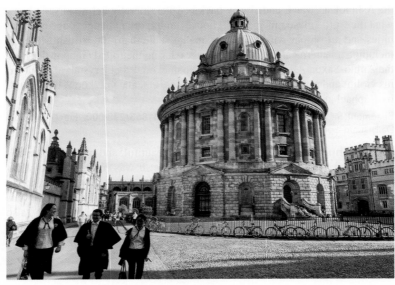

Oxford students stroll by the Radcliffe Camera.

Magdalen College was founded in 1458 and is alma mater of Thomas Wolsey (Henry VIII's chief minister), C. S. Lewis, Oscar Wilde, Andrew Lloyd Webber, and nine Nobel Prize winners.

Punting on the River Cherwell is an essential if slightly eccentric Oxford pastime. From mid-March to October at the **Cherwell Boathouse,** Bardwell Road (www.cherwellboathouse.co.uk; *℡* **01865/515-978**), you can rent a punt (a flat-bottomed boat for up to five people, maneuvered by a long pole and a small oar) for £20 per hour. **Magdalen Bridge Boathouse,** the Old Horse Ford, High Street (www.oxfordpunting.co.uk; *℡* **01865/202-643**), charges £25 per hour weekdays, £30 per hour Saturday and Sunday, daily 10am until dusk. Both outfits offer basic training.

The Pitt Rivers Museum ★

An imposing 1886 cast-iron cathedral-like building, not unlike a railway station, houses a blend of folk art and anthropology—think African headdresses, masks, and bundles of poisoned arrows. Most of the collection was brought back by plundering British explorers over hundreds of years and now gives the curators fits about how to display it sensitively.

Parks Rd. www.prm.ox.ac.uk. *℡* **01865/270-927.** Free admission. Mon noon–5pm; Tues–Sun 10am–5pm.

OUTSIDE OXFORD

Blenheim Palace ★★★ Before Winston Churchill was famously born here in a makeshift cloakroom during a party, this eye-popping pile (in the rare English baroque style) was commissioned in 1705 as a reward for his triumphant military ancestor, John Churchill, the first Duke of Marlborough. Winston, who wasn't in line to inherit it, would nevertheless try to impress girls by bringing them to visit, a tactic that finally paid off when he proposed to Clementine Hozier in its garden's Temple of Diana. There's an artifact-packed biographical museum about Winston in the cellar, but mostly, the audio guide of the lavish Palace State Rooms of this rightful UNESCO World Heritage Site is obsessed with the intricacies of lineage and noble titles. You could spend all day (there's a cafe for lunch) gawping at bygone English indulgence by ambling through the glorious 2,000-acre gardens, both formal and falsely naturalistic, which were designed with such extravagance that they helped ruin the reputation of playwright-cum-architect John Vanbrugh (when he died, the wry poet Abel Evans wrote an epitaph for him: "Lie heavy on him, Earth! for he Laid many heavy loads on thee!"). The British rarely remind you that the oh-so-English savior of World War II was, in fact, half American: Winston's mom, Jennie, was from Brooklyn and married an English lord, *Downton Abbey*-style. A few decades later, the home was saved from financial ruin when the 9th Duke of Marlborough married another wealthy American, Consuelo Vanderbilt; their descendants still live here for part of the year, which may account for the family-obsessed audio tour.

Hensington Rd., Woodstock, Oxfordshire. www.blenheimpalace.com. *℡* **01993/810-530.** Admission palace and grounds £32 adults, £27 seniors, students, and young people 17–25, £18.50 children 5–16, £83.50 family ticket; £7–£10 less for grounds only. Daily 10:30am–5:30pm; last admission 4:45pm. Take half-hourly S3 bus (www.stagecoachbus.com; 30 min.; around £4.50) from the Oxford train station or Gloucester Green to Hensington Road, Woodstock.

It took years to build Blenheim Palace (1705–1722), and it's still one of the largest residential buildings in the U.K. The UNESCO World Heritage Site is also the only non-royal manor house in the nation permitted to use the word "palace" in its name.

BLETCHLEY PARK: ENIGMA no more

For decades, it was top secret. Few people realized what had happened here during World War II in these rotting temporary wooden huts, so they were nearly bulldozed for a housing development. But in time, we learned what codebreaker Alan Turing and his brilliant team accomplished at **Bletchley Park** (https://bletchleypark.org.uk; ℂ **01908/640-404**), hidden from the world on a former estate 88km (55 miles) northwest of London. Here they cracked the Enigma machine code, breaking the German blockade that threatened to starve an entire country. In 2014, the year a film about their story, *The Imitation Game*, was released, the fully restored Bletchley Park campus was opened as a fascinating large-scale day out. A visit is like a spy novel set in a park, suffused with the urgency, intrigue, and excitement of those terrifying years when computers were born and Nazis were a few chess moves away from storming England. You can tour more than a dozen buildings around its soothing central pond, exploring the methods, experiments, and lucky breaks that enabled round-the-clock workers—including many gifted women—to translate a jumble of meaningless letters into life-saving intercepted secrets. The cramped, rudimentary Huts 3, 6, and 8, dressed to look like they probably did then (no one is sure—photographs were forbidden), were the heart of the operation, but you can also tour the ground floor of the mansion that served as its command post and outbuildings that housed the computers, which were later dismantled down to the rivets to prevent anyone from duplicating them. Head to the basement of Block B, where modern fans have rebuilt one. The number of Enigma-related artifacts and the level of codebreaking detail can be head-spinning, so children may tire quickly, but interested adults could spend 3 or 4 absorbed hours wrapping their heads around it, a pursuit made easier by the three cafes spread around its grassy acres. Admission is £24.50 adults, £22 seniors and students, £16 children 12–17, and £41–£65.60 family ticket. It's open daily, from 9:30am to 5pm, March to October (9:30am–4pm Nov–Feb); last admission 2 hours before closing.

Trains to Bletchley leave Euston a few times an hour (50 min.; £17 return in advance), and the gates are only 182m (200 yards) from the station; sit on the left of the carriage for good views of the Grand Union Canal as you go. If you fancy a country drive, Avis, Enterprise, and Budget are clustered near the Bletchley train station.

CAMBRIDGE

Oxford is a city in its own right, but Cambridge, in the marshes 79km (49 miles) northeast of London, would barely have a pulse without its university. That makes Cambridge manageable—it's also cheaper to visit. It feels in some ways like a typical English town, with a daily market for crafts and food on its central square, Market Hill. Its best rewards come when you wander through randomly chosen iron gates or along a river path—that's when the inviting little town really opens up.

Essentials

GETTING THERE Nonstop **coaches** from National Express (www.national express.com; ✆ **08705/80-80-80;** 2½ hr.; £7–£8 single) leave hourly from Victoria Coach Station; don't get off at Trumpington, but wait for the city center stop. There are **trains** from Liverpool Street or King's Cross, but be warned that Cambridge's station is several miles from the city center, so you will need to bike or call a taxi; coaches are the smarter way to travel. If you insist, though, note that some trains take about 45 minutes and some take twice that, so ask about journey times (www.nationalrail.co.uk; ✆ **08457/48-49-50;** 45–90 min.; £10–£23).

VISITOR INFORMATION Download a free map from **Visit Cambridge** (www.visitcambridge.org; info@visitcambridge.org); sometimes Cambridge City Ambassadors are on hand at the railway station to distribute info and maps.

TOURS **Cantab Tours** runs 90-minute walking tours of the city (www.cantabtours.com; daily 11am and 2pm; £20 adults, and up to £12 for children 15 and under). **City Sightseeing** runs hop-on, hop-off bus tours with prerecorded audio (https://city-sightseeing.com; ✆ **01789-299-123;** from £17; daily 10am–6pm).

Exploring Cambridge

Like Oxford, Cambridge's glory is the elaborate and ancient architecture of its colleges. However, unlike in Oxford, it's easy to venture into the cloistered grounds of many of Cambridge's colleges, though doing so usually requires a few quid. (Cambridge took shape in the early 13th c., after a squabble in Oxford drove several scholars to leave there and establish a second educational capital. The oldest Cambridge College, Peterhouse, was founded in 1284.) Mill Lane leads to the River Cam, where you can rent a punting boat for £6 or sit at The Mill pub overlooking the water. (If you want to seem savvy to Cambridge traditions, punt from the back of the boat. In Oxford, they punt from the front.) The meadows along the Cam, known as the **Backs,** make for idyllic walks.

The head of Oliver Cromwell, which was impaled outside Westminster Hall in London as a warning against regicide (albeit 3 years after the man died of natural causes), was finally buried within an antechapel (not open to visitors) at Sidney Sussex College in 1960. It's in an unmarked grave to keep pranksters from pinching the much-abused thing. That's Cambridge in a nutshell: It has many secrets, but since it's still a working university town, marvels won't be handed to you. You have to wander, wonder, and ask questions. Outside of term (terms run mid-Jan to mid-Mar, late Apr to mid-June, and Oct to early Dec), colleges aren't open, and street life is at a minimum.

Queens' College (www.queens.cam.ac.uk) and its famous **Mathematical Bridge** closed to visitors during Covid-19; check to see if it has reopened to outsiders.

Fitzwilliam Museum ★★★ Cambridge's most storied attraction is a first-rate neoclassical building full of applied arts and Old Masters that a city 10 times Cambridge's size (population 118,000) would covet. If a colonial Englishman could carry it home on a ship, it's here: precious antiquities from Rome, Greece, Egypt, and Asia, and paintings by every famous name under the European sun.

Trumpington St., near Peterhouse. www.fitzmuseum.cam.ac.uk. ℭ **01223/332-900.** Free admission, but booking timed admission is requested. Tues–Sat 10am–5pm; Sun and bank holidays noon–5pm. Closed Mon, Good Friday, Dec 24–26 and 31, and Jan 1.

King's College Chapel ★★ For some reason, the marauding Puritans neglected to smash the 16th-century stained-glass windows of this chapel— they probably thought they were too divine to destroy, just as you will. The chapel's fanned and vaulted ceiling, a work of craftsmanship that stuns even those who care little for such things, was completed at the behest of Henry VII. Its famous choristers sing at services during term time. Some Saturdays (check ahead), there's a £6 guided tour upgrade.

King's Parade. www.kings.cam.ac.uk. ℭ **01223/331-100.** Admission £10 adults, £8 students and young people 6–17, free for children 5 and under. Generally daily 9:30am–4:30pm, last entry to chapel 3pm, but check website calendar in advance for frequent closures and changes.

The soaring interior of King's College Chapel.

THE TRADE-OFF WITH escorted tours

With so many tour options, renting a car for day trips is a lousy idea. Arranging your own day trips using public transportation will almost always be the most cost-effective method, but there are cogent reasons for choosing a guided coach tour. It's simply quicker to allow someone else to drive you around, making sure you cram a laundry list of major sights into a short time span and consume spoon-fed nuggets of information about each place. At least you'll have been there. And some sights have a cache of tickets not accessible to the public—places like Highclere Castle (p. 344) may be easier to do as part of a coach tour.

Most tours cost about £70 to £130 for 6–11 hours out of London. You get a richer experience (and one that doesn't have you waiting for other tour members to catch up) when you do it yourself. But some people desperately want to soak up as many sights as they can, even if it means viewing sights as a blur from the motorway. For them, here are the major players in the coach-tour biz, sold aggressively through concierges at expensive hotels (who love getting the commissions). Most tours depart from Victoria Coach Station.

- **Evan Evans Tours** (www.evanevans tours.co.uk; © 020/7932-8385 in the U.K., 800/422-9022 in the U.S.)
- **Gray Line's Golden Tours** (www. goldentours.co.uk; © 020/7630-2028 in the U.K., 800/509-2507 in the U.S.)
- **Premium Tours** (www.premiumtours. co.uk; © 020/7713-1311 in the U.K., 800/815-4003 in the U.S.)
- **Rabbie's** (www.rabbies.com; © 0131/226-3133 in the U.K.) tends to use small-group vans more than large coaches, and tends to be a little less expensive.

Pembroke College ★★ The third-oldest college in town is one of the best, distinguished by the oldest gatehouse in Cambridge and by a chapel with an ornate plaster ceiling, which was the first completed work by Christopher Wren (after finishing this, the man seemed never to rest again). Unlike many of the colleges, Pembroke never charges visitors to poke around its common areas.

Trumpington St. www.pem.cam.ac.uk. © **01223/33-81-00.** Free admission with advance bookings made via porters@pem.cam.ac.uk. Daily 10–5pm, except mid-May to mid-June when closed for exams.

Trinity College ★★ Trinity is the largest and most endowed of Cambridge's 31 colleges. Sir Isaac Newton first calculated the speed of sound here, at Neville's Court, and Lord Byron used to bathe naked in the Great Court's fountain with his pet bear. (The university forbade students from having dogs, but there was no rule against bears.) In *Chariots of Fire*, sprinters tried to get around the .8-hectare (2-acre) yard in the time it took for its clock to strike 12. Your attempts will not be appreciated.

Trinity St. www.trin.cam.ac.uk. © **01223/338-400.** Free admission. Grounds: daily 9:30am–5pm. The Wren Library: Mon–Fri noon–2pm; Sat 10:30am–12:30pm, but check website calendar in advance for frequent closures and changes.

Punting on the River Cam.

STONEHENGE & SALISBURY

Stonehenge is a circle of rocks. If it's raining, it's a damned circle of rocks. But people still ask to go, and if that's their dream, then they should do it. Just understand that it may not blow you away.

Most coach tours offer an itinerary that combines Stonehenge with Bath (p. 325); bus and train connections make it difficult to do that if you're traveling independently. However, it's quite doable to combine Stonehenge with a visit to Salisbury, a lovely and relatively well-preserved cathedral town.

Essentials

GETTING THERE This one's a pain. Trains don't go directly to Stonehenge; the nearest station is in Salisbury, nearly 16km (10 miles) south. So the easiest way to get here is to catch a group tour (see box, above) or drive. The rocks are located 3.2km (2 miles) west of Amesbury in Wiltshire on the junction of A303 and A344/360. If you must do public transportation, take a half-hourly **train** (www.nationalrail.co.uk; © **08457/48-49-50; **90 min.; £25 return with advance purchase) from Waterloo station to Salisbury station. There used to be a cheap public bus to the rocks from there, but it says a lot about the values of local tourism authorities that they replaced that route entirely with the expensive but convenient **Stonehenge Tour Bus** (1 hr. 10 min. for return transportation; www.thestonehengetour.info; ☎ **01202/338-420;** bus only: £17 adults, £11.50 children 5–15; add tours of Salisbury Cathedral and Old Sarum for more; buy online or in cash from driver), which leaves from Salisbury station seven times a day between 10am and 4pm. Many tour companies offer round-trip all-day coach tours from London that take about 7 hours. One of them is **Premium Tours** (see above) for £62 adults, £59 seniors, and £52 children 3 to 16. Fast-moving versions that also include Bath cost about £30 more.

VISITOR INFORMATION   **Visit Wiltshire** (Fish Row, Salisbury; www. visitwiltshire.co.uk; ☎ **01722/342-860**) provides info on both Stonehenge and Salisbury.

TOURS   You can easily see Salisbury on foot, either on your own or by taking a guided daytime or evening walk, run by **Salisbury City Guides** (www. salisburycityguides.co.uk; ☎ **07873/212-941;** Fri Apr–Oct). Tickets are £10 for adults, £5 for students and children 12–18, and free for kids 11 and under.

Exploring Stonehenge & Salisbury

Stonehenge ★   Construction on this bucket-list site began about 5,000 years ago; the first recorded day trips to the megalith were in 1562. Arranged in such a way that it aligns with the rising of the sun during the midsummer solstice, this Neolithic circle of stones is certainly Britain's most important ancient wonder, and it's a UNESCO World Heritage Site (together with Avebury, a far less interesting, but still important, line of rocks 39km/24 miles north). Whether its builders, who remain anonymous despite growing theories, worshiped the sun or merely appreciated astronomy is only the beginning of the mystery. We also can only make educated guesses as to how these prehistoric people, using only rudimentary tools, managed to hoist these slabs from Wales to here, and then into place. Even if you don't salivate over such long-ago feats of ingenuity, the distinctive profile of the stones, surrounded by empty plains, "henge" earthworks, and hundreds of lumpen burial mounds, will surely feel iconic.

You're not allowed to walk among the rocks the way visitors once were; you have to stick to a footpath that curves near the circle but keeps the formation at a safe distance, good for pretty photographs but bad for curiosity. Most tourists like you and me are kept at arm's length (exception: Clark Griswold, who managed to topple them like dominoes in *National Lampoon's European Vacation*), but you can apply in advance for a 1-hour "Stone Circle Experience" pass to stroll with about 29 others among the rocks—no touching—timed in the very early morning or after it closes for the day. The application is at the English Heritage website (see below). Otherwise, you'll have a limited experience—a disappointment for many who trudge 129km/80 miles west of London to have it. Alternatively, climb **Amesbury Hill,** clearly visible

Mysterious Stonehenge has drawn visitors for centuries.

2.4km (1½ miles) up the A303. From here, you'll get a free panoramic view. Check opening times before heading out; closings are occasional.

At the junction of A303 and A344. www.english-heritage.org.uk/stonehenge. © **08703/ 331-181.** Admission £20 adults, £18 seniors and students with ID, £12 children 5–15, £32–£52 family ticket; Stone Circle Experience £48 adults, £29 children 5–17; higher posted prices include a "voluntary donation." June–Aug daily 9am–8pm; Apr–May and Sept–mid-Oct daily 9:30am–7pm; mid-Oct–Mar daily 9:30am–5pm; last admission 2 hr. before closing. Train: Salisbury, then Stonehenge Tour Bus.

Old Sarum ★ Believed to have been an Iron Age fortification, Old Sarum was used again by the Saxons and flourished as a walled town into the Middle Ages. The Normans built a cathedral; parts of that were taken down to build the city of "New Sarum," later known as Salisbury, leaving behind dramatically sited remains with unforgettable views of Salisbury and rolling green hills, not to mention the opportunity to commune with grazing sheep.

2 miles north of Salisbury, off A345. Castle Rd. www.english-heritage.org.uk/oldsarum. © **01722/335-398.** Admission £6 adults, £5.30 seniors and students, £3.60 children 5–17; higher posted prices include a "voluntary donation." Apr–Sept daily 10am–6pm; Mar and Oct daily 10am–5pm; Nov–Feb daily 10am–4pm. Bus: X5, 8, or 501, every 30 min. during the day, from Salisbury bus station.

Salisbury Cathedral ★★ Built with uncommon efficiency between 1220 and 1258 and barely touched since, this early English Gothic masterpiece is considered by many to be the most breathtaking church in the world. The

Salisbury Cathedral's spire is 404 feet tall—the tallest such structure in the U.K. You can climb its 332 winding steps, many of them wooden and spiraling, to the foot of the spire for a view over the marshes.

HIGHCLERE CASTLE, THE real DOWNTON ABBEY

The 8th Earl and Countess of Carnarvon still dwell under the sandstone turrets of **Highclere Castle** (Highclere Park, Newbury; www.highclerecastle.co.uk; ℂ **01635/253-204;** admission £27.50 adults, £25.50 students and seniors, £16 children 4–16; last admission at 4pm, grounds close at 6pm), known to TV viewers as the idyllic and stately Downton Abbey. Time and spendthrift earls took their toll on this historic home, and as recently as 2009, more than 50 rooms were uninhabitable due to mold and leaks. The current Earl faced repair bills running around £12 million, so he welcomes visitors to spend the day exploring the estate's 1,000 acres of private rolling Berkshire countryside.

He also rents out to film production: The upstairs scenes of the ITV/PBS show Downton Abbey were shot on the ground floor and first floor using the house's actual furniture, though downstairs scenes were shot on a soundstage in Ealing, West London. That's partly because at Highclere, the basement is full not of kitchens but of mummy stuff: The 5th Earl was the guy who bankrolled Howard Carter's 1923 emptying of King Tut's tomb in Luxor, so unseen beneath Lord Grantham's feet lie items taken from the tombs of Egypt. The grounds are generally accessible, but Highclere house is open only on predetermined days, and they're scattered all over the calendar—typically Easter Week, bank holiday weekends, and from July to mid-September (closed Fri and Sat).

Taking a group tour guarantees a ticket, but those sell out months ahead and herd you along. If you show up independently at 10am or by 2pm at the latest, you can usually get a walk-up ticket even though advance tickets are sold out. Only once you have a ticket can you also sign up for the afternoon tea (£60 for two) in its Coach House (no children for that). Getting here on your own involves taking a 52-minute train from Paddington (from £24) or a National Express bus

---

cathedral complex's octagonal Chapter House shelters one of four surviving copies of the Magna Carta signed by King John in 1215. (Two more are in London at the British Library; p. 122.) After you've seen the cathedral, and lost yourself in gazing at it and sighing, the rest of your time in Salisbury will be contentedly spent walking medieval streets, which were laid in a loose grid and give the city an airy character.

The Close. www.salisburycathedral.org.uk. ℂ **01722/555-120.** Admission £9 adults, £6 students 17 and up, £5 students 13–16, free for children 12 and under. Mon–Sat 9am–5pm; Sun 12:30–4pm; last entry 1 hr. before closing.

CANTERBURY

The ecclesiastical capital of England, Canterbury (62 miles southeast of London) feels like a seat of English charm itself, with the squared spire of its great Gothic cathedral rising from the cobbled cluster of its village. You can still find traces of the original city walls and punt on the calm water that meanders through town. It's also easy to explore on foot; start your explorations at The Goods Shed, a market for luscious English dairy, meat, and alcohol (with its

(1¾ hr.; from £10) to the adorable town of Newbury (stop to admire the long-boats on the Kennet and Avon canal and peruse the century-old village department store, Camp Hopson) and then a £20-ish taxi (try www.cabco33333.com, *C* **01635/33333;** or www.newburytaxi.co.uk, *C* **01635/224466**). The coach tour companies make it a lot easier, and Premium Tours (p. 339) throws in a signed copy of one of Lady Carnarvon's books.

Highclere Castle, better known to TV and movie fans as Downton Abbey.

own gourmet restaurant; www.thegoodsshed.co.uk), beside the Canterbury West railway station.

Essentials

GETTING THERE   Two National Rail stations, Canterbury East and Canterbury West, are both conveniently just outside the city walls. High-speed trains from Charing Cross, St Pancras, and Victoria take 60 to 90 minutes (www.nationalrail.co.uk; *C* **08457/48-49-50;** £38 return in advance). Buses are not recommended for a day trip; trains are quick and deliver you right to the town.

VISITOR INFORMATION   **Canterbury Visitor Information** is at the Beaney House of Art and Knowledge, 18 High Street (www.canterbury.co.uk; *C* **01227/862-162**).

TOURS   The popular **Canterbury Punting Company** (Water Lane; www.canterburypunting.co.uk; *C* **07786/332-666;** £10–£20) lets you ply the River Stour on a wide, flat boat past medieval buildings under hanging bowers—an ideal outing.

Exploring Canterbury

Canterbury Cathedral ★★★   The original modern tourist attraction, it's where the pilgrims were headed in Chaucer's *The Canterbury Tales* (1478).

The square Gothic tower of Canterbury Cathedral rises above the town's cobbled medieval lanes.

They were going to pay their respects to Archbishop Thomas Becket, who was murdered in the northwest transept, next to what is now the Chapel of Our Lady Martyrdom. Henry VIII tore down that shrine in a typical fit of pique, but this transporting place is still one of the most visited sites in Britain. The cathedral, along with **St Augustine's Abbey** and **St Martin's Church** (the oldest still-functioning church in the English-speaking world; both were founded around 597), form a World Heritage Site. Look for the medieval tombs of King Henry IV and Edward the Black Prince; Becket lies in the Trinity Chapel, near the high altar. The stained glass depicting his reported miracles is regarded as some of England's finest; fortunately, the cathedral's windows survived Hitler's bombs by being removed and hidden away.

The Precincts. www.canterbury-cathedral.org. ℰ **01227/762-862.** Admission £17 adults, £11 students, £9 children 7–18, free for ages 6 and under. Mon–Sat 9am–5pm; Sun 11:30am–5pm; last admission 1 hr. before closing.

PLANNING YOUR TRIP TO LONDON

F irst of all, you'll be fine. Getting to London isn't as tricky as it used to be. Some 20 million tourists journey to London in a normal year, so it can't be that hard. London hospitality and tourist industries know a thing or two about helping foreigners. Finding airfare isn't much harder than finding a cross-country flight, and communicating is as easy as opening your mouth to speak. Being ready for the rest (money, electricity) is simply a matter of having the facts.

GETTING THERE

By Plane

Transatlantic flights usually land at **Heathrow,** Europe's busiest international airport (LHR; 17 miles west of London), or **Gatwick,** perhaps the most disliked (LGW; 31 miles south). With a few minor exceptions, the other four airports—**Stansted** (STN; 37 miles northeast), **Luton** (LTN; 34 miles northwest), **London City** (LCY; in London's Docklands area), and **Southend** (SEN; 42 miles east)—serve flights from Europe; they're where cut-rate flyers and executive jets tend to go.

FINDING THE LOWEST AIRFARE

The central question here is *when* are they? London is such a popular destination (it's served by more flights from the United States than any other European city) that plenty of airlines vie to carry you across—although the ones that are not American-run are usually of higher in-flight quality. And because international routes are prized among crew with seniority, flights across the ocean are usually less likely to be canceled than domestic routes back home. To minimize the chances of your schedule being ruined by delays or cancellations, try to stick to nonstop flights if you can. If you're not redeeming frequent-flier miles (book very far ahead if you are), there are six rules to finding bargains:

1. **Fly on days when traffic is lightest.** Some airlines post calendars that show you when their best prices are, or test fare trends on a site such as **Hopper.com.**

The Cashless Revolution

The Covid-19 pandemic accelerated the everyday use of tap-and-go credit and debit purchases to such a degree that you can't ignore it anymore. Do not rely on cash. Even simple items like coffee and theater programs may only be available if you pay by plastic. In London, it's now possible to conduct an entire vacation without using cash or coins a single time—in fact, many vendors won't even accept loose change anymore. It's possible to pay by card swipe, but your life will be much easier if you're set up for tap-and-go transactions. Before leaving home, ensure your cards can be used for contactless transactions: A little Wi-Fi symbol on the card usually denotes the capability, but you may have to ask your bank for a contactless version of a card. You can also use smartphone-centric payment such as Apple Pay or Google Pay (even for the Tube—but set it up in your phone before leaving home) as long as your associated credit cards work internationally.

2. **Depart after dinner.** This saves you from paying another hotel night, since you'll arrive in the morning. You're also likely to find lower fares, because business travelers like day flights.

3. **Go off-season.** London's weather isn't extreme, so there's really not a no-go month. November through March yield the lowest airfares and hotel rates, although the late-December holidays and the last week of November (Thanksgiving in U.S.) can be busy, too. Summer prices (June–Sept) soar over a grand.

4. **Search for fares for or on a weekend.** Many major airlines post lower prices to fly then. You might also save money by booking your seat at 3am. That's because unpaid-for reservations are flushed out of the system at midnight, and prices often sink when the system becomes aware of an increase in supply.

5. **Try a bargain airline.** Norse (flynorse.com) and Icelandair (www.iceland air.com) are worth checking.

6. **Don't buy last-minute.** Desperation has a price.

Monitor airline emails, sale pages, Twitter accounts, and sites for sales. Sign up with a flight tracker notification service (there are plenty online, such as Skyscanner or Google Flights) that will spit out emails when airfare drops.

Primary websites that collect quotes from a variety of sources (whether they be airlines or other websites) include **Skyscanner.com, Kayak.com,** and **the app Hopper.** Always canvas multiple sites, because each has odd gaps in coverage because of how they obtain quotes. Always compare your best price with what the airline is offering, because that price might be lowest of all. Many sites force you to accept nonrefundable tickets with no luggage allowance for the cheapest prices, so be prepared for the extra fees to make those flights workable. If you're hitting a wall, search for transatlantic itineraries that allow for one or two stops, since routes that include stops in Reykjavik or Frankfurt (on Icelandair or Lufthansa, respectively) can produce hidden bargains. No matter which airline you go with, prepare yourself for added taxes and fees, which are usually $500 or higher round-trip from the U.S.—London's airport fees are truly noxious.

Most times of the year, the least expensive way to reach London is with an **air-hotel package** (p. 66), which combines discounted airfare with discounted nights in a hotel. Most air-hotel deals will allow you to fly back days after your hotel allotment runs out, and at no extra charge. Keep in mind that for those, solo travelers always pay a little more, typically $250.

AIRPORT TRANSPORTATION OPTIONS

Fares and trip duration can be found in the chart, p. 350.

BY TRAIN   Always take the train. This is how nearly everyone does it here. Every airport offers some kind of rail connection to the central city, and that's the smartest option to take. Tickets can be bought at kiosks in the arrivals halls, at machines before the platform, or online or via an official app ahead of time (almost always the cheapest way, when you'll get a discount). You'll rarely have to wait more than 20 minutes for the next train, and you don't have to pre-book.

Opened in 2022, the newly built **Elizabeth Line,** which has plenty of room for your luggage, takes you from Heathrow to Paddington Station in 28 minutes (£10.70) using the same Oyster card (p. 357) you'll be using to ride the Tube and buses during your trip. You can remain on the Elizabeth Line to continue at any other station it calls on in central London, including Bond Street (for Marylebone and Mayfair), Tottenham Court Road (for Bloomsbury and the West End), Farringdon, Liverpool Street (for the City), Whitechapel (for East London), and the Canary Wharf business district.

Faster but more expensive, **Heathrow Express** trains (www.heathrow express.com; ✆ **0345/600-1515**) zoom to Paddington in 15 minutes every quarter-hour. First Class is a waste of money; Express, the cheapest option (purchasing online or on its app is cheapest, but there are also vending machines at the stations), is plenty plush. Weekend one-way tickets go as low as £5.50 if you book at least 90 days ahead. It uses commuter-style carriages and departs every 15 minutes to and from Paddington, where you can hop the Tube system or a taxi.

The slowest but cheapest train from LHR is the **Piccadilly Line** (£6.30 cash or £5.50 Oyster, which is explained on p. 357), which takes a slow 75 minutes to plod to the West End in an old-fashioned Tube carriage with very little luggage space. *Bus option:* If you need to go in the middle of the night and the trains aren't running (they tend to shut down after midnight and return before dawn), Night Bus N9 goes to and from Trafalgar Square and Heathrow, taking about 75 minutes.

Gatwick Express trains (www.gatwickexpress.com; ✆ **0345/850-1530**) run from Victoria. On **ThamesLink** (www.thameslinkrailway.com; ✆ **0345/026-4700**), you can get to Gatwick via Blackfriars, London Bridge, City Thameslink (near St Paul's), Farringdon, or St Pancras stations five times an

AIRPORT	COST/AVG. TIME USING NATIONAL RAIL	HOURS OF RAIL SERVICE
Heathrow (LHR), www.Heathrow.com	Heathrow Express (www.heathrow express.com): £5.50–£25 single, £37 return, kids 14 and under free*/15 min.	5:10am to 11:33pm
Gatwick (LGW), www.Gatwick Airport.com	Gatwick Express (www.gatwickexpress. com): £18.50 single/£36.80 return (booked online), kids 5–15 £9.25/ £18.50/30 min. OR ThamesLink (www.thameslinkrailway.com): £12.90–£23.10 single/37–54 min.	Five times hourly ~5am to ~12:30am
Luton (LTN), www.London-Luton.co.uk	ThamesLink (www.thameslinkrailway. com): £19.10 single including 10-min. shuttle bus, 22–45 min.	Seven times hourly 5am to midnight; hourly midnight to 5am
Stansted (STN), www.Stansted Airport.com	From £20.70 single/47 min.	Every 30 min. 4:40am to 12:30am (also a 3:40am train on Mon, Fri, and Sat)
London City (LCY), www.LondonCity Airport.com	N/A	DLR: 5:30am to midnight
London Southend (SEN), www.south endairport.com	Greater Anglia: About £19 single/ 53 min.	4am to midnight

Discounts for purchasing online in advance and avoiding rush hour departures.

hour—service usually ends just after midnight, but check ahead, because timings change.

Stansted Express (www.stanstedexpress.com; ☎ 085/600-7245) runs from Liverpool Street station. **Luton** has rail service from St Pancras, Farringdon, City ThamesLink, and Blackfriars stations by **ThamesLink** (www.thames linkrailway.com; ☎ 0345/026-4700). The correct stop is Luton Airport Parkway Station, linked by a 10-minute shuttle (5am–midnight and included in your train fare) to the terminals.

City Airport is linked so expediently and affordably by the Docklands Light Railway that it doesn't support commuter rail or coach service. **London Southend** (www.southendairport.com) is so well-connected to a shiny new station by **Greater Anglia** rail from Liverpool Street that buses don't bother to go there.

BY BUS There's not enough of a speed or price advantage to take a bus into London. Still, if you love fumes and traffic, **National Express** (www.nation alexpress.com; ☎ 0871/781-8181) buses will take you from all airports (except

RAIL SERVICE TO	COST/TIME USING TUBE OR DLR	COST/AVG. TIME TO AIRPORT BY TAXI
Paddington	£6.30 cash or £5.50 Oyster on Piccadilly Line (75 min.) £10.70 on Elizabeth Line (28 min.)	£75–£95/70 min.
Gatwick Express: Victoria; **ThamesLink**: St Pancras, Farringdon, Blackfriars, or London Bridge	N/A	£100/70 min.
St Pancras, Blackfriars, Farringdon, or City ThamesLink	N/A	£110/80 min.**
Liverpool Street	N/A	£100/80 min.**
N/A	£6.30 cash, £3.60 Oyster/25 min. on Docklands Light Railway	£25–£40/20–40 min.
Liverpool Street	N/A	£80–£110 (£28 shared)/ 60 to 80 min.**

** As if you'd be daft enough to want a taxi after seeing those prices and drive times, you're more likely to find one by booking ahead. Check www.london-luton.co. uk, www.stanstedairport.com, and www.southendairport.com for list of the latest approved companies. Addison Lee (www.addisonlee.com) is an established minicab giant, and Heathrow has a partnership with WeKnow London (U.K.: ✆ **0800/310-0442;** www.weknowlondon.com). All services offer discounted prices for children.

Southend or City) for around £8. With extreme advance purchase, **easyBus** (www.easybus.com) can be a few pounds cheaper (from Gatwick, Stansted, and Luton).

BY TAXI OR CAR SERVICE Because of traffic and price, taking a metered **taxi** (£46–£100) to the city the way you might do at home does not have our hearty recommendation. **Uber** drivers can only be hailed once you leave the terminal, and then they pick you up at the pickup point indicated by the app. All other road transport should be booked at least a day ahead, if possible. Door-to-door **car service** (£60–£80) is cheaper than a metered taxi and can take 45 minutes to 2 hours. The train-taxi or train-Tube combo is often faster (although on trains you'll have to contend with your luggage). You can book cars ahead, which often saves about 25% off the price of a taxi: Check each airport's web-site for a current list of the latest approved companies. **Addison Lee** (www. addisonlee.com; ✆ **020/7387-8888;** book via its app) is an established minicab company; the website **Minicabit.com** surveys companies for the best prices. Also try sustainable **Green Tomato Cars** (www.greentomatocars.com; book

driving IN LONDON?

Don't! Roads are clogged. In bad traffic, a trip from Heathrow to the western fringe of London can take 2 hours. And once you're in the city, just about every technology is deployed against you. There's a hefty fee just to drive to the city center and if you're driving an older, fuel-inefficient car, it's even heftier. Roads are confusingly one-way. Cameras capture and ticket the most honest driving errors. Parking is a fantasy when you're looking for it and a nightmare when you find it and have to pay. The only time to *maybe* drive a car is if you're on a cross-country tour—but in cities, it won't be easy for you.

The cheapest coach and van services usually drop you off at standardized stops such as major train stations. For Gatwick, Heathrow, Stansted, and Luton, in addition to the usual National Express coach options, there's the no-frills **easyBus** (www.easybus.com). Unless you book far in advance, it may not be much cheaper.

If you insist upon wheels (don't!), reserving ahead from home yields the best prices. Try to return your car outside the congestion-charge zone to avoid charges and aggravation. You will find similar rates among **Auto Europe** (www.autoeurope.com), **Europcar** (www.europcar.com), and **Holiday Autos** (www.holidayautos.com). Also check the major names like Avis, Hertz, and Budget, in case they can do better. Air-conditioning, something you won't need, adds about £5 to the daily bill. Fuel, or *petrol*, is priced like liquid gold, and although most rentals include unlimited mileage, not all do. It's smart to have your own GPS unit because your mobile phone's roaming data is likely to be so throttled that maps won't render fast enough. Do not add anything to a reservation once you're at the rental counter or you may negate that great deal you thought you had. **Note:** Many rental cars are stick-shift models, which means you'll be driving on the left in a foreign land with a stick shift. Don't!

via its app); **Chaufferit** (www.chaufferit.com); and **Carrot Cars** (www. carrotcars.co.uk; ℂ **020/7005-0557**), which serve all airports.

By Long-Distance Rail

For trips from northwestern Europe, the train is the dignified way to go. Train stations are right in the middle of town. We're living in marvelous times: The Channel Tunnel opened in 1994 (although they *still* seem to be working out the kinks), so you can reach the heart of London in an incredible 2 hours and 16 minutes from Paris. You can literally ride both the Tube and the Métro before lunch. In fact, you can ride both a black taxi and Space Mountain before lunch, because one Eurostar route alights in the middle of Disneyland Paris Resort. Eurostar links London's St Pancras station with Paris, Brussels (less than 2 hr.), Lille, and Calais, and from there, you can go just about anywhere using other trains. In 2018, after decades of dreams, it finally finished the line to Amsterdam, too (just under 4 hr.), although that route can still be unreliable.

Book via **Eurostar** (www.eurostar.co.uk; ℂ **03432/186-186** in the U.K., or ℂ **646/934-6454** in the U.S.; phone bookings incur a surcharge) itself or the

U.S.–based **Rail Europe** (www.raileurope.com; ℂ **800/361-7245** in North America), which also sells European rail passes. Check both sites, since prices can differ, but do it early, because rates boom as availability decreases. Advance-purchase deals to Paris regularly go as low as £29 each way, but standard bookings cost several times that.

By Bus

A few coach companies also travel between the U.K. and the continent, usually crossing the English Channel with a ferry. Because of the pressure put on the market by mushrooming no-frills airlines, rates are extremely low, but because the ferry industry is in disarray and delays are common, **we don't currently recommend this method.** You'll pay as little as £21 one-way to Paris via **Eurolines** (www.eurolines.eu; info@eurolines.eu; 8–10 hr. each way). Brussels or Amsterdam is £15 with a 7-day advance purchase. Also look at **Flixbus** (which absorbed some Megabus routes; www.flixbus.com), which goes from Victoria to multiple destinations around Europe (say, Antwerp from 50€). The trade-off: It can take all day, sunrise to sunset, to reach Paris by this method. Discouraged? The website **CheckMyBus.com** searches all the available carriers.

Some other companies arrange full-on organized tours of Europe's greatest hits—but never for less than you could do independently; choose one only because you'd enjoy having company: **Contiki** (www.contiki.com; ℂ **833/670-9198**) is geared toward a party-hearty under-35 crowd, and **Fanatics** (www.thefanatics.com; ℂ **020/7240-3233**) is for followers of organized sports.

By Boat

Ferry travel was already nearly obsolete, and then pandemic woes made ferries even more unreliable. We don't think you should rely on them right now unless you have a very loose travel schedule. Besides, no ferry to Europe or Ireland sails directly to London. You'll have to get down to the southern coast (for France), Portsmouth (for Spain), or Liverpool or Wales (Ireland). Fares are around £56 each way with a car and including taxes (150 min.) on **P&O Ferries** (www.poferries.com; ℂ **01304/44-88-88**) or **DFDS** (www.dfds.com; ℂ **0208/127-8303**), both of which do Dover–Calais. Ferries between Wales and Ireland are operated by **Irish Ferries** (www.irishferries.ie; ℂ **0818/300-400** in the Republic of Ireland, or ℂ **353/818-300-400** in Northern Ireland/U.K.) and **Stena Line**

Keep Up-to-Date

Americans and Canadians often write dates as month / day / year, as in June 1, 1957. But the default way to express a date in the U.K. is day / month / year, à la 1 June 1957—which, honestly, makes more sense because the units of time are ordered by increasing size. When you make reservations for anything online, don't accidentally swap the day and month—if you can, select the day from a calendar grid to ensure you've got it right.

(www.stenaline.com; ✆ **+46/31-85-80-00**). The aggregator **DirectFerries. co.uk** sells European routes from a rapidly diminishing roster of offers.

If you despise flying, one ocean liner still makes the storied 7-day trip between New York City and Southampton, which connects by rail to London in an hour. That's the ***Queen Mary 2*** (www.cunard.com; ✆ **800/728-6273**), intermittently scheduled. Fares start around $1,200 per person one-way, including all your meals. Pack your tuxedos and gowns for the formal nights.

GETTING AROUND LONDON

There are three practical methods for taming London's sprawl: by Tube (historic and enchanting, but expensive); by bus (less expensive and less glamorous, but more edifying and often quicker); and by foot (the best method, but not always possible). Taxis are overpriced, and driving a car is lunacy.

A significant savings strategy is to choose a hotel that's within walking distance of lots of the things you want to do. Fortunately, the city is extremely walkable. Tube trains go shockingly slowly (34kmph/21 mph is the *average* and has been for more than 100 years); in the center of town, stops are remarkably close together and the stairs can wear you out. In fact, if your journey is only two or three stations, you'll often find it less strenuous to simply walk.

The Underground

Londoners call their 402km (249-mile) metro system the Underground, its official name, or just as commonly, "the Tube." Its elegant, distinctive logo—a red "roundel" bisected by a blue bar—debuted in 1913 as one of the world's first corporate symbols, and it remains one of the city's most ubiquitous sights. The Tube is much more dignified than most American systems. In fact, seats are upholstered—because the British know how to take care of nice things. And yet there's no older subway system—the first section opened in 1863 while America was fighting its Civil War—and it often acts its age, with frequent delays and shutdowns. Check posters and whiteboards in the ticket hall to see what "engineering works" are scheduled.

The Tube is an attraction unto itself. It's fun to seek out vestiges of the early system (1907 tilework on the Piccadilly Line; the fake house facades built at 23–24 Leinster Gardens to hide exposed tracks; abandoned stations like the one at Strand and Surrey Street). If such "urban archaeology" fascinates you, visit the **London Transport Museum** in Covent Garden (p. 136), one of the city's family-friendly highlights.

There are 13 named lines, plus the new Elizabeth Line; the Docklands Light Railway (DLR), which serves East London; and a tram line in South London. Lines are color-coded: The Piccadilly is a peacock purple, the Bakerloo could be considered Sherlock Holmes brown, and so on. All told, the Underground serves nearly 300 stations.

In May 2022, after a controversial five-year delay, the newly dug £15-billion **Elizabeth Line** (once called **Crossrail**) created a quick train line linking

East London to West London. Before its opening, most commuters had to laboriously hop various Tube lines to get across the city. Now, you can use the new line to connect to all of the train stations that serve nearly all of London's airports. What's more, all the Elizabeth Line's stops in central London have step-free access, something many Tube stops can't claim.

The Tube shuts down nightly from Sunday to Thursday. Exact times for first and final trains are posted in each station (using the 24-hr. clock), but the Tube generally operates from 5:30am (0530) to just after midnight (0000), and Sundays 7am (0700) to 11:30pm (2330). On Friday and Saturday nights, many lines in central London run every 10 minutes all night long: **"Night Tube"** trains are the Victoria, Central, and Jubilee lines, plus the Charing Cross branch of the Northern line and a slice of the Overground between Islington and New Cross Gate. (The Piccadilly Line overnight service was suspended for the pandemic; check to see if it's back.) Still, if you plan to take the train after midnight, always check the Night Tube map and schedule beforehand. **Transport for London** (TfL) offers 24-hour information at ✆ **0343/222-1234.**

What happens if you miss the last train? Don't worry—you're not stranded, although your trip may take longer or cost more. Just turn to the city's network of 24-hour and Night Bus routes (p. 359).

HOW TO FIND YOUR WAY ON THE TUBE

Navigating is mostly foolproof. Look for signs pointing to the color and name of the line you want. Pretty soon, more signs separate you according to the direction you want to go in, based on the Tube map. If you know the name/color of the line you want, as well as the direction of your destination, the signs will march you, anthill-like, to the platform you need. Nearly every station is combed with staircases. You'll shuffle through warrens of cylindrical tunnels, many of them faced in custard-yellow tiles and overly full of commuters, and you'll scale alpine escalators lined with ads. Stand to the right so "climbers" can pass you.

On the DLR (the Overground) and trains that stop outdoors, the carriage may not automatically open. Push the illuminated button and it will.

Electronic signs on platforms tell you how long it'll be until the next train. A 24-hour information service is also available at ✆ **0343/222-1234.** You can use the TfL Journey Planner online at **https://tfl.gov.uk/plan-a-journey**, but the best resource is the free app **Citymapper,** which tells you which Tube, bus, or train to use and how long it takes. It also includes mapped walking directions to the appropriate stop. Transport for London has its own free app, **TfL Go,** that's good for determining which lines are working (or closed). The **UK Bus Checker** app shows 3D maps of routes and where the next bus is.

The most confusing lines for tourists are the Northern line (black on the maps) and the District line (green). Owing mostly to the petty backbiting of the Victorians who built these lines as individual businesses, those lines split into several paths through the city (but there are places to jump off and change

frustrations OF THE TUBE

The Tube lists everything about itself in exhaustive detail at **https://tfl.gov.uk**, which contains more maps, planners, and FAQs than a normal person can use. As endearing as the Tube is, it is not perfect. In fact, it can be so dehumanizing that it has had to put up signs begging people not to abuse its staff (sad but true). Be prepared for a few things:

1. **Stairs.** Most stations are as intricate as anthills. Passengers are sadistically corralled up staircases, around platforms, down more staircases, and through still more staircases. Even stations equipped with extremely long escalators (Angel has the longest one in the system—59m/194 ft.) perversely require passengers to climb a final flight to reach the street. So, if you bring luggage into the Tube, be able to hoist your stuff for at least 15 stairs at a time. (This is where backpacks make sense—but don't be the person who keeps wearing it on a crowded carriage.) For a list of which stations are step-free, contact **Transport for London Access & Mobility** (https://tfl.gov.uk/accessibility; (*) **0343/222-1234**) or consult the TfL Go app.

2. **Delays.** The TfL Go app will tell you if anything is amiss. Or, when you enter a station, look for a standing sign before the fare gates. You'll see status bars reading "Good service," "Severe delays," or the like. If you note "Minor delays," don't worry. *Do* worry about labor strikes—they're unpleasantly common.

3. **Heat.** The network can be stuffy. In summer, health advisories are issued to passengers. The worst lines: Bakerloo, Central, and Northern. The best: Elizabeth Line, Circle, and District. Air-conditioning is being added—slowly.

4. **Hellish rush hours.** Shoulder-to-shoulder, silently shuffling through airless underground cylinders. It's memorable in the wrong way.

5. **Tough weekends.** Unlike modern systems, which generally have two sets of rails in each direction, London's ancient system has one set, so entire lines have to shut down when maintenance is required. Weekends are when this happens. This is a major reason why it's smart to stay in central London, where you don't depend on a single Tube line. Check in the ticket hall to see what "engineering works" are scheduled.

in case you mess up). Platform displays and signs on the front of the trains tell you its final destination before you board, so you can figure out the direction. If you ride the DLR (and you should—it provides a lovely rooftop-level glide through the brickwork of the old East End and the monolithic towers of Canary Wharf), those lines split variously, too, but there are lots of chances to rectify mistakes.

The **Underground's website** provides the excellent "London's Rail and Tube Services" map at https://tfl.gov.uk/maps/track/national-rail. It's a truer picture than the Tube map alone because it shows all the places your fare card can take you by rail. (Buses are on separate maps.) The site also has terrific simplified bus maps that show you routes from any neighborhood.

FARES, PASSES & TICKETS

London Underground (**https://tfl.gov.uk/tickets**) provides 1.1 billion rides in a normal year—and seemingly every passenger pays a different fare. Rates go up regularly (these rates were current at press time and will give you a sense of proportion). Britain's system is so complicated that it's accused of having been engineered to bewilder travelers into paying more than they have to. But it can be boiled down to this: **Get an Oyster card and load it with money.** I'll explain.

Zones determine cost: The center of town—basically everything the Circle line envelops, plus a wee bit of padding—is zone 1. Heading outside of town, in a concentric pattern, come zones 2 through 6. Most tourists stick to zones 1 and 2; very few major sights are outside those (Wimbledon, Hampton Court, and Kew being the main exceptions). Your fare is calculated by how many zones you go through, and the lower the zone number, the less you pay. If a station appears to straddle zones, you'll pay the cheaper zone's rate. One-way tickets are called "singles" and round-trips are "return."

Astonishingly, **kids 10 and under travel for free** when accompanied by an adult. Adults must buy their own ticket and then ask the staff to wave their kid through the entry gate. Ask an agent about the going discounts for kids.

There are essentially three ticket types for visiting adults.

1. **Via Oyster Pay As You Go (PAYG).** You *could* buy a Travelcard fare pass, but don't—and I'll explain why. Getting an Oyster card is the best option, and it's what locals use. Tap the credit card–size Oyster pass on yellow dots at the turnstiles and you get the lowest fares. You load it with cash and it debits as you go, no tickets required, on all forms of in-city public transit. No matter how many times you ride the Tube (debited at £2.50 in zone 1—that's a lot better than the £6.30 "cash" fare you pay if you don't use Oyster!) and bus (debited as £1.65—you can't pay cash on a bus), the maximum taken off your card in a single day will **always be less** than what an equivalent Day Travelcard (see below) would cost. Which makes it the cheapest. Nonstop Oyster use will always peak at £7.70 for anytime travel in the center city (£4.95 if you only took buses), versus the flat rate of £14.40 you'd have paid if you'd bought a Travelcard pass instead. That benefit is called "price capping," and it resets daily at 4:30am. Getting an Oyster usually requires a £5 deposit, but that can pay for itself in a single day vs. buying a Travelcard. The card won't get erased if you keep it beside your mobile phone. And if you don't use up all the money you put on it, you can get a refund as long as there's less than £10 value left on your card. (Travelcards offer no refunds for unused monies.) So. **Buy an Oyster card.** They're sold at vending machines when you enter the Tube and then you can use it on buses, Thames Clipper ferries, and other trains within the city, too.

2. **Via Travelcard.** Aimed at tourists, this is an unlimited pass for 1 or 7 days on the Tube, rail, and bus. "Day Anytime" Travelcards for zones 1 through

4 with no timing restrictions are £14.40. If you find you have to pop into a zone that isn't covered by your card, buy an extension from the ticket window before starting your journey; it's usually a couple pounds more. A 7-Day Travelcard costs adults £38.40 for travel in zones 1 and 2. For Travelcard prices that include more zones, visit **https://tfl.gov.uk/tickets**. You can load a Travelcard purchase onto an Oyster. *Downside:* Unlike PAYG, you may end up paying for rides you never use.

3. **In cash, per ride.** You could, but don't. To travel a mile in zone 1 on the Underground, the cash fare is £6.30 (more than $7.50). I did the math: It can cost 3½ times more to pay cash to go a mile on the Tube than to fly a mile in transatlantic First Class. What's more, bus drivers don't even take cash anymore. They *do* take Oyster.

The Tube does offer **contactless payment** on turnstiles' yellow dots—charges are exactly the same as with Oyster—but there's no telling if your card issuer or bank supports it. Apple Pay and Google Pay should work. Visit **https://tfl.gov.uk/fares** and confer with your issuer to make an educated guess whether you can use this method. If you do use your phone to pay, complete fingerprint or facial recognition before you approach the turnstiles or you'll hold everyone else up. Frankly, for visitors, an Oyster card is more surefire.

If you accidentally overspend the cash you have stored on your Oyster during a ride, the exit turnstile will deduct the overage from your deposit.

How to use tickets: Since pricing depends on how far you've gone, you must touch your Oyster card to the big yellow reader dot both before you board *and* after your trip—even if there are no turnstiles and even if turnstiles are wide open (so don't forget). On the DLR, the dot may be at the bottom of the stairs to the street. The same goes if you have a paper ticket for any train; keep it handy because you'll need it to get back out at the end. If you can't find it or if you forget to touch out, you'll pay the maximum rate as if you had ridden to the end of the line. Inspectors regularly check passengers' tickets and they won't hesitate to fine you. They feast on the power.

How to pay at a vending machine: If you are using a credit card to buy tickets from a vending machine, don't pull your card out of the vending machine until you're told to, or it will falsely tell you it's declined. (Underground machines never hesitate to claim something is wrong with your card. Don't believe them. Try a few times.) Vending machines usually accept cash and coins. Cards embedded with a SIM make transactions infinitely easier in London, so make sure yours are.

> **From *Europe on $5 a Day*, 1969–1970**
>
> "For those who have played the sardine in New York's subway, the London 'underground' is a revelation. Quiet, clean, comfortable; the normal fare ranges from 6 to 18¢, depending on the length of the ride, but your average trip should cost no more than around 9¢."

Buy ahead?: Although TfL will mail Oysters or Travelcards ahead of time, that's a waste. You can purchase them at any Tube stop, including at airports, without shipping fees.

Buses

The Tube and buses are seen as one piece, so the same payment systems work on both. Buses are what smart Londoners use. The buses in your city may not come often, but London's are frequent (every 5 min. or so on weekdays), plentiful (some 100 routes in central London and 700 in the wider city), and surprisingly fast (many zoom in dedicated lanes). Sitting on the second level of a candy-apple red double-decker, watching the big landmarks roll past, is one of London's priceless pleasures. Best of all, the bus is cheaper than the Tube.

Single trips are just £1.65. The most you can possibly spend in a day on bus travel using Oyster PAYG is £4.95, no matter the zone. (If you mix bus and Tube travel in the same day, you'll max out at £7.70.) You can make **free transfers** between as many buses as you want within a 1-hour window. Don't ride without tapping in on that yellow disc (on buses, you don't have to tap *out* when you leave): Surprise card inspections are common. Bus passes and Travelcards expire at 4:30am the day after you buy them. The TfL supplies 24-hour information at ℂ **0343/222-1234.**

Important: Everyone in your party must use their own card, whether it's Oyster or a contactless card. Parents cannot use their own cards for their kids' fare.

Bus drivers do not accept money. You **must** have an Oyster card or Travelcard (get one in any Tube stop; bus stops with vending machines are super rare). All stations have easy-to-read poster maps that tell you where to catch the buses going to your destination and where the routes go. Major intersections might have multiple stops named with letters, and each stop will service different routes, so check the map in the bus shelter to find the lettered stop you need. Many shelters even have electronic boards that approximate the arrival time of the next bus.

Once you're aboard, an automated voice announces stops with plenty of warning. Press a button on a handrail to request a halt before the next one. Get off via the door at the middle. Some buses have reinstated a rear-door design, so on those, you can leap off that back entrance and break your neck whenever you like.

Routes that start with N are Night Buses, which tote clubbers home after the Tube stops around midnight; many connect tediously in Trafalgar Square, so pee before setting off. London has trams, too, charged like buses, but they're in areas where tourists are unlikely to go.

National Rail

These are the rail lines that aren't operated by the Underground but they are as useful as the Tube within the city. These comfortable, standard-size trains go to suburbs and distant cities, and they operate on a regular, reliable, published timetable—on maps, they are denoted by two red parallel lines with a zigzag line connecting them. These lines are covered by Travelcards and Oyster PAYG for roughly the same price as the Tube as long as you stay in the zone system. (The major stations have information desks if you're unsure about Oyster's validity on any journey.) You must tap Oyster at the start *and* at the completion of each journey or you'll be charged as if you took the train to the end of the line. If you accidentally tap in for a wrong or missed train, alert staff. They can ensure you aren't penalized.

There are many termini, but you don't have to hunt by trial and error. Check **TheTrainLine.com** website or app, call the 24-hour operators at **National Rail Enquiries** (www.nationalrail.co.uk; ✆ **08457/48-49-50**), or plug your journey into your favorite directions app such as the free **Citymapper,** which will enlighten you. Alternatively, each station posts timetables. Schedules are listed by destination; find the place you're going, and the departures will be listed in 24-hour time.

National Rail stations (not Eurostar or the Underground) accept discount cards for certain folks. Each card requires proof of eligibility (passport, ISIC student ID), but since they can be used for trips to distant cities, they pay for themselves quickly if you're doing lots of rail-riding. Get them at rail stations:

- The **Senior Railcard** (www.senior-railcard.co.uk; £30 a year): Discounts of about 33% for those 60 or over.
- The **16–25 Railcard** (www.16-25railcard.co.uk; £30 a year): Discounts of 33% for those 16 to 25, plus full-time students of any age. It requires a passport-size photo, which may be uploaded from a computer. If you're applying in the U.K., bring a passport photo for that purpose.
- The **Family & Friends Railcard** (www.family-railcard.co.uk; £30 a year) is for at least one adult and one child age 5 to 15, with a maximum of three

RED-LETTER double-deckers

A few routes are truly world-class, linking legendary sights. With routes like these, you won't need to splurge on those tedious hop-on, hop-off tour buses:

- The **15 bus,** which crosses the city northwest to southeast, takes in Paddington, Oxford Street, Piccadilly Circus, Trafalgar Square, Fleet Street, St Paul's, and the Tower of London.
- The **10** passes Royal Albert Hall, Kensington Gardens, Knightsbridge (a block north of Harrods), Hyde Park Corner, Marble Arch, Oxford Street, Goodge Street (for the British Museum), and King's Cross Station.

- The **159** links Paddington, Oxford Circus, Trafalgar Square, and Westminster.
- The **RV1** hits Covent Garden, Waterloo, the Tate Modern, and as a bonus, you get to ride over the Tower Bridge to the Tower of London.

adults and four kids on one ticket; at least one child must travel at all times. It awards adults 33% off and kids 60% off. But know that two kids age 4 and under can travel with an adult for free at all times, even without this card.

Ferries

Partly thanks to the dedication of a series of mayors, London's river ferry services are now one of the most pleasurable ways to get around. The Clipper boats, nicknamed River Bus, cover a surprising amount of terrain quickly. Some of their most useful stops include right outside the London Eye, the Tate Modern, the Tower of London, Greenwich, and the O_2. Getting from Greenwich to Embankment takes all of 45 idyllic minutes (but on weekends, you may have to wait 30 min. for a boat back). You can go right under the famous Tower Bridge—and because it's intended for commuters, the ride comes at a fraction of the price of a tourist boat.

Fares depend on how far you're going, but for a trip from Westminster to Greenwich, expect a one-way fare around £8.70 (£7.50 with Oyster). You will always save money if you buy a return trip instead of two one-ways, and always ask if your Oyster card or Travelcard grants a discount. The fast catamarans of **Thames Clippers,** now branded as **Uber Boat** (www.thames clippers.com; ✆ **020/7930-2062;** generally 6:30am–10:30pm; bookable via its app), go every 20 minutes during the day and are much cheaper and plentiful than the narrated tour boats. The RB1 route is particularly useful, hitting most of the major tourist stops plus Greenwich and the O_2. *One snag:* On weekends, the queue to return from Greenwich can be 40 minutes to an hour long. River Roamer passes, which allow you to take as many trips as you want on a single day after 9am, cost £18.90 for adults, £9.45 kids, £37.80 for a family of two adults and up to three kids. You can buy at the piers or, for a discount of a few quid, buy ahead via the Thames Clippers Tickets app, downloadable via www.thamesclippers.com/route-time-table/book-tickets-with-ticketing-app.

Thames River Sightseeing (www.thamesriversightseeing.co.uk; ✆ **020/7930-4097**) is a touristy version of the Clippers (it looks similar, but this one has a roof deck for passengers) and offers a £14 single/£18.50 return ride from Westminster to Greenwich. It calls these "sightseeing" trips but note that it's not fully guided and the Clippers are just as good.

You can pay for ferries with Oyster, but keep in mind that whatever you spend on a boat will not count toward your daily Oyster price capping.

Bikes

Scattered in 839 places throughout town, you'll see racks of identical red bikes in racks. They're in London's main bikeshare system. They're called **Santander Cycles** (www.tfl.gov.uk/modes/cycling/santander-cycles), but Londoners call them **Boris Bikes,** after the blowsy former mayor-cum-ousted prime minister who brought them here, and they provide more than 10.9 million rides a year. Bikeshare is ubiquitous today, but in 2010, London was one of the first cities to try it.

It works like this: You choose one and pull it out of the rack by lifting the seat. You ride it to any other docking station in the city with a free space, and you park it by slotting the front wheel in until a green light appears on the dock. When you're ready to ride somewhere else, just get another bike. You buy the right to borrow bikes for 24 hours for £2, and that gets you 30 minutes (payments are on your credit card) every time you pull a bike out of the rack. Go past that, and you pay the same rate: £2 per extra 30 minutes. The idea is for you to use a bike as you need it, not to keep it with you all day. You are required to follow the same traffic rules that cars do, which won't be easy, although the city's huge parks are safer places to cycle. Locations of nearby docks are listed on every pylon. Use the free apps **Santander Cycles** or **Citymapper** to find nearby stations with space.

Taxis

Even Londoners think taxis are crazy expensive. It's not the fault of the cabbies. They're the best in the world. Before they're given their wheels, every London taxi driver (there are some 24,000 of them) must go through a grueling training period so comprehensive that it's dubbed, simply, "The Knowledge." On Sundays, you'll see trainees zipping around on mopeds with clipboards affixed above their dashboards. Cabbies arrive inculcated with directions to every alley, mews, avenue, shortcut, and square in the city, and if they don't know, they'll find the answer so discreetly you won't catch the gaffe. They're even trained in first aid, childbirth, and assisting after an acid attack—so breathe easy. And then there are those adorable vehicles: bulbous as Depression Era jalopies, roomy as a studio apartment, yet able to do complete U-turns within a single lane of traffic.

But for this admittedly peerless carriage, you'll pay a £3.80 minimum. Trips of up to 1.6km (1 mile) cost £6.40 to £10 during working hours; 3.2km (2-mile) trips are £9 to £15.80; 6.4km (4-mile) trips are £17 to £25; and trips of around 9.6km (6 miles) hit you for a painful £26 to £33. Rates rise when

CAN I do that?

Some things that are considered sins back home may lead to legal pleasures in London. Which means they're not sinful as long as you're on British soil! To wit:

- The drinking age is 18. But if you're having your first legit night out, take it easy, because beers here have higher alcohol content than in many countries.

- There are no open container laws. That means you can drink beer in public. The one exception is on

public transportation, where, ironically, you need a drink the most.

- You may smoke Cuban cigars. Get them at any tobacconist and puff away. If you're American, though, don't try smuggling them home.

- Absinthe, the brutal quaff nicknamed "The Green Fairy," is available here. Drink up because American Customs frowns on many versions of it.

- The age of consent is 16 no matter the sexual preference.

If You Need to Fake a British Postcode

When you're online in the U.K., such as when you sign up for free Wi-Fi, you may be asked for a mobile number and a postcode before you access a signal. Of course, you don't have those things—you're visiting! Bulldoze through this shortsightedness by giving a fake email address and a fake number you can invent at https://fakenumber.org/generator/mobile. As for a postcode, use your hotel's. Better yet, use the following code: SW1A 1AA. After all, if that postcode is good enough for Buckingham Palace, it's good enough for you!

you're most likely to need a taxi: by about 10% from 8 to 10pm or all day on weekends, and roughly another 20% from 10pm until dawn. Trips that start at Heathrow cost an extra £3.60, and trips around Christmas and New Year's Day tack on £4. Mercifully, there is no charge for extra passengers or for luggage. It has become customary to tip 10%, but most people just round up to the nearest pound. Some taxis accept credit cards (don't count on it), but mostly they are a cash-only concern.

Taxis are often called "black cabs," although in fact 12 colors are registered, including "thistle blue" and "nightfire red." **Minicabs,** which are hire cars that operate separately from the traditional black cab system, are easy to find using apps. Don't accept a ride from an unsolicited one. Among the top free apps that can hail the nearest ride: **Minicabit** (www.minicabit.com); taxi-calling app **Free Now** (www.free-now.com/uk); independent ride-share app **Uber** (www.uber.com); and London's reigning power minicab operator, **Addison Lee** (www.addisonlee.com). Lyft does not operate in London.

Renting a Car

Are you insane? Rare is the local who drives in central London, where there's a mandatory weekday "congestion charge" of £15 (Don't believe me? See **www.cclondon.com**.), where cars that don't meet low-emission standards pay *another* £12.50 a day, and where parking rates look like your rent back home. Streets were cramped enough when people rode horses, and now they're dogged with one-way rules and police cameras that will ticket you for even honest errors, which you'll definitely make since you're just visiting. You'll go crazy and broke, so why do it? If you're driving out of the city for a tour of the country, fine, pick up a rental on the outskirts, but *do not* rent a car for a central London vacation.

GETTING AROUND THE U.K.
By Train

The original railway tycoons plowed their stations into every town of size, making it easy to see the highlights of the United Kingdom without getting near a car. The British whine about the declining quality of the service, but Americans, Canadians, and Australians will be blown away by the speed (and the cost, unfortunately, if they don't book ahead) of the system. Find tickets to all destinations through **National Rail** (www.nationalrail.co.uk; ✆ **08457/ 48-49-50**) or the indispensable **TheTrainLine.com.** Early-bird bookings can yield some marvelous deals, such as £26 for a 4-hour trip to Scotland (£125 last-minute is common). When hunting for tickets, always search for "off-peak" (non-rush hour) trips going or coming from London in general, not a specific London station, because each London terminal serves various cities. **SplitTicketing.com** also searches the rail companies' byzantine fare schedules to tell you journey configurations that can save you many pounds. Trainline accepts international credit cards.

Tickets bought reasonably well in advance will still be cheaper than what you'd pay for the same trips on a **BritRail pass** (www.britrail.com; must purchase outside the U.K.), good on long-distance trains but not on local London transport. Few tourists ride rails with the near-daily regularity that would make a timed pass pay for itself. Check prices against the U.S. seller **Rail Europe** (www.raileurope.com; ✆ **800/622-8600**), as quotes vary.

By Bus

National Express (www.nationalexpress.com; ✆ **0871/781-8181**) is the least expensive way to get from city to city in Britain (but not the fastest—that's usually the train). Because the country is not very big, it rarely takes more than a few hours to reach anyplace by bus. Even Scotland is only 5 hours away. A major carrier with scads of departures, **Megabus** (https://uk.megabus. com; ✆ **090/0160-0900,** or 44-141-352-4444), which serves more than 100 cities across Europe, charges as little as £1.50 for early bookings, although £19 to £45 for Edinburgh is a more typical rate. It accepts bookings 2 months ahead; book online to avoid phone fees. Both coach services depart from the miserable Victoria Coach Station, located behind Victoria railway station (www.tfl.gov.uk/coaches).

What's the best place to hear about inexpensive ground tours? Hostels. Drop into one; most of their lobbies are papered with brochures. Don't neglect their bulletin boards, either, because you may catch wind of a shared-ride situation that'll often cost you no more than your share of the gasoline (in Britain, *petrol*).

By Car

The only reason you might want to rent a car is if you're headed out of town (see "Driving in London?" on p. 352 for car rental tips).

WHEN TO GO

CLIMATE   It's always time to visit London. It doesn't rain as much as they say and it hasn't been foggy since they got rid of coal. Even though it's approximately at the same latitude of Edmonton, Alberta, weather patterns keep the environment from being extreme. It gets cold in the winter, but rarely snowed in. It gets warm in the summer, but only occasionally blisteringly so (in fact, most buildings don't even have air-conditioning), although climate change is noticeably changing that quickly. The winter months are generally more humid than the summer ones, but experience only slightly more rain. Locals use the free, reliable **Met Office Weather Forecast app,** by the U.K.'s national weather service, to pinpoint forecasts by GPS.

London's Average Daytime Temperatures & Rainfall

	JAN	FEB	MAR	APR	MAY	JUNE	JULY	AUG	SEPT	OCT	NOV	DEC
TEMP. (°F)	39	39	43	46	52	58	62	62	57	51	44	42
TEMP. (°C)	3	3	6	7	11	14	16	16	13	10	6	5
RAINFALL (in.)	1.6	1.4	1.6	1.6	1.7	1.8	1.3	2.1	2	2.4	2.2	1.9
RAINFALL (mm)	41	36	41	41	45	47	34	54	51	61	57	48

SEASONAL CONSIDERATIONS   The principal indoor arts season (for theater, concerts, art shows) falls between September and May, leaving the summer months for festivals and park-going. A few royal attractions, such as the state rooms of Buckingham Palace, are only open in the summer when the Royal Family decamps to Scotland. In summer, when the weather is warmest, the sun sets after 10pm, and half of Europe takes its annual holiday, when airfares are higher, as are hotel rates. Summertime queues for most tourist attractions, such as the London Eye and the Tower of London, might make you wish you'd come in March. For decent prices and lighter crowds, go in spring or fall—April and October seem to have the best confluence of mild weather, pretty plantings, and tolerable crowds. Prices are lowest in midwinter, but a number of minor sights, such as historic houses, sometimes close from November to March, and the biggest annual events take place during the warmer months.

London's Public Holidays

England observes **eight public holidays** (also known as "bank holidays"): New Year's Day (Jan 1); Good Friday and Easter Monday (usually Apr); May Bank Holiday (first Mon in May); Spring Bank Holiday (usually last Mon in May, but occasionally the first in June); August Bank Holiday (last Mon in Aug); Christmas Day (Dec 25) followed by Boxing Day (Dec 26)—you'll find it hard to even get around on those last two dates. If a date falls on a weekend, the holiday rolls over to the following Monday.

London Calendar of Events

Special events are an integral part of London's calendar, and many regular happenings draw tourists from around the world. Find even more events at London's **city website** (www.london.gov.uk/events), at the **official tourism site** (www.visitlondon.com), the blogs **Londonist** (www.londonist.com) and **IanVisits** (www.ianvisits.co.uk), and *Time Out* **magazine** (www.timeout.com/london).

JANUARY

London New Year's Day Parade. As many as 10,000 dancers, acrobats, musicians, and performers (heavy on the marching bands) promenade from Parliament Square to Piccadilly for 500,000 spectators and TV audiences. www.lnydp.com, ☎ 020/3275-0190. January 1.

Chinese New Year Festival. In conjunction with the Chinese New Year, the streets around Leicester Square come alive with dragon and lion dances, children's parades, performances, screenings, and fireworks displays. 2023: Late January.

Get into London Theatre. Theatre gets a jolt of new audiences during this promotional period during which producers cooperate to sell some 75,000 tickets at big discounts. www.getintolondontheatre.co.uk. Early January to February.

London International Mime Festival. Have you heard? It's not just for silent clowns, but also for funky puppets and ingenious physical tomfoolery, and it's held at venues around town. www.mimelondon.com, ✆ **020/7637-5661.** Mid-January.

MARCH

St Patrick's Festival. When you're this close to Dublin and you consider England's long rivalry with the Emerald Isle, you can expect several days of raging Irish pride—parades, music, and food stalls around Trafalgar Square, where the fountains gush green. The city also sponsors concerts and craft fairs promoting Irish culture and heritage. It's not just about drinking—it only looks that way. www.london.gov.uk, ✆ **020/7983-4000.** Weekend around March 17.

BADA Antiques & Fine Art Fair. Sponsored by the British Antique Dealers' Association, it's considered to be the best in Britain for such collectors. Some 100 exhibitors move into a mighty tent in Duke of York Square, in Chelsea, for the 7-day sales event. Don't expect a bargain. www.badafair.com, ✆ **020/7589-6108.**

Oxford and Cambridge Boat Race. This popular annual event (since 1829), held on the Thames in Hammersmith, takes less than 30 minutes, but the after-party rollicks into the night and the good-natured rivalry is undying. www.theboatrace.org. Late March or early April.

APRIL

London Marathon. Although it draws some 35,000 runners, the marathon is also a kick for spectators, so hotels tend to fill up ahead of it. The starter pistol fires in Blackheath; the home stretch is along Birdcage Walk near Buckingham Palace. If you want to run, apply by the previous October. www.TCS londonmarathon.com. 2023: April 23.

Udderbelly Festival. Famously mounted in a giant inflatable purple cow's udder by the London Eye (really), this offshoot of Edinburgh Fringe Festival's variety venue the Underbelly is now at Earl's Court and Cavendish Square (off Oxford Street) and sells well over a million tickets. Dozens of acts range from comedy to musicals to circus, plus there's food, beer, and other amusements. It grows bigger and more beloved by the year. www.udderbelly.co.uk, ✆ **0844/545-8282.** April to late September.

MAY

Regent's Park Open Air Theatre. Forget stuffy auditoriums. There's little shelter from sudden downpours, but in good weather the four-show season of high drama, musicals, and Shakespeare sparkles under a canopy of blue skies, towering trees, and natural beauty. www.openairtheatre.com, ✆ **0333/400-3562.** Mid-May to September.

Chelsea Flower Show. The Royal Horticultural Society, which calls itself a "leading gardening charity dedicated to advancing horticulture and promoting good gardening" (don't you just love the English?), mounts this esteemed show for 5 days on the grounds of the Royal Hospital in Chelsea. The plants, all raised by champion green thumbs, are sold to attendees on the final day, but sadly, foreigners aren't usually able to get their plants past Customs. Tickets go on sale in November for this lilypalooza, and they're snapped up quickly. The event is so celebrated that it is covered on nightly prime-time TV. Really. www.rhs.org. uk, ✆ **020/3176-5800.** Late May.

JUNE

Beating Retreat. Drum corps, pipes, and plenty of bugle calls: This anachronistic twilight ceremony, held for two evenings at Horse Guards Parade by St James's Park, involves the salute of the monarch and the appearance of many red-clad marchers. Scholars trace its origins to 1554—so for tradition's sake, it's deeply meaningful. It's the nearest relative to the better-known Trooping the Colour, but without the crowds. Reserve ahead starting in mid-December. www. householddivision.org.uk, ✆ **020/7839-5323.** Early June.

SUMMER festivals

With many major music festivals taking over London's green spaces, summer is like one long Woodstock. The pandemic put a pause on most, but many are returning. Only the highlights (and check for the month if it's not listed here, as things can change):

o **May: All Points East.** Three days in Victoria Park. Past acts: Björk, The Chemical Brothers, Christine and the Queens, Nick Cave. www.allpointseastfestival.com.

o **August: Field Day.** Alternative acts (Erykah Badu, Charlotte Gainsbourg, Kraftwerk 3D) over 2 days. www.fielddayfestivals.com.

o **Hampton Court Palace Festival.** High-end names (Lionel Richie, Van Morrison, George Benson, Tom Jones) in a temporary theater on palace grounds. www.hamptoncourtpalacefestival.com.

o **Lovebox.** A weekend in Gunnersby Park. Sunday is a virtual Pride festival. Past acts: Mark Ronson, Chance the Rapper, Frank Ocean, Cypress Hill. www.loveboxfestival.com.

o **Wireless Festival.** Held alfresco in Finsbury Park for 3 days. Recent years: Cardi B, Megan Thee Stallion, The Weeknd. www.wirelessfestival.co.uk.

London Fashion Week. Collections are unveiled for press and buyers. It's tough to get a runway show ticket, but there's a raft of slick events and parties across the city. www.londonfashionweek.co.uk. June.

The Royal Academy Summer Exhibition. Artists have been in a frenzy to win entry to this blind competition since 1768. Paintings, sculpture, drawings, architecture—if you can dream it, you can enter it, and if you're one of the most talented, your piece is anointed as the best that year. The show is what the Royal Academy is known for, and although it's not envelope-pushing, it's a seminal event in British art culture and shouldn't be missed if you're in town. www.royalacademy.org.uk. Late June to late Aug.

Trooping the Colour. Never mind that the king was born in November. Since 1748, this is the "official" birthday of the British sovereign, and as a present, they get the same thing every year: soldiers with big hats. A sea of redcoats and cavalry swarm over Horse Guards Parade, 41 guns salute, and a flight of Royal Air Force jets slam through the sky overhead. Until her latter years, Queen Elizabeth herself led the charge, waving politely to her subjects before they lost themselves in a hearty display of marching band prowess. Try for grandstand seats instead of standing in the free-for-all along the route, where you'll only get a fast glimpse of passing royalty. Tickets are only sold by random draw, which closes at the end of February. www.householddivision.org.uk/trooping-the-colour, (C) **020/7414-2479.** Mid-June.

Taste of London Festival. The city's top chefs and the region's finest farmers convene in Regent's Park for 5 days of belly-stuffing. https://london.tastefestivals.com, (C) **087/1230-7132.** Mid-June.

Pride London. A signature event on the world's LGBTQ calendar, in a good year London Pride can pull nearly a million revelers, many of them heterosexual, with a buoyant roster of concerts and performances by famous names plus a parade (the U.K.'s largest) in the center of the city. The gay pride week, co-sponsored by the mayor's office, also makes an excellent excuse for some blowout dance parties. www.prideinlondon.org, (C) **0844/344-5428.** Late June or early July.

Wimbledon Championships. Why watch on television yet again? Check p. 211 for how to be one of the 500,000 to witness it in person. www.wimbledon.org, (C) **020/8944-1066.** June or July.

Greenwich+Docklands International Festival (GDIF). An ambitious program of free theatrical and musical pieces, many of them developed by artists expressly for the spaces they're performed in. www.festival.org, ✆ 020/8305-1818. Late June and early July.

Meltdown. A compendium of hip prestige arts held at the Southbank Centre, curated in the past by such notables as Patti Smith, David Bowie, Grace Jones, and Yoko Ono. www.southbankcentre.co.uk/meltdown, ✆ 020/3879-9555. Summer.

BBC Promenade Concerts. The biggest classical music festival of the year, held primarily at the Royal Albert Hall, "the Proms" consists of orchestral concerts for every taste. Up to 1,350 standing places are available starting under £10. www.bbc.co.uk/proms, ✆ 020/7070-4441. July to September.

The Lambeth Country Show. A free, old-fashioned farm show overtakes Brixton's Brockwell Park (for a single weekend, anyway) with farm animals, jam-making contests, a fun fair, tractor demonstrations, and Punch and Judy puppet shows. Very English stuff. Free. www.lambethcountryshow.co.uk, ✆ 020/7926-7085. Third weekend in July.

London Triathlon. Some 11,000 participants cycle through the city from Westminster, sprint around the ExCeL center in Docklands, and swim in Royal Victoria Dock in this annual event. Sir Richard Branson attends. www.thelondontriathlon.co.uk, ✆ 020/8233-5900. Late July or early August.

Notting Hill Carnival. In August 1958, roving bands of white racists combed the slums of Notting Hill in search of Caribbean-owned businesses to destroy. Resulting community outrage and newly rediscovered cultural pride led to the formation of this festival, now Europe's largest street parade, attracting some 2 million people. It's a smorgasbord of cultures spanning the Caribbean, Eastern Europe, South America, and the Indian subcontinent. Sunday is kids' day, with scrubbed-down events and activities, but on Monday, the adults take over, costumes get skimpy, floats weave through small streets, and rowdy hordes celebrate into the wee hours. www.thelondonnottinghillcarnival.com. August Bank Holiday weekend.

Great British Beer Festival. Just like it sounds: More than 1,000 British ales and ciders from some 400 breweries are available to try at Olympia London—after all those tastings, you'll be relieved to learn the Tube is within easy reach. It runs 5 days. www.gbbf.org.uk, ✆ 01727/867-201. August.

The Great River Race. Always over too soon, the race is the aquatic version of the London Marathon, with rowers vying to beat out 300 other vessels—Chinese dragon boats, Canadian canoes, Viking longboats, and even Hawaiian outriggers—on a morning jaunt upriver from the Docklands to Richmond. www.greatriverrace.org.uk, ✆ 020/8398-8141. Saturday in mid-September.

Totally Thames. In conjunction with the Great River Race (above), nearly half a million souls attend London's largest free open-air arts festival, with more than 150 events. Southwark Bridge is closed for a giant feast, and there's a flotilla of working river boats, circus performers, and antique fireboats, tugs, and sailboats. Sunday sees the Night Carnival, a lavish procession of thousands of lantern-bearing musicians and dancers crawling along the water. Everything is topped off with barge-launched fireworks. www.totallythames.org, ✆ 020/7928-8998. September.

Open House London. More than 800 buildings, all of them deemed important but normally closed to the public, yawn wide for free tours on a single, hotly anticipated event. Past participants have included the skyscraper headquarters of Lloyd's, Crossrail tunnels, the new U.S. embassy, and even No. 10 Downing St. The list of open buildings comes out in August. Some require timed tickets, but for most, the line forms at dawn. Open House also organizes year-round walking tours. www.openhouselondon.org.uk, ✆ 020/7383-2131. September.

Dance Umbrella. For 4 decades, one of the world's best contemporary dance festivals, with plenty of standing-room seats for as little as £5. www.danceumbrella.co.uk, ✆ 020/7257-9380. October.

Frieze Art Fair. More than 160 galleries vie for big money from collectors in a colossal 4-day tent show in Regent's Park. It has become influential in the contemporary art world. www.frieze.com, ✆ 020/3372-6111. Early October.

Diwali. One advantage of visiting a multicultural city like London is that it affords you the chance to sample major international holidays in an English-speaking environment. One such treat is Diwali, the Indian "festival of light," when Trafalgar Square is transformed with lights, floating lanterns, massive models of the elephant god Ganesh, music, dance, and DJs. It's free. Mid- to late October.

BFI London Film Festival. An important stop on the cinema circuit, this event, sponsored by the British Film Institute, is geared toward media exposure for more than 200 features, but there are plenty of tickets for the public, too. www.bfi.org.uk/lff, ✆ 020/7928-3232. Mid-October.

NOVEMBER

Guy Fawkes Night. In 1605, silly old Guy Fawkes tried to assassinate James I and the entire Parliament by blowing them to smithereens in the Gunpowder Plot. Joke's on him: To this day, the Brits celebrate his failure by blowing up *him*. His effigy is thrown on bonfires across the country, fireworks displays rage in the autumn night sky, and more than a few tykes light their first sparklers in honor of the would-be assassin's gruesome execution. Although displays are scattered around town, including at Battersea Park and Alexandra Palace, get out of the city for the weekend nearest November 5, also called Bonfire Night—the countryside is perfumed with the woody aroma of burning leaves on this holiday. Mount Primrose Hill or Hampstead Heath for a view of the fireworks around the city. November 5.

Lord Mayor's Show. What sounds like the world's dullest public access program is actually a delightfully pompous procession,

about 800 years old, involving some 140 charity floats and 6,000 participants to ostensibly show off the newly elected Lord Mayor to the king or his representatives. The centerpiece is the preposterously carved and gilt Lord Mayor's Coach, built in 1757—a carriage so extravagant it makes Cinderella's ride look like a Toyota Corolla. That's a lot of hubbub for a city official whose role is essentially ceremonial; the Mayor of London (currently Sadiq Khan) wields the true power. All that highfalutin' strutting is followed by a good old-fashioned fireworks show over the Thames between the Blackfriars and Waterloo bridges. www.lordmayorsshow.org. Second Saturday in November.

EFG London Jazz Festival. Some 165 mid-November events attract around 60,000 music fans for 10 days. Many performances are free, and tickets are distributed by the venues. www.efglondonjazzfestival.org.uk, ✆ 020/7324-1880. Mid-November.

Remembrance Sunday. Another chance to glimpse a monarch. The prime minister and the monarch, as well as many royals, attend a ceremony at the Cenotaph, in the middle of Whitehall, to honor the war dead and wounded, of which Britain has borne more than its share. Those red flowers you'll see everywhere—red petals, black centers—are poppies, the symbol of remembrance in Britain. Sunday nearest November 11.

DECEMBER

Carols at the Royal Albert Hall. Royal Albert Hall's annual evening of candlelight Christmas carols, readings from Dickens, and music by Handel, Bach, Mozart, and Corelli played by the Mozart Festival Orchestra—in period costume. www.royalalberthall.com, ✆ 020/7589-8212. Late December.

New Year's Eve Fireworks. As Big Ben strikes midnight, London usually rings in the New Year with 12 minutes of fireworks over the Thames and the Eye. The pandemic suspended the tradition, so check if it's back: A few tickets are usually released via www.london.gov.uk/nye in mid-June, with the rest available in September.

[FastFACTS] LONDON

Accessible Travel London can't seem to strike the balance between preserving old buildings and making sure they're accessible to all. With the laudable exception of the Docklands Light Railway, only a few Tube stations have lifts (although the new Elizabeth Line is very accessible), and those with plenty of escalators still require passengers to climb flights of stairs. Research your options at **AccessAble** (www.accessable.co.uk) and **Transport for London** (www.tfl.gov.uk/accessibility; ℂ **0343/222-1234**). In the map section of its **TfL Go** app, you can tap the wheelchair icons to show you only the stations that offer step-free access—sadly, the West End is pretty poorly served by lifts. The website **UpDownLondon.com** keeps tabs on step-free access at Tube stations, including temporary maintenance obstacles.

Many London hotels, museums, restaurants, and sightseeing attractions have dedicated wheelchair access, all taxis and buses do, and persons with disabilities often get admission discounts. Generally speaking, the more expensive a hotel is, the more likely it is to be wheelchair accessible, but not always. The website for **Nationwide Disabled Access Register** (www.directenquiries.com) lists the accessibility features of a wide range of facilities, from attractions to car renters.

Travelers who are blind or partially sighted will find useful advice from the **Royal National Institute of Blind People** (www.rnib.org.uk; ℂ **0303/123-9999**). **Tourism for All** (www.tourismforall.org.uk; ℂ **084/5124-9971**) has accessibility information for older travelers as well as travelers with disabilities.

The British agency **Can Be Done** (www.canbedone.co.uk; ℂ **020/8907-2400**) runs tours adapted to travelers with mobility needs.

Area Codes The country telephone code for Great Britain is **44.** The area code for London is **020.** The full telephone number is usually 8 digits long. Businesses and homes in central London usually have numbers beginning with a **7;** those that are farther out begin with an **8.** For more info, see "Telephones," p. 377.

ATMs/Banks See "Money," p. 374. *One quirk to note:* Retrieve your card immediately from ATM slots; many machines suck them in within 10 to 15 seconds, for security. Cards that are thicker than the norm, lack raised numbers, or are not made of standard plastic may also be gobbled up by confused ATMs. Should that happen, you'll have to petition the bank to have it returned to you.

Business Hours Businesses are generally open weekdays between 9 or 10am and 5 or 6pm. Some remain open a few hours

longer on Thursdays and Fridays. Saturday hours for stores are the same; Sunday store hours are generally noon to 5 or 6pm. Banks are usually open from 9:30am to 4 or 5pm, with some larger branches open later on Thursdays or for a few hours on Saturday mornings. Stores and restaurants are more likely to close on Sundays, Mondays, or both.

Cellphones See "Mobile Phones," p. 374.

Credit Cards Many places only accept cards now (see p. 348). Credit cards are accepted nearly everywhere, but if you can, bring **Visa** or **Mastercard,** because **American Express** is accepted less widely. (If you try to use it at a place that doesn't accept it, you may be mistakenly told your card has a problem or you've been declined; don't panic.) Many credit card issuers levy an annoying international transaction fee on top of your purchase—many **American Express** cards have dropped that fee, as have **Capital One Venture** (www.capitalone.com; ℂ **800/695-5500**) and several options from **Chase** (www.chase.com). If you are given a choice between being charged in British pounds or your home currency, always choose GBP (pounds); as long as your card has no international fee, the exchange rate will likely be better. Try not to use credit cards to withdraw cash—you'll pay a currency exchange fee, and worse, you'll be charged interest from the moment your money leaves the slot.

It is now illegal for vendors to charge you a transaction fee to defray the cost of dealing with the card companies. Minimum purchases and clearly labeled service fees, however, remain legal.

The fastest way to pay is with a card that can make contactless payments. If yours doesn't, you may have to take extra steps when you buy things. Europeans use **"chip and PIN" cards** requiring a code number. Some vending machines won't accept swipe-only cards and may incorrectly inform you that you were declined. Most U.S. cards now come with such a chip, but if yours doesn't, ask your lender to send you one for free. If you do not normally use a PIN to make credit card purchases, inform clerks you're using a "Signature card," as they will usually have to scramble around for a pen (Europeans don't sign anymore). Using mobile payment such as Google Pay or Apple Pay speeds up transactions to a mere tap of your phone, no signature required—I strongly urge you to set yours up with a Visa or Mastercard before leaving home. Restaurants will usually process your payment at your table wirelessly—the British consider it standard security practice not to let your card out of your sight and to check ID along with signature.

Customs Rules about what you can carry into Britain are standard but ever-shifting, so get the latest restrictions from **HM Revenue & Customs** (www.hmrc.gov.uk). Your own government is responsible for telling you what you can bring back home.

Doctors Ask your hotel first. Then try the G.P. (General Practitioner) finder at **www.nhs.uk**. North American members of the **International Association for Medical Assistance to Travelers** (IAMAT; www.iamat.org; ☎ **716/754-4883** in the U.S., or 416/652-0137 in Canada) can consult that organization for lists of local approved doctors. *Note:* U.S. and Canadian visitors who become ill while they're in London are eligible only for free *emergency* care. For other treatment, including follow-up care, you'll pay £60 to £150 just to see a physician.

Drinking Laws Legal drinking age is 18. Children 15 and younger are allowed in pubs if accompanied by a parent or guardian. Drinking on London's **public transport network** is forbidden; on-the-spot fines are issued to transgressors.

Electricity The current in Britain is 240 volts AC. Plugs have three squared pins. Foreign appliances operating on lower voltage (those from the U.S., Canada, and Australia use 110–120 volts AC) will require an adapter and possibly a voltage converter, although the range of capability will usually be

printed on the plug. Many modern phone chargers and laptops can handle the stronger current with only an adapter. A few hotels provide North American–style outlets for a non-heating appliance such as a shaver, but don't count on one.

Embassies & Consulates In 2017, the **U.S. Embassy** moved from Grosvenor Square to an elaborate 4.9-acre complex in West London's Wandsworth district (33 Nine Elms Lane, SW11; https://uk.usembassy.gov; ☎ **020/7499-9000;** Tube: Vauxhall). Standard hours are Monday to Friday 8:30am to 5:30pm. All visits require an appointment. You may bring mobile phones but not tablets or laptops. For passport information, call ☎ **877/487-2778** in the U.S.

The **High Commission of Canada** (1 Trafalgar Sq., London W1; www.canadainternational.gc.ca/united_kingdom-royaume_uni/index.aspx; ☎ **020/7004-6000;** Tube: Charing Cross) handles passport and consular services for Canadians. Hours are Monday, Wednesday, and Friday 8 to 10:30am.

The **Australian High Commission** is at Australia House, Strand, London WC2 (www.uk.embassy.gov.au; ☎ **020/7887-5776;** Tube: Temple). Hours are Monday to Friday 9am to 4:30pm.

The **New Zealand High Commission** is at New Zealand House, 1 Pall Mall East, London SW1 (www.mfat.govt.nz; ☎ **020/7930-8422;** Tube: Charing Cross or Piccadilly Circus). Hours are

Monday to Friday 9am to 5pm.

The **Irish Embassy** is at 17 Grosvenor Place, London SW1 (www.dfa.ie/irish-embassy/great-britain; ℭ **020/7235-2171;** Tube: Hyde Park Corner). Hours are Monday to Friday 9:30am to 12:30pm and 2 to 4pm.

Emergencies The one-stop number for Britain is ℭ **999**—that's for fire, police, and ambulances. It's free from any phone, even mobiles. Less urgent? Call 111.

Family Travel Attractions cater to the family market. The kingly treatment starts, at many places, with the so-named **Family Ticket,** which grants a reduced price for parents and kids entering together. For any length of stay, you can rent baby equipment from **Tiny Tots Rentals** (www.tinytotsrentals.co.uk; info@tinytotsrentals.co.uk) and **The London Baby Equipment Hire Company** (www.babyequipmenthirelondon.co.uk; ℭ **07807/932-206**). If you need babysitting, **Sitting Pretty Babysitters** (www.sittingpretty babysitters.com; ℭ **07971/083-207**) will come to your hotel for a minimum of 3 or 4 hours, depending on the time of week; rates are around £10 an hour with a £6.50 booking fee and a £18.50 membership fee.

If you are a **divorced parent** traveling with your children, bring proof to the airport that you are entitled to take your kids out of the country.

Resources for family-specific travel tips include the **Family Travel Network** (www.familytravelnetwork.com). **The Family Travel Files** (www.thefamilytravelfiles.com) lists tour operators and packagers geared to families, but its suggestions aren't always the most economical or efficient. *Time Out* (www.timeout.com/london) includes a section on kids' activities.

When it comes to **baby supplies,** pacifiers are called "dummies," diapers are "nappies," a crib is a "cot," and Band-Aids are "plasters."

Fitness PureGym (www.puregym.com) offers contract-free passes for 1 day, 3 days, or a week for as little as £20; it has facilities open 24 hours in Piccadilly (Rex House, 4–12 Regent St., SW1; ℭ **345/013-3386;** Tube: Piccadilly Circus), Waterloo (11–15 Brad St., SE1; Tube: Waterloo), and Holborn (Lacon House, 84 Theobalds Rd., WC1; ℭ **345/013-3502;** Tube: Holborn). Additional locations are in Marylebone, Tower Hill, and Farringdon, plus others.

Health Traveling to London doesn't pose specific health risks. Common drugs are generally available over the counter and in large supermarkets, although visitors should know the generic rather than brand names of any medicines they rely on. For example, the generic general-purpose painkiller known in North America as

acetaminophen is called **paracetamol** in the U.K.

Pack **prescription medications** in carry-on luggage and in their original containers, with pharmacy labels—otherwise they may not pass airport security. Also bring copies of your prescriptions, just in case. If you require **syringes,** always carry a signed medical prescription. Don't forget an extra pair of contact lenses or prescription glasses.

If you need the advice of a doctor or a nurse, the national health care system operates a free, 24-hour hotline: **National Health Service Direct** (www.nhs.uk; ℭ **111**). Citizens of many European countries are entitled to free health care while in Britain (www.dh.gov.uk/travellers), but not everyone is. Non-EU citizens should carry health or travel insurance. Also see "Doctors," p. 371.

Health Insurance U.K. **nationals** receive free medical treatment countrywide; visitors from overseas qualify only for free **emergency** care. **U.S. visitors** should note that most domestic health plans (including Medicare and Medicaid) do not provide coverage, and the ones that do often require you to pay for services upfront and file for reimbursement after you return home. You might want to buy international medical coverage from companies such as **UnitedHealthcare SafeTrip** (www.UHCsafetrip.com; ℭ **800/732-5309**) or **Travel Assistance**

International (www.travel assistance.com; 📞 **410/987-6233**). **Canadians** should check with their provincial health plan offices or call **Health Canada/Santé Canada** (www.hc-sc.gc.ca; 📞 **613/957-2991**) to find out the extent of their coverage and what documentation and receipts to bring home if they are treated overseas. **E.U. nationals** (and nationals of E.E.A. countries and Switzerland) with a European Health Insurance Card (EHIC) from their home country can use it until it expires. If you don't have an EHIC or you can't obtain a Provisional Replacement Certificate (PRC) for it, you may be charged 150% the standard NHS rate for treatment. Norwegians are entitled to medically necessary health care in the U.K.

Hospitals In the U.K., the ER is usually called A&E, or Accident and Emergency. If your need is urgent, dial 📞 **999** (it's free no matter where your phone is registered) rather than risk going to a medical center that doesn't offer A&E. You can search **www.nhs.uk** for the nearest A&E, or go to the 24-hour, walk-in A&E departments at **University College Hospital,** 235 Euston Rd., London NW1 (www.uclh.nhs. uk; 📞 **020/3456-7890;** Tube: Warren Street) or **St Thomas's Hospital,** Westminster Bridge Road, entrance on Lambeth Palace Road, London, SE1 (www. guysandstthomas.nhs.uk; 📞 **020/7188-7188;** Tube: Westminster or Waterloo).

For less serious needs, visit **Soho NHS Walk-In Centre** (1 Frith St., W1; www.clch. nhs.uk; 📞 **020/7534-6500;** Tube: Tottenham Court Road), which is open Monday through Friday 8am to 8pm and Saturday to Sunday 10am to 8pm. Bear in mind it was closed to walk-ins during the pandemic, so you may need to call it for a referral.

Innoculations Unless you're arriving from an area known to be suffering from an epidemic, inoculations or vaccinations are not required for entry into the U.K.

Insurance You may want special coverage for **apartment stays,** especially if you've plunked down a deposit, and for any **valuables** you may bring with you; airlines are only required to pay up to $2,500 for lost luggage domestically, less for foreign travel. Compare policies at **Insure MyTrip.com** (📞 **800/487-4722**), or contact one of the following reputable companies: **Allianz** (www.allianz travelinsurance.com; 📞 **866/884-3556); Generali Global Assistance** (formerly CSA Travel Protection; www. generalitravelinsurance.com; 📞 **800/874-2442); Travel Guard** (www.travelguard. com; 📞 **800/826-5248);** or **Travelex** (www.travelex insurance.com; 📞 **800/228-9792**). Note that most insurers require you to purchase plans soon after you buy your trip and *before* you leave home. If you seek Covid-19-related coverage, make sure it's included in the

policy that you purchase, because some exclude it.

Internet Wi-Fi flows freely at pubs, cafes, museums, and nearly all hotels. Usually, you will have to fill in an email address to activate it, but often it's a data collection ploy and you can write dummy information. (See box on p. 363.)

Laundry Launderettes are not easy to find in central London anymore, and expensive hotels will only clean your garment for roughly as much money as it would take to simply buy a new one. Look into the app **Laundrapp,** which will pick up and drop off to your hotel for free. Prices start at £2 per article or £2.50 for 1kg (2.2 lb.).

Legal Aid If you find yourself in trouble abroad, contact your consulate or embassy (see "Embassies & Consulates," p. 371). It can advise you of your rights and provide a list of local attorneys (for which you'll have to pay if services are used), but they cannot interfere on your behalf in the English legal process. For questions about U.S. citizens who've been arrested abroad, telephone the **Citizens Emergency Center** of the Bureau of Consular Affairs in Washington, D.C. (📞 **202/501-4444,** or 888/407-4747).

LGBTQ Travelers Gay and lesbian people have equality and marriage rights in England. Public displays of affection are barely noticed in the center of the city, although in the outer suburbs couples should show more restraint. Gay bashings are rare enough to be newsworthy, but it's true that an element of society can, once full of ale or vague political rage, become belligerent. Particularly in parks at night, be aware of your surroundings and give wide berth to gaggles of drunken lads. This advice holds irrespective of your sexuality.

For nightlife planning, the best sources for information are **Boyz** (www.boyz.co.uk), which publishes a day-by-day schedule on its website, and the free **QX International** (www.qxmagazine. com). Also see nightlife listings on p. 280.

Luggage Storage Useful if you're taking those cheap European flights with steep luggage fees, **Left Baggage** (www.left-baggage.com; ☏ **0800/077-4530**) has locations at Heathrow, Gatwick, and the big railway stations: It costs £12.50 per item per 24 hours, available for up to a week, then £5 per item per day thereafter. The apps **Bounce** (https://usebounce. com) and **Luggage Hero** (www.luggagehero.com) arrange with local businesses to keep your bags during business hours for a small hourly fee.

Mail An airmail letter or postcard to anywhere outside Europe costs £1.85 for up to 20g (⅔ oz.) and generally takes 5 to 7 working days to arrive. Within the E.U., letters or postcards under 20g (⅔ oz.) also cost £1.85.

Mobile Phones Anytime you call a mobile phone in Britain, the fee will be higher than calling a landline, although there is no fee to *receive* a call or text.

Apart from renting a phone (not recommended to the casual visitor), many tourists simply enable their international **roaming** feature. North American carrier T-Mobile offers standard packages that include calls and texting for free, although data is limited and throttled unless you pay extra for a special add-on data plan. Depending on your contract, your allowance may be scanty and your provider may bleed you for extra data, so it's crucial to know what your subscription includes and what your limits are. If you don't know, put your phone on airplane mode before you land in the U.K. and only use free Wi-Fi signals.

The other solution, if you have an unlocked phone that uses the GSM system, is to pop into any mobile phone shop or newsstand and buy a cheap **pay-as-you-talk** phone number from a mobile phone store. This method is rapidly losing favor and is increasingly hard to manage, so it's not recommended. But if you must: You'll pay about £5 for a SIM card, which you stick in your phone, and then you buy vouchers to load your new U.K. phone number with as much money as you think you'll use up (no refunds). That will give you a British

number, which you can e-mail to everyone back home, that charges local rates (10p–40p per minute). Just call your provider before you leave home to make sure your phone is "unlocked" (last-generation phones are more likely to allow this as a default), so that the British SIM card will function in it. That service is usually free. U.K. mobile providers with pay-as-you-talk deals, all comparable, include **Vodafone** (www.vodafone.com), **O₂** (www.o2.co.uk), **Lebara** (www.lebara.co.uk), **EE/T-Mobile** (www.ee.co.uk), and **Virgin Mobile** (www.virgin mobile.com). Annoyingly, purchased SIMs come with automatic child content locks, which may block certain social sites. To remove the censorship, go to a mobile phone store run by your SIM provider to prove you're an adult. Bring your hotel's details—you must supply a U.K. address.

Even if your home mobile company won't permit you to unlock your phone, you can use its Wi-Fi features for Skype, FaceTime, WhatsApp, and on some phones, even free texts and calling.

Money British pounds are divided into 100 pennies (p), the plural of which is called "pence." Coins come in 1p, 2p, 5p, 10p, 20p, 50p, £1, and £2 (the 2-pound coin is commonly called a "quid"). Notes come in £5, £10, £20, and £50. The government recently completed a redesign of its money. The new British pound (£1), a small, chunky, gold-colored coin with silver faces, looks round but is actually subtly 12-sided. The previous version, truly round and golden without shiny faces, was phased out in 2017. Paper notes were replaced with polymer versions in recent years, so if someone tries to pass you a paper bank note, *refuse it!* If you find yourself holding outdated money and a local bank refuses to exchange it, go to the Bank of England on Threadneedle Street (Tube: Bank) to try to exchange it, but be warned that queues are long. Now and then, you'll receive notes printed by the Bank of Scotland; they're valid, but an increase in forgeries means some shops refuse them, so we recommend you decline them as well. Banks will exchange them.

In 2022, the exchange rate hovered in the vicinity of £1 = US$1.20 but the trials of modern times have thrown that rate into flux; consult a currency exchange website such as **www. oanda.com/currency/ converter** or the Oanda or XE apps.

All prices (including at most B&Bs but not at all hotels) are listed including tax, so what you see is what you pay. No guesstimating required.

Every visitor should have several sources for money, but cash is still a fail-safe. The simple solution is to pull cash from an ATM upon arrival; rates are the cheapest there. Before leaving home, find out if you need to warn your bank and your credit card issuers that you

intend to travel internationally so that they don't place a stop on your account. You may also need to adjust your PIN, because English banks require 4-digit codes. (If you know your PIN as a word, memorize the numerical equivalent.) Most banks hit you with fees of a few pounds each time you withdraw cash, and your own bank may toss in a small fee of its own; gauge for yourself how much you feel comfortable withdrawing at a time to offset that fee. Also ask your bank if it has reciprocal agreements for free withdrawals anywhere.

Paying with **a mobile wallet** such as Google Pay or Apple Pay is fast, but it may only be accepted for individual purchases, generally up to £100.

Traveler's checks are dead—most places reject them—but creditors have come up with **traveler's check cards,** also called **prepaid cards,** which are essentially debit cards loaded with however much money you choose to put on them. They work in ATMs, and should you lose one, you can get your cash back in a matter of hours. You can reload the card mid-trip by calling a number or visiting a website, although there may be fees of a few dollars for ATM transactions. Try **NetSpend** (www.netspend.com; 𝄞 **866/ 387-7363**). The cards are not capable of contactless payment, but they can connect to digital wallets on your smartphone that are.

Changing cash is also on the outs. Old-fashioned

cambios/bureaux de change are few and far between, although you'll still find a few at the airport and around Leicester Square. If you must change money, better rates are offered by banks (open 9:30am–4pm).

Newspapers & Magazines London offers more publications than one would think a city of its size could support. The broadsheets, ordered from left to right, politically speaking, are the *Guardian,* the *Independent,* the *Daily Telegraph,* and the *Times.* On the Tube, *Metro* is free in the morning and *Evening Standard* is free in the afternoon. The salmon-colored *Financial Times* covers business. The tabloids are fluffier and more salacious: They include the *Sun,* the *Mirror, Daily Star,* the *Daily Mail,* and *Daily Express. Time Out* publishes a free listing of events and entertainments.

Other popular magazines include the *Big Issue* (written and sold by homeless and formerly homeless people), *Radio Times* (TV listings and celebrity interviews), and *Hello!* and *OK!* (fawning celebrity spreads planted by publicity agents).

Packing For your wallet's sake, pack sparingly! It's not as easy as it used to be to wink your way through the weigh-in. **British Airways,** for example, grants coach passengers a puny 23kg (51 lb.); if you exceed that, you will be smacked with a flat fee of £65 per flight. Bags over 32kg (71 lb.) will be rejected outright. Some airlines, such as **Virgin Atlantic,** can be ruthless about making sure even your *carry-on* baggage weighs no more than 10kg (22 lb.). If you're taking multiple airlines, stick to the tightest restrictions of the lot. Many airlines (even the no-frills) discount for booking baggage at least 24 hours early, and charge more at the airport.

Pare toiletries to essentials. You're not going to the jungle—you will find staples like toothpaste, contact lens solution, and deodorant everywhere. Women should bring a minimum of make-up; the British don't tend to use very much themselves. Brits are also more likely to wear trousers than blue jeans. If you plan to go clubbing, pack some fashionable duds—Londoners love to look natty.

You'll be most comfortable if you dress in clothing that layers well. Even in winter, London's air can be clammy, and dressing too warmly can become uncomfortable. No matter what the average temperature is (see weather box on p. 365), the air can grow cool after the sun sets; plan for that. A compact umbrella is wise year-round, as is an outer coat that repels water, because you never know when you're going to find yourself in one of those misty rains that make the British Isles so lush and green.

Don't bring illegal drugs (duh) or medical marijuana (duh), and also leave the pepper spray and mace at home; they're banned in the U.K.

Passports To enter the United Kingdom, all U.S. citizens, Canadians, Australians, New Zealanders, and South Africans must have a passport valid through their length of stay. No visa is required. A passport will allow you to stay in the country for up to 6 months. The immigration officer may also want to see proof of your intention to return to your point of origin (usually a round-trip ticket) and of visible means of support while you're in Britain (credit cards work). If you're planning to fly from the U.S. or Canada to the U.K. and then on to a country that requires a visa (India, for example), secure that visa before you arrive in Britain.

Pharmacies Every police station keeps a list of pharmacies (chemists) that are open 24 hours. Also try **Zafash,** a rare chemist that is open 24 hours (233–235 Old Brompton Rd., SW5; www.zafashpharmacy.co.uk; ✆ 020/7373-2798; Tube: Earl's Court). For non-emergency health advice, call the NHS at ✆ **111.**

Police Dial ✆ **999,** or 112 if the matter is serious. London has two official police forces: the City of London police (www.cityoflondon.police.uk), whose remit covers the "Square Mile" and its 8,600 residents; and the Metropolitan Police ("the Met"), which covers the rest of the capital. Opening hours for all the Met's local police stations are listed at www.met.police.uk. In a non-emergency, you can contact your local police station by dialing ✆ **101.** Losses, thefts, and other criminal matters should be reported at the nearest police station immediately. You will be given a crime number, which your travel insurer will request if you make a claim against any losses.

Safety Crossing the street is the most perilous thing you'll do. Always look down to see which way traffic is flowing—the street will be painted "Look right" or "Look left" so you'll know. Also, a steady-lit green man on the crosswalk signal means it's safe, but when the green man flashes, do not begin crossing—it means cars are about to gun it again.

Few places in London are unsafe. Neighborhoods that might be called sketchy are usually distant from the Tube lines, and they only feel tense after dark, when shops close. Simply be sensitive to who's around you and you'll do fine.

The biggest nuisance tourists might encounter—besides tipsy locals—are drive-by snatch muggings. Each day, dozens of people are so absorbed in their smartphones that they don't notice the moped-driving pickpockets zoom up, snatch their phone, and speed off. Simply be smart about how you use your phone and, of course, where you put your cash and what you leave sitting in the open.

London is always on the lookout for terrorists, and it has been since the days of IRA violence. Don't leave a bag unattended even for seconds or you may lose it.

Guns are banned in London—even on most police officers—so you don't often see the kind of violence taken for granted in the United States. Londoners cite knife crime as a problem, but the victims are almost always young men who themselves carry knives. Some male tourists have gotten fleeced at "hostess bars" in Soho. If you do suffer a lapse of judgment and accept the barker's invitation to go into one, understand that you might have cash exacted by lunkheaded yobs with tattooed fingers.

Should you find yourself on the business end of the legal system, you can get advice and referrals to lawyers from **Legal Services Commission** (www.legalservices.gov.uk; ☏ **0300/200-2020**). Crime victims can receive volunteer legal guidance and emotional fortification from **Victim Support** (www.victimsupport.org.uk; ☏ **0808/168-9111**). In the event of a sexual assault, find help through the **Rape Crisis Federation** (www.rapecrisis.org.uk; ☏ **0808/902-9999;** many caseworkers will only assist females).

Senior Travel Don't hide your age! Seniors in England—usually classified as those age 60 and over—are privy to all kinds of price breaks, from lower admission prices at museums to a third off rail tickets (to apply for the **Senior Railcard,** go to www.senior-railcard.co.uk). You may hear seniors referred to as OAPs, which stands for Old Age Pensioners, although that acronym is falling out of use—perhaps because it's rare to find a solvent pension fund anymore. Don't be offended if you're referred to as a "geezer"—in England, it's a compliment, meaning a fun-loving (if sometimes rowdy) bloke.

If you're over 50, you can join **AARP** (601 E St. NW, Washington, DC, 20049; www.aarp.org; ☏ **202/434-3525**) to wrangle discounts on hotels, airfare, and car rentals. Elderhostel's well-respected **Road Scholar** (www.roadscholar.org; ☏ **800/454-5768**) runs many classes and programs in London designed to delve into literature, history, the arts, and music. Packages last from a week to a month and include airfare, lodging, and meals.

Smoking Smoking is prohibited by law in any enclosed workplace, including museums, pubs, public transportation, and restaurants. If in doubt, ask permission.

Student Travel Have ID on hand, and always mention you're a student—it'll save you cash. Attractions gladly offer discounts of around 25% for full-time students. However, your high school or university ID may not cut it where clerks haven't heard of your school: Before leaving home, obtain a recognized ID such as the **International Student Identity Card** (ISIC; www.isic.org). Those 25 and under who are not in school can obtain an **International Youth Travel Card,** also through ISIC, which performs many of the same tricks as a student discount card.

Taxes Prices of all goods in the U.K. are quoted inclusive of taxes. Since 2011 the national value-added tax (**VAT**) has stood at 20%. This is included in all hotel and restaurant bills, and in the price of most items you purchase.

Options for tourists to get some VAT refunded for certain shopping purchases have changed. Refunds are no longer possible at the airport. See p. 255 for details and see the latest information on www.gov.uk/tax-on-shopping/taxfree-shopping.

Telephones When dialing a number in this book from abroad, precede it with your country's international prefix (in the U.S. and Canada, it's 011), add the U.K.'s country code (44) and drop the first zero in the number.

To make an **international call** from Britain, dial the international access code (**00**), then the country code, then the area code, and finally the local number. When calling from a mobile phone, dial the full number including area code.

Directory assistance is at www.bt.com or ☏ **118-500.** Local calls start with 020.

The main **toll-free** ("freephone") prefixes are 0800, 0808, and 0500. Numbers starting with 07 are usually for mobile phones and will be charged at a higher rate. Numbers starting with 09 are premium-rate calls that will usually be very expensive (around £1.50/minute) and may not even work from abroad.

Many attractions, hotel companies, and services have changed their standard phone numbers to profit-generating ones that charge for every minute you call them. You often can't reach 0845, 0870, and 0871 numbers (charged at 10p a minute or less) from abroad, and when you can, you're charged more. Use the Web instead to get information.

The majority of London's **payphones** are gone or derelict. You can barely find a working one, let alone rely upon them.

Phonecards, though rarely used today, can be an economical method for both international and national calls. They are reusable until the total value has expired. Cards can be purchased from newsstands and post offices, and offer rates of a few pence per minute to most countries.

Hotels routinely add outrageous surcharges onto calls made from your room. Rather than dial directly using a hotel phone, use the Wi-Fi to make Internet calls.

Time London is generally 5 hours ahead of New York City and Toronto, 8 hours ahead of Los Angeles, 11 hours behind Auckland, and 9 hours behind Sydney. It is 1 hour behind western

continental Europe. Greenwich Mean Time is London time.

Tipping **Waiters** should receive 10% to 15% of the bill unless service is already included—*always* check the menu or bill to see if service was already added. At **pubs,** tipping isn't customary unless you receive waiter service (not food drop-off). Fine **hotels** may levy a service charge, but at the finest ones, grease the staff with a pound here and there. Staff at B&Bs and family-run hotels don't expect tips. **Bartenders** and **housekeepers** need not be tipped. There's no need to tip **taxicab drivers** but most people round up to the next £1, although a 10% to 15% tip is becoming increasingly standard.

Toilets London doesn't have enough of them. Washrooms can be found at any free museum in this guide, any department store, any pub or busy restaurant (though it's polite to buy something), and at Piccadilly Circus and Bank Tube stations. Train stations may also have toilets; they're free at Charing Cross, Victoria, and London Bridge but may charge 50p elsewhere. On weekends, open-air *pissoirs* for men are placed throughout the West End.

VAT See "Taxes," above.

Visas No E.U. nationals require a visa to visit the U.K. Visas are also not required for travelers from Australia, Canada, New Zealand, or the U.S. To be sure that hasn't changed, search

"visa" at **www.gov.uk** long before your travel dates. The usual permitted stay is 90 days or fewer for tourists, although some nationalities are granted stays of up to 6 months. If you plan to work or study, though, or if you're traveling on a passport from another country, you'll need to obtain the correct paperwork.

Visitor Information Three official information units supported by British taxes are set up to help tourists, but only online: **Visit Britain** (www.visitbritain. com); **Visit England** (www. visitengland.com); and **Visit London** (www.visitlondon. com). The only official information bureau with a public office is across the road from St Paul's Cathedral north of Millennium Bridge: The **City of London Information Centre** (St Paul's Churchyard; www.visitthecity.co.uk; ✆ **020/ 7332-1456;** Fri–Sat 10am–4pm, but check to see if hours have expanded) sells attraction tickets and Oyster cards, runs tours, and supplies brochures and counsel for day trips throughout the country. It publishes walking tours, a free City Visitor Trail audio walking tour app, and children's discovery trail maps.

Excellent independent sources for things to learn and things to do include **Londonist.com, Culture Calling.com, TimeOut.com/ London,** and the Twitter account **@SkintLondon**.

Women Travelers First and foremost, lone women

should avoid riding in **unlicensed London taxicabs,** especially at night. Flag down a black cab or call a minicab instead. **Addison Lee** (www.addisonlee.com; ✆ **020/7387-8888**) has a huge, efficient fleet, and will text you the registration plate of your cab for added security. Its free app is faster than the phone for arranging rides.

A true club and not an agency, **Women Welcome Women Worldwide** (www. womenwelcomewomen.uk; ✆ **01494/46-54-41**) connects travelers worldwide and costs £40 a year to join, £30 a year to renew.

Index

Photo Credits